GOVERNING GLOBALIZATION

Governing Globalization

Issues and Institutions

Edited by
DEEPAK NAYYAR

A Study prepared for the World Institute for Development Economics Research of the United Nations University (UNU/WIDER)

OXFORD
UNIVERSITY PRESS

OXFORD

UNIVERSITY PRESS

Great Clarendon Street, Oxford OX2 6DP

Oxford University Press is a department of the University of Oxford.
It furthers the University's objective of excellence in research, scholarship,
and education by publishing worldwide in

Oxford New York

Auckland Bangkok Buenos Aires Cape Town Chennai
Dar es Salaam Delhi Hong Kong Istanbul Karachi Kolkata
Kuala Lumpur Madrid Melbourne Mexico City Mumbai Nairobi
São Paulo Shanghai Taipei Tokyo Toronto

Oxford is a registered trade mark of Oxford University Press
in the UK and in certain other countries

Published in the United States
by Oxford University Press Inc., New York

World Institute for Develoment Economics Research of the
United Nations University (UNU/WIDER), Katajanokanlaituri 6B,
00160 Helsinki, Finland

The moral rights of the authors have been asserted
Database right Oxford University Press (maker)

First published 2002

A catalogue record for this title is available from the British Library

Library of Congress Cataloging in Publication Data
(Data available)
ISBN 0-19-925403-6 (Hbk.)
ISBN 0-19-925404-4 (Pbk.)

3 5 7 9 10 8 6 4 2

Typeset by Newgen Imaging Systems (P) Ltd., Chennai, India
Printed in Great Britain
on acid-free paper by
Biddles Ltd., Guildford and King's Lynn

Foreword

The United Nations system and the Bretton Woods institutions were created more than fifty years ago. Since then, the world has changed almost beyond recognition. And so have its governance needs. In the sphere of economics, national economies have become ever more closely integrated. The rapid growth of international trade, financial flows, direct investments, migration, tourism, and communication flows over the last 50 years has sharply boosted global interdependence and increased the scope for intervention by global institutions.

However, at the same time, globalization has de facto reduced the effectiveness of the interventions by global institutions and created the need for new, different types of interventions. Global institutions have indeed experienced a gradual erosion of their capacity to 'govern'. The IMF now controls only 2 per cent of the world's liquidity and is able to impose some monetary discipline only on a few developing countries while its ability to prevent recurrent and highly damaging financial crises is seriously questioned. Similar problems affect the World Bank whose management of the problem of African debt is seriously questioned, the WTO, and the UN. As for the latter, the erosion of original mandates has been accompanied by the lack of a clear agenda and uncertainties over the objectives and institutional arrangements for the tackling of new problems.

In the realm of politics, the collapse of communism has created a unipolar world. Some old problems, such as poverty, inequality, and deprivation persist. Some new problems have surfaced. Transitional economies and new states remain economically fragile and politically unstable. There is no system in place to take care of, let alone prevent, complex humanitarian emergencies. The need for stronger governance has been heightened by the emergence of new supranational problems (such as those in the environment and crime) which have brought to the fore the limitations of national states in dealing with these new challenges.

As a result of all this, for several years now, an increasing gap has been emerging between the changing problems of the world economy on the one hand and the policy agenda and the ability of world institutions to govern on the other. This book is the first to examine, in depth, the governance needs of the world economy and polity. It evaluates the past and considers the present to develop a vision about the future. The first part explores the international context and the national setting, in a changed world, to set the stage. The second part analyses selected issues of emerging significance in the contemporary world such as global macroeconomic management, transnational corporations, international capital flows and cross-border movements of people. Its object is to examine whether the present institutional framework is adequate or appropriate for governance and to identify the emerging institutional gaps. The third part provides a critical evaluation of the existing institutions, in retrospect, with a focus on the United Nations, the International Monetary Fund, the World Bank, and the

World Trade Organization. Its object is to explore how existing rules need to be modified or existing institutions need to be restructured to meet the present and future governance needs of the world. The fourth part explores some important elements of governance, which are critical for any vision about the future. It suggests some changes in, and highlights important issues for, existing institutions. It also points to emerging governance needs where new norms, rules, or institutions may have to be created.

In reflecting upon the emerging governance needs of the world economy and polity, this book makes an important and significant contribution to understanding. It is also most timely, for it comes at a time when the world community is thinking about, and engaged in, a debate on global governance. I strongly commend this book to the academic community with an interest in international economics, development economics and international relations. The volume would also be of enormous value to practitioners, whether policymakers or diplomats, and observers, whether individuals or institutions, concerned with problems of global governance.

Professor Giovanni Andrea Cornia
University of Florence and
Director of WIDER when this research was initiated

Contents

Part I. Context

Part II. Issues

Part III. Institutions

Contents

List of Figures

List of Tables

List of Contributors

Yilmaz Akyüz, UNCTAD, Geneva, Switzerland

Amit Bhaduri, Centre for Economic Studies and Planning, Jawaharlal Nehru University, Delhi, India

Andrew Cornford, UNCTAD, Geneva, Switzerland

Richard Falk, Center for International Studies, Princeton University, Princeton, USA

Gerald K. Helleiner, Department of Economics and Munk Centre for International Studies, University of Toronto, Toronto, Canada

Devesh Kapur, Department of Government, Harvard University, Cambridge, USA

Sanjaya Lall, Queen Elizabeth House, University of Oxford, Oxford, UK

Deepak Nayyar, University of Delhi, Delhi, India

José Antonio Ocampo, Economic Commission of Latin America and the Caribbean (ECLAC), Santiago, Chile

S. P. Shukla, Independent Consultant, Delhi, India

Joseph E. Stiglitz, Columbia Graduate School of Business and the School of International and Public Affairs (SIPA), Columbia University, New York, USA

Lance Taylor, Department of Economics, New School University, New York, USA

Jong-Il You, School of Public Policy and Management, Korea Development Institute, Seoul, Korea

Preface

This book is the outcome of a UNU/WIDER research project on 'New Roles and Functions for the United Nations and the Bretton Woods Institutions' which began life in June 1998. I am indebted to Giovanni Andrea Cornia, the then Director of WIDER, for suggesting the theme. It was his commitment to the idea that persuaded me to accept what seemed to be an exceedingly difficult task at the time. It turned out to be a challenging and rewarding endeavour. In the journey to completion, the unstinted support from Andrea Cornia was invaluable.

At the outset, a paper which conceptualized the volume was discussed with Amit Bhaduri, Andrea Cornia, Bob Deacon, Gerry Helleiner, and John Langmore, in Helsinki in June 1998. Their comments and suggestions were indeed constructive. The preliminary drafts of the papers written for the project, most of which are included in this volume, were discussed in a meeting of the authors at WIDER, Helsinki, in May 1999. The wide-ranging discussion among the contributors was enriched by the presence of Jacques Baudot, Andrea Cornia, John Langmore, and Ramesh Thakur. Critical comments and helpful suggestions from the participants at that stage were most valuable. An informal brainstorming meeting with Nitin Desai, Inge Kaul, John Langmore and some of the contributors, in New York in December 1999, provided useful suggestions particularly for the concluding chapter. Comments from referees, at different stages, also helped improve the quality of the volume. Above all, I am grateful to the contributors for their patience and their effort in putting up with my demands for successive rounds of revisions.

The staff at WIDER in Helsinki lent wonderful support even though I lived in far-away New Delhi. I would like to thank, in particular, Philip Matthai, Barbara Fagerman, Ara Kazandjian, and Adam Swallow. It is difficult for me to find the words to thank Liisa Roponen, the Project Secretary, who provided superb administrative support, with tireless effort, complete dedication and commendable initiative, throughout the life cycle of the project.

Gratitude is also extended to acknowledge the financial contributions to the project by the Ministry for Foreign Affairs of Finland and the United Nations, Department of Economic and Social Affairs, Division for Social Policy and Development.

This book seeks to examine the governance needs of the world economy and polity, situating them in the wider context of the contemporary unipolar world characterized by liberalization and globalization. In doing so, it provides a comprehensive analysis of the emerging issues and the existing institutions, to sketch the contours of reform and change necessary in the present system. It is clear from the essays in the volume, however, that we have not reached the end of the debate on governing globalization. There are unexplored themes and unsettled issues. This endeavour, it is hoped, will contribute to our understanding of, and stimulate further thinking on, the subject.

Historical experience suggests that crises are the catalysts of change. The last time around it was the aftermath of a world war and a worldwide economic depression that led to the foundation of the United Nations system and the creation of the Bretton Woods institutions. This book is written in the hope that the world need not wait for another crisis of such proportions to contemplate and introduce the much needed changes in global governance.

Deepak Nayyar
New Delhi
October 2001

PART I

CONTEXT

1

Towards Global Governance

DEEPAK NAYYAR

1. A CHANGED WORLD

It is now more than fifty years since the foundation of the United Nations system and the creation of the Bretton Woods institutions in 1945. During the second half of the twentieth century, however, the world has changed almost beyond recognition, not only in the sphere of economics but also in the realm of politics. For one thing, national economies have become ever more closely integrated through cross-border flows of trade, investment, and finance. The technological revolution in transport and communications, which has eroded the significance of barriers implicit in distance and time, has facilitated this process. For another thing, there has been a profound change in the political situation, as communism has collapsed and capitalism has emerged triumphant. The world of competing political ideologies has given way to a world with a single dominant political ideology. In both domains, the past decade has been particularly eventful. The context has obviously changed. But thinking about development is also very different. And, even as some old problems persist, several new problems have surfaced.

The United Nations and the Bretton Woods institutions were created in an altogether different context. The concerns of the industrialized countries were strongly influenced by memories of the great depression, which created the desire for full employment and also the conception of a welfare state, and the legacy of the Second World War, which motivated the quest for peace. This juncture in time was also the beginning of the end of colonialism. It shaped the aspirations of the newly independent countries about economic development and national sovereignty. These countries wanted to improve the living conditions of their people through rapid industrialization and to participate in a more democratic world where the structure of governance treated nations as equal partners. In the pursuit of these objectives, the role of the nation state was perceived as critical everywhere.

The perspectives on management of economies in the industrialized world and strategies of development in the developing world, or in the erstwhile socialist bloc, are now very different. In the industrialized countries, the Keynesian consensus has vanished. The rise of monetarism has meant that macroeconomic policies have sought to maintain price stability at the expense of full employment, while the welfare state is being slowly eroded. The retreat of the state from the economy is matched only by the advance of the market. The change is just as dramatic elsewhere in the world.

In the post-colonial era, most underdeveloped countries adopted strategies of development that provided a sharp contrast with their past. There was a conscious attempt to limit the degree of openness and of integration with the world economy, in pursuit of a more autonomous, if not self-reliant, development. The state was assigned a strategic role in development because the market, by itself, was not perceived as sufficient to meet the aspirations of latecomers to industrialization. Both represented points of departure from the colonial era, which was characterized by open economies and unregulated markets. This approach also represented a consensus in thinking about the most appropriate strategy of industrialization. There were a few voices of dissent, but it was, in effect, the *development consensus* at the time. Four decades later, by the early 1990s, the pendulum had swung the other way in terms of perceptions about development.[1] Most countries in the developing world, as also in the erstwhile socialist bloc, had begun to reshape their domestic economic policies so as to integrate much more into the world economy and to enlarge the role of the market *vis-à-vis* the state. This was partly a consequence of internal crisis situations in economy, polity, and society. It was also significantly influenced by the collapse of planned economies and excessive or inappropriate state intervention in market economies. The widespread acceptance of this approach, it would seem, represented a new consensus in thinking about development that came to be known as the *Washington consensus*. Despite many voices of dissent, it remained the dominant view, in part because it was propagated by the IMF and the World Bank, which exercised enormous influence on economies in crisis. This belief system was somewhat shaken by the financial crisis in Asia. But the Washington consensus has also lost some of its lustre as development experience during the 1990s has belied expectations. Its prescriptions are now subjected to question.[2] And the questions have not come from the critics alone.[3]

Changes in thinking mirror changes in reality. Privatization, liberalization, and globalization have gathered momentum. This process has placed new players centre stage in the world economy. There are two main sets of economic players in this game: transnational corporations which dominate investment, production, and trade in the world economy, and international banks or financial intermediaries which control the world of finance. This has induced a strategic withdrawal on the part of the nation state in some important spheres. They remain the main political players but are no longer the main economic players. Even the political milieu is not the same in nation states. For *market economy* is not the only buzzword of our times. So is *political democracy*. This is attributable, in part, to a concern about authoritarian regimes, particularly in countries where there has been no improvement in the living conditions of the common people, but even in countries where economic development has been impressive there has been no movement towards a democratic polity. Of course, it must be

---

[1] For an analysis of contending views about openness and intervention, see Nayyar (1997).

[2] The critical literature on the subject is extensive. See, for example, Cornia *et al.* (1987), Taylor (1988) and Cooper (1992). [3] See Stiglitz (1998).

recognized that the very rapid marketization of economies is combined with a much slower democratization of polities.

2. PROBLEMS: OLD AND NEW

The economic and political changes in the world, highlighted above, have been associated with, or have led to, a number of often severe problems. Some old problems persist and may have intensified. Poverty, inequality, and deprivation persist. And there is poverty everywhere. One-eighth of the people in the industrialized world are affected by, or live in, poverty. Almost one-third of the people in the developing world, an estimated 1.5 billion, live in poverty and experience absolute deprivation insofar as they cannot meet their basic human needs. The same number do not have access to clean water. As many as 840 million people suffer from malnutrition. More than 260 million children who should be in school are not. Nearly 340 million women are not expected to survive to the age of 40. And, as we enter the twenty-first century, more than 850 million adults remain illiterate. Most of them live in the developing world. But, in a functional sense, the number of illiterate people in the industrialized world, at 100 million, is also large.[4] Globalization may have created opportunities for a few countries and some people in the developing world, but a very large proportion of both countries and people have remained untouched or have been marginalized by the same process. Such exclusion has had social consequences as some of those deprived have turned to crime, drugs, or violence. Similarly, environmental destruction continues. The accent on deregulation has possibly accelerated the overexploitation and degradation of common property resources.

New problems have surfaced. The transition in Eastern Europe remains grossly incomplete and has been accompanied by a large increase in poverty, inequality, and mortality.[5] At the same time, political tensions have mounted. Indeed, many of these new states remain economically fragile and politically unstable. Elsewhere, nation states have fractured as they have slipped into ethnic strife or civil war. The number of humanitarian crises, with their legacy of death, displacement and destruction, has risen dramatically over the past decade. The response of the international community and of the United Nations (in peacekeeping, helping refugees, de-mining, reconstruction and so on) has been *ad hoc*, inadequate or simply not forthcoming. There is still no system in place to take care of, let alone prevent, complex humanitarian emergencies. Some new problems are a direct consequence of globalization. In their endeavour to attract direct foreign investment, developing countries compete with each other in a 'race to the bottom', by offering tax holidays, diluting labour laws, repressing trade unions, or turning a blind eye to environmental concerns. The rapid integration of, and into international financial markets, combined with the explosive growth in portfolio investment flows and short-term capital movements, has led to a volatility in capital flows and an instability in exchange rates so that the danger of capital flight is ever

---

[4] The evidence cited in this paragraph is drawn from UNDP (1999).   [5] See Cornia (1999).

present.[6] These problems can only in part be addressed at the domestic level as attempted in Chile. Thus, as the recent series of currency crises establish, unrestricted capital mobility means that penalties for even moderate macroeconomic imbalances (as in Thailand, Malaysia, or South Korea) can be disproportionate and excessive. Indeed, such economic crises (as events in Indonesia show) can easily acquire political dimensions.

It need hardly be stressed that this enumeration of problems—old and new—is illustrative rather than exhaustive. It is also abundantly clear that the world economy and polity at the present juncture are fundamentally different from those that existed half a century ago when the United Nations system and the Bretton Woods institutions were created. This institutional framework has, of course, evolved over time. However, the underlying construct, which was based on the world view of its architects, has remained the same. It should come as no surprise that there are no systemic solutions, yet, for the old problems that persist and the new problems that confront the world. And if the world has changed so much since then, so must have its governance needs in terms of institutions and rules.[7]

The main object of the book is to address this issue, in an endeavour to sketch the contours of institutions and governance that would meet the needs of the world economy, as also polity, at least for the first quarter of the twenty-first century, just as the system and the institutions created in 1945 served the world during the second half of the twentieth century. In doing so, it is essential to pose, and attempt to answer, the following questions. First, is the institutional framework created *c*.1945 adequate, or even appropriate, for the economy and the polity of the contemporary world? Second, if there are gaps, do we need to redefine the role of, or adapt the existing institutions to meet the needs of our times? Third, if this is not sufficient because there are missing institutions, do new institutions also need to be created?

3. GLOBALIZATION AND GOVERNANCE

The world economy has experienced a progressive international economic integration since 1950. However, there has been a marked acceleration in this process of globalization during the last quarter of the twentieth century. There are three manifestations of this phenomenon—international trade, international investment, and international finance—which also constitute its cutting edge. But there is much more to globalization. It refers to the expansion of economic transactions and the organization of economic activities across the political boundaries of nation states. More precisely, it can be defined as a process associated with increasing economic openness, growing economic interdependence, and deepening economic integration between countries in the world economy.

---

[6] For an analysis of this proposition, see Eatwell and Taylor (2000) and Nayyar (2000). For a discussion of, and evidence on, the financial crises in South-East Asia and East Asia, as also elsewhere, see UNCTAD (1998).

[7] The problems and challenges arising from these changes in the world are explored in the Report of the Commission on Global Governance (1995).

Economic *openness* is not simply confined to trade flows, investment flows, and financial flows. It also extends to flows of services, technology, information, and ideas across national boundaries. But the cross-border movement of people is closely regulated and highly restricted. Economic *interdependence* is asymmetrical. There is a high degree of interdependence among countries in the industrialized world. There is considerable dependence of the developing countries on the industrialized countries. There is much less interdependence among countries in the developing world. It is important to note that a situation of interdependence is one where the benefits of linking and the costs of delinking are about the same for both partners; where such benefits and costs are unequal between partners, it implies a situation of dependence. Economic *integration* straddles national boundaries as liberalization has diluted the significance of borders in economic transactions. It is, in part, an integration of markets (for goods, services, technology, financial assets, and even money) on the demand side, and, in part, an integration of production (horizontal and vertical) on the supply side.

It is important to situate our analysis of governance, through institutions and rules, in the wider context of globalization. For the process of globalization in the world economy has brought about profound changes in the international context which have far reaching implications for development.[8] The need for governance is greater than before. But the task has become more difficult.

The United Nations and the Bretton Woods institutions were at the core of the institutional system for global governance that was created in 1945. The nation state was the foundation of both the conception and the design. Indeed, even if they were unequal partners, nation states were not only the actors onstage but also the directors backstage. Now, more than fifty years later, the world is different. For one thing, globalization has constrained the role of the nation state. The autonomy of the nation state is much reduced in matters economic if not political. For another, there are significant players apart from nation states. Governments now share the stage with corporate entities and civil society. The system of institutions and rules for governance of the world economy created then is, therefore, less compatible with the changed reality now.

Globalization, however, is not new. There was a similar phase of globalization which began a century earlier, *c.*1870, and gathered momentum until 1914 when it came to an end. In many ways, the world economy in the late twentieth century closely resembled the world economy in the late nineteenth century.[9] The parallels between the two periods are striking. The integration of the world economy through inter-national trade, reflected in the share of world exports in world GDP, was about the same. The story was similar for international investment, as the stock of direct foreign investment at constant prices or as a proportion of world output was about the same. The integration of markets for international finance was also comparable, in so far as

---

[8] For a detailed discussion on the implications of globalization for development, see Nayyar (2000).

[9] This historical parallel was the theme of my Presidential Address to the Indian Economic Association (Nayyar 1995). Sachs and Warner (1995) make a similar comparison but from a very different perspective. The supporting evidence cited in this paragraph draws upon Nayyar (1995).

D. Nayyar

the cross-national ownership of securities, international bank lending and net international capital flows, in relative terms, were about the same. In the late nineteenth century, the missing dimension was international transactions in foreign exchange, which are massive now, given the past regime of fixed exchange rates under the gold standard. In the late twentieth century, the missing dimension was the almost unrestricted movement of people across national boundaries, which was massive then, given the present regime of restrictive immigration laws and consular practices. In terms of governance, however, there is a fundamental difference between these two phases of globalization. The late nineteenth century was the age of empire. The rules of the game were set by the military strength of the few imperial powers. And the risks associated with trade, investment, and finance across national boundaries were, in effect, underwritten by the imperial nation states. The early twenty-first century is a different world. The earlier forms of governance are neither feasible nor desirable, in part because the nation state does not have the same strength and in part because the contemporary world would prefer to set the rules of the game to manage the risks associated with globalization.

Globalization, both then and now, has been associated with an exclusion of countries and of people from its world of economic opportunities.[10] The irony of this reality is captured eloquently by what Joan Robinson once wrote: 'There is only one thing that is worse than being exploited by capitalists. And that is not being exploited by capitalists.' Much the same can be said about markets and globalization which may not ensure prosperity for everyone but may, in fact, exclude a significant proportion of people. Markets exclude people as consumers or buyers of goods and services if they do not have any incomes, or sufficient incomes, which can be translated into purchasing power. This exclusion is attributable to a lack of *entitlements*.[11] Markets exclude such people as producers or sellers if they have neither *assets* nor *capabilities*. People experience such exclusion if they do not have assets, physical or financial, which can be used (or sold) to yield an income in the form of rent, interest, or profits. Even those without assets can enter the markets as sellers, using their labour if they have some capabilities.[12] Such capabilities, which are acquired through education, training, or experience, are different from natural abilities, which are endowed. But the distribution of capabilities may be just as unequal if not more so. It is these capabilities which can, in turn, yield an income in the form of wages. Hence, people without

---

[10] See Rodrik (1997).

[11] This term was first used by Sen (1981) in his work on poverty and famines.

[12] In this chapter, I use the word *capabilities* to characterize the mix of natural talents, skills acquired through training, learning from experience and abilities or expertise based on education, embodied in a person and which enable him or her to use their capabilities (as a producer or worker) for which there is not only a price but also a demand in the market. It is essential to note that the same word, *capabilities*, has been used in a very different sense by Amartya Sen, who argues that the well-being of a person depends on what the person succeeds in *doing* with the commodities (and their characteristics) at his/her command. For example, food can provide nutrition for a healthy person but not to a person with a parasitic disease; or a bicycle can provide transportation for an able-bodied person but not a disabled person. Thus, for Sen (1985), *capabilities* characterize the combination of functionings people can achieve, given their personal features (conversion of characteristics into functionings) and their command over commodities (entitlements).

capabilities—the poor, who cannot find employment—are excluded. In fact, even people with capabilities may be excluded from employment if there is no demand for their capabilities in the (labour) market. And, in the ultimate analysis, such capabilities are defined by the market. That is the problem. In a national context, the state may introduce correctives to pre-empt exclusion or interventions to limit the adverse effects of exclusion.[13] The reason is simple. Governments are accountable to their people, whereas markets are not. Globalization, also, is a market-driven process which may reinforce or accentuate exclusion. In the changed international context, however, the increased openness, interdependence, and integration attributable to globalization have made it more difficult for governments to intervene, particularly through economic policies, to combat such exclusion.[14]

4. THE INSTITUTIONAL FRAMEWORK

An assessment of the United Nations system and the Bretton Woods institutions, over five decades in retrospect, is obviously difficult but clearly necessary. And there are bound to be differences in judgement. Even so, most would agree that the performance of these institutions presents a mixed picture with some important successes and some major failures. It is also reasonable to suggest that as the world has changed, and new global problems have surfaced, the evolution or development of institutions for governance has simply not kept pace. Indeed, it would seem that the capacity of the old institutions is not quite a match for the complexity of the new challenges.

An emerging institutional gap is discernible in a wide range of symptoms. For example, there are conflicts in mandates, between the Bretton Woods institutions on the one hand and the United Nations on the other, in the reconstruction of war-torn societies, in the management of crisis-ridden economies, or in the development of democratic institutions. These situations need not only a clearer division of labour but also responses which blend humanitarian assistance, economic management, and political leadership in ways that the narrow and somewhat rigid approach of the IMF and the World Bank is unable to provide. Even where the United Nations has received mandates without such constraints (as in the area of peacekeeping), it is hamstrung by a range of problems from inadequate resources to political disagreements. And the real problem, often, is that the United Nations is a watchdog without teeth. The Bretton Woods institutions also have their problems, as private capital flows have turned them into marginal providers of resources while international financial markets have undermined their ability to manage international liquidity and preserve monetary

---

[13] For an analysis of such correctives and interventions, see Nayyar (2000).

[14] Countries, which are integrated into the world financial system are constrained in using an autonomous management of demand to maintain levels of output and employment. Expansionary fiscal and monetary policies—large government deficits to stimulate aggregate demand or low interest rates to stimulate investment—can no longer be used because of an overwhelming fear that such measures could lead to speculative capital flight and a run on the national currency (Nayyar 2000). And when financial crises do surface, deflationary economic policies adopted by governments accentuate the exclusion of the poor (UNCTAD 1998).

D. Nayyar

stability.[15] Most important, perhaps, there are areas such as organized crime, pollutant emissions, environmental degradation, portfolio investment flows, and so on, where controls and regulations are necessary to cope with their cross-border consequences and national authorities are manifestly unable to operate alone. Yet, no international authorities or coordinating bodies have been created. It needs to be said that such examples can be multiplied with ease.

The questions posed earlier asked whether the present institutional framework is adequate, appropriate, or sufficient to meet the governance needs of the contemporary world economy and polity. The obvious way of seeking answers to these questions is to consider the existing institutions, evaluate their experience, analyse their problems, recognize their limitations and, if possible, identify their gaps. In doing so, we need to focus on: (a) the United Nations system which spans a wide range of activities from peacekeeping, human rights and disarmament (UN), through social development (UNICEF), education and culture (UNESCO), health (WHO), labour (ILO), refugees (UNHCR) and famine prevention (WFP) to technical assistance (UNDP), and there are several others; (b) the Bretton Woods twins, the International Monetary Fund and the World Bank (together with its affiliates); and (c) the General Agreement on Tariffs and Trade, incorporated into the World Trade Organization in 1995.

Such an evaluation of the institutional framework for global governance is clearly necessary. But this approach is characterized by an important limitation. It views the world and its problems through the eyes of these institutions. Two difficulties arise. For one, it could miss out on problems beyond their defined jurisdiction or established scope. For another, it would not be possible to identify the institutional gaps let alone the missing institutions.

5. EMERGING ISSUES AND MISSING INSTITUTIONS

Obviously, a focus on the existing institutions alone cannot suffice. It must be combined with a focus on issues, which have acquired a new significance in the contemporary world. Given the increasing economic openness associated with globalization, it would be logical to consider changes in the nature and the scope of international economic transactions as a starting point. The reason is simple enough. It may highlight the emerging issues even if it cannot pinpoint the missing institutions. The past five decades have witnessed not only a phenomenal expansion of, but also considerable structural change in, international trade flows and international capital movements. Cross-border transactions in technology and movements of people have experienced significant changes in their dimensions or composition, which suggest a considerable potential. These changes may have created new governance needs.

The rules governing trade, which began life with the GATT five decades ago, have evolved over time, but the system has not quite kept pace with the changing reality and the increasing complexity of world trade. An increasing proportion of world output enters into world trade. An increasing proportion of world trade is made up of

---

[15] For a discussion of these issues, see Eatwell and Taylor (2000). See also UNCTAD (1998).

intra-firm trade. Trade flows have moved much beyond the simple world of goods, just as trade barriers have moved far beyond the simple world of tariffs. Trade is more and more an arena for conflicts and claims from other spheres. And, in a world of unequal partners, where bargains are struck among the major players, a large number of countries are spectators rather than participants in multilateral negotiations.

The composition of long-term capital flows has changed significantly from concessional development assistance through commercial bank lending to direct foreign investment. Short-term capital movements and portfolio investment flows are, of course, a more recent phenomenon which has been driven, in part, by the explosive growth in, and the rapid integration of, international financial markets and, in part, by the domestic deregulation of the financial sector within countries. Despite the series of crises unleashed by their inherent volatility or instability, there is no prospect so far of rules or institutions that might govern such capital movements.

International transactions in technology are modest by comparison, but the scope spans a wide range while the potential for expansion in an integrated and inter-dependent world economy is enormous. However, the recently introduced rules are confined to the protection of intellectual property rights. In these, there is a striking asymmetry between the interests of technology-leaders or technology-exporters, which are the subjects of attention, and the interests of technology-followers or technology-importers, which are the objects of neglect. A view of the totality, with an eye to the future, is essential.

Cross-border movements of people are constrained by immigration laws and consular practices. But, in a world where income disparities and population imbalances between countries are vast, pressures for migration across national boundaries are considerable. And these pressures may have been reinforced by the spread of education and the revolution in transport, which has led to a significant increase in the mobility of labour. In this sphere, there are distinctions to be drawn between: legal migration and illegal migration, permanent emigration and temporary migration, or voluntary migration and distress migration. This issue is not confined to the sphere of economics. It extends to the realm of politics. And there are problems, serious problems, which surface time and again. Yet, apart from the UNHCR, there is little in the form of institutions let alone governance.

It must be recognized that issues extend beyond cross-border movements or transactions. National policies of governments have international consequences, just as international activities of firms have national consequences. Economic interdependence means that macroeconomic policies adopted in a national context, particularly by the major industrialized countries, exercise an important influence on economies in the rest of the world through interest rates, exchange rates, or inflation rates. But there are almost no mechanisms, let alone institutions, which would facilitate the coordination of national macroeconomic policies or the introduction of global macroeconomic management. Similarly, economic integration means that investment, production, trade, and technology in the world economy are increasingly dominated by transnational corporations. Yet, these large international firms are not governed by any rules or institutions. It is worth noting that there is more to issues than the consequences of actions by governments or firms. For actions of individuals also have effects that spill over across national boundaries, just as global developments influence the lives of people everywhere.

6. GOVERNANCE NEEDS

It is important to recognize that governance of the world economy, through institutions or rules, is necessary but difficult. There are two reasons why it is necessary now perhaps more than it was earlier. First, national laws are applicable to resident individuals or registered firms but their jurisdiction does not extend to individuals or firms across national boundaries. This was probably sufficient in a world where economic space coincided, broadly, with geographical space. As a consequence of globalization, however, economic space extends much beyond geographical space. Yet, rules or laws do not. Second, rational economic behaviour by individuals (utility-maximization) and firms (profit-maximization) leads to externalities in production and in consumption so that the whole is different from the sum total of the parts. In a world economy characterized by ever increasing openness and integration, such externalities are much more prone to spillovers across national boundaries. Even if the need for governance is greater, it is somewhat difficult to put in place. The reason is simple. Individuals or firms are subject to national laws enacted by their parliaments. But countries are not subject to similar international laws for there is no world government or parliament that can enact laws binding on nations. Indeed, nation states are very conscious of national sovereignty. Thus, creating rules or laws that are binding on sovereign nation states is a matter for international negotiations and mutual acceptance by governments. That, we know from experience, is both complex and slow.

In contemplating governance needs, it is perhaps appropriate to make a distinction between: (i) existing rules or institutions and how they need to be changed or adapted; and (ii) missing rules or institutions and why they need to be introduced or created.

In a world of unequal partners, it is not surprising that the rules of the game are asymmetrical in terms of construct and inequitable in terms of outcome. The strong have the power to make the rules and the authority to implement the rules. In contrast, the weak can neither set nor invoke the rules. The problem, however, takes different forms.

First, there are different rules in different spheres. The rules of the game for the international trading system, being progressively set in the WTO, provide the most obvious example. There are striking asymmetries. National boundaries should not matter for trade flows and capital flows but should be clearly demarcated for technology flows and labour flows. This implies more openness in some spheres and less openness in other spheres. The contrast between the free movement of capital and the unfree movement of labour is the most stark. Second, there are rules for some but not for others. The conditions imposed by the IMF and the World Bank provide the most obvious example. There are no rules for surplus countries, or even deficit countries, in the industrialized world which do not borrow from the multilateral financial institutions, but the IMF and the World Bank set rules for borrowers in the developing world and in the transitional economies. Third, the agenda for new rules is partisan, but the unsaid is just as important as the said. The attempt to create a multilateral agreement on investment in the WTO, which seeks free access and national treatment for foreign investors with provisions to enforce commitments and obligations to foreign investors, provides the most obvious example. Surely, these rights of foreign investors must be matched by some obligations. Thus, a discipline on restrictive business practices of transnational corporations, the importance of conformity with antitrust laws in home countries, or a level playing field for domestic firms in host countries, should also be in the picture.

It need hardly be said that the nature of the solution depends upon the nature of the problem. Where there are different rules in different spheres, it is necessary to make the rules symmetrical across spheres. Where there are rules for some but not for others, it is necessary to ensure that the rules are uniformly applicable to all. Where the agenda for new rules is partisan, it is imperative to redress the balance in the agenda.

The momentum of globalization is such that the power of national governments is being reduced, through incursions into hitherto sovereign economic and political space, without a corresponding increase in effective international cooperation or supra-national government, which could regulate this market-driven process. In sum, national economies are much less governable while the global economy is almost ungoverned. Yet, there are no rules in some spheres while needed institutions are missing. This is possibly because the conflict between national sovereignty and global governance is a critical issue in the realm of politics.

The non-existent rules also have implications for the world economy. If each nation acts in its own perceived self-interest, the outcome could be suboptimal in terms of world welfare simply because each country would rely on others to bear the costs of arrangements that benefit every country in the world. Consequently, *public goods* would be in excess demand, while *public bads* would be in excess supply. Consider an example of a *public good* (say environmental conservation) which requires a contri-bution from all countries. The order of preferences, in the pursuit of self-interest, would be as follows: (1) our country does not contribute but others do (*free rider* problem); (2) our country contributes as do all other countries and everybody is better off (*cooperative solution*); (3) no country contributes and everybody is worse off (*Prisoners' Dilemma* outcome); and (4) our country contributes but no other country does (the *isolation paradox* in reverse). Although every country prefers 2 to 3, the hope for 1 and the fear of 4 lead to 3. Strategies based on self-interest would, inevitably, lead to a Prisoners' Dilemma outcome. This cannot be mitigated by the Coase Theorem solution, for even in situations where there are no transaction costs, there is complete information and there are well-defined property rights, those who gain may not be in a position to, or may not wish to, make compensation payments to those who lose. A cooperative solution outcome can only be ensured if there are penalties for non-contribution and rewards for contribution.

Under the present system, where there is no supranational government or dominant world power imposing restraint, or cooperation requiring self-restraint, we are bound to end up with *public bads* (such as environmental degradation, the arms trade, or drug

traffic). It follows that where there are no rules, which can impose restraint or discipline, it would be desirable to create new rules in the interest of *public goods* (such as a
sustainable environment or world peace). But this may not always be feasible. Yet, in
a world where the pursuit of self-interest by nations means uncoordinated action or
non-cooperative behaviour, suboptimal solutions, which are ultimately self-damaging
or self-destructive and leave everybody worse off, can only be prevented through the
creation of institutional mechanisms for cooperation. This requires more than rules. It
needs a consensus, as the regulation of *public bads* requires self-restraint while the
promotion of *public goods* requires a contribution from all countries. Global governance, then, is not so much about world government as it is about institutions and
practices combined with rules that facilitate cooperation among sovereign nation states.

There are, indeed, many spheres in the world economy where coordination between
countries, outside and beyond the market, might make everybody better off or
minimize the costs (maximize the benefits) associated with globalization. The example,
which comes to mind instantly, is environmental preservation. But there are others in
the more mundane world of economics. Greater international coordination of macroeconomic policies, particularly among the industrialized countries, would not only help
raise levels of output and employment but would also contribute towards maintaining
stability in the short term and sustaining growth in the long term.[16] The regulation of
speculative financial flows, constituted mostly by short-term capital movements, sensitive to exchange rates and interest rates, in search of capital gains, would help both
the industrialized countries and the developing countries. In the industrialized world,
financial deregulation has raised real interest rates and discouraged investment, while
financial markets have forced governments to follow low growth or even deflationary
policies. In the developing world, a rapid integration into international financial
markets has introduced a vulnerability that comes from volatility with far reaching
consequences for economy and polity.

Governing globalization, or steering the process, is a possible starting point that is
less abstract and more concrete than global governance. The endeavour should be to
make the market-driven process of globalization conducive to a more egalitarian
economic development and a more broad-based social development. The object of
such a design should be to provide more countries with opportunities to improve
their development prospects and more people within these countries to improve their
living conditions. It would have to be supported by a new institutional set-up. This
would mean providing *global public goods*, such as world peace and a sustainable

---

[16] It was such coordination that helped sustain rapid growth and maintain full employment in the
industrialized world during the 1950s and the 1960s. The institutional arrangements in the world economy
at the time were conducive or supportive but not causal. Thus, the IMF and the World Bank were not so
important in the economic recovery of Europe and Japan. The strategic economic response of the United
States to the actual or perceived threat from the then Soviet Union was far more important. This was not
simply the Marshall Plan. It extended to measures that permitted European countries and Japan to
discriminate against goods from the United States but provided them with complete access to the market in
the United States. But such coordination, or cooperation, is much more difficult in the post-cold war world
which is not characterized by competition between two systems. The challenge now is to create a political
milieu and an institutional framework for cooperation between countries that extends beyond the market.

environment.[17] This would mean regulating *global public bads*, such as international crime whether trade in drugs, arms, people, or organs. But that is not all. In so far as the pursuit of self-interest by nations leads to non-cooperative behaviour, which increases *public bads* and decreases *public goods* in the world, it may be necessary to introduce new rules or create new institutions. It would also require a system to correct for the failures of unregulated or liberalized international markets (say regulating short-term capital movements or portfolio investment flows and controlling harmful emissions or wastes through environmental regulations). And the design would not be complete without some initiatives to build up missing markets.

7. STRUCTURE AND SCOPE

The preceding discussion sets out the rationale and the objective of this volume. It also outlines the analytical approach. The structure and the scope of the book are as follows.

The first part seeks to situate the subject in the wider context of globalization, which has shaped development in the world economy, affected the living conditions of people and constrained the role of nation states. And, even as some old problems persist, several new problems have surfaced. If we wish to understand these problems and search for solutions, the international context and the national setting are both important. This introductory chapter explores the changed international context to highlight the governance needs of the contemporary world. Chapter 2, by Amit Bhaduri, is concerned with the national setting to analyse the implications and consequences of globalization for the nation state especially in terms of economic policy. These chapters are meant to set the stage before the play begins.

The second part endeavours to analyse selected issues, which have acquired a new significance in the contemporary world. Its object is to examine whether the present institutional framework is adequate or appropriate for governance and to identify the emerging institutional gaps. It was obviously difficult to keep such an exercise within manageable proportions, for even a short list would have been long. A choice was inevitable. And, any selection is, to some extent, subjective. The choice of issues was, nevertheless, based on two criteria: where problems are of a recurring nature and are not random or unpredictable occurrences; and where governance, however difficult, is in the realm of the possible. Chapter 3, by Lance Taylor, addresses the complex theme of global macroeconomic management. Chapter 4, by Sanjaya Lall, analyses the implications of international systems of governance for transnational corporations and technology flows. Chapter 5, by Yilmaz Akyüz and Andrew Cornford, studies capital flows to developing countries to highlight emerging problems associated with financial crises and outlines possible solutions, which would require new forms of governance. Chapter 6, by Deepak Nayyar, analyses cross-border movements of people, an unexplored theme, to consider issues and problems of governance. The discussion on these issues endeavours to answer the following questions: How has the world changed

---

[17] Global public goods, as also global public bads, are analysed and discussed, at some length, in Kaul *et al.* (1999).

since 1945? What have been the implications for development? Are there any rules or institutions for governance? If so, how have they performed? Is there a need to modify present rules or adapt existing institutions? Is it necessary to formulate new rules or create new institutions for governance?

The third part attempts a critical evaluation of the existing institutions in retrospect. In doing so, it analyses their problems, recognizes their limitations and, wherever possible, identifies their gaps. But the main object is to explore how existing rules need to be modified or existing institutions need to be restructured to meet the present and future governance needs of the world economy and polity. Chapter 7, by Richard Falk, considers the record of the United Nations system since its inception with an eye on prospects for renewal and reform at the present juncture. Chapter 8, by Jong-Il You, discusses the evolution of the Bretton Woods institutions, pinpoints their limitations and their failures, to suggest directions for reform and change. Chapter 9, by Joseph Stiglitz, stresses the logic of international collective action in the context of globalization to re-examine the role of the Bretton Woods institutions. Chapter 10, by Shrirang Shukla, examines the evolution of the international trading system from its inception as the GATT to its new incarnation as the WTO, evaluates the experience so far, and reflects on future governance needs. The discussion on these sets of institutions endeavours to answer the following questions: Why were they created? What were the context and the rationale? What were their objectives? How have they functioned in terms of successes and failures? If they have not realized their objectives, is it attributable to structural problems of the institutions or to political constraints on the functioning of the system? Has the exclusion of the countries from their membership or of issues from their domain made a difference? How have they responded to the problems of developing countries? Is there a structural flexibility that allows for the needs of development? Do they need to adapt any response to changing circumstances and new problems? Is it necessary to contemplate radical change or new institutions?

The fourth part seeks to develop an overview about the present and a vision about the future. In an ideal world, the object would have been to sketch the contours of institutions and governance that would meet the needs of the world economy, as also polity, over the next two, if not five, decades. But this is an exceedingly difficult, if not impossible, task. Even a modest beginning, therefore, would make a contribution. Chapter 11, by José Antonio Ocampo, argues that there should be a thorough reform of the international financial architecture. Chapter 12, by Gerald Helleiner, considers the role and objectives of developing countries in global economic governance with an emphasis on negotiation processes rather than on the specific objectives of improved governance. Chapter 13, by Devesh Kapur, examines processes of change in international institutions to develop generalizations about causal mechanisms and trajectories of change. Chapter 14, by Deepak Nayyar, on the existing system and the missing institutions, suggests some changes in, and highlights important issues, for existing institutions; it also points to emerging governance needs where new institutions may have to be created.

It is clear from the essays in this volume that we have not reached the end of the debate on governing globalization let alone global governance. There are unexplored themes and unsettled issues. This endeavour, it is hoped, would contribute to our understanding and stimulate further thinking.

8. TOWARDS A WORLD VIEW

As we approach the twenty-first century, it is time to reflect on a new world view and search for a new consensus on development, which can only be based on a vision about the future of economy, polity, and society in the world. In this reflection, the concern for efficiency must be balanced with the concern for equity, just as the concern for economic growth must be balanced with a concern for social progress: for efficiency and growth are means not ends. They need to be combined with economic stability, full employment, poverty eradication, reduced inequality, human development, and a sustainable environment. It is also time to evolve a new consensus on development in which the focus is on people rather than economies. Such a consensus must be built on a sense of proportion, which does not reopen old ideological battles in terms of either-or-choices and on a depth of understanding which recognizes the complexity and diversity of development. This thinking should not be limited to the sphere of economics. It must extend to the realm of politics. The eradication of poverty from the world is an imperative. In 1945, when the United Nations system and the Bretton Woods institutions were created, there was an underlying world view about peace in the world, full employment in the industrialized countries, and economic development in the newly independent countries. If there is to be another world view fifty years later, which could provide the core of a new development agenda for the twenty-first century, it must surely begin with humankind where ensuring decent living conditions for people, ordinary citizens of the world, is a fundamental objective.

In pursuit of these objectives, the new paradigm for world governance could derive some inspiration from the expected (not actual) role of government (within countries) in an ideal world (set out in standard public economies). It could also derive some inspiration from the conception of political democracy so as to create a more democratic structure of world governance. In a world of unequal partners, inevitably, it is the rich and the powerful nations that can create institutional systems for global governance. And historical experience suggests that crises are the catalysts of change. The last time around, it was the aftermath of a world war and a worldwide economic depression that led to the foundation of the United Nations system and the creation of the Bretton Woods institutions. This book is written in the hope that the world need not wait for another crisis of such proportions to contemplate and introduce the much needed changes in global governance.

REFERENCES

Commission on Global Governance (1995). *Our Global Neighborhood*. The Report of the Commission on Global Governance. Oxford University Press, Oxford.
Cooper, Richard N. (1992). *Economic Stabilization and Debt in Developing Countries*. The MIT Press, Cambridge, MA.

Cornia, Giovanni Andrea (1999). Liberalization, globalization and income distribution. *WIDER Working Paper*, No. 157. UNU/WIDER, Helsinki.

——Richard Jolly, and Frances Stewart (1987). *Adjustment with a Human Face*. Clarendon Press, Oxford.

Eatwell, John and Lance Taylor (2000). *Global Finance at Risk: The Case for International Regulation*. The New Press, New York.

Kaul, Inge, Isabelle Grunberg, and Marc A. Stern (eds) (1999). *Global Public Goods: International Cooperation in the 21st Century*. Oxford University Press, New York and Oxford.

Nayyar, Deepak (1995). Globalization: The past in our present. *Indian Economic Journal*, 43(3), 1–18.

——(1997). Themes in trade and industrialization. In D. Nayyar (ed.), *Trade and Industrialization*. Oxford University Press, New Delhi.

——(2000). Globalization and development strategies. *High-Level Roundtable on Trade and Development at UNCTAD X*. TD X/RT.1/4. United Nations, New York and Geneva.

Rodrik, Dani (1997). *Has Globalization Gone Too Far?* Washington, DC: Institute for International Economics.

Sachs, Jeffrey and Andrew Warner (1995). Economic reform and the process of global integration. *Brookings Papers on Economic Activity*, 1, 1–118.

Sen, Amartya K. (1981). *Poverty and Famines: An Essay on Entitlement and Deprivation*. Clarendon Press, Oxford.

——(1985). *Commodities and Capabilities*. North-Holland, Amsterdam.

Stiglitz, Joseph E. (1998). More instruments and broader goals: Moving toward the post-Washington consensus. *WIDER Annual Lectures* 2. UNU/WIDER, Helsinki.

Taylor, Lance (1988). *Varieties of Stabilization Experience: Towards Sensible Macroeconomics in the Third World*. Clarendon Press, Oxford.

UNCTAD (1998). *Trade and Development Report 1998*. United Nations, New York and Geneva.

UNDP (1999). *Human Development Report 1999*. Oxford University Press, New York.

2

Nationalism and Economic Policy in the Era of Globalization

AMIT BHADURI

The *raison d'être* of the nation state is the ideology of nationalism. Yet, nationalism is a complex notion, which encompasses the society, the state, and the economy. It comprises a complex nexus of multiple loyalties of an individual as a member of the society, duties and rights of the citizen in a reciprocal political arrangement with the state, and the role of the individual as a producer and consumer in the economy. While the balance among these different aspects of nationalism evolved historically, in the present area of globalization this balance seems to be shifting in favour of global market forces. Its consequences for the nation state, and the new role that it needs to define for itself, especially in terms of economic policy, is the theme of this chapter.

1. AN INTELLECTUAL BACKGROUND TO THE RISE OF THE NATION STATE

The three-way merger of the state as a political entity, the nation as a historical or cultural concept, and the economy as an organization of production and exchange activities has always been problematic. Through several centuries in Western political philosophy, the relationship between the political authority of the state and the historical formation of the society, viewed as the voluntary association of individuals, posed a major problem. Coinciding almost exactly with the date of publication of Adam Smith's *Wealth of Nations* (1776), Thomas Paine gave one of the clearest, if somewhat dramatic expression of the view which tended to treat the state almost as a 'necessary evil'.

Society is produced by our wants and government by our wickedness; the former promotes our happiness positively by uniting our affections, the latter negatively by restraining our vices. (Paine 1776: 66)

To the modern proponents of the 'minimalist state', this might sound like an echo from the distant past of their theories. Nevertheless, this would be a misinterpretation. In classical political philosophy, the counterposing of society as widening the individual's freedom of action against the role of the state needed for restricting the scope of the individual's negative impulses, had a more subtle intellectual basis. Indeed, the shaping of Adam Smith's political economy—his journey from the *Theory of Moral Sentiments* (1759) to the *Wealth of Nations* (1776)—illustrates this point well.

Unless we postulate oversimplistically, in line with modern 'methodological individualism', that all social as well as economic interactions are reducible only to the self-interest of the individual, the notion of the society can be embedded in a wider range of human moral sentiments, that is, the Smithian composite notion of 'sympathy'. Sympathy, in his view, is not just altruism, but a complex range of coexisting, often conflicting human motives. In particular, it combines 'fellow-feeling' which involves the desire to be socially engaged, with a 'rational' evaluation of the consequences of such engagements. An important social outcome of this is the emergence of mutual 'trust' and reciprocity without which no commercial society can function.

The consequence that follows from this analysis provides a necessary clue to our understanding of the role of the state. It is not altruism vs egoism, or community feeling vs selfishness which is the relevant issue. Neither the society nor the economy can function exclusively on the basis of either. Selfishness is moderated invariably by social 'norms' like trust and reciprocity of behaviour, which may even be the outcome of longer-term enlightened self-interest. They are absolutely essential for production with specialization, trade, and exchange on an extensive scale. Thus, norms for social behaviour having their origin in the Smithian notion of 'sympathy' go beyond narrow selfishness, but do not necessarily contradict enlightened self-interest; instead, self-restraint may be imposed on enlightened self-interest. This raises doubts about the popular view of a Leviathan state whose main purpose is to restrain self-seeking individuals in times of destructive conflict with each other (Hobbes 1957: especially chapters 14 and 15).

Viewed in the context of our preceding discussion, a central misleading feature of modern economic theory is not so much in the act of commission, as in the act of omission. The celebrated Arrow–Debreu model purports to demonstrate rigorously the Smithian proposition that the unintended outcome with (Pareto) optimal properties results through entirely selfish actions of individuals in a (competitive) market. What could be misleading about this analysis is not the string of unrealistic assumptions needed to establish the optimal properties of the market mechanism; but the implicit neglect of the complementary Smithian proposition that market exchange is sustained by the underlying social 'norms' resulting from sympathy, for example, trust in exchange, respect for contracts, etc. By leaving out the role of social norms in our formal analysis of exchange and production, we tend to exaggerate on the one hand, the efficiency of an abstract market mechanism based on an invented 'auctioneer'. On the other, we tend to neglect the roles which the state could play in either reinforcing or destroying these norms which are essential for the functioning of the market economy.

Within the framework of methodological individualism, some writers have tried recently to incorporate the notion of social norms as the informal constraints which the otherwise selfish individual faces (e.g. North 1990, chapter 5). Some others have seen these social norms as the emergence and evolution of cooperation which individuals learn in their enlightened, longer-term self-interest, especially in situations of repeated games of short-term conflictive interests (e.g. Axelrod 1984). In addition to the self-imposed restraint, either perceived by the individual as informal constraints or learnt as cooperative behaviour through repeated experience in social interactions, there is, however, a wider set of cultural limits that may be imposed by the norms of the society. They originate in different spheres like religion, language, or a common historical memory of the people. Juridical interpretations of such norms, in which the state plays an important role, may either reinforce or weaken them over time. The conflict between the church and the state in Europe, the curbing of the absolute power of the monarch during the European Enlightenment, the attempt even in recent times to establish the authority of the state either by adopting an official religion or by emphasizing its secular character bear testimony to the complexity of this process evolving continuously through time.

However, there is perhaps a general feature in this evolution. Broadly speaking, the more homogeneous a society is, say in terms of language, religion, ethnicity, and a shared history, the stronger is likely to be the intensity with which social norms apply to the individual members. It is not by accident that close-knit tribal societies have more powerful social norms, which typically tend to be reinforced by the political authority of a tribal or village headman. Obversely, social norms may be reinforced by a feeling of togetherness against a common enemy that operated in many liberation struggles against colonial powers. However, they tend to weaken after political freedom is achieved. Commercial societies, often in the interest of trade and commerce, deviate from such rigid and explicit social norms, apparently bestowing the individual with greater social freedom. At the same time, however, a commercial society creates other norms reinforced continuously by the needs of trade and commerce, like respect for commercial contracts. The modern 'nation state', which tries to fuse together the state, the society, and the economy under the overriding norm or ideology of 'nationalism' needs to be understood in this context.

In terms of starkly schematized intellectual history, Hobbes saw relatively little space between the individual and the state for the operation of the civil society. Hegel's philosophy of the statecraft (*staatswissenschaft*) can be seen as the culmination of this intellectual tradition. By separating the private from the public sphere, and by assigning moral supremacy to the latter, the Hegelian view celebrated the authority of the state which is engaged in the public sphere over the society which is engaged in the private sphere (Knox 1964).

Hegel's metaphysical justification of the moral supremacy of the state with its overriding authority over the private sphere became a powerful idea in the shaping of the nation state. This was especially feasible in situations where the (civil) society and its diverse norms could be compatible with the political objectives of the state. Thus, somewhat imperceptibly over almost the last two centuries, the political concept of the 'nation' has come into use to replace gradually the concept of the (civil) society. As pointed out already, the society generates its formal and informal norms of behaviour for social interaction, but it is hardly the natural place to forge any collective ideology like 'nationalism'. Multiple affinity or loyalty to groups, in terms of ethnicity, language, religion, or culture, is more easily understandable than 'nationalism' as an abstract construction which overrides these particular loyalties. This is given a tangible form in terms of loyalty to the geographical territory controlled by the state.

Territorial loyalty, however, is only a surface phenomenon; its content derives from the fact that the state is meant to assign and protect the 'rights' of its 'nationals' within that territory. The nation state is, therefore, based on a reciprocal arrangement. Nationals accept territorial loyalty as overriding, while the nation state protects their rights within that territory. However, in this reciprocal arrangement, the rights which the nationals of a particular territory enjoy is determined by the sovereign state according to the vague principle of 'self-determination of a people'. National sovereignty, therefore, leaves ambiguous the question of what these rights are or should be. In particular, it leaves open the question of how a sovereign state should deal with the multiple loyalties of its nationals in terms of ethnicity, language, religion, or culture which often make conflicting demands. The Hegelian requirement of placing the civil society with its multiple loyalties as the 'private' domain, and therefore, under the political authority of the state which belongs to the 'public' domain, becomes a particularly convenient ideology for the nation state in this context. Like Voltaire's God, the idea of loyalty to the nation, had to be invented, to suit the requirements of the nation state in dealing with multiple loyalties in the civil society.

The emphasis on the territorial integrity of the nation state meant that its laws and regulations applied also to the commercial activities carried out within its territory. Most importantly, national currency as a 'legal tender' within its territory became the symbol not merely of commercial trust, but also of the authority of the state over the economy. Nevertheless, these newer commercial norms and arrangements, often encouraged by the state, weakened at the same time many traditional social norms. As a result, the nation state consolidated itself by extending its control over the civil society through the economy. Nevertheless, the requirements of foreign trade, investment, and technology never allowed this control over the economy to be complete. The Aristotelian doctrine, that the optimum size of the state is determined according to the level of self-sufficiency (Aristotle 1912, Book 7), was reinterpreted centuries later by Machiavelli as self-sufficiency in arms and the ability of the state to defend itself (Meinecke 1957). In our century, it came to be redefined as the right to self-determination and sovereignty of a 'nation', which permits the state to become the ultimate decision maker within its territory. And yet, with respect to national sovereignty, foreign trade, investment, or finance can play a contradictory role. It may undermine the political authority of the economically weaker nation states by making them crucially dependent on foreign trade, investment, and finance; contrariwise, it may enhance the political authority of the economically stronger states in so far as the weaker nation states are crucially dependent on them. This links inextricably the economic and the political aspect of the authority of the nation state in its national and international context.

The policies of mercantilism recognized this possibility of furthering economic nationalism through trade. Closer to our time the political importance attached by national governments to the 'strength' of their national currency might reflect a similar sentiment. The current phase of globalization is important in the evolution of the nation state precisely from this angle. Economic globalization challenges the political authority, which the nation state had attained by undermining gradually many of the norms of the traditional civil society. The political authority of the nation state was consolidated in the process of expansion of commerce, as its laws and jurisdiction extended over the national economy. This strengthened economic nationalism as a complement to territorial nationalism. A paradoxical turn in history now confronts most nation states, as the further spread of trade, commerce, finance, and information obliterates many economic boundaries among nations. The same commercial logic, almost ironically, tends to undermine today the economic authority of the nation state, which it once helped to consolidate.

2. ECONOMIC NATIONALISM AND THE MARKET SYSTEM

The enormous political authority, which the nation state has acquired gradually is encapsulated conveniently in popular imagination as the 'sovereignty' of a nation. Viewed from above, each government is the ultimate source of authority and arbiter of disputes among its people. And, viewed from below, the nation, as a body of citizens, enjoys rights, which are given and defended by the state. In turn, this gives the population a stake in 'their country' to reinforce the ideology of patriotism, in defence of the nation of a sovereign nation (Hobsbawm 1990). At the same time, the political authority of the national government seeks legitimacy in one form or another. The more repressive and undemocratic a national government denying rights to its citizens, the more it needs to appeal to some version of 'nationalism' or patriotism for legitimizing its exercise of power over its people. The ideology of national sovereignty becomes important not only for democracies but also for dictatorships; paradoxically both need nationalism to maintain an arrangement of reciprocal advantage between the state and its citizens, and the latter usually by exaggerating the threat from 'others'.

The need for legitimacy and the search for a legitimizing ideology for the exercise of authority by the nation state proceeds in two somewhat different directions. As argued in Section 1, the umbrella ideology of nationalism and national interest is an intellectual construction, which is meant to override the diverse cultural, religious, and social norms that evolve from interactions in the civil society. Thus, one obvious way to legitimize the ideology of nationalism and the authority of the nation state is through an appeal to reinforce particular loyalties. Cultural or religious nationalism, or nationalism based on the ethnicity of a 'common' people, provides examples of this tendency in recent history.

At the same time, however, an almost opposite tendency is also in operation. Increasing specialization in production and exchange, the expansion of trade and commerce, and the spread of a commercial society, weaken many earlier social bonds and norms, while creating new commercially-oriented norms. Aided by the nation state, this contributes to the growth of economic nationalism. It is a process of convergence of 'norms' dominated by their economic content. These market-oriented norms like respect for contract also seem capable of adapting themselves faster to new requirement and circumstances, compared to traditional social norms that tend to change more slowly.

In many newly formed nation states of the developing world, both tendencies operate and pull the emerging nation state often in opposite directions. The tensions of 'modernization' in the 'building of a nation' arise largely from these opposing tendencies of relying on the traditional cultural, social, and religious norms on the one hand, and the requirements of strengthening economic nationalism driven by the logic of a commercial society on the other. What appears as a relapse into tribalism, or a drive for ethnic purity, or religious fundamentalism usually means the triumph of the former tendency over the latter. The tension is further accentuated by the discrepancy between the faster pace of change in the market-oriented, and the slower pace of change in traditional social norms. In contrast to this, in industrially advanced countries, the norms of the commercial society are far more well-established; indeed, they tend to become the organizing principle of various other social norms. From this point of view, the distinction in terms of nationalism between the 'developed' and the 'developing' economies is largely a matter of the relative strength of the two opposing tendencies, both of which rely on strengthening different aspects of nationalism. However, it is only the sustained success of capitalism in the course of the rise of the nation state that inclines us towards that particular version of nationalism, which has a dominant economic content, that is, 'economic nationalism' for short. Nevertheless, this economic nationalism is still embedded in the particular historical and cultural contexts of different societies. And, the power of economic nationalism is often at its height, not when it opposes other social or cultural norms, but when it moulds them to reinforce the requirements of a commercial society.

The acceptance of the commercial values by the individual and the dominance of the 'market culture', which drives modern economic nationalism is the outcome of a complex system of beliefs, economic arguments, and historical experiences. Recent analytical works have helped to clarify the 'belief-system' which sustains the market culture. Four important components may be distinguished for expositional convenience (Schotter 1989):

(1) individualism;
(2) rationality;
(3) the 'invisible hand' as the guiding principle of the market mechanism;
(4) and finally, belief in the market process, and not merely in the ultimate equilibrium outcome of the market (e.g. Pareto-optimal outcome in a competitive market).

To elaborate, social outcomes are believed to be an expression of aggregated individual preferences implying 'individualism'. But this aggregation procedure includes only 'rational' individuals. Not only those considered lunatics or psychopaths are excluded by the criterion of 'rationality' but all those who do not subscribe sufficiently to economic calculations based on material well-being, create a difficulty for such a procedure of aggregation. The principle of the 'invisible hand', postulated by Adam Smith, and articulated rigorously by the so-called fundamental theorem of welfare economics, suggests that the aggregation of the preferences of self-interested rational individuals is done optimally by the market. Finally, this is believed to be optimal, not simply as the ultimate equilibrium outcome, but even as a process. Note that such a process may be stable with optimal equilibrium outcome, but only very slowly convergent. In contrast, another process may not have a strictly optimal outcome, but may achieve more rapidly some reasonably satisfying configuration. It is far from clear that the former, slowly convergent process would be more desirable to a rational participant in the market. Nevertheless, belief in the market culture might require this as a condition of rationality (cf. Hurwicz 1989). In a simpler allegory, the 'rational' bellboy brought up in the market culture needs to believe that he too has as fair a chance as anyone else of becoming the chairman of the corporation, provided he sticks resolutely to the routine market-based process 'long enough'!

Even if the fragility of the belief system underlying the market culture can be demonstrated analytically, there is a danger in overdoing this. Because, subjected to analytical scrutiny, almost all belief systems would turn out to be questionable. And yet, a belief system persists by the force of experience and in the absence of an alternative, plausible belief system. It is called into question only when experience shows it to be disastrously wrong. Thus, the recent experiences of the collapse of a centrally planned economic system strengthened the belief in the market as the only viable alternative. Nevertheless, the belief in the market system would not have spread so widely, if the market economies were to face economic disasters frequently like the great depression of the 1930s. Similarly, a market system, which marginalizes over time an increasing proportion of the population steadily is unlikely to sustain itself, except by default until a plausible, alternative belief system is created.

3. THE CONTENT OF ECONOMIC NATIONALISM: THE INTERNAL AND THE EXTERNAL MARKET

Economic nationalism tends to manifest itself in two interrelated ways. First, because the nation state depends to a large extent on the market forces in matters of international trade, investment, and finance, it naturally tries either to adapt or mould those external market forces to its advantage. The age-old debate between the free traders and the mercantilists is an expression of this. However, at the same time, by its very nature the nation state exerts far greater control on the internal market defined within the national boundaries than on the external market. This gives rise to the second aspect; the nation state, particularly if it is a weak player in the international economic scene, has a tendency to rely more heavily on the internal rather than on the external market.

The relative importance attached to the internal and the external market in the policies pursued by the nation state provides a useful indicator of how economic nationalism is shaped under different circumstances. Since the relative importance of the internal and the external market depends both on the size of a country and the stage of its development, relying heavily on the internal market is not a feasible option for many countries. However, Keynes's theory of effective demand (Keynes 1936) was set almost self-consciously in the context of a closed economy without foreign trade, focusing almost exclusively on the internal market. And yet, it had an intellectual link with mercantilism, which Keynes himself recognized. Mercantilism was largely a product of economic nationalism of the emerging nation state of an earlier time. One of its most articulate, early proponents, Friedrich List (1841) discussed the problem of industrial development of his country, Germany, in an age when Germany was still fragmented politically, and faced Great Britain as the hegemonic economic power of the day. List argued in favour of a policy of tariff protection with at least temporary deviation from free trade to 'conquer the internal market'. Free trade might still be the longer-term national goal, but only when the weaker nation catches up more or less to the same level of economic and industrial development. This argument for protecting domestic 'infant industries' provided the intellectual justification in more recent times for an import-substituting, inward-looking strategy for the industrial development of the economically weaker nations. They invariably perceived the free trade doctrine as the weapon of the stronger nations, against whom protection of the domestic market was the only option. Fallows (1993) stresses that all the US presidents whose effigies decorate today's dollar notes supported such protectionist policies. He quotes Abraham Lincoln in the context of the conflicting views of the Northern and the Southern States on tariff: 'I do not know much about tariff. But, I know this much. When you buy manufactured goods abroad, we get the goods and the foreigner gets the money. When we buy the manufactured goods at home, we get both the goods and the money' (Fallows 1993: 82). At that time, the average import tariff in the newly industrializing United States was around 30 per cent.

The argument for protecting the domestic market runs two serious dangers. First, it is logically incomplete in so far as it points to the importance of supplying to the domestic market from domestic industries, but fails to examine what determines the size of aggregate domestic demand. As is well known, Keynes's theory made its most important contribution precisely here. It logically completes an important aspect of the mercantilist-free trade debate. Until the Keynesian formulation of effective demand, economists and policy makers alike might have debated over the virtues and vices of protecting the domestic market, but neither side had any precise idea about what determined its size.

There is a second danger of the protectionist doctrine in so far as it tends to overstate the danger of economic openness. While in its more extreme version conventional theory argues for indiscriminate free trade and passive insertion into the world economy, more judicious and selective integration with the world economy can be of advantage to even a poor nation, as experience has shown repeatedly. Conventional trade theory highlights the problems of consumers' welfare, which is enhanced through control over cost and quality. These controls are most effectively managed through the discipline of international competition. While this argument is valid in many circumstances, it is misleadingly incomplete, because it fails to recognize that consumers' welfare may or may not be enhanced through competition among the producers, particularly if the market size shrinks. Thus, unless we assume full employment, it is not clear why international competition will leave the levels of domestic employment unaffected. If the size of the domestic market and economic activity decline as foreign producers capture a larger share of the market, the level of consumers' welfare within the nation state may decline due to lower employment. Moreover, with serious unemployment, efficient utilization of economic resources is not possible. Consequently, the conventional support for free trade in enhancing consumers' welfare by allocating resources more efficiently is open to question, unless we assume the level of domestic employment to be unaffected.

The problem with the free trade doctrine in particular, and with the free market mechanism in general, however, lies deeper. Each individual nation state tries to mould the international market mechanism in its favour, not because of what it receives, but, because of what is denied to it by the international market mechanism. The international market mechanism is not merely about what the individual nation state receives, but what is denied to it. In this respect, it is similar to 'majority rule' in a democracy, which is not merely about what the majority wants, but what is denied to the minority (Schotter 1989). The enhancing of the market mechanism through free trade appears to be justified in the eyes of the domestic participants only when the denials, including marginalization and exclusion from the labour market are accepted by them as justified. It is at this more fundamental level that the market mechanism is criticized by those who are economically weaker, and feel threatened with marginalization, exclusion, or other forms of denial by the market. This applies to individuals, groups, and regions within a nation state or to the state itself. Consequently, economic nationalism can either favour or turn against free trade depending on the benefit the nation receives, and the cost of denials by the international market mechanism.

The distributional implications of participating in the international market with or without free trade has been a familiar theme through centuries, almost since the birth of political economy. The power of a nation to settle international disputes or denials in its favour depends largely on its economic position. For developing countries their ability to resist international pressure is limited by their economic weakness. Moreover, often torn between tradition and modernization, between social, religious, and cultural norms on the one hand and the norms of an encroaching international commercial society on the other, they face a paradoxical situation. Without accepting, largely, the norms of the commercial world, and undermining the cohesion of the traditional society, they cannot often hope to acquire the minimal economic strength needed to assert their nationalism. It is this paradoxical choice which many developing countries try to make the best of, by surrendering to 'impersonal' market forces. In this sense, globalization is not imposed but accepted by them.

For the industrialized nations, the situation is less paradoxical. With the logic of a commercial society historically well-entrenched, reliance on the market becomes more a matter of routine which usually entails the acceptance of a form of nationalism with a dominant economic content. It is the relative economic performance *vis-à-vis* other nations which increasingly defines the 'nationalism' of an industrially developed country. Accordingly, the legitimacy of the government in power also depends usually on the relative economic performance of the country.

'Globalization' in this context becomes an uneasy meeting point of opposites. The developing nation state feels the compulsion to globalize to assert internally within the country the supremacy of economic over social norms to strengthen some form of economic nationalism. Externally *vis-à-vis* other nation states, however, its economic nationalism suffers in so far as it is economically less powerful, and is compelled to play more or less passively by the rules set by the more powerful industrial nations. The same tension is less intense, but no less real, for the industrially developed nation. Its relative economic performance depends crucially on external conditions in many ways. However, while economic performance is the main vehicle of expressing its nationalism, within the domestic economy, internal economic compulsions may become incompatible with better external economic performance. Thus, consolidation of economic nationalism through globalization operates as a double-edged weapon, which often wounds the nation state, developing or developed, which tries to wield it. The danger is usually greater for developing nation states; but it is also real for advanced industrial nations.

The political significance of the Keynesian theory of demand management can be appreciated in this context. The theory showed how mass unemployment and acute economic depression could be avoided through the management of demand in the internal market by the national government. It was a model of cooperative capitalism because output expansion through higher demand results in more profit as well as more wage income without necessarily generating distributive conflicts. That the size of the internal market is governed largely by the purchasing power of the working population had been a well known economic doctrine long before Keynes. According to this under-consumptionist doctrine, a high wage and a more equal distribution of income are favourable not only to the workers, but even to the capitalists, in so far as they maintain high demand in the internal market. Keynes distanced himself from this narrow under-consumptionist position by pointing out that either consumption or investment could be raised to increase aggregate demand, to avoid disastrous economic depressions with mass unemployment. Contrasting his views from those of early under-consumptionists like Malthus and Sismondi, he writes:

Practically I only differ from these schools of thought in thinking that they may lay a little too much emphasis on increased consumption at a time when there is still much social advantage to be obtained from increased investment. Theoretically, however, they are open to the criticism of neglecting the fact that there are *two* ways to expand output.   (Keynes 1936: 325; emphasis in original)

Kalecki (1944) pointed out more precisely the entire range of possibilities for managing demand by the national government. Each of the three major components of aggregate demand—private consumption, private investment, or government expenditure—could be manipulated through a different set of policies to influence the level of aggregate demand. To these 'three ways to full employment' must be added also the possibility of generating demand through a larger export surplus in an economy open to foreign trade.

Of all these different routes to demand management, by far the speediest and the most convenient way for the national government is to increase the level of government expenditure through deficit financing. Understandably, governments of very different political persuasion took repeated recourse to this method for averting serious unemployment. Thus, the share of government spending in GDP in major OECD countries rose from about 18 per cent before the outbreak of the Second World War to 27 per cent in 1950, and to 37 per cent in 1973 (Maddison 1991; see also Tanzi 1998 for an alternative set of calculations). However, more important than the actual method of demand management was the intellectual confidence that governments acquired to fight economic depression. Keynesianism brought about this dramatic change in the climate of opinion, as more or less continuous full employment came to be viewed as an achievable goal under capitalism. Thus, following the publication of the Beveridge Report in 1942, the maintenance of 'a high level of employment' was recognized by 1944 as a primary objective of the British government.

Its implications for the growth in the economic stature of the nation state was tremendous. The economic role of the state in maintaining high employment through high state expenditure became the accepted norm for the conduct of economic policy across a wide political spectrum. It also meant an expanding role for the welfare state. This was rooted in the implicit consensus that cooperative capitalism among the contending classes is practicable, because both sides stand to gain through the expansionist fiscal and monetary policies of the state in maintaining high demand. More than two decades of sustained near-full employment with high growth seemed to reinforce this view. It was the golden age of capitalism. Perhaps, it was also the golden age for the nation state in its conduct of economic policy.

When the Keynesian theory of aggregate demand is extended to incorporate the influence of international trade, its limit becomes immediately obvious. Considered in isolation, a country with an export surplus would experience an expansion in its market and economic activity, just as a country with an import surplus would experience a contraction. However, since one country's export surplus is another country's import surplus in the global balance of trade, this immediately points to a source of conflict of interests among the trading nations. The model of cooperative capitalism within the nation state as the main political attraction of the Keynesian theory, seems to run into serious difficulty in the international context.

The conflict of interests among the trading nations is, however, more moderate than might appear at first sight. This is because the export-surplus nation with its higher level of income would spend a part of that higher income on imports, that is, on export from the import-surplus nation. This, in turn, would stimulate to some extent the external demand in the import-surplus nation. The net effect of an export surplus would still be an expansion in income, but the expansion would be moderated by higher imports induced by higher income through the so-called 'foreign trade mul-tiplier'. Obversely, the import-surplus nation would experience a more moderate net contraction in income, as it experiences higher exports due to higher induced imports by its export-surplus trading partner. Schematically speaking, conflict of interests still remains the dominant theme among trading nations, but it tends to be moderated by an undercurrent of their complementarity of interests through mutual dependence on trade (Bhaduri 1986: chapter 5).

Management of demand by the nation state through fiscal expansion runs into a similar difficulty. As the country expands its demand and income, importation is increased by the higher income which, in turn, leads to a deterioration of the trade balance. As a result, the model of cooperative capitalism in an economy closed to foreign trade does not extend easily to open economies. Despite the mutual interdependence that trade creates, conflict of interests among nation states engaged in trade seems unavoidable.

The problem might seem to be moderated by the international market mechanism in two different ways, especially in a regime of flexible exchange rates. If the export-surplus country experiences an appreciation of its currency while the import-surplus country undergoes depreciation, there might be a tendency for the balance in trade to be restored through the international exchange rate mechanism, provided the 'trade elasticities' are sufficiently large (that is, the Marshall–Lerner condition is satisfied for both the countries). The effective exchange rate, adjusted for the comparative rates of inflation in the two countries, might also set in motion a similar equilibrating mechanism. Thus, as demand expands in the export-surplus country, if it experiences a higher rate of inflation at home, its exports become more expensive to foreign buyers to reduce the initial export surplus. An obverse sequence of events reduces the import surplus of the deficit country. Its analogy with the equilibrating discipline of the Gold Standard, first postulated by David Hume (1739), should be apparent. A trade surplus was supposed to lead to an inflow of gold, which in turn would result in a corresponding expansion of the domestic money supply linked to the gold stock. Under the Quantity Theory of Money, this was expected to raise the price level of all domestic, including exported, goods and reduce its international price competitiveness until the trade surplus got more or less wiped out.

The reliance on any automatic international price mechanism to restore the trade balance often runs contrary to experience. The fault lies with both the theoretical formulation, and neglect of economic nationalism that permeates international economic relations. Theoretically, the postulate that an increase in demand resulting from an export surplus would necessarily lead to an increase in the domestic price rather than output is open to question. It is indeed one of the fundamental propositions of Keynesian economics that higher demand may cause output to expand with the price level relatively stable in situations of substantial unemployment or excess capacity. Therefore, the efficacy of the price mechanism would require the assumption of full employment, or at least the implicit assumption that output is constrained by supply and not by demand, so that the effect of higher demand would be felt in higher prices and not in higher output levels. Moreover, the price mechanism would fail to do its job if the trade elasticities are sufficiently low (violating the Marshall–Lerner condition). And such low trade elasticities are a common feature of many least developed countries which depend on essential imported items, but have only some primary products to export in the international market.

However, these theoretical problems are only one side of the story, and not always the most important side. As we have already argued, trade among nations almost invariably involves some conflict of interests. Consequently, the working of the price mechanism may be manipulated in the interest of economic nationalism. Thus, an export-surplus country may accumulate reserves of other currencies and engage in 'financial diplomacy' to bring down the international economic position of another country, especially in the earlier regime of non-floating exchange rates. Britain's return to the Gold Standard in 1925, and abandonment of it in 1931 illustrates how such financial diplomacy used to be played out among the major nation states, each governed by its economic nationalism. Britain returned prematurely to the Gold Standard in 1925, pegging the pound at the old pre-war rate of gold parity. However, since the competitive position of Britain in world trade had declined considerably in the meantime, between 1926 and 1930 both the United States and France ran large trade surpluses, and the Bank of France also began to convert steadily the payments surplus into sterling claims for a final showdown with Britain over the British attempt to reinstate the sterling internationally. The impending 'run' on the small gold reserve of the Bank of England began in early 1931, when France brought matters to a head by converting her accumulated sterling claims into gold. Britain was forced to abandon the Gold Standard in the summer of 1931.

A more blatant case in history was the manipulation of the market mechanism to suit imperial trading interests. In the later phase of the Industrial Revolution (from around 1880), enforced trade, irrespective of international competition on a bilateral basis between the imperialist metropolis and the colonial periphery, began surfacing on an extensive scale. With several capitalist countries of Europe emerging as rival industrial powers, the doctrine of free trade became less acceptable to the economic nationalism of Britain. A pattern evolved gradually in which each major imperialist country of Europe tried to retain and expand its share of the captive formal or informal colonial market, which was more or less its exclusive sphere of economic influence (Klieman 1976; Hobsbawm 1972). The conflict among the imperialist nation states to expand or retain their spheres of influence led not merely to trade war, but ultimately to open war. It might be added that the 'financial diplomacy' of the interwar period was a step forward compared to the 'imperialist war' of the earlier phase.

Historically, in those periods of intense economic nationalism, the imperialist nation states played a major role, both as a vehicle for organizing direct foreign investment and as a defender of foreign investments and loans. It was a twilight zone between formal and overt imperialism, often taking the form of 'gunboat diplomacy' which characterized the economic relations between the stronger and the weaker nation state. The stronger nation states themselves went through phases. The situation degenerated at times to open territorial wars over spheres of influence, especially until the First World War and gave way later to 'financial diplomacy' in various forms. On the whole, it was an ugly face of economic nationalism.

The return to the 'closed' economy emphasized by the Keynesian theory redirected economic nationalism internally, but it did not reduce the importance of the nation state. As a matter of fact, with national governments engaged in maintaining a high level of employment at home through demand management, the legitimate economic role of the nation state got enhanced over time. The emergence of the 'welfare state' as a widely accepted ideology in the advanced industrial nations strengthened this process further. Following the Second World War, almost three decades of unprecedented economic growth with near-full employment assigned to the nation state an undisputed economic position. On the political level, it seemed to reconcile two apparently irreconcilable tendencies. On the one hand, the Keynesian model of cooperative capitalism contained within limits the conflict between capital and labour, as the state managed aggregate demand, usually to the advantage of both. On the other, by giving economic nationalism an internal orientation, by focusing on the internal market and the welfare state, it reconciled to a large extent the economic nationalism of the individual nation state with some degree of mutualism in international relations. It needs to be emphasized also that the cold war contributed to this process indirectly. The threat of socialism acted as a cementing factor to unite ideologically the capitalist market economies (Hobsbawm 1994). Rising expenditure on armaments, especially in the United States, helped in sustaining aggregate demand, while the perceived threat of socialism stimulated welfare programmes to moderate the intensity of capital–labour conflict within the capitalist nation state. It was in many ways an exceptionally favourable configuration for the nation state. The subsequent limitations of the nation state emerged as conditions became less favourable.

4. THE EVOLVING NATURE OF THE NATION STATE AND GLOBALIZATION

The gradual erosion in the authority of the nation state, from its past height achieved during its golden age in the decades following the Second World War, is attributable to several intertwined tendencies. They impose serious limitations on the economic role of the state. Although they coincide in time with the current phase of 'globalization', it would be a misleading oversimplification to suggest that these tendencies are generated entirely by the world economy globalizing at a rapid pace. This is because some of these tendencies are the consequence of the economically active role which the nation state played in the past; others are attributable to the process of globalization. For expositional clarity, it may be useful to distinguish these tendencies under four different heads, while bearing in mind that they interact with each other in the process of eroding and reorienting the authority of the nation state. They are:

(1) the resurfacing of capital–labour conflict, especially in an era of sluggish growth and high unemployment in several industrially advanced nations;
(2) the consolidation of multinational corporations in production related activities as well as in the field of international finance;
(3) the overwhelming quantitative importance of international financial capital flows, mostly from private sources; and,
(4) finally, technological development, especially in communication technology.

Each of these tendencies requires some elaboration which follows.

4.1. *Capital–Labour Conflict: Unemployment and Inflation*

It is perhaps not too misleading to evoke the image of the biological evolutionary process to understand the economy. Economic policy, that deals successfully with the immediate problems of the economic environment is likely to change that environment by its very success. Somewhat like the grand algorithm of natural selection, successful adaptation at each round of evolution might call for a different type of adaptation at the next round, precisely because adaptation was successful enough in the preceding round to change the environment! This analogy applies with some force to the Keynesian theory of demand management. Its sustained success in dealing with the problem of unemployment in a framework of cooperative capitalism generated new problems.

The problem was not altogether unforeseen. As early as 1943, Kalecki expressed his scepticism about the political sustainability of long periods of full employment (Kalecki 1971). As he saw it, a shift of power in favour of the workers generated through long periods of sustained full employment would create new problems of workers' 'indiscipline', as the fear of job-loss as an enforcement device in the labour market begins to erode. This problem of shift in the balance of power between the classes would arise despite the fact that high employment and capacity utilization might be good for both profit- and wage-earners. As a consequence, Kalecki argued, the government supported by captains of industry would retreat from time to time from demand management, perhaps in the name of 'sound' public finance and balancing the budget, to precipitate 'political trade cycles' in order to impose discipline on the workers.

The idea of 'political trade cycles' is an astute variation on the classical Marxian theme of the maintenance of the 'reserve army of the labour' as an integral feature of capitalist development. However, the precise economic consequences of workers' indiscipline in the political trade cycle were left somewhat vague. Marx had postulated that the presence of a 'reserve army' of labour would prevent real wages from rising. That prediction, literally interpreted, had turned out to be false. Nevertheless, its implication that cooperative capitalism has an inherent tendency to degenerate into conflictive capitalism over the distribution of income under conditions of low unemployment and increased bargaining power of the worker, cannot be so readily dismissed. Thus, workers' indiscipline can take the particular form of demand for higher money wages, out of line with labour productivity growth, to threaten the economy with inflation, and a squeeze on profits. This idea got a sharper quantitative focus in Phillips's (1958) statistical analysis which showed that money wages generally tend to rise faster at lower levels of unemployment. This presents an awkward choice between the two economic objectives of maintaining a higher level of employment, and a reasonable degree of price stability—the 'unemployment–inflation trade-off', as it came to be known in policy debates. The first crack in the model of cooperative capitalism had appeared.

The terms of the policy debate changed dramatically when 'monetarist' economists led initially by Friedman (1968) denied the very possibility of any trade-off in the longer run between the rates of inflation and unemployment. Economic models were constructed to demonstrate that the economic policies of the state would necessarily be ineffective in the long run to reduce unemployment below its 'natural rate' or the related concept of the 'non-accelerating inflation rate of unemployment' (NAIRU). It again became respectable in 'new classical' economics to argue that all unemployment is 'voluntary', that is, the outcome of intertemporal leisure-income choice by the individual workers (e.g. Barro 1993; Lucas 1981; Phelps 1970; Sheffrin 1996).

The interesting political question is, what made these various models, all of which had the common unifying thrust against the expanding economic role of the state, so widely acceptable politically at this juncture of history? At the most obvious level, constructs like the 'natural rate' or NAIRU played on the fear of inflation triggered off by higher wage claims at sustained near-full employment. In essence, they justified the need for maintaining a 'reserve army' of labour under capitalism, an old idea recycled in new theoretical terms.

It should be remembered that three decades of near continuous full employment, the welfare state, and sustained growth had largely transformed advanced capitalist economies into property owning democracies with extensive rentier interests. This transformation was sustained by the growing presence of the state in economic life; government expenditure as a share of GDP in the industrial countries increased from about 22 per cent in 1937 to 28 per cent in 1960 to 46 per cent in 1996 (Tanzi 1998: table 1). It was financed partly by taxes; but also by the issue of interest-bearing government securities, which helped in strengthening rentier interests on the one hand, and the need to raise taxes to finance the growing interest payments on the other. Both the resistance to paying higher taxes, and the fear that inflation would hurt rentier interests in particular, combined to undermine the attractiveness of still higher public expenditure to fight unemployment in this transformed social structure of advanced capitalism. It was not only the 'captains of industry' who wanted to discipline organized labour through maintaining a 'natural rate' of unemployment. A wider middle class with rentier interests supported them, fearing that inflation triggered off by excessive wage claims might erode the value of their accumulated savings.

There is, however, a more subtle political reason for the breakdown of the Keynesian consensus. The wide acceptability of the Keynesian theory is accounted for partly by its political ambiguity. Its vision of cooperative capitalism presupposed a neutral state which will manage aggregate demand to reconcile the interests of capital and labour. However, once their distributive conflict begins to fuel a process of inflation driven by conflicting claims, the neutral stance of the state may become increasingly untenable; indeed, even traditional fiscal instruments like a progressive direct tax structure may contribute to, instead of abating, the inflationary process by involving the state as one of the parties in the conflicting claims (Bhaduri 1986: chapter 6; Jackson *et al.* 1975; Rowthorn 1980).

The policy of demand management is also politically ambiguous, in so far as either the state or private business can be relied upon to undertake the necessary investment for expanding aggregate demand. Since the stimulation of private investment is an alternative route to managing demand, measures aimed at achieving this, for example reduced taxes on corporate profits or restraint on wages, become justifiable in the Keynesian framework. These measures constitute the case for a politically conservative style of demand management based on profit, and private investment driven economic expansion within the Keynesian intellectual tradition. Moreover, in so far as such private investment-led economic expansion also creates sufficient jobs with a relatively slow rise in real wages in relation to the growth in labour productivity, private profitability is increased; at the same time, however, the working class might also gain in terms of higher real wages and expanding employment opportunities.

The original under-consumptionist thesis of wage-led and consumption driven economic expansion, which argued essentially that a 'high wage' is beneficial to both the classes, finds its antithesis in this case of profit and private investment driven economic expansion. Ironically, both can be interpreted as models of cooperative capitalism. And, both are based on the Keynesian theory which assigns centrality to aggregate demand in determining output and employment (Bhaduri and Marglin 1990). Keynesianism in this wider sense also leaves ambiguous the economic basis of social democratic politics or the necessity of the welfare state, by accommodating different forms of cooperative capitalism. Helmut Schmidt, as the social democratic chancellor of the then West Germany, articulated this conservative alternative by pointing out, 'The profits of the enterprises today are the investments of tomorrow, and the investments of tomorrow are the employment of the day after' (*Le Monde*, 6 July 1976). It symbolized complete reliance on private industry, and its willingness to invest to solve the problem of unemployment, rather than creating jobs through direct expansion of public investment. The economic role of the nation state was thus circumscribed by the need to maintain, above all, a favourable climate for private investment. This view was also an intellectual watershed. It marks the beginning of a new conservative era in advanced capitalist countries, when it becomes increasingly difficult to distinguish social democratic from conservative policies, in so far as the economic role of the state becomes directed towards strengthening the role of private business. According to this new conservative view of demand management, if cooperation between capital and labour is at all to be attained, it is better attained through the agency of private business, but not through direct state intervention, as the earlier version of social democracy had advocated.

4.2. *The Rise and Consolidation of Multinational Corporations*

At the level of the relevance of theory, there can be little doubt that the Kalecki–Keynes model of the closed economy became increasingly obsolete as world trade, particularly among the industrialized countries, began to grow rapidly in the post-war years. In an economy significantly open to foreign trade, arguments in favour of mass consumption-led growth through a 'high wage' policy become less compelling. Because, in so far as higher wages through higher prices also lead to lower international price competitiveness, aggregate demand may actually decline through adverse trade balance. Therefore, with the increased relative importance of the external compared to the internal market under globalization, policies aimed at promoting aggregate demand through 'high wage' policies are less likely to be effective. A basic tenet of welfare capitalism thus becomes questionable. In contrast, in an open economy conservative policies in favour of a 'low wage' policy directed at propelling economic expansion led by profit, private investment, and trade surplus seem more likely to succeed (Bhaduri and Marglin 1990).

International trade has grown at roughly double the rate of world GDP on an average, since the Second World War. This growth is linked intimately with the internationalization of production by the multinational corporations; some 40 per cent of the volume of trade in manufacturing is accounted for by intra-firm trade among the subsidiaries of these corporations. As a result, attracting direct foreign investments of the corporations assumes a special significance for improving the trade performance of nations. Since footloose corporate investments would tend to choose the most profitable locations, a 'race to the bottom' follows among the nations by reducing corporate tax rates competitively, and offering other tax breaks. This reinforces further the limitations on the nation state in conducting economic policy, by reducing the collection of tax revenue on the one hand, and by promoting policies for an attractive investment climate for the multinationals on the other.

Nevertheless, the quantitative importance of foreign direct investment (FDI) in terms of its share either in fixed capital formation, or the accumulated stock of FDI as a share of GDP, is not overwhelmingly large. For all economies, its share in fixed capital formation roughly doubled from 4.4 to 8.7 per cent on a four-year average between 1981–85 and 1991–95 (UNCTAD 1997: table B5), and as a ratio of GDP the accumulated FDI stock increased over the same period from about 11 to 20 per cent (UNCTAD 1997: table B6). Even for the more 'open' industrializing economies, the figures are not very different, the former share was about 10.7 per cent in South-East Asia and 10 per cent in Latin America in 1991–95, but highest at 13.6 per cent in Europe (UNCTAD 1997: table B5).

It raises an interesting puzzle: Why are multinationals perceived to be so important, if their presence in terms of FDI is not proportionately large? The answer to this question lies, perhaps, in two parts. First, multinational corporations are involved increasingly in activities like licensing, outsourcing, and joint ventures, including international marketing, which are not captured in the measures of FDI. They become important in influencing the trade performance of the nation state through these channels, and in updating technologies in newly industrializing nations. Moreover, multinational corporations are increasingly engaged not only in international production activities, but also in finance. It is often easier for a domestic firm in a developing country to raise commercial loans internationally through joint ventures, and to obtain a better, internationally approved credit-rating, if it is linked to a well-known multinational. Even the credit-rating as well as the Bretton Woods institutions usually tend to use the attitudes of the multinationals to the host country as an index of its economic health and market-friendliness. Thus, the cost of noncompliance by the nation state to the requirements of the multinationals—the 'enforcement cost' imposed by the international corporations on the conduct of economic activities by the nation state—tends to be large, and indirectly magnified by the nexus between international trade and investment on the one hand, and international credit-worthiness on the other (Crotty *et al.* 1998).

In the second place, multinational investment is also assigned somewhat disproportionate importance by national governments because it is growing at a relatively faster rate in recent years. Through this fast growing route, developing countries hope to attract both modern technologies, and an increasing share of other forms of international capital inflow, including portfolio investments. On the other hand, in making their investment location decisions multinational corporations are involved in a guessing game about the 'investment climate', not only *vis-à-vis* the potential host country but also by watching the behaviour of other multinationals. Like in so many other situations of marked uncertainty and incomplete information, this tends to generate behaviour governed by the 'herd instinct', and looking for safety in the crowd. As a result, a well-publicized refusal by one multinational can set off a chain reaction of refusals by many other multinationals. Strategic negotiations by setting one multinational against another become all the more difficult for the national government in these circumstances. It feels circumscribed, paradoxically not because of 'coordination failure' but, because of too much informal coordination among multinational corporations, banks, and Bretton Woods institutions!

4.3. *International Financial Capital Flows*

As is widely recognized nowadays, the most dramatic face of contemporary globalization is presented neither by international trade nor by investment. It is in the field of internationalization of finance by private players on a scale altogether unprecedented in history. Global turnover in foreign exchange trading, excluding trade in derivatives, rose from the average daily figure of 18.3 billion dollars in 1977 to 1.23 trillion dollars in 1995, a figure which increases to about 1.30 trillion dollars per day including foreign exchange options and related derivatives. During the same period, 1977–95, the ratio of global foreign exchange turnover to the value of global exports rose from 3.5 to 64, while official reserves declined from 15 days of daily foreign exchange turnover to less than that of a day (Felix 1998: also tables 1A and 1B).

Given the astronomically vast magnitudes, all nation states tend to view this process of globalization of finance as enormous, opportunities mixed with equally serious dangers, reminding one of an old Buddhist proverb: 'It is the same key that opens the gate to heaven or hell.' So long as the nation state can play on the right side of the international financial market, its opportunities for getting finance are enormous; but placed on the wrong side of the same market the danger is equally serious, as the financial power of any national government or central bank to intervene is pitifully limited. The resulting compulsion to be friendly to the day-to-day sentiments of the international financial market has curtailed, more than anything else, the traditional autonomy of the nation state in conducting economic policies.

The erosion of authority of the nation state in the face of globalized finance occurs in several ways. Of these the following four are probably most important. First, the national governments have far less control in managing aggregate demand, because fiscal or monetary policies aimed at expanding demand spill over partly into higher imports and current account deficit. The fear on the part of the national governments that this might destabilize the financial markets triggering off massive speculative capital flights, has an almost paralytic effect on expansionary fiscal and monetary policies.

Second, import liberalization in developing countries, sustained, at least temporarily, by international capital inflows can often result in a higher trade deficit which contracts aggregate demand and output (Bhaduri and Skarstein 1996). And, the obverse of this contractionary output adjustment is the lack of price, or exchange rate adjustment in such cases. If the global financial market sentiments are in favour of import liberalization, which seems to be the usual case, many national governments in developing countries would have to accept contractionary pressures on domestic economic activity with an artificially boosted exchange rate in a liberal trade regime.

Third, national governments would have little autonomy to increase domestic corporate tax rates for raising additional revenue, just as they would have little freedom in lowering interest rates. The more integrated the international financial markets, the greater is the danger that a comparatively higher tax rate or lower interest rate would induce disproportionately large capital flights that might become explosive as speculation feeds on speculation.

Finally, and overriding the preceding considerations, national governments in both developing and developed countries have a strong compulsion to pander to the widely held sentiments, beliefs, and prejudices of the globalized financial markets. Like the self-fulfilling prophesies in 'sun-spot' theories, if the financial market holds, rationally or irrationally, that fiscal or government budget deficit is 'bad' or current or capital account liberalization is 'good', the governments would have a strong compulsion to indulge those market sentiments. This single factor, more than anything else, has probably been the most important reason for the 'convergence' of economic policies across nations, and in driving the global economy towards rapid liberalization of trade, investment, and finance. Without gross exaggeration, it is probably on the basis of such convergence that the foundations of the neoliberal economic regime is being laid.

4.4. *Communication Technology*

Economists seldom try to analyse the social processes that generate widely held economic beliefs and sentiments that govern the financial markets. They marvel at the lightning speed and efficiency with which vast funds can be transferred across national borders with the aid of modern communication technology, but seldom turn their attention to the tremendous power of the electronic media in shaping and influencing the sentiments that drive transactions in financial markets. And yet, it is these sentiments which impose the most serious constraints on the conduct of national macroeconomic policies.

Nevertheless, the media itself is not in the business of formulating the theories and hypotheses around which the sentiments in the market crystallize. They merely package attractively and propagate views, while the theories underlying them originate mostly in individual creative thinking, often in academia (Enzensberger 1988). In the inimitable and oft-repeated words of Keynes:

The ideas of economists and political philosophers, both when they are right and when they are wrong, are more powerful than is commonly understood. Indeed the world is ruled by little else. Practical men, who believe themselves to be quite exempt from any intellectual influences, are usually the slaves of some defunct economist. Madmen in authority, who hear voices in the air, are distilling their frenzy from some academic scribbler of a few years back.   (Keynes 1936: 383)

If anything, these words are more true in our media age.

Rightly or wrongly, the dominant economic theories of our time, since the disintegration of the Keynesian consensus around the early 1970s, believe in the efficiency and wisdom of the market, and in the inefficiencies of the government. Thus, restraining government spending through a balanced budget, or by putting an upper ceiling on fiscal deficit and public debt, accepting a 'natural rate' of unemployment, etc. are ideas that originate in particular models and theories, which are propagated by the media to become popular beliefs. From finance ministers to ordinary participants and practical men in the financial market, these beliefs become the 'distilled truths' continuously served by the media. This was also the case in the past. The real difference today is that those 'distilled truths', when they become sufficiently popular in a globally integrated financial market, force national governments to act according to those beliefs. This social process, enormously strengthened by the advances in communication technology, makes national governments unable or even unwilling to act with determination in the face of poverty, unemployment, or environmental degradation. The particular theories propagated in recent times by the media also show a rather systematic bias in favour of private capital, against a sufficiently active role by the state in defence of the economically weaker sections of the society. This bias is not accidental; it reflects a shift in favour of the interest of corporate capital on the one hand, and the discrediting of bureaucratic central planning on the other. And the 'free' media, often a part of the corporate world, tends to propagate as theories, beliefs that are especially convenient to these powerful interests.

5. THE NATION STATE AND DEMOCRACY: ACCOUNTABILITY, SELF-CORRECTION AND ECONOMIC NATIONALISM

As markets have become globally integrated, their major actors, the multinational corporations, have global reach while the nation state remains local by its very nature. It is understandable why so many contemporary observers find the nation state to be an anachronism in this global setting. Like the prehistoric dinosaur, the once powerful national state seems to have almost outlived its time as an institution.

The view that the nation state is moving inexorably towards its demise during the present era of globalization is misleadingly oversimplistic for two reasons. First, it misunderstands the economic role that the state plays with respect to the market. Second, it fails to see the way in which the relationship between the nation state and economic nationalism is evolving over time. The first aspect is discussed quite extensively in debates over the relative roles of the state and the market. It is best understood in terms of how the state and the market relate to one another in terms of the extent of accountability and self-correction embodied in the two institutions. The second aspect as to how economic nationalism is affected by, and affects globalization in turn, has received relatively little attention from economists and political commentators.

5.1. *The State and the Market: Accountability and Self-Correction*

We emphasized earlier that the acceptance of the 'market culture' depends on the participants seeing as justified, not merely what they receive, but also what is denied to them by the market. And yet, the most important feature of the market mechanism is that it is not directly accountable to the participants; in contrast the state is. In a political democracy, the majority cannot trample on the rights of the minority, simply in the name of majority rule. And, in this sense, the notion of democratic legitimacy and accountability involves not just majority rule, but extends also to the protection of rights for the minority. A similar argument applies to the functioning of the market economy. If its functioning marginalizes and denies almost everything to a significant minority, the state as the accountable institution may have to intervene, if only for the sake of legitimizing the market. Otherwise, the political authority of the state itself would be in question for supporting an unjustifiable market system which deprives the significant minority of almost everything. And if there is one thing to be learnt from the unfolding experiences of the post-Soviet reform, it is precisely this. A state which pays little attention to the economic sufferings and marginalization of a significant proportion of its population, not only discredits itself but also the market process through which such marginalization occurs.

The problem is distressingly acute in many economically poor countries because, in the more extreme cases, not merely a minority, but even the majority may be denied the very minimum of economic life through extensive poverty, unemployment, illiteracy, and lack of health care. The staggering magnitudes of the problem on a global scale can be judged from the facts that, of some 4.4 billion people in developing countries, almost three-fifths live without basic sanitation, one-third without safe drinking water, a quarter lack minimum housing facilities, and one-fifth live beyond the reach of any modern health services. And at least one-fifth of the children are condemned to illiteracy, as they do not get as far as grade five in school (UNDP 1998).

As the state is accountable and the market is not, the state seeking legitimacy should feel compelled to act under such circumstances. There has been a great deal of discussion in recent years about the extent of state versus market failures. Theories like public choice and rent-seeking have rightly drawn our attention to the fact that, in many circumstances the failures of the state can be even more severe than the failures of the market mechanism. However, they ignore the basic issue: being accountable, the state has compulsions to act which are absent in the workings of the market mechanism. And, this accountability is a basic criterion for any democracy.

However, accountability is no guarantee for a self-corrective mechanism. A state might continue to perform very poorly on the economic front, and yet try to improve its 'image' of accountability by taking recourse to cruder forms of nationalism like religious fundamentalism or increased military might. In contrast, proponents of the market mechanism would argue that the market has an in-built self-correcting mechanism, an argument flawed on two counts. First, the self-correction of the market mechanism is based upon a string of unrealistic assumptions which need not hold in practice, especially the fact that the lack of adequate aggregate demand is not subject to automatic self-correction. What conventional theory claims to show is the efficient allocative equilibrium properties of a well-functioning market (e.g. the so-called 'fundamental theorem' of welfare economics), when full employment of resources is ensured by adequate aggregate demand. Second, even granting such allocatively efficient equilibrium, the speed of adjustment to the equilibrium may be too slow to be of practical relevance (see Section 2). While the proponents of liberalization in favour of the market might claim that liberalization and integration with the global market is necessary 'now' to reap benefits in the 'future', there is nothing in economic theory to establish how close or distant that 'future' might be!

In contrast, the accountability of the government, at least in a democracy, has a well-specified timescale. Its failure to correct gross mistakes becomes accountable in times of election. The government has to act, wisely or unwisely, because of that definite time constraint; but the market does not. As a matter of fact, the collapse of bureaucratic central planning was largely due to the fact that it was neither accountable nor subject to correction within a specified timescale. Similarly, dictatorial rules, even apparently benevolent ones that try to legitimize themselves in the eyes of the population, are dictatorial precisely because they accept no definite time constraint. A dictator can promise a better 'future' without committing himself to when that future would come. And, in this respect, the trajectory of a competitive market towards the desired 'optimum' may represent something like a dictatorial promise! In contrast, the time-constrained political accountability of the nation state may force it to act in a manner not necessarily replicated by the market. From this perspective, a fundamental issue, therefore, is not whether state actions are 'market-friendly', but whether they conform to the time-constrained accountability criterion of a democracy.

5.2. *Economic Nationalism and Globalization*

It is largely a myth of our time that both the market and globalization would weaken many aspects of narrow economic nationalism. Since, like the market, globalization creates its losers and gainers among the nation states, the losers would naturally have a tendency to create a defence mechanism against globalization by taking recourse to different aspects of nationalism. Thus, the tension between tradition and modernization may be heightened through the reinvention of the 'nation' in terms of ethnic purity or homogeneity in terms of religion, language, or a shared history. That these tendencies have actually surfaced far too frequently in the recent political history of many developing countries might not be just an accident, but partly the result of being confronted with global market forces.

Even for the nations that expect to be gainers from the current process of globalization, there is a paradoxical element. These nation states are geared increasingly towards serving the demands and requirements of a process of globalization which is driven not primarily by their political authority but by the multinational corporations and powerful anonymous private traders in the international capital market. Viewed from this angle, the nation state today does not merely face more severe constraints in the conduct of independent economic policies (Section 4). In a more subtle fashion which typically escapes the attention of most commentators on the subject, the economic activities of the nation state are being reoriented, and many of its economic institutions are being strengthened systematically in the interest of globalization. The point may be illustrated with only a few selected examples.

There is a growing tendency for stronger central banks to emerge as independent decision makers to establish the supremacy of monetary over fiscal policies. Their main objective is to maintain the stability of the exchange rate and the value of the currency by curtailing government expenditure, rather than fighting unemployment or alleviation of poverty. In a parallel vein, many countries are centralizing institutions and strengthening regulations for facilitating international transactions in financial assets, but are underplaying at the same time the need for strengthening other institutions and regulations needed for improving corporate tax collection or their socio-economic infrastructure. Even the larger regional groupings that are being formed among countries often have a central motivation of developing a more integrated market for trade, investment, and finance in the interest of large corporations which produce and trade across national boundaries. In other words, two opposing tendencies are being fused together. The nation state is apparently being constrained and weakened on the one hand in exercising its economic and political authority. On the other, however, the nation state is being strengthened in certain respects in so far as it suits global corporate interests in trade, investment, and finance. In this sense, it is not the demise, but a systematic reorientation of the nation state that we may be witnessing as one of the most striking features of the current process of globalization. Nevertheless, it tends to create a growing hiatus between the democratic governments of the nation states that have to be accountable for their performance within the electoral timeframes, and the multinationals as central actors in globalizing markets who are not accountable to the wider body of ordinary citizens of any nation.

Viewed from this perspective, the emerging challenge both to the process of globalization, and to the nation state and its nationalism can be appreciated in a different light. On the one hand, the global 'rules of the game', especially for multinational business, have to become more sensitive to the democratic accountability of national governments; indeed, they may even play a part in enhancing this accountability by following a more transparent code of conduct that discourages corrupt and unfair trade and business practices, especially in dealing with weaker national governments. On the other hand, national governments need to recognize the gains that can be made from selective, greater international interdependence through trade, investment, and finance. In particular, the dynamic sources of gains that are attainable through international learning about technology, taste, and quality and are typically carried by the vehicles of international trade and investment should not be minimized. The challenge to economic nationalism is to devise ways and means by which it can take advantage of the international interdependence in various ways without compromising democratic accountability.

6. TOWARDS A POLICY FRAMEWORK

The drift of the preceding argument seems to be leading to a puzzle at first sight. How can the nation state define a practicable economic role for itself in the global setting without rooting itself in narrow economic nationalism? An answer may be found in the recognition that an intelligent policy of shifting the balance globally, by relying more on the internal and less on the external market by all nations can become the guiding principle of macroeconomic policy without generating conflicting economic nationalism. In contrast, the contemporary process of globalization is increasingly shifting the balance in an opposite direction, from the internal to the external market. The nation states are acting as passive or even complying agents in this process, with the result that economic nationalism is degenerating into mere competition among nation states. Nation states today help in setting up an international regime of trade, investment, finance, and technology transfer in the name of globalization, more in the interest of multinational corporations who are accountable at best only to the narrow sectional interest of their managers and shareholders. It has been rightly pointed out in this context that the concept of competition applies to companies, not to nation states. The most beneficial and important objective of competition is to enhance productivity. This very reasonable objective can be pursued independent of a competitive international trade policy: because an increase in productivity raises the general living standard, and the average per capita GDP with or without trade; because quantitatively trade plays a relatively inconsequential part in this (Krugman 1996). Only because of the competition among corporations, have we come to the surprising view that this reasonable objective of raising productivity is a means and not an end. It is needed only to enhance international competition and is related to the external, but not to the internal, market. And yet, increased productivity of one nation need not by any means imply decreased productivity of another. Productivity gain is not a zero sum game, once taken out of the context of competition in international trade.

The extent of the division of labour as a source of productivity growth, Adam Smith observed, is limited by the size of the market. If the market is primarily the external market, increase in productivity can materialize mostly through conflicting economic nationalism, over international market shares in a zero sum game. However, if the market is internal, the nation state has a paramount role to play in expanding the size rather than the share of the market, without necessarily generating conflicting forces of economic nationalism. It is from this perspective of the link between productivity gain and the expansion of the international market that demand management by the nation state needs to be recognized to redefine the role of the nation state. There are two types of constraints normally perceived on demand management—the fear of inflation, generated mostly by domestic capital–labour relations (e.g. 'natural rate' of unemployment, NAIRU, etc.), and the fear of an external payments imbalance that might deteriorate unmanageably into speculative capital flights on a massive scale (Section 4).

For a democratically accountable national government, the way to contain the capital–labour distributive conflict as the main source of inflation cannot be to precipitate unemployment in the name of a 'natural rate' of unemployment. Expansionary fiscal policies aimed at increasing the internal market on the one hand, and raising labour productivity on the other, are still the valid ways to fight unemployment. Rising labour productivity, which usually goes with expanding market and output also provides more room to accommodate the distributive conflict between labour and capital, as the size of the cake to share expands. An institutionalization of 'incomes policy' has a far greater chance of success in an expanding economy with rising labour productivity. In this sense, demand management focused on an expanding internal market is a precondition for a less conflictive capital–labour relation. To emphasize the difference, one has only to contrast this with some recent corporate strategy of 'downsizing' of firms by shedding labour to raise labour productivity at the microlevel. It generally increases the market share of the successful corporation by reducing its unit cost, but tends to reduce the overall size of the market through a reduction in employment and purchasing power. And, if the size of the market is not reduced due to 'capturing external markets', the size of one nation's market is expanded only at the cost of another. Thus, increasing labour productivity through downsizing would tend to accentuate distributive conflict between capital and labour, and trade conflict among nations, precisely because its focus is on market share and the external market, rather than on the internal market. This cannot be the route to a more harmonious process of globalization, as it would unleash forces of conflictive economic nationalism.

The ideal way to deal with the problem of external balance would have been to encourage an International Clearing Union arrangement, by which all member states would accept the debt obligation of the Clearing Union ('banker', as the Keynes Plan of 1942 called it). The logic is obvious—'No depositor in a local bank suffers because of balances, which he leaves idle, are used to finance the business of someone else' (UNO 1948; quoted from article 12 of the 'proposals by British experts for an International Clearing Union' dated 18 April 1943). This implies symmetrical treatment of surplus and deficit nations. The proposal was unacceptable, not because its logic is faulty, but because it runs against narrow economic nationalism—the use of trade surplus or the privilege of the use of the national currency as international money to dominate other nations. It must also be pointed out that, trying to institute an International Clearing Union is no more difficult in principle than trying to set up, say, a world trade organization or complex rules for international protection of intellectual property rights. The real difference is that while the latter is in the interests of dominant nations and their corporations, the former is not.

The severity of the constraint of the balance of payments on internal demand management would tend to be lower, if policies of internal demand management could be internationally, or at least regionally, coordinated, especially with respect to their timings. When all countries expand simultaneously to raise each other's demand for exports, the net effects on trade deficit and surpluses are likely to be smaller, even if they are unevenly distributed among countries. Similarly, simultaneous lowering of interest rates in support of expansionary monetary policies reduces the danger of capital flights from an individual country.

It should be recognized that proposals for international monetary reform along the lines of a Clearing Union assume even greater importance in a world without any coordination in international demand management. However, it should be a stated complementary objective of any such international Clearing Union arrangement to promote such coordination in demand management, because the Clearing Union was essentially devised to allow countries to pursue, unilaterally, policies of demand management without coming up against the crippling constraint of the balance of payments. Although in an ideal world, one would like to see both a Clearing Union arrangement and coordination of demand management, fortunately international agreement or even debate, discussion, and negotiations can begin separately on either front (e.g. in the United Nations). For instance, in the absence of any international agreement or even debate on any Clearing Union-type arrangements, countries may be allowed to impose capital controls in the interest of demand management. At the same time attempts should be made to discourage international speculative foreign exchange transactions through schemes like the Tobin Tax (Tobin 1978) which is a variation on the 'government transfer tax on all transactions in the stock exchange' as suggested originally by Keynes (1936: 160). A first step in this direction will be for the IMF to recognize that capital or even current account convertibility is not an objective in itself. It needs to be tailored to the requirement of internal demand management by the nation state. Similarly, international negotiations may be initiated by the IMF to permit 'stand-still' agreements between private international lenders and the nation state in case of a speculative attack on its currency to provide more room for demand management and investment for development through the expansion of the internal market.

Plans relating to wide ranging international financial reforms such as the International Clearing Union are not even on the current international political agenda for discussion. This raises two questions in turn whose practical relevance cannot be overemphasized in the present context. First, are there other forms of international governance and policy coordination that might be more feasible in the foreseeable future? Second, without feasible agreements in the sphere of international governance in the near future, can the nation state find a way to empower itself in a way which will enhance its democratic accountability to its people, especially the economically weaker and more vulnerable sections? These two questions are usually separately addressed, somewhat like the 'first-best', and the 'second-best' alternative. And yet, a main thrust of our economic policy perspective with its repeated emphasis on the importance of the internal market has been to question implicitly the usefulness of any such dichotomy. It does not seem particularly useful in actual decision-making to separate the 'best' alternative that might be achievable in the unforeseeable long run from the 'next-best' alternative that might be worth attempting in the foreseeable short run. We should look for ways by which policies pursued in the short run are not only compatible, but reinforce the process of change in favour of the longer-term objectives.

It has been the main thrust of our argument that for countries with sufficiently large size, a determined effort to manage their internal markets more effectively rather than leaving it to the forces of global capital would be a way to empower their national governments politically in the eyes of their electorate, especially the economically weaker section of the electorate.

This implies, taking recourse to internal demand management to deal directly with problems like unemployment and business cycles in advanced industrial countries. It is also the main route to the re-empowerment of the welfare state. To the extent larger regional groupings such as free trade areas facilitate rather than hinder progress along this route, especially to overcome the problem of size, they are a step in the desirable direction. However, if regional groupings or unions impose rules whose main purpose is to strengthen currencies or to help corporate business (like a bureaucratic limit to budget deficit or national debt) but restrict the ability of the nation state in managing demand in the internal market, they should be considered counterproductive.

The problems are somewhat different in developing countries where issues like poverty, basic education, and health care are naturally far more pressing. Yet, it is worth emphasizing that employment expansion through public works and the simultaneous creation of productive assets is the best way known to deal with these problems on a more sustained basis. Pure welfare programmes, however desirable, soon run into problems of resource constraints, unless the resource base can be expanded simultaneously through these programmes. Thus demand management, but with a view to productive employment creation, should also be a focus of policy formulation in developing countries.

In the present intellectual climate of neoliberalism at the start of the twenty-first century, the policy framework and perspective in favour of which we argue may seem to run contrary to conventional wisdom. Yet, conventional wisdom usually reflects not the truth but the mood and the dominant interests of the time. A natural harmony between public and private interest was the earlier conventional wisdom justifying conservative policies. It was the very cornerstone of nineteenth century liberalism. Harmony between public and corporate interests in the name of globalization became the cornerstone of the late twentieth-century neoliberalism. And yet, it is a contrived harmony, a harmony not meant to enhance the welfare of the people, but mostly to extend the global reach of the multinational business. It is time, this fact is faced candidly, to redefine the role of democratic nation states in the interests of their citizens.

REFERENCES

Aristotle (1912). *Politics—A Treatise on the Government* (translated by H. Ellis) by E. Rhys (ed.) Dent, London and Toronto.

Axelrod, Robert (1984). *The Evolution of Cooperation*. Basic Books, New York.

Barro, Robert (1993). *Macroeconomics*, 4th edn. John Wiley & Sons, New York.

Bhaduri, Amit (1986). *Macroeconomics: The Dynamics of Commodity Production*. Macmillan, London.

—— and Stephen A. Marglin (1990). Unemployment and the real wage: The economic basis for contesting political ideologies. *Cambridge Journal of Economics*, 14, 375–93.

—— and R. Skarstein (1996). Short-period macroeconomic aspects of foreign aid. *Cambridge Journal of Economics*, 20, 195–206.

Crotty, J., G. Epstein, and P. Kelly (1998). Multinational corporations in the neoliberal regime. In Dean Baker, Gerald Epstein and Robert Pollin (eds), *Globalization and Progressive Economic Policy*. Cambridge University Press, Cambridge.

Enzensberger, Hans M. (1988). The industrialization of the mind. In Hans M. Enzensberger (ed.), *Dreamers of the Absolute: Essays on Politics, Crime and Culture*. Radins, London.

Fallows, James (1993). How the world works. *The Atlantic Monthly*, December.

Felix, David (1998). Asia and the crisis of financial globalization. In Dean Baker, Gerard Epstein and Robert Pollin (eds), *Globalization and Progressive Economic Policies*. Cambridge University Press, Cambridge.

Friedman, Milton (1968). The role of monetary policy. *American Economic Review*, 58, 1–17.

Hobbes, Thomas (1957). *Leviathan* (originally published in 1651), edited with an introduction by M. Oakeshott. Oxford University Press, Oxford.

Hobsbawm, Eric (1972). *Industry and Empire: The Birth of the Industrial Revolution*. Pelican, Middlesex.

—— (1990). *Nations and Nationalism since 1780: Programme, Myth, Reality*. Cambridge University Press, Cambridge.

—— (1994). *The Age of Extremes: A History of the World, 1914–1991*. Pantheon Books, New York, NY.

Hume, David (1739). *A Treatise on Human Nature* (ed.) L. A. Selby-Bigge (1978), 2nd edn. Clarendon Press, Oxford.

Hurwicz, L. (1989). Mechanisms and Institutions. In T. Shiraishi and S. Tsuru (eds), *Economic Institutions in a Dynamic Society*, pp. 87–101. St. Martin's Press, New York.

Jackson, Dudley, H. A. Turner, and S. F. Wilkinson (1975). *Do Trade Unions Cause Inflation?* Cambridge University Press, Cambridge.

Kalecki, Michal (1944). Three ways to full employment. In *The Economics of Full Employment*. Oxford Institute of Statistics Edition. Blackwell, Oxford.

—— (1971). Political aspects of full employment. In *Selected Essays on the Dynamics of the Capitalist Economy, 1933–1970*. Cambridge University Press, Cambridge.

Keynes, John M. (1936). *The General Theory of Employment, Interest, and Money*. Macmillan, London.

Klieman, Ephraim (1976). Trade and the decline of colonialism. *Economic Journal*, 86.

Knox, T. M. (1964). *Hegel's Political Writings*. Oxford University Press, Oxford.

Krugman, Paul (1996). *Pop Internationalism*. The MIT Press, Cambridge, MA.

List, Friedrich (1841). *National System of Political Economy* (translated by G. A. Matile). London.

Lucas, Robert E. (1981). *Studies in Business Cycle Theory*. The MIT Press, Cambridge, MA.

Maddison, Angus (1991). *Dynamic Forces in Capitalist Development*. Oxford University Press, Oxford.

Meinecke, Friedrich (1957). *Machiavellism, the Doctrine of Raison d'Etat and its Place in Modern History* (translated by D. Scott). Routledge, London.

North, Douglass C. (1990). *Institutions, Institutional Change, and Economic Performance*. Cambridge University Press, Cambridge.

Paine, T. (1776). Common sense. In M. Foot (ed.), *The Thomas Paine Reader*, pp. 65–115. Penguin, Middlesex.

Pasinetti, Luigi L. (1981). *Structural Change and Economic Growth*. Cambridge University Press, Cambridge.

Phelps, Edmund (1970). The new macroeconomics in employment and inflation theory. In E. Phelps (ed.), *Microeconomic Foundations of Employment and Inflation Theory*. Norton, New York.

Phillips, A. W. (1958). The relation between unemployment and the rate of change of money wage rates in the United Kingdom, 1861–1957. *Economica*, 25, 283–99.

Rowthorn, Robert (1980). *Capitalism, Conflict and Inflation: Essays in Political Economy*. Lawrence and Wishart, London.

Schotter, A. (1989). Comment. In Takashi Shiraishi and Shigeto Tsuru (eds), *Economic Institutions in a Dynamic Society*. St. Martin's Press, New York.

Sheffrin, Steven M. (1996). *Rational Expectations*, 2nd edn (Cambridge Surveys of Economic Literature). Cambridge University Press, Cambridge.

Smith, Adam (1759). *The Theory of Moral Sentiments*. Oxford 1976 bicentenary edition. Oxford University Press, Oxford.

——(1776). *An Inquiry into the Nature and Causes of the Wealth of Nations*, 2 vols. Oxford 1976 bicentenary edition. Oxford University Press, Oxford.

Tanzi, Vito (1998). The demise of the nation state? IMF Working Paper WP/98/120. IMF, Washington, DC.

Tobin, James (1978). A proposal for international monetary reform. *Eastern Economic Journal*, 4, 153–9.

UNCTAD (1997). *World Investment Report: Transnational Corporations, Market Structure and Competitive Policy*. United Nations, New York and Geneva.

UNDP (1998). *Human Development Report 1998*. Oxford University Press, New York and Oxford.

UNO (United Nations Organization) (1948). *Proceedings and Documents of the United Nations Monetary and Financial Conference*, volume 2. Government Printing Office, Washington, DC.

PART II

ISSUES

3

Global Macroeconomic Management

LANCE TAYLOR

The most important development in the global macroeconomic system over the past several decades has been the liberalization of international capital markets that got underway in the 1970s. This sea change from the Bretton Woods system has had enormous consequences for both developed and developing economies. This chapter begins by recalling the history of world capital markets—especially the changes that have occurred since the Second World War. It then summarizes some of the outcomes, and concludes with current policy problems. The presentation draws heavily on Eatwell and Taylor (2000).

One important outcome has been a marked increase in the volatility of capital movements and asset prices, amplified by international contagion. Exchange rate fluctuations, in particular, have been highly destabilizing—they are major transmitters of shocks. It is argued in this chapter that spot rates have no 'fundamentals' in the sense of price or quantity variables that can determine rate levels when they are permitted to float. The only prices a spot rate 'floats against' are expected future values of itself and other asset values. In forward markets, conventions about the future determine these expectations. They can shift very rapidly, adding instability to the system.

International payments flows have been profoundly affected by liberalization, and the peculiar role the American economy plays in regulating them. The United States is now beginning to encounter the same sorts of disequilibria among stocks and flows of assets and flows of output and trade that triggered the recent crises in developing economies. It too can be subject to destabilizing speculation, if conventions move against the notion that its imbalances are sustainable. Exchange rate bands for the major currencies and capital controls are means available to dampen such shifts. Regardless of whether they are imposed, the United States is soon likely to be forced in the directions of depreciation and fiscal expansion, which could have significant international repercussions.

How shifting conventions led to crises in developing economies is the next topic. A stylized model of cycles of capital movements and macroeconomic performance is sketched. It captures much of the drama of recent events, and suggests policies to avoid future repetitions.

How these trends can be managed for the common good is at the centre of current debate. The chapter closes with a review of international financial regulation and governance.

1. THE EVOLUTION OF CAPITAL MARKETS

Volatility and contagion are intimately related to the 'stability' of financial and other markets, that is, their resistance to big fluctuations in prices, asset rates of return, and in volumes of claims or commodities lent, borrowed, and sold. It is these fluctuations that destroy confidence, and hit investment and growth. Much can be learned about market instability from the experiences of the world economy when it has operated within a liberal financial framework over the past century or so.

Since around 1870, there have been three periods during which cross-border movements of financial capital were substantially unregulated: first, under the 'high' gold standard before the First World War; second, the gold exchange standard between the wars; and, third, the new liberal financial order existing today. Was global macro-economic stability assured during the two gold standard episodes? In the first it was, after a fashion. In the second it most clearly was not.

The high gold standard was the linchpin of the late Victorian world economic order.[1] Under its rules, most countries fixed their currencies in terms of gold (thus maintaining fixed exchange rates among themselves), held gold reserves to settle their international accounts, and often used gold coins as well. Between 1870, when gold triumphed over silver as the monetary standard, and the outbreak of the First World War, international macro-adjustment pivoted on the Bank of England, often acting in cooperation with other central banks. Capital flows stabilized the system, because they tended to move out of the UK when it was at the bottom of its business cycle and the London interest rate was low. Import demand was down in the UK, but the low interest rate stimulated real investment in borrower countries of European settlement and the colonies. In time, the British economy would recover or the Bank of England would raise the discount rate to counter reserve losses. Capital would move back toward London and high rates would force raw materials exporters to sell off stocks on unfavourable terms, improving the British terms of trade and trade balance as well. The system operated counter-cyclically, stimulating demand outside Britain when UK demand was low, and reducing demand outside Britain when UK demand was high.

This overall stability did *not* rule out national crises. When their capital inflows dried up, capital-importing countries in many cases could not raise exports sufficiently to avoid suspending debt payments or abandoning gold parity. But such local financial volcanoes erupted without threatening the system as a whole. Even repeated crises in Britain itself failed to topple the gold standard, primarily because of the financial support of the Banque de France, the investment of the Indian surplus in London (to the detriment of the Indian economy), and South African gold production. Nonetheless, by the outbreak of the First World War, the gold standard was becoming unsustainable as more countries established central banks, complete with gold reserves that were no longer susceptible to the free-flowing influence of London interest rates.

The adjustment mechanisms central to the operation of the gold standard resulted in the *real* interest rate (that is, the nominal rate minus the rate of inflation) being very

---

[1] de Cecco (1984) is a good summary reference.

high. Between 1870 and 1890, average long-term real rates in the major industrial countries were around 4 per cent. From 1950 to 1970, during the so-called 'golden age' of rapid economic growth worldwide—and a time when capital markets were highly regulated—real interest rates were about 2 per cent. They fell to near zero in the inflationary 1970s. In the period 1981–93 when the international financial market was once again deregulated, the average real rate in major industrial countries was at the historic high of 5.1 per cent. Free international capital markets appear to go hand-in-hand with high real interest rates, that is, high returns to rentiers. Some of the reasons why are taken up here.

Under the 'gold exchange standard' as it functioned between the wars, stability properties were very different (Eichengreen 1998; Temin 1993). The United States had become the biggest international lender, meaning that its national saving (the 'source' of funds directed toward financial markets) exceeded its domestic investment (the major domestic 'use' of funds after they filter through the financial system). Because the excess of sources over uses had nowhere else to go, it had to take the form of international lending. Moreover, the US aggregate savings supply rose substantially during a business cycle upswing, so that at the peak both its exports of financial capital and its import demand were high. In contrast to Britain under the high gold standard, capital movements out of and trade flows into the US economy both moved *with* the trade cycle. They thereby tended to stimulate economies elsewhere, with further positive feedback effects on the United States—both upswings and downswings were strongly amplified. The United States also competed directly in export markets with financial capital importers such as Germany, in contrast to pre-First World War Britain, which exported sterling to the countries that produced its imports.

In the interwar years international cooperation was weak, in contrast to the earlier period when the Bank of England could always rely on help from counterpart institutions on the continent. One crucial example was the wave of banking crises that spread across Europe in 1931. Following bank failures in Austria, Germany encountered difficulties in mid-year, throwing the Reichsbank into dire need of external credit. France had ample gold reserves (built up through annual trade surpluses that resulted in part because the franc was pegged at a weak level when it re-entered the gold standard). But it attached such political strings to the credits it offered that the Germans would not accept—money with strings is not liquid. A continent-wide crisis and the spread of the great depression worldwide followed in turn.

This collapse was deepened by 'currency' or 'locational' imbalances in balance sheets of the financial systems in many of the affected countries. In Germany (and elsewhere), a large share of domestic bank deposits was held by foreign investors and banks. At the same time, the German banks' assets were largely domestic. Rising fears of devaluation would lead almost automatically to deposit withdrawals, possibly igniting a bank run and subsequent crisis. Sixty-six years later and half the world away, these same factors exacerbated the Asian crisis of 1997 and spilled over into Russia the following year.

In the United States, the major creditor country, the financial system was fragile for a different reason. Many of its clients had borrowed heavily to undertake financial investments. In the jargon, they were highly 'leveraged' or 'geared'. In principle, such a position cannot be maintained when the value of the collateral assets an investor holds falls below the level of his or her debt. In practice, he or she often fails when current income flows (including capital gains) fall short of current interest obligations. After the 1929 crash, the first condition applied. Through 'margin calls' on the loans they had taken out to buy shares when their prices were rising, falling share prices turned many previously creditworthy borrowers into bankrupts. This process of 'debt-deflation' (the Yale economist Irving Fisher's term from 1933) was another contributing factor to the great depression. A similar process was clearly visible in Asia in 1997–98.

One effect of the competitive devaluation and beggar-my-neighbour policies of the 1930s was to encourage wartime economists (led by John Maynard Keynes from the UK and Harry Dexter White from the United States) to design a system with fixed exchange rates that did *not* rely on anachronistic national gold hordes. At the famous Bretton Woods, New Hampshire, conference in 1944 they replaced the liberal international financial markets of the gold standard with strict controls on capital movements. These controls were a fundamental characteristic of the new Bretton Woods system. Insofar as its institutional structure reflected the Keynesian theoretical concerns of the time, Bretton Woods may be interpreted as a set of rules under which national authorities might, if they wished, pursue full employment policies, free of some of the anxieties that accompany open capital markets.[2]

The success of the Bretton Woods design must be a key factor in the evaluation of the impact of the subsequent, post-1971, liberalization. Growth and employment rates in the 25 years of the system's effective operation from after the Second World War until about 1970 were at historic highs in most countries, whether developed or developing. Productivity growth was also at an historic high, not only in countries that were 'catching-up' but also in the technological leaders. It *was* a golden age. How the Bretton Woods system broke down after 25 years of extraordinary economic success is a well-known story. For present purposes, the objective is not the resurrection of Bretton Woods—that is economically and politically impossible. Rather, the post-Second World War system provides a point of reference from which to study the impact of the reduction in barriers to international capital movements that got underway as it started to fail.

2. TWENTY-FIVE YEARS OF CAPITAL MARKET LIBERALIZATION

The present wave of capital market liberalization began with the opening of Eurocurrency markets in the 1950s. But it was with the breakdown of Bretton Woods and the consequent privatization of foreign exchange risk that the explosion of foreign exchange markets began, followed by the creation of global bond markets in the 1980s, and global equity markets in the early 1990s (Eatwell 1996; D'Arista 1998).

---

[2] Block (1977) and Helleiner (1994) give useful synopses of the Bretton Woods period.

The international financial flood of the past 25 years rose from a tiny spring—Eurodollar (later Eurocurrency) markets in the 1950s. A Eurodollar deposit is just a deposit denominated in dollars in a bank outside the political jurisdiction of the United States. British and American authorities winked and nodded at such placements at the outset because they seemed like a sensible way for commercial banks to make use of their excess reserves. Many of the early deposits were made by banks operating for Soviet bloc countries. They moved funds to London because they feared that their assets might be expropriated in the United States following the failure of the Soviet Union to pay wartime debts. As the name implies, offshore banking operations were originally limited to Europe (with London as the major trading point), but they soon could be carried out worldwide. Net Eurocurrency deposit liabilities amounted to around $10 billion in the mid-1960s and grew to $500 billion by 1980. By the mid-1980s in the industrial countries, bank deposits in currencies other than each nation's own currency amounted to around one-quarter of the total.

A major contributing factor to growth in Eurocurrency markets was the American 'interest equalization tax' of 1964–73, which raised costs for banks to lend offshore from their domestic branches. The resulting higher external rates led dollar depositors such as foreign corporations to switch their funds from onshore US institutions to Eurobanks. A second massive Eurodeposit inflow came in 1973–74 with the onset of 'recycling' of OPEC trade surpluses after the first oil shock. The developing country debt boom followed in turn, as rich countries' banks used OPEC's deposits to back massive loans to middle-income economies in Latin America and elsewhere. The subsequent crash after the Mexican default of August 1982 led to a 'lost decade' of growth in most of the developing world (with Asian economies as the major exceptions until 1997, for reasons discussed below).

Eurocurrency transactions rapidly taught market players that they could shift their deposits, loans, and investments from one currency to another in response to actual or anticipated changes in interest and exchange rates. These moves were early warnings of a pervasive regulatory problem that dominates the world economy today: *any nation's financial controls appear to be made for the sole purpose of being evaded.* Even the ability of central banks to regulate the supply of money and credit was undermined by commercial banks' borrowing and lending offshore. This process accelerated after the shock of 1973–74. Within 10 years, national authorities were forced to scrap long-established interest rate ceilings, lending limits, portfolio restrictions, reserve and liquidity requirements, and other regulatory paraphernalia. These instruments acted on the supply side of financial markets by limiting the ability of private sector players to seek capital gains, hedge risk, or undertake arbitrage. They all could be circumvented by the new freedom to pursue offshore transactions. All finally had to be abandoned.

Dropping their supply-side regulatory tools meant that central banks could now operate only on the demand side of the money market. The only instrument of monetary policy available to them was buying and selling securities to influence short-term interest rates. The result has been higher and more volatile real interest rates. The 1995 *Annual Bulletin* of the Bank for International Settlements (BIS) commented,

'. . . interest rates generally have to become higher and more variable' as they are managed to influence demands for financial assets. The new interest rate regime became the norm in every major economy. The result was a powerful inducement for even greater cross-border surges of portfolio investment. As under the interwar gold standard, central banks in the advanced economies lost much of their power to pursue counter-cyclical monetary policies. And as under the nineteenth-century gold standard, high interest rates seemed to settle in for good.

3. VOLATILITY AND CONTAGION

Instability has bedevilled not just interest rates. Liberalization has been accompanied by increased volatility of all prices and quantities, and its spread (or 'contagion') across markets and national borders. In the recent period, increased volatility stands out whether it is measured by short-term movements in exchange and interest rates, or by longer swings in market activity. In the major industrial countries short-term volatility, as measured by movement in prices at two-weekly intervals, has tripled in most markets in the past 25 years. And long-term swings have taken the real value of the dollar from an index of 100 in 1980, to 135 in 1985, down to 94 in 1990, and up again to 134 in 1998.

Volatile financial markets generate economic inefficiencies. Volatility creates financial risk, and even if facilities exist for hedging that risk, the cost of capital formation is raised. The impacts show up in developed and developing economies alike. In the face of higher and more volatile real interest rates along with the emergence of 'junk bonds' in a deregulated financial system, defaults on US corporate bonds spiked upward after the breakdown of Bretton Woods in 1970, fell back, and then rose steadily through the 1980s. Similarly, corporate bankruptcy, at an all time low in the stable years from 1950 to 1970, has now returned to a level characteristic of the deregulated markets of the 1930s.

Volatility fuels contagion. Microeconomic responses can easily escalate worldwide. The stock market crash of 1987 spread rapidly from New York to all financial markets. Recent studies of the 1992 ERM (exchange rate mechanism) crisis have concluded that systemic contagion makes the link between domestic macroeconomic conditions and the size of currency devaluation, let alone the likelihood of a crisis, tenuous. Indeed, the link may even have the 'wrong' sign, with the financially virtuous suffering the greater punishment. The Mexican crisis of 1994 propagated the 'tequila effect' throughout Latin America. The Asian financial crisis of 1997 spread throughout emerging markets, including Eastern Europe, Latin America, and South Africa.

4. EXCHANGE RATES

This sequence of crises was accompanied by major exchange rate realignments (if rates were initially fixed) or fluctuations (if they were flexible). The key issue arising is that under a floating rate regime the exchange rate has no anchor; it only floats against its expected future values. And in a fixed rate system, if the peg is out of line with expectations, then there is a danger of external attack. In both cases, the root cause of volatility is an unregulated capital market.

In other words, the exchange rate has no 'fundamentals.' To see why, we can run through the standard list of the forces that are supposed to 'equilibrate' a floating rate system; with fixed rates, market perceptions that these fundamentals are out of line can lead to an attack. A model independently proposed 40 years ago by the Australian economists W. E. G. Salter (1959) and Trevor Swan (1960) is the standard for the trade account. It suggests that a low ratio of traded to non-traded goods price indexes will be accompanied by a trade deficit. The price incentive to produce non-tradeds instead of tradeds could be corrected by devaluation. The resource allocation logic is impeccable but the problem is that in the world today, the volume of annual currency trading is around eighty times as large as the yearly value of foreign trade and long-term investment. The trade account makes up such a tiny fraction of total external transactions that it cannot possibly play a central role in determining the exchange rate. Either the exchange rate is fixed by the authorities, or it is determined in currency markets. With the rate determined one way or the other, domestic prices and output flows adjust so that markets for non-traded goods clear. The current account of the balance of payments comes out as a consequence.

Similar observations apply to another relative price warhorse, purchasing power parity (or PPP). The basic idea is that the dollar should buy as much of a traded good in a foreign country as at home. If P and P^* are the home and foreign price indexes respectively, then the spot exchange rate e should satisfy the relationship $e = P/P^*$. If P exceeds eP^*, then the home country should be inundated with goods from its foreign providers until P is forced down or e up to restore market balance. Purchasing power parity is a 'fundamental' that is conventionally supposed to hold. In the 'over-valued' $P > eP^*$ case, violation of PPP should be associated with a widening trade deficit, so that two well-known fundamental indicators reinforce one another. However, such concordance is not observed in practice. By most price comparisons the United States is 'under-valued'. In one familiar example, price quotations in the local currency for many consumer goods in the UK and United States are just about the same, although in exchange markets it costs about \$1.60 to buy one pound. At the same time the chronic US trade deficit signals that the dollar is too strong.

If the exchange rate is determined in asset markets, then which ones? We must distinguish between forward and current transactions. Uncovered interest rate parity (or UIP) is an arbitrage condition originally proposed by Keynes (1923) that supposedly describes the former. In the short run, it is represented by the equation

$$e = \varepsilon/(i - i^*) \tag{1}$$

in which e is the current spot rate (home currency to foreign currency), i and i^* are the home and foreign interest rates, and ε is the expected change in the rate. For a foreign investor, a positive vale of ε portends a capital loss if he or she moves into the home currency. Hence i has to exceed i^* to compensate. For given interest rates and expectations, eqn (1) provides a formula that is supposed to determine e.

'Testing' the validity of UIP has been a playground for econometricians for the past few decades (Blecker 1999). They have infinite fun trying to formulate and quantify expectations. The general conclusion seems to be that UIP does not hold in the data. But that does not mean that expectations are irrelevant. Rather, expected future values of the exchange rate provide the only point of reference against which it can be measured. Moreover, as discussed below, wide spreads between foreign and domestic asset returns were key factors underlying payments crises in developing countries. The problem is that they provided no clear guidance as to when and how the fixed exchange rate regimes in question would get into trouble.

For current (or temporary equilibrium) asset market relationships among i, i^*, and e, the portfolio balance model is the standard. It is usually set up with four financial assets—money and bonds in the home and foreign countries (the 'rest of the world' or ROW). Three market clearing conditions are traditionally assumed to be independent and thereby able to determine the three variables. Because a market cannot be out of balance just with itself, an economic truism known as Walras's Law asserts that if $N - 1$ of N markets clear in any economic system, then the Nth market will clear as well. In the portfolio balance set-up, the Law supposedly assures that the fourth market clears when the others are satisfied.

In fact, when its complete wealth accounting is respected, the portfolio balance model has just two independent equilibrium conditions, say for bonds in the two countries. Although no one seems to have noted it since the model was proposed in the 1960s, this observation is no surprise (Taylor 1999). It is an extension of the equivalence of money and bond markets in the standard macro model for an economy closed to international finance and trade—if money and bonds are the only financial assets, then when one of the two markets clears, Walras's Law says the other will clear as well. Just adding a foreign economy scaled to the one at home by the exchange rate does not alter the basic situation. If the local interest rate clears each country's asset market(s), then contemporary portfolio adjustments *cannot* determine the exchange rate.

To trace through the details with a *given* spot rate, suppose that the central bank creates money (deposits it in bondholders' accounts) to buy home bonds in an open market operation. The bond price will rise and in a standard market response the home interest rate will fall. Home portfolios will shift from home bonds toward money and ROW bonds until the home money market clears. Foreign portfolios will also shift toward ROW bonds. The combined new demands from home and the ROW will drive up the latter's bond price or reduce its interest rate until the foreign bond market clears. But by Walras's Law applied to the foreign economy, then its money market has to clear as well. All four financial markets re-balance *without* any need for the exchange rate to change—it is irrelevant to the adjustment process.

This same indeterminacy carries over to another 1960s model proposed by Robert Mundell and J. Marcus Fleming. Their 'IS/LM/BP' system is the open economy macro standard (Williamson and Milner 1991). If asset market stock equilibrium conditions vary smoothly over time (that is, stock equilibria are built up smoothly from flows), the results just quoted carry over to Mundell–Fleming. Its balance of payments or BP equation is not independent of the model's two other market balances (for goods and money)—when they are satisfied, the balance of payments is automatically satisfied as well.

To see why, we have to consider how the balance of payments interacts with home's flows of funds and flow asset market balances. The former are relationships stating that for each aggregate group of economic actors (households, firms, the financial sector, government, and the ROW), its savings plus increases in liabilities (e.g. new borrowing) must equal increases in assets (e.g. new loans or capital formation). The flow asset market balances state that new loans economy-wide are equal to new borrowing, new money issued by the banks appears as new deposits, and so on.

Now suppose that the home country is running up external arrears by not meeting contracted payment obligations on outstanding debt—its capital account surplus is less than its deficit on current account. There are two possible forms of repercussion on home's flow asset market balances and flows of funds. One is that some other flow of funds relationship will not balance. The other is that if home's domestic flows of funds equalities hold, then some flow market balance for a financial asset must fail to clear.

Consider the second case. The obvious counterpart to a non-clearing balance of payments is the domestic bond market. The run-up in external arrears would be reflected into a flow excess supply of home bonds—foreigners are not picking up enough domestic securities to provide home with the wherewithal to meet its external obligations. Under such circumstances, a spot devaluation of appropriate magnitude could be expected to cut the cost of acquiring home's bonds, increase their demand, and remove the disequilibrium. The balance of payments would clear.

The rub is that if home's other financial markets are clearing, then this sort of adjustment *cannot* happen—we know from the analysis of the portfolio balance model that if the home money market clears then so will the market for bonds. And with both money and bond markets in balance, there is simply no room in the accounting for an open balance of payments gap.

The other possibility is that the non-clearing balance of payments is reflected into another flow of funds relationship. For example, one can imagine and even observe (as in recent developing country experiences) situations in which the home country is running up external arrears at the same time as the domestic business sector is borrowing in anticipation of investment projects that are not working out. An exchange rate realignment might even reverse such simultaneous build-ups of external and internal bad debt. But at the macroeconomic level such situations are unusual—the banking sector at home is *not* usually in the business of providing non-performing loans to corporations. In harmonious times, the balance of payments emerges automatically from output and asset market equilibria. There is *no* need for the exchange rate (or any other variable) to adjust to ensure that external balance is satisfied.

The bottom line is that neither the traded/non-traded goods price ratio, nor PPP, nor UIP, nor portfolio balance, nor a balance of payments disequilibrium serves to determine the exchange rate. The same conclusions apply to the fiscal deficit in 'twin deficit' analyses and 'overly expansionary' policy in the 'trilemma' involving a fixed rate, liberalized capital markets, and a country's fiscal and monetary stance.

So where does the spot rate come from, if there are no fundamentals? From the Sherlock Holmes procedure of eliminating all possibilities until only one remains, the answer has to be that the spot rate is determined in forward markets, as it varies against expected future values of itself and other asset prices. In the real world, forward markets are intrinsically unpredictable and subject to a mix of rational and irrational behaviours.

Another way of parsing this statement is to observe that there is no real difference between the market's 'conventions' about future values of the exchange rate, and the rate's 'fundamentals.' There are no clear causal channels open between the factors listed in the preceding paragraphs and the spot rate. Yet, if market players come to believe that a floating rate will depreciate because some fundamental is 'wrong', then they will revise expectations accordingly and force the rate to move. One is reminded of a famous passage from Keynes's *General Theory* (1936): 'Speculators may do no harm as bubbles on a steady stream of enterprise. But the position is serious when enterprise becomes the bubble on a whirlpool of speculation. When the capital development of a country becomes a by-product of the activities of a casino, the job is likely to be ill-done.'

Liberalization of international capital markets and speculation in exchange rates have extended the reach of the casino from mere countries to the entire world. The record of the 1990s shows that the resulting tendencies toward destabilization and the hindrance of 'capital development' are of enormous policy concern.

5. MACROECONOMIC BALANCES

So far, the casino has mostly fed upon developing countries, as discussed later. But it is just not the periphery that is subject to destabilization; the centre (and the central country) may be at risk as well.

Analogous to foreign lending by the UK and United States under the high gold standard and gold exchange standard respectively, the key driving force in the world economy is the American current account deficit. The United States has been able to run large deficits for many years because global financial markets have been open and increasingly dominant institutional investors in all countries initiated a large and sustained flow of foreign capital into the United States. But the persistent American deficit has produced a peculiarly unbalanced structure of financial stocks and flows, which may well threaten the future stability of the world economy.

At the world level, there are three main financial actors—the United States, the fifteen countries in the European Union (EU) functioning as a rather tightly coordinated group, and Japan. At the core of the EU is Euroland, with eleven members that now share a single currency, the euro. China and the other historically rapidly growing economies in East Asia play supporting roles, with the rest of the world (ROW) picking up the slack. Table 3.1 summarizes their current account performances during the 1990s.

The first point to note is that international payments data do not add up as they should. As shown in the last line the world seems to run a substantial current account

Table 3.1. *Current accounts in major areas (billions of US dollars)*

	1990	1991	1992	1993	1994	1995	1996	1997	1998	1999
USA	−92	−6	−56	−91	−134	−129	−148	−166	−211	−249
Japan	45	68	112	132	131	110	66	95	125	147
EU-15	−31	−80	−81	9	23	52	91	126	125	137
East Asia	5	−2	3	6	−3	−22	−31	0	52	33
China	12	13	6	−12	7	2	7	23	12	6
ROW	−196	−249	−228	−200	−177	−137	−148	−150	−205	−206
World total	−257	−256	−244	−156	−153	−124	−163	−72	−102	−132

Source: OECD (Figures for 1998 and 1999 are estimates from the *OECD Economic Outlook* No. 64, December 1998).

deficit with itself—an impossibility because the sum of all nations' current accounts should be zero. After all, one country's exports are another country's imports. The error is comparable in magnitude to the flows of the major players. So the scales, though probably not the directions, of the forces about to be discussed are imprecise.

The two surplus players in the late 1990s were the EU-15 and Japan. Europe ran a current account deficit earlier in the decade, but then switched to a surplus partly as a consequence of the contractionary macro-policy packages most countries adopted as part of the run-up to the introduction of the euro on 1 January 1999. Aside from 1991 to 1992 when the Bush recession, prior depreciation, and payments for mercenary services rendered during the Persian Gulf War generated a transient surplus, according to the estimates in Table 3.1, the United States has run the major deficit. An American current account gap in the $200–300 billion range injects effective demand to the tune of about 1 per cent of world GDP into the global macro system. This is a non-trivial amount. The world economy can be very sensitive to 'one percent' shocks. That was about the size of the 1973 oil price shock.

There are four key international financial flows:

1. The United States has a structural deficit, financed by borrowing from abroad. It has used the resulting capital inflows to support steady if unspectacular GDP growth beginning in the early 1990s, based on stable although not low real interest rates. Calling the decade's results a 'boom' is an exaggeration. All around the world, trend output growth during recent decades has been around two-thirds as fast as in the 1960s.

2. Japan has been stagnant since its 'bubble' economy burst around 1990, and runs a secular surplus. As a consequence of the collapse of the bubble, its internal credit supply has been limited, leading to slow growth, a weakening yen through 1997, and a strong current account surplus with corresponding capital outflows.

3. In recent years, Europe's growth has been slow and its foreign surplus large. Since the middle of the decade, the sum of the European and Japanese surpluses has exceeded the American deficit.

4. The ROW is the main sink for surpluses originating elsewhere. China/East Asia ran deficits in 1995–96 and then switched to a surplus position after the Asian crisis,

as the countries of the region attempted to export their way out of depression. The region's famous bilateral current account surplus with the United States consistently exceeded its overall surplus. The difference is the deficit that the East Asian economies ran with the EU and with Japan. In effect, they were absorbing some of the excess saving in the EU and Japan and recycling it toward American shores. After all, the US external deficit *had* to be financed from somewhere.

How do the national economies supporting these flows interact? In terms of its output dynamics, the US current account deficit is pro-cyclical. When world activity is low, the US deficit, and hence US borrowing, rises, pumping demand into the rest of the world. Similarly, when world activity is high, the US deficit falls, limiting the injection of demand into the rest of the world. America's net borrowing therefore varies against the cycle, meaning that its incoming financial flows have behaved in a globally stabilizing fashion (as did Britain's outgoing flows of loans when it was the pivot of the system under the 'high' gold standard of the nineteenth century).

6. THE AMERICAN PREDICAMENT

For a nation that borrows, however, capital movements are not a matter of its own volition. A better way to describe the current role of the United States is to say that its creditors—Japan directly and the EU at one remove—have agreed to lend pro-cyclically to finance the American injection of global effective demand. The inflows have built up a huge stock of debt. At the end of 1997, gross US external 'liabilities' (in a broad sense, including foreign holdings of corporate equity) were about $4.8 trillion. According to Federal Reserve data, a rough breakdown was government debt, $1.5 trillion; corporate debt, $0.5 trillion; corporate equity, $0.9 trillion; financial sector, $0.7 trillion; and 'miscellaneous' (mostly obligations of business and finance), $1 trillion. These sums could lie at the root of at least three potential imbalances among stocks and flows of assets and liabilities, and output and trade flows from the real side of the economy:

1. First, the consolidated government sector's foreign debt was 27 per cent of its total obligations of $5.5 trillion. But less than 50 per cent of the $1.5 trillion it owed externally was owed to foreign governments. Most corporate debt was held privately. Foreign governments' holdings of US debt are at least subject to international negotiation. The same cannot be said of the US debt and equity held by the private sector in the rest of the world. A jump downward of just 6 per cent of total foreign holdings of American liabilities (as of 1997) would equal the projected current account deficit in 1999. Just as in East Asia before 1997, there is the potential for huge, rapidly destabilizing capital outflows. The federal government's T-bills, in particular, could be sold off very rapidly.
2. A second potential source of trouble would be an interest rate increase. If the short-term rate went from its current 5 per cent to 10 per cent, for example, American payments to foreigners on government and corporate debt of $2 trillion would go

up by $100 billion. To pay these bills the projected 1999 foreign borrowing would need to be increased by one-third. In this sense, the external position of the United States resembles Brazil's in 1998.

3. A third source of concern is who is actually to do America's borrowing in the future. The main component of *net* US external liabilities (including equity) of $1.3 trillion is government debt, built up during the long period of fiscal deficits from 1980 until 1997. Future external borrowing can only take the form of new liabilities issued by the government and/or the three main private sub-sectors: finance, corporate business, and non-corporate business and households. The consolidated government sector has been in fiscal surplus since 1997, so reducing both its domestic and foreign liabilities. The corporate sector largely finances its capital formation with retained earnings and over the medium term keeps its annual increments of financial assets and liabilities in rough balance (within a range of $200 billion or so). At most, its contribution to the growth in the stock of liabilities available to the rest of the world will be considerably less than the current account deficit. Similar statements apply to the financial sector's and 'miscellaneous' claims, for which foreign assets and liabilities are broadly offsetting. By a process of elimination, households emerge as the *only* major sector in a position to borrow from the rest of the world in the future. But in 1999 households were beginning to demonstrate financial distress just as they were supposed to begin a foreign borrowing spree that would be the fundamental corollary of a reasonable rate of growth in the United States.

So a household stock–flow imbalance threatens. Household debt is approaching $6 trillion (roughly 70 per cent in the form of mortgages, 25 per cent consumer credit, and the balance miscellaneous). At the end of 1997, the ratio of household debt to personal disposable income was 0.98, up from 0.89 in 1993.

Given the structure of global trade and payments, the United States will have to borrow $200–300 billion externally every year for the foreseeable future. The government sector seems intent on running an annual budgetary surplus in the $100–200 billion range. If they follow their traditional borrowing patterns over the cycle, the business and finance sectors will soon start saving more than they invest. It is the spending of households that must offset all these savings. If household income is (optimistically) assumed to grow steadily at 2.5 per cent per year, then the household debt/income ratio would rise to about 1.12 by the end of 2002. It is impossible to say how households and their creditors would respond to new borrowing of such magnitude, especially if a fall in the stock market (which must happen some time) results in a serious plunge in personal sector wealth ($33.6 trillion at the end of 1997, up from $19.6 trillion ten years before).

To illustrate the potential American debt trap(s), it makes sense to take a look at how the external position is likely to evolve if business continues as usual. At the end of 1997, the breakdown of US *net* foreign assets by type of instrument was monetary, $0.1 trillion; credit market, −$1.7 trillion; equity, $0.1 trillion; and miscellaneous, $0.2 trillion. Historically, the United States has received a strong positive return on its equity and similar holdings, with profits on net direct foreign investment (DFI) exceeding interest on America's net debt. However, that surplus vanished in 1997, when portfolio and DFI income were −$82 billion and $68 billion respectively.

Forward projections under fairly conservative assumptions about the trade deficit, volumes of DFI, and investment income flows, suggest that net foreign liabilities may rise from $1.3 trillion at the end of 1997 to $2.5 trillion at the end of 2002 *if current levels of macroeconomic activity and hence foreign borrowing are sustained.* Which of the major economic sectors—business, government, or households—will directly or indirectly run up this new foreign debt per year is a key policy question. For the reasons already discussed, households may not be able to shoulder the burden. If they do not and deep recession is to be avoided, the federal budget will have to move into substantial deficit. This is not a question of 'fine-tuning'. It is a question of whether the government will be capable of moving to counter a potentially very deep recession when the private sector's borrowing spree runs out. The popular prejudice against government deficits suggest that it will not.

7. EXTERNAL DANGERS?

The most recent runs on the dollar took place in the 1970s and 1980s. The former helped provoke the Volcker interest rate shock, a significant recession worldwide, the developing country debt crisis, and other major adjustments. Doubts about the dollar in the mid-1980s were instrumental in triggering the 1987 stock market crash. A decade is a long time span in terms of such events; after all, the Bretton Woods system lasted for only about 25 years. What scenarios may unfold if the United States in particular and the world system more generally get into trouble once again?

So far, the United States has managed to borrow in a globally stabilizing fashion and faces only potential flow–flow and stock–flow disequilibria. There are risks, however, on both fronts. With regard to borrowing, the real decisions will be made in Europe and Japan. The latter has been under international pressure for years to restructure its economy so that aggregate demand can be driven by domestic spending as opposed to exports. Through early 1999, very little had been achieved and the Japanese current account surplus continued to be recycled via Wall Street. This situation may very well continue.

Europe, on the other hand, may grow more rapidly now that the Maastricht process has ended and the euro has been born. In that event, higher activity levels and interest rates in the EU would draw in imports and capital flows. US borrowing could begin to be squeezed as the European trade surplus declines. It is also possible that the introduction of the euro, the only currency with a potential status in international trade and finance similar to that of the dollar, will create a potentially unstable currency duopoly. It is argued below that international arrangements might be put into place to limit fluctuations among the dollar, euro, and yen. But suppose this does not happen, and speculative pressure mounts against the dollar.

A sell-off of the dollar would produce sharp falls in US bond prices, and hence a rise in interest rates. Would higher interest rates stop the rot, would they be 'credible'? The potential disequilibria—portfolio shifts away from the United States, bigger interest obligations on its debt, and growing financial stress on the household sector—could begin to feed on one another, and on the views of the markets. At that point, with an expectational run on the dollar fuelled and not staunched by higher interest rates, dollar devaluation, austerity, and the other usual policy moves, all hopes for global macro stability could disappear. A massive international rescue campaign would certainly be required, with worldwide implications impossible to foretell.

A medium-term policy mix for the United States, then, will require an expansion in government spending to offset the solvency problems that the private sector (especially the household sector) will soon confront. Monetary expansion will not do the trick, since *some* domestic sector has to borrow to offset the current account deficit. But still more is required. The dollar is perhaps not so 'over-valued' as it was in the mid-1980s, but a real exchange rate correction could help reduce the external deficit and slow the debt accumulation process just described. Talk of depreciation in the 20–30 per cent range was in the air in the first part of 1999.

8. THE ROLE OF EXCHANGE RATES

We are back to exchange rates as high-voltage transmission lines for volatility and contagion. The mixed records of both fixed and floating exchange rates in the 1990s reflect a fundamental problem. In a world in which stocks of international debt are so large, and potential capital flows so overwhelming, something needs to be done to lessen the foreign exchange risk, which is undermining confidence and reducing growth and employment. In a completely liberal financial world, a return to fixed exchange rates is just not possible. Fixed rates need to be buttressed by exchange controls. What might be feasible would be to raise market confidence by establishing broad bands in the 5–10 per cent range above and below agreed midpoint bilateral exchange rates of the major currencies (the dollar, euro, and yen). Rates would be subject to 'dirty floats' within the bands, but the authorities would make clear to the markets their official intention to maintain the limits by joint interventions.

Management of markets would be unavoidable because (to repeat) exchange rates have no clear and direct linkages to fundamentals such as trade and fiscal deficits, or relative price levels. They are the outcome of a financial beauty contest of the sort famously described by Keynes in chapter 12 of *The General Theory*. The linkages that do exist are in the minds of market players, subject to the moving expectations and possibilities for rapid jumps in conventions that are the hallmark of the financial beauty game. The management of the bands would therefore be a management of conventions, with all the potential fragility that it implies. To move rates up and down within their permitted ranges, policy coordination (including coordination among central banks jealous of their 'independence') would be required. To steer them away from the bounds, international collaboration would be essential.

A system of bands would require close monitoring of markets, but it could yield considerable benefits. Private capital flows would be stabilized because the authorities would have explicitly stated their degree of tolerance of fluctuations. The entire history of liberal capital markets clearly indicates that a lack of government guidance encourages contagion when a currency is subject to speculative attack. Third countries would gain because they could peg their currencies to one of the big three without running the risk of major misalignment such as occurred in East Asia in the 1990s.

If the public sector were to re-adopt some of the foreign exchange risk that was privatized when the Bretton Woods system fell apart in 1973, then the authorities would need to create a system to manage that risk. In the absence of capital controls this would require a commitment to defend the limits of the bands by supporting to an indefinite degree any currency which is speculated against. This, in turn, would require international collaboration in the conduct of monetary policy. The absorption of risk by the public sector would also encourage the private sector to take excessive currency risks. So the bands would need to be complemented by a regulatory regime, which would diminish the moral hazard implicit in the public sector guarantee. The interrelationship of greater exchange rate stability and regulatory control will be a central policy concern for the foreseeable future.

9. DEVELOPING COUNTRY EXPERIENCES

Are there common factors that underlie the tidal waves of volatility, contagion, and crisis that have hit developing countries beginning with the Mexican events of 1994–95? Contrary to widely held perceptions, the crises were *not* caused by an alert private sector pouncing upon the public sector's foolishness, whether in pursuing overly expansionary fiscal and monetary policies, or setting up moral hazards. They are better described as private sectors (both domestic and foreign) acting to make high short-term profits when policy and history provided the preconditions and the public sector acquiesced. Mutual feedbacks between the financial sector and the real side of the economy then led to crises. By global standards, the financial flows involved were not large—$10–20 billion of capital flows annually (less than one month's external borrowing for the United States) for a few years are more than enough to destabilize a middle-income economy. The outcomes have been visible worldwide.

To see how they occurred, we can follow Frenkel (1983) and Neftci (1998) by thinking in terms of a stylized model in which initially the exchange rate is 'credibly' fixed, that is, $\varepsilon = 0$ in eqn (1) and the central bank enters the market to support a chosen value of e. It is easy to sketch how an unstable dynamic process can unfold. The cycle begins in local financial markets, which set up incentives that generate capital inflows. They spill over to the macroeconomy via the financial system and the balance of payments as the upswing gains momentum. At the peak, before a (more or less rapid) downswing, the economy-wide consequences can be overwhelming.

To trace through an example, suppose that a spread on interest rates (e.g. on Mexican government peso-denominated bonds with a high nominal rate but carrying an implicit exchange risk) or asset prices (e.g. capital gains from booming Bangkok real estate) opens. A few local players take positions in the relevant assets, borrowing abroad to do so. Their exposure is risky but *small*. It may well go unnoticed by regulators; indeed, for the system as a whole the risk is negligible.

Destabilizing market competition enters in a second stage. The pioneering institutions are exploiting a spread of (say) 10 per cent, while others are earning (say) 5 per cent on traditional placements. Even if the risks are recognized, it is difficult for other players not to jump in. A trader or loan officer holding 5 per cent paper will reason that the probability of losing his or her job is close to 100 per cent *now* if he or she does not take the high-risk/high-return position. Such potentially explosive behaviour is standard market practice. In one description from an interview study, '... the speculative excesses of the international investors in the Asian financial crisis were not an exception, ... but instead the result of normal business practices and thus to a certain degree inevitable' (Rude 1998).

After some months or years of this process, the balance sheet of the local financial system will be risky overall. It will feature 'short' (indebted) positions in foreign claims and 'long' positions in local assets. There may also be problems with maturity structures of claims, especially if local players borrow from abroad short-term. Nervous foreign lenders may then contrast a country's total external payment obligations over the next year (say) with its international reserves. Such comparisons proved disastrous for Mexico in 1995 and several Asian countries in 1997.

But the real problem lies with the currency or locational mismatch of the balance sheet—in light of developing country experience it emerges as a convention/fundamental that can lead to exchange rate crises. Potential losses from the long position are finite—they at most amount to what the assets cost in the first place. Losses from short-selling foreign exchange are in principle unbounded—who knows how high the local currency-to-dollar exchange rate may have to climb?

In a typical macroeconomic paradox, individual players' risks have been shifted to the aggregate. Any policy move that threatens the overall position—for example cutting interest rates or pricking the real estate bubble—could cause a collapse of the currency and local asset prices. The authorities will use reserves and/or regulations to prevent a crash, consciously ratifying the private sector's market decisions. Unfortunately, macroeconomic factors will ultimately force their hand.

In a familiar scenario, suppose that the initial capital inflows have boosted domestic output growth. The current account deficit will widen, leading at some point to a fall in reserves as capital inflows level off and total interest payments on outstanding obligations rise. Higher interest rates will be needed to equilibrate portfolios and attract foreign capital. There will be adverse repercussions for both the private and public sectors. Business saving will fall or turn negative as illiquidity and insolvency spread, threatening a systemic crisis. Bankruptcies of banks and firms may further contribute to reducing the credibility of the exchange rate. If the government has debt outstanding, escalating interest payment obligations as rates shoot up can provoke a fiscal crisis—witness events in Russia and Brazil in the late 1990s.

A downturn becomes inevitable, since finally no local interest rate will be high enough to induce more external lending in support of what is recognized as a short foreign exchange position at the economy-wide level. Shrewd players will unwind their positions before the downswing begins (as Mexican nationals were said to have done before the December 1994 devaluation). They can even retain positive earnings over the cycle by getting out while the currency weakens visibly. But others—typically including the macroeconomic policy team—are likely to go under.

The dynamics thus involves both the financial and real sides of the economy. Movements in the spread itself feed into cyclical changes that finally provoke massive instability. A classic engineering parallel is the Tacoma Narrows suspension bridge. Opened in July 1940, it soon became known as 'Galloping Gertie' because of its antics in the wind. Its canter became strong enough to make it disintegrate in a 41-mile-per-hour windstorm in November of that year. The best efforts of economists are beginning to produce systems that can fail almost as fast.

10. POLICY OPTIONS

What can local authorities do to avoid the Galloping Gertie syndrome? One step is to avoid the sort of balance sheet problems just mentioned. The list includes the following:

1. *Stock–flow imbalances*: Have some asset or liability stocks become 'large' in relation to local flows? East Asia's short-term debt exceeding 10 per cent of GDP was a typical example. It was a stock with a level that could change rapidly, with sharply destabilizing repercussions. Rapid expansion of bank credit to the private sector as a share of GDP while booms got underway in the Southern Cone, Mexico, and Thailand might have served as an early-warning indicator, had the authorities been looking. The causes included monetization of reserve increases and growth of loans against collateral assets such as securities and real estate with rapidly inflating values.

2. *Stock–stock relationships*: Besides locational or currency mismatches in balance sheets in the financial sector, indicators such as debt/equity ratios and the currency composition of portfolios (including their 'dollarization' in Latin America recently) become relevant here. They can signal future problems with financing investment-saving differentials.

3. *Quality of debt*: Finally, there is a question about the quality of collateral assets that borrowers hold. Much of the credit expansion in Thailand and Russia went to players holding assets with rapidly rising prices such as real estate and shares. With an asset price collapse in a crisis, such loans suddenly became 'non-performing'. In early 1999, China was in a similar situation. Although its capital controls and massive reserves kept that country out of the first Asian crisis, its internal financial imbalances may yet change investors' conventions enough to provoke an external crisis.

When seen as 'excessive', any of these factors can become 'fundamental' in the eyes of external investors, and feed rapidly into capital outflows. But in recent developing country experience, more than a simple reversal of conventions has been involved. There have been clear cyclical patterns leading to a collapse. How can they be avoided or damped?

The key control variables for the external accounts in any economy are its exchange rate, quality of financial regulation, and capital and exchange controls. Especially for a middle-income country, 'small' in terms of the global macro system, all have sub-stantial international implications.

11. EXCHANGE RATES IN DEVELOPING ECONOMIES

In developing countries, there are often very good reasons why the exchange rate should be fixed (or limited to fluctuations within a narrow band). A pegged rate is anti-inflationary, a factor crucially important to Latin American stabilization packages beginning with Mexico's in the late 1980s. It can also enhance export competitiveness, as happened when countries in Southeast Asia pegged to the falling dollar after the Plaza Accord in 1985.

However, a fixed rate can create severe problems. Obviously, it can be an easy target for speculation. Another problem stems from the fact that it is often convenient for a country to peg its rate to just one of the major global currencies (rather than a 'basket'), if only to give clear signals and simplify calculations for its importers and exporters. The risk is that the 'anchor' currency can drift out of line. Although the Asian eco-nomies benefited from their dollar peg in the late 1980s, they were badly hurt by the strengthening dollar after 1990. Such problems can be reduced if the dollar, euro, and yen maintain relatively stable exchange rates among themselves, as discussed above. Then pegging to a single one of the trio will not be destabilizing.

The benefits and costs of floating rates for developing countries remain to be assessed, although several important economies adopted such regimes after the wave of financial crises in the late 1990s. The main difficulty for developing countries is that markets in their currencies tend to be rather 'thin', and hence the currency will be prone to large, destabilizing fluctuations. Middle-income economies often lack deep future markets to generate forward values of the exchange rate against which the spot rate can float. Mexico, which after its 1994 crisis adopted a managed float with some degree of capital market regulation, provides a sobering example. An index of the real exchange rate was 71 in 1993, 107 in 1995 just after the crisis, and back down to 85 in 1998. Were currency markets truly self-stabilizing, such worrisome fluctuations would be less likely to occur.

Moreover, any exchange rate regime has to be consistent with fiscal and monetary policies. The required linkages will vary according to the regime chosen, and may require complementary measures. In the absence of widespread capital and exchange controls, fixed rates demand large international reserves to be viable (and note how even Brazil's billions did not save its pegged rate after serious capital outflows got underway in late 1998). Intermediate regimes require more active intervention in the management of the capital account. Flexible rates can be highly unstable. Certainly, all regimes can be aided by some control over capital movements.

12. FINANCIAL REGULATION

The crises demonstrate that there are few greater problems than those confronted by financial regulatory authorities in developing and transition economies. Their own capacities are underdeveloped, they lack a suitable number of qualified personnel, and, given their small size relative to the volume of international financial transactions, the risks they confront are proportionately far greater than those of the United States, Europe, or Japan.

As noted above, much of the instability in capital flows in and out of developing and transition economies can be traced to wide spreads between foreign costs and national returns to assets. Under a fixed exchange rate regime, it is easy to see a 10 per cent differential between local and foreign short-term interest rates or a similarly sized gap between the growth rate of the local stock market index or real estate prices and a foreign borrowing rate. Such yields are an open invitation to capital inflows that can be extremely destabilizing. Whether policy makers feel they are able to reduce interest rates or deflate an asset market boom is another question, one that merits real concern.

Another source of potential spreads is through off-balance sheet and derivative operations. Here, local regulators can be at a major disadvantage. It is difficult to keep up with the latest devices and most (but one hopes not all) of any nation's skilled financial operators will be on the other side, inventing still newer devices to make more money. Staying up-to-date as far as possible and inculcating a culture of probity in the local financial system are the best defences here.

There is thus a serious question as to whether many developing country macro-policies and regulatory systems can meet such goals, especially in the wake of capital market liberalization. Another difficulty arises with timing. It is very difficult to put a stop to capital flows *after* convention has decreed that fundamentals have become adverse. At such a point, interest rate increases or a discrete devaluation can easily provoke a crash. The authorities have to stifle a potentially explosive cycle early in its upswing; otherwise, they may be powerless to act. The problem with all indicators of a threatening crisis is that they often lag behind an unstable dynamic process. By the time they are visibly out of line, it may be too late to attempt to prevent the crisis. Its management becomes the urgent task of the day.

13. CAPITAL CONTROLS

The fixed exchange rate regime of the Bretton Woods era was buttressed by capital controls. It is difficult to imagine such extraordinary stability without them. In the new international financial order, controls have a somewhat different role. They are for the management of risk. The volatility and contagion associated with uncontrolled markets is highly inefficient. Capital controls are simply part of the regulatory framework for the management of risk at both macroeconomic and microeconomic levels. This is why so much attention has been focused of late on the control of capital inflows, rather than the traditional concern with outflows.

It is important to recognize that there is a significant difference between limiting short-term capital flows into a country on the one hand, and closing markets to foreign goods on the other. In the latter case a country may attempt to acquire a beggar-my-neighbour advantage. The same argument does not apply in the case of limitations on short-term inflows of capital.

14. THE PROBLEMS AT HAND

A long list of concerns is on the table (United Nations 1999):

(1) How to deal with international volatility and contagion;
(2) How to manage exchange rates, when in floating rate regimes they are only determined by forward market expectations about their changes over time and fixed rates are subject to attack if conventions/fundamentals veer the wrong way;
(3) The need to cope with a system of global payments flows in which the richest country absorbs the bulk of available international saving, and is itself building up massive stock–flow and stock–stock imbalances. Depreciation and fiscal expansion by the United States look inevitable when its household spending spree comes to an end, with implications for the rest of the world that are difficult to foresee;
(4) Proposals for exchange rate bands for the trio of major currencies emerge naturally at this point in time; how to manage rates in developing economies is also of immediate concern;
(5) Developing countries also have to build up regulatory capabilities, including the intelligent use of capital controls on inward movements.

15. INTERNATIONAL FINANCIAL REGULATION

Regulatory issues are at the centre of these concerns. The 1999 US *Economic Report of the President* got part of the story right:

Traditionally, supervision and regulation of financial systems have been domestically based. But the increased global integration of financial markets and the proliferation of institutions doing cross-border transactions suggest the desirability of enhanced *international* financial supervision and surveillance (p. 277, emphasis in original).

Timidly, the Group of Seven—big industrialized countries—is taking up this task. At a meeting in Bonn in early 1999, their finance ministers accepted a report by Hans Tietmeyer, governor of the Bundesbank, recommending the establishment of a financial stability forum (or FSF) to 'foster stability and reduce systemic risk in the international financial system'.

The new institution was proposed in September 1998. Tietmeyer got the job of sorting out how 'a permanent standing committee... charged with delivering the global objective of a stable financial system' might work. He came up with the Forum, plus an action plan for reforming the world's financial 'architecture'. The question now is whether, as the G-7 communique suggests, these moves can 'improve the functioning of markets' and 'reduce systemic risk'?

'Systemic risk' is what volatility, contagion, and unpredictable exchange rates are all about. Systemic risk is to finance what dirty smoke is to the environment. Like power plants that do not bear the social costs of their emissions, financial firms do not price into their activities the costs that their losses might impose on the economy as a whole.

Yet, there are familiar consequences of financial failures. The blow-up of one house can create a conflagration as loss of confidence sweeps away the entire street. Taking risks is what financial enterprises do to make money, but markets underprice the risk they generate for the rest of society.

National authorities try to contain risk by establishing regulators. They are supposed to ensure that investors recognize the dangers their activities create. Firms may be required to bear their full costs by meeting capital adequacy and risk management standards, or that they may be directly regulated. By forcing businesses to behave *as if* they took systemic risk into account, regulators strive to enable finance to weather normal storms. However, their precautions fail when the system confronts abnormal storms. A complete loss of confidence will sink even the most prudent and secure. Then regulation is not enough. A lender of last resort is required.

Today, financial markets know no borders. Yet, regulatory power remains trapped within irrelevant national boundaries. Since the mid-1970s standing committees based at the Bank for International Settlements (BIS) in Basle have sought to establish common standards for banking supervision, supported by greatly enhanced information flows. In 1999, the BIS extended the scope of its activities with its first report on the supervision of financial conglomerates, including securities firms and insurance companies in an international perspective.

The new FSF will be based at the BIS. It will take coordination and provision of information several steps further. It will bring together national central bankers and regulators, the major international institutions, and international regulatory bodies in order to achieve 'a better understanding of the sources of systemic risk . . . , ensure that international rules and standards of best practice are developed . . . , ensure consistent international rules . . . and a continuous flow of information amongst authorities having responsibility for financial stability'.

All the above is worthy. But the Asian crisis and its spread to Russia and Latin America demonstrate that information, cooperation, and coordination are not enough. It does not matter how many numbers are available or how transparent financial institutions might be, the market still underprices risk and is still systemically inefficient. It does not matter how many national regulators sign up to common standards if there is no enforcement procedure to ensure that those standards are met. And it does not matter how competent national authorities might be, if, when the global financial crises demand concerted action, they cannot provide a swift, unified response.

What is required is the power to enforce and to act, and that is what the FSF conspicuously lacks. This is understandable. National governments, especially G-7 governments, do not look kindly on the idea of surrendering their surveillance, regulatory, and intervention powers to an international body. But the die has been cast. In a world of open financial markets, national governments cannot effectively regulate the risks to which their economies are exposed. That can only be done by an international body with policy-making and policy-enforcing powers. And certainly not by an FSF that plans to meet only twice a year.

16. A WORLD FINANCIAL AUTHORITY

It will probably take a couple more big crises before governments face up to the need to endow an international regulator with real powers. One of the proposals currently being debated is to establish a World Financial Authority (or WFA) with regulatory and surveillance powers as well as the ability to coordinate with central banks and the IMF when international lender-of-last-resort interventions may be needed (on the unassailable proposition that the lender of last resort should only inject funds into institutions, which in the judgement of the regulatory authorities are creditworthy). Indeed, the FSF can be interpreted as an initial step toward a WFA.

Policy cooperation and coordination have probably been taken to a limit in the formation of the FSF. In the next few years international financial regulation will have to enter into a phase of control. International surveillance, regulation, and intervention will be performed by someone, somewhere. Developed countries need the WFA as much as do developing countries. Of course the shocks to developing countries are more severe, but the long-term impact of volatility and contagion on developed countries has been no less costly. Moreover, the rising scale of exposures in highly leveraged markets is ratcheting up systemic risk throughout international financial markets, developed or developing alike.

The institutional framework of the WFA, and the role it would perform in the international economy derive both from analysis of the sort presented here, and from historical experience. Historical experience has confirmed the necessity of regulation and of the lender of last resort in domestic markets. The same sorts of measures are now required internationally. These measures are required if a broadly liberal world order is to survive.

17. TASKS AND LEGAL BASIS OF A WFA

If a World Financial Authority is established, what tasks should it perform? What should be the legal foundation of WFA action? How are the tasks to be performed? Because for market efficiency the tasks of the WFA must be performed by someone, answering these questions in the context of the WFA provides a template for policy development.

A national financial regulator performs five main tasks: authorization of market participants; the provision of information to enhance market transparency; surveillance to ensure that the regulatory code is obeyed; enforcement of the code and disciplining of transgressors; and the development of policy that keeps the regulatory code up to date (or at least not more than 10 yards behind the market in a 100-yard race). These tasks now need to be performed at international level, ideally *as if* performed by a unitary WFA.

For example, criteria for authorization should be at the same high level throughout the international market: ensuring that a business is financially viable, that it has suitable regulatory compliance procedures in place, and that the staff of the firm are fit and proper persons to conduct a financial services business. If high standards are not uniformly maintained then firms authorized in a less demanding jurisdiction can impose unwarranted risks on others, undermining their high standards of authorization.

Similarly, as far as the information function is concerned, the failure to attain not only transparency but also common standards of information undermines the efficient operation of international financial markets, and creates risk. The persistent inability of national regulatory bodies to agree upon international accounting standards is a prime example of just such a failure.

Surveillance and enforcement are the operational heart of any effective regulatory system. Without effective, thorough policing of regulatory codes, and uniform enforcement of standards by appropriate disciplinary measures (including exclusion from the market place) the international financial system is persistently exposed.

Finally, the policy function is the essential driving force of effective regulation. Regulatory codes must be adapted to a continuously changing marketplace. An important component of that change is international. As national financial boundaries dissolve, and as new products are developed that transcend international boundaries by firms with a worldwide perspective, the policy function must ensure that the regulator is alert to the new structure of the marketplace, the new systemic risks created, and to the new possibilities of contagion. This requires a unified policy function, capable of taking a view about the risks encountered in particular markets and by the international market place as a whole.

All five core activities involve the exercise of authority, and hence trespass into sensitive political arenas. Nation states are naturally reluctant to cede powers to an international body, even if this might mean the acquisition of (collective) sovereignty over activities otherwise beyond their control. When this is done it is done typically by treaty, confirming collective rights and responsibilities, and, at least in principle, accountability. It is also done by the consensus and by the mutual recognition of self-interest that produces 'soft law'.

As Alexander (2000) explains:

International soft law refers to legal norms, principles, codes of conduct and transactional rules of state practice that are recognized in either formal or informal multilateral agreements. Soft law generally presumes consent to basic standards and norms of state practice, but without the *opinio juris* necessary to form binding obligations under customary international law . . . . Soft law may be defined as an international rule created by a group of specially affected states which had a common intent to voluntarily observe the content of such rule with a view of potentially adopting it into the national law or administrative code.

Even with this potential 'legalization' of international policy-making and of surveillance (which includes some standardization of the information function in the drive for 'transparency'), authorization and, for the richer countries, enforcement remain national activities—though even here agreements on home–host division of responsibilities inject an international dimension.

There is, in effect, a creeping internationalization of the regulatory function in international financial markets—witness the FSF. This internationalization is federal in character, with national jurisdictions being the predominant legal actors guided by international soft law, and by the pressures of the marketplace. So some of the functions of a WFA are being performed. But they are being performed haphazardly. Authorization is still essentially national, the information function is highly imperfect, surveillance (by the IMF) is as yet 'experimental', enforcement is national, and the policy function is predominantly driven by an exclusively G10 consensus. As measured against the template of a proper WFA there is a long way to go.

While the template of a WFA clarifies the tasks that must be performed if international financial markets are to be regulated efficiently, it does not provide much guidance as to how the tasks are actually to be performed in the absence of a unitary authority. In practical terms many tasks can and must be delegated to national authorities. But it is important that national authorities should operate within common guidelines. That is the importance of the WFA—not to tell national authorities what to do, but to ensure that in a single world financial market they behave in a coherent and complementary manner to manage the systemic risk to which, in a seamless market, they are all exposed. Effective international regulation will necessarily be federal, with different responsibilities at appropriate levels of the system. But there must be a coherent federation with common principles and common values, resulting in (converging) national codes enforced by national authorities to attain common goals.

18. BEYOND A WFA

Even so, a world financial authority is not enough. Among the problems listed above, better regulation can certainly help contain the negative externalities created by excessive volatility and contagion in financial markets. However, an international regulator is not automatically a lender of last resort (or LLR), with the ability to mobilize massive resources to offset extreme financial collapses. Interestingly enough, although Euroland has seen fit to launch a new currency, it has not explicitly considered the establishment of an LLR to deal with internal financial crises that may arise. The same path may well be taken by the rest of the world—until a crisis hits. This will also leave the issue of 'orderly workouts' for developing countries in abeyance, despite the manifest failures of IMF packages in East Asia and Russia (United Nations 1999).

For developing economies, a WFA can certainly offer advice and technical assistance on decisions involving exchange rate regimes and capital controls. It can also help with internal financial market regulation. The key issue regarding governance of such activities is whether that informal Basle committees/FSF approach to these questions can be extended to give a voice to representatives from the non-OECD world. There is perhaps room for guarded optimism on this front.

A WFA could give technical input to the formulation of exchange rate bands for the three key currencies, but would scarcely be in a position to manage a system. As a non-treaty-based institution, it would have scant leverage on the international economic decisions of the United States. These latter problems reflect the fundamental weakness of the current system for management of international finance. Basically, managerial responsibility resides with the finance ministers and central bank governors of the

United States/Europe/Japan triad, with some mechanisms for giving modest voice to countries outside this small group.

This management system is not entirely market-based and permits some room for institutional innovation—the creation of the euro, for example, was at least in part a response to the exchange rate instability displayed during the ERM crisis. However, as just noted, the space for such manoeuvres is circumscribed and leaves many potentially important issues unattended.

Nothing is quite so effective in concentrating the political mind as a financial crisis—fear of systemic collapse can help drive significant reforms when a crisis strikes. If the current semi-system fails to muddle through, in particular if the US economy is significantly damaged, then steps such as explicit creation of a WFA, formation of a system of exchange rate bands, and establishment of proper provisions for LLR interventions and orderly workouts could well become politically feasible and even desirable. But there is no sense in anticipating major changes in the present system until untoward events force them upon it.

REFERENCES

Alexander, Kern (2000). The role of soft law in the legalization of international banking supervision. *Oxford Journal of International Economic Law*.

Bank for International Settlements (BIS) (1995). *65th Annual Report*. BIS, Basle.

Blecker, Robert (1999). *Taming Global Finance*. Economic Policy Institute, Washington, DC.

Block, Fred L. (1977). *The Origins of International Economic Disorder*. University of California Press: Berkeley, CA.

D'Arista, Jane (1998). Financial Regulation in a liberalized global environment. Center for Economic Policy Analysis, New School for Social Research, New York.

de Cecco, Marcello (1984). *The International Gold Standard: Money and Empire*. Francis Pinter, London.

Eatwell, John (1996). International financial liberalization: The impact on world development. *Discussion Paper No. 12*. Office of Development Studies, UNDP, New York.

——and Lance Taylor (2000). *Global Finance at Risk: The Case for International Regulation*. The New Press, New York.

Eichengreen, Barry (1998). *Globalizing Capital: A History of the International Monetary System*. Princeton University Press, Princeton.

Fisher, Irving (1933). The debt-deflation theory of Great Depressions. *Econometrica*, 1, 337–57.

Fleming, J. Marcus (1962). Domestic financial policies under fixed and floating exchange rates. *International Monetary Fund Staff Papers*, 9, 369–79.

Frenkel, Roberto (1983). Mercado Financiero, Expectativas Cambiales, y Movimientos de Capital. *El Trimestre Economica*, 50, 2041–76.

Helleiner, Eric (1994). *States and the Reemergence of Global Finance: From Bretton Woods to the 1990s*. Cornell University Press, Ithaca NY.

Keynes, John M. (1923). *A Tract on Monetary Reform*. Macmillan, London.

——(1936). *The General Theory of Employment, Interest, and Money*. Macmillan, London.

Mundell, Robert (1960). The monetary dynamics of international adjustment under fixed and flexible exchange rates. *Quarterly Journal of Economics*, 74, 227–57.

Neftci, Salih N. (1998). FX short positions, balance sheets, and financial turbulence: An interpretation of the Asian financial crisis. Center for Economic Policy Analysis, New York.

Rude, Christopher (1998). The 1997–98 East Asian financial crisis: A New York market-informed view. UNDESA, New York.

Salter, W. E. G. (1959). Internal and external balance: The role of price and expenditure effects. *Economic Record*, 35, 226–38.

Swan, Trevor (1960). Economic control in a dependent economy. *Economic Record*, 36, 51–6.

Taylor, Lance (1999). Neither the portfolio balance nor the Mundell–Fleming model can determine the exchange rate—each has one fewer independent equation than people usually think. Center for Economic Policy Analysis, New School for Social Research, New York.

Temin, Peter (1993). Transmission of the Great Depression. *Journal of Economic Perspectives*, 7(2), 87–102.

United Nations Task Force (of the Executive Committee on Economic and Social Affairs of the United Nations) (1999). Towards a new international financial architecture. ECLAC, Santiago.

Williamson, John and Chris Milner (1991). *The World Economy*. New York University Press, New York.

4

Transnational Corporations and Technology Flows

SANJAYA LALL

1. INTRODUCTION

This chapter analyses international systems of governance for transnational corporations (TNCs) and for technology transfer in the emerging world. This world provides a very different setting for industrial growth from that of half a century ago, when much of 'development strategy' was launched. Technical change is now more rapid and pervasive, affecting most activities in developing countries. It is shrinking economic distance dramatically, exposing enterprises to intense and immediate competition unprecedented in history. Trade plays a much larger role in economic life, and much of it is handled by large transnationals—and an increasing proportion of trade and production is integrated across national boundaries under TNC aegis. Governments are, willingly or otherwise, liberalizing economic policies. In this new setting, market competitiveness is the lifeblood of industrial growth. But markets are harsh taskmasters. For those unprepared for open competition, it imposes severe penalties, and there is clearly growing divergence rather than convergence in industrial and technological performance in the developing world.

Technology and direct investment flows are now not subject to much direct regulation at the international level—traditional controls on these flows are one of the casualties of liberalization and globalization. The forces regulating technology and investment flows are now the general economic setting and the 'rules of the game'. The rules are framed to support greater economic integration driven by free market forces, to provide level playing fields for all participants regardless of their size and competitive capabilities. This does improve resource allocation and provide a bracing competitive environment, but it also ignores the costs resulting from deficient markets and weak institutions. Where countries have very different structural abilities to cope with free competition, a level playing field is bound to result in continuing and growing inequities.

By outlawing many important policy tools (many of which were used very effectively in East Asia) the new rules may force countries to grow less than if they could

I am very grateful to Deepak Nayyar and Pedro Roffe for their detailed suggestions, and to the other contributors for their comments at an initial presentation. The usual disclaimer applies.

improve markets and their supply capabilities by deliberate interventions. The rules do offer some benefits, in particular constricting the more egregious policy errors that characterized the early days of import-substitution and planning. However, they also impose (largely unnecessary) costs by insisting that countries at vastly different levels of development follow the same rules. There is, in other words, a valid and growing case for differentiating the rules to take account of legitimate development needs. The rest of this chapter spells out these arguments.

2. THE NEW SETTING

The global economy is undergoing a series of sweeping changes, driven by rapid technical progress and widespread policy liberalization. So broad and far-reaching are the developments that analysts see the emergence of a new technological 'paradigm' (Freeman and Perez 1988). This new paradigm involves not only new technologies in the traditional sense but also new management techniques, different forms of enterprise linkages and relations between industry and science, and intensification of information flows between economic agents. These technological changes are transforming international economic relations: patterns of trade and comparative advantage, flows of capital, technology and people, generation and ownership of information, and property rights. While the main locus of technological dynamism is the industrialized world, all developing countries are also directly affected as economic actors. The environment in which they have to operate is now very different from that in which most development strategies and institutions were formed.

Section 3.2 discusses the uneven impact of technology and globalization, as a backdrop to the analysis of governance issues. Section 3.3 describes how investment and technology flows are regulated. It argues that while the Bretton Woods and UN institutions play a small *direct* role in these flows, they are important *indirectly*, by setting the rules for trade and capital flows. The new rules have benefits: they impose market discipline, liberate private enterprise and encourage greater private capital flows to developing countries. They also have costs (Section 4). They leave steadily diminishing scope for industrial policies, many of which were effective in the Asian newly industrializing economies (NIEs). This penalizes less industrialized countries and can inhibit their future technological and industrial development. At the same time, few countries have been able to mount effective industrial policies in the past, and the new rules can prevent some of the more glaring policy errors that have held back economic progress.

3. PARTICIPATION IN INTERNATIONAL TRADE AND TECHNOLOGY FLOWS BY DEVELOPING COUNTRIES

3.1. *Overview*

The context for technology and trade within which developing countries function is changing rapidly. Different countries are adopting different strategies (consciously or by default) to cope. Some are succeeding spectacularly, some others are failing miserably, and many are somewhere in between. It is useful to consider these strategies, since the emerging systems of governance for TNCs and technology affect their scope and feasibility.

Let us start with the main trends on the competitive performance of developing countries, with the following sections providing more empirical evidence.

Technology is increasingly the driving force behind global competitive advantage. New technologies affect all manufacturing and service industries, making it imperative for every country to raise its abilities to access and deploy such technologies. However, technology-intensive activities are growing faster than others in production and trade, and sustained growth requires countries to shift their competitive structure into such activities.

Technological change is accelerating, and technology diffuses more rapidly than before. At the advanced end its creation and transmission are concentrated in a small number of TNCs that dominate (increasingly costly) R&D in industrial countries. This raises the significance of FDI to technology transfer, since many new technologies are not available at arm's length and since, with policy liberalization, TNCs represent a convenient way of securing the entire package of knowledge, skills, capital, and marketing needed even for available technologies. TNCs are increasing their role in world production and trade, integrating their production systems globally and rationalizing their distribution systems; thus, belonging to such systems can lead countries to share in technical change and international trade. However, FDI is highly concentrated (export-oriented FDI more so): few developing countries participate in TNC-generated industrial dynamism; many are increasingly marginalized. As a result, globalization accentuates national disparities rather than reducing them.

The strategies deployed by successful developing countries have important lessons for the rest of the developing world. Successful countries have used two broad export and technology development strategies: FDI-dependent and autonomous.

3.1.1. *FDI-dependent Approaches*

FDI-dependent approaches have two sub-strategies, passive and targeted. Passive export strategies mean opening up to FDI and attracting investors to exploit existing advantages—natural resources or cheap unskilled labour—for export markets. This has worked well in several countries. TNCs have set up many assembly facilities aimed at world markets, particularly in simple consumer goods like clothing and footwear. A small number of countries have also attracted FDI in the final assembly of technology-intensive products like electronics. The two sets of 'passive' countries have diverged over time. Those in simple consumer goods have largely failed to upgrade from simple labour-intensive undifferentiated goods into higher quality products or into more dynamic, technology-based activities. Those in electronics assembly have managed to upgrade technologies, but without significant local technological or skill inputs or supply linkages. The former group faces serious problems of sustaining growth as wages rise or the special trade rules that made their exports profitable (the Multi-Fibre Agreement) expire. The latter group faces skill and technological constraints to further upgrading. The presence of export-oriented FDI *per se* does not ensure the continued evolution of dynamic comparative advantages.

Active FDI-dependent strategies involve strong strategic and targeted interventions by the host government, both to direct FDI into higher value activities and to raise the quality of domestic factors, suppliers, and institutes. Very few host countries, led by Singapore (and Ireland in the OECD), have implemented such proactive FDI strategies, but these have been very successful in sustaining growth in advanced activities. However, their indigenous technology base remains weak.

3.1.2. *Autonomous Strategies*

Autonomous strategies have minimized or selectively reduced reliance on FDI as a means of technology transfer and development. This has entailed pervasive interventions, including infant industry protection and credit direction, to facilitate difficult technological learning by domestic firms. It has worked well where disciplined by strong export orientation and implemented by a skilled and independent bureaucracy. The technological base produced by autonomous strategies is far broader and deeper than that yielded by FDI-dependent strategies. However, pervasive interventions have often created inefficiencies, where pursued as import-substitution strategies with no regard for efficiency and competitiveness. Only two mature Asian Tigers stand out as successful cases of efficient industrial policy.

All this is relevant because many successful strategies are under threat from the emerging governance regime for international investment and technology transfers.

3.2. *Export Performance and Technological Change*

Let us start with recent trends in the export performance to gauge how developing countries are faring with this aspect of globalization: competitiveness is a good (and readily available) means of comparing the effects of technology transfer and FDI across regions and countries. We later deal with the strategies adopted to foster competitiveness, and how the new systems of governance affect the ability of countries to launch those strategies.

Table 4.1 shows the structure and growth of world exports over 1980–97 by technological categories.[1] Primary exports are separated from manufactures. The determinants of primary exports (natural resource endowments) do not need any specific analysis; nor do they raise interesting issues in terms of technology transfer. TNCs do play an important role in primary resources, particularly where large-scale mining or plantations are involved, but the governance issues involved are largely covered by the discussion below on FDI in manufacturing. Thus, we do not examine primary products in any detail below. Service trade is not shown for lack of comprehensive data; technological classifications are also very difficult for services (OECD 1999*a*). FDI in services is a large and rapidly growing part of international investment flows, and some of the important issues that arise in terms of governance are touched on below.

---

[1] For an earlier analysis see Lall (1998). The present figures have been updated from that paper. I am grateful to the World Bank for processing the data from the UN Comtrade database.

S. Lall

Table 4.1. *Growth rates and shares of exports by technological categories, 1980–97*

	Growth rates (% p.a.)				Developing country shares (%)		
	World	Industrialized countries	Developing countries	Developing less industrialized	1980	1997	Change in share
Primary products	2.3	3.1	1.6	−1.5	52.5	46.3	−6.2
Manufactures	7.9	6.8	13.5	6.7	10.1	24.0	13.9
Of which							
Resource based	5.7	5.1	8.1	3.0	16.9	24.7	7.8
Low technology	7.8	6.2	12.4	6.2	17.0	35.1	18.1
Medium technology	7.4	6.6	16.4	9.8	4.1	15.9	11.8
High technology	11.4	9.8	21.2	11.4	6.7	27.8	21.1
All exports	7.0	6.5	8.5	2.0	20.7	26.3	5.6

Source: Calculated from UN Comtrade data.

Manufactures are the dynamic engines of trade growth. Exports of primary products grew at around 2 per cent per annum during 1980–97, compared to 8 per cent for manufactures. Interestingly, primary exports by developed countries grow faster than by developing ones, reflecting different rates of productivity increase and perhaps the impact of discriminatory trade barriers. The growth of manufactured exports, grouped in four categories,[2] is strongly driven by technology: high-technology exports are the fastest expanding group. However, low-technology products grow slightly faster than medium-technology products over the period, suggesting that the relocation of production from high to low wage areas has been a significant factor in trade expansion.

The correlation between technology intensity and export growth is expected.[3] Innovation leads to rapid new product introduction. Innovative products generally have high income-elasticities of demand and create new demands. They also stimulate the demand for related technology-based products (especially in information technology and electronics). New materials and processes substitute for existing ones and take market share from technologically stagnant activities. These are *dynamic* sources of

---

[2] Resource-based products like processed foods or beverages tend to be simple and labour-intensive, but there are segments using capital, scale, and skill-intensive technologies (e.g. petroleum refining). Since competitive advantages in these products arises generally—but not always—from the local availability of natural resources, they do not raise particularly interesting issues for competitiveness. Low-technology products (e.g. garments, textiles, footwear, travel goods, simple metal and plastic products) have stable well-diffused technologies, with low technological expenditures and simple skill requirements. Labour costs tend to be a major element of cost; barriers to entry are relatively low and final markets tend to grow slowly, though there can be some items that enjoy bursts of rapid growth. Medium-technology products (e.g. standard machinery, automobiles, chemicals, and basic metals) are the heartland of industrial activity. They tend to have complex technologies, moderately high levels of R&D and advanced skill needs. High-technology products (e.g. advanced electronics, precision instruments, aircraft, and pharmaceuticals) have fast changing technologies with particular emphasis on new products. They are highly dependent on high R&D investments, highly specialized technical manpower and well-developed technology institutions. However, high-tech electronics products also have simple labour-intensive processes that can be relocated in low wage areas.

[3] The same factors that drive trade also drive the growth of high-tech production and services within industrialized economies. See the US National Science Foundation (NSF 1998) and OECD (1999a).

new comparative advantage. The relocation of labour intensive processes, by contrast, leads to export growth by exploiting *static* comparative advantages—the final market generally grows slowly and technologies are relatively stable. Relocation has been stimulated by recent trade and FDI liberalization, falling transport and communication costs, and the spread of export-oriented TNCs (many from the developing world). Such structural adjustments take time to work out (as the growth of textile and garment exports over the past 2–3 decades shows), but they slow down as the advantage offered by low wages is 'used up', and other competitive forces (e.g. skills and technology) come into play. However, that relocation is *not* confined to low-technology products. It also applies to many high-technology products, particularly in electronics, where certain processes (final labour-intensive assembly) are economical to shift to poor countries. The exceptional growth of high-tech exports in fact reflects the interaction of technological and relocation factors.

Developing countries do surprisingly well in technologically complex products, partly as a result of this interaction. While their overall share is largest in low-technology products, their growth rate is highest in high-tech products, as is their relative lead over developed countries. The value of their high-technology exports exceeds that of low-technology exports ($287 and $256 billion respectively in 1997). If this suggests that developing countries as a whole are well placed to benefit from technological change and globalization, it would be misleading. Only a few countries account for the technological dynamism of exports in the developing world, and within those even fewer display domestic technological capabilities. The above figures conceal enormous *concentration* in competitive performance.

Thus, East Asia by itself accounts for 91 per cent of high-tech exports by the developing world (and for 75 per cent of total manufactured exports and 77 per cent of low-technology exports). At the other extreme, Sub-Saharan Africa (excluding South Africa) accounts for only 0.5 per cent of total manufactured exports, 1.4 per cent of resource-based manufactured exports, 0.6 per cent of low-technology exports and zero per cent of high-technology exports. Only 15 countries—the four mature Asian Tigers, four new Tigers (Indonesia, Malaysia, Philippines, and Thailand), China, India, Turkey, South Africa and the three large Latin American economies—account for over 92 per cent of total manufactured exports from the developing world. The level of concentration has risen over time: in the mid-1980s their share was 80 per cent. Concentration also rises with technological sophistication. The leading five countries account for 62 per cent of the developing world's manufactured exports; their share is 46 per cent in resource-based, 63 per cent in low-technology, 69 per cent in medium-technology, and 78 per cent in high-technology, exports. This shows clearly the unevenness in the spread of competitive abilities.

There are also significant differences in national patterns of specialization by technology. Five countries—Philippines, Singapore, Malaysia, Mexico, Korea, and Taiwan—have very high (over 60 per cent) shares of advanced (high- plus medium-technology) products in their manufactured exports. India, China, Indonesia, Turkey, South Africa, and Argentina are the technological laggards (with shares of below 40 per cent). Even these laggards are far more advanced than developing countries as a whole, around half of which have shares of advanced exports below 20 per cent, and around one-quarter below 10 per cent.

The main agents of export activity (TNCs vs local enterprises) differ. Domestic enterprises account for the bulk of manufactured exports from Korea, Taiwan, Hong Kong, India, Turkey, and South Africa. TNCs dominate exports from the other countries. Of technology-intensive exporters, only Korea and Taiwan show significant domestic competence—the others depend heavily on foreign affiliates mainly to assemble imported components and to transfer new technologies and skills. Korea and Taiwan developed their position by heavy investments in skills, technology, and capability development, guided by pervasive industrial policy (Lall 1996). Their larger enterprises are now leading TNCs in their own right, with considerable technological and marketing muscle. The TNC-reliant economies also differ in how far they have advanced along the skill and technology ladder. Singapore has moved furthest, followed by Malaysia. China remains at an intermediate level, the bulk of its exports consisting of assembly operations by investors from the Tigers. Singapore's success is traceable to selective industrial policy on investment, skills, and infrastructure.

3.3. *Determinants of Competitive Success*

3.3.1. *Strategic Options*

The factors accounting for competitive success in the developing world are intimately related to technology transfer and FDI, and the lessons from successful countries are vital to assessing the relevant governance mechanisms. Competitive success and upgrading of manufactured exports depend on the ability of countries to access new technologies, assimilate them, and build upon them over time (Lall 1992). While many factors affect this ability, among the critical ones are inflows of foreign technology, both via FDI and in other forms. Such inflows must be supplemented by domestic efforts to create skills and technical capabilities if they are to result in sustainable development. There are different ways of doing this: we can group them into FDI-dependent and autonomous strategies.

FDI-dependent strategies: In developing countries, all strategies to export manufactures start with labour-intensive activities. The main explanation is not that given by textbook theory—they have ample labour relative to capital—but is related to technological learning. Activities with 'easier' technologies (that they can master best, given their low levels of technological capabilities) tend to be labour-intensive and have low skill needs. Labour costs *per se* become important because these activities have low entry barriers and scale economies, and products tend to be undifferentiated. In these conditions, pure wage differences do matter to competitiveness (unlike other manufacturing activities where skills, scale, technology, and product differentiation are more important to competitiveness). Entry into more complex technologies entails not just more advanced equipment, but also costly, prolonged and risky learning, with greater requirements of skill and technical effort. The differences between the two strategies for learning lie in the different degrees of access they provide to new technologies, the learning processes they face, and the access they enjoy to world markets.

An FDI-dependent strategy initially facilitates entry into easy export activities in countries without a base of technical skills and capabilities. TNCs can provide the 'missing elements' relatively easily and upgrade them over time. They have the skills, experience and resources to facilitate local learning. They can stimulate exports in developing host countries by letting them specialize in the simplest processes within internationally integrated operations. In many advanced industries the direct entry of TNCs may be the only feasible way of accessing technology and markets. All these give TNCs an edge over comparable local entrants in terms of building competitive capabilities (in cases where local firms are in the running at all).

There are, however, disadvantages in the FDI-dependent strategy. While it creates local capabilities for simple processes, its competitive edge (essentially in assembly activities) lasts only as long as relative wages remain low. Having such assembly operations do not ensure that capabilities deepen over time to allow more complex activities to be undertaken competitively. TNCs relocate as wages rise: they place the simple processes in lower cost countries and the more advanced ones in countries with the requisite skills and supplier bases. To sustain competitive development, the country must ensure the creation of more advanced skills, supply capabilities, and technology systems. In addition, it must induce TNCs to transfer advanced activities and strike deeper local roots (UNCTAD 1999*f*). Even this process of upgrading faces limits. TNCs have established bases in the industrial world for such functions as design, R&D, and marketing: they are reluctant to transfer these to developing host countries because of the difficult learning and institutional linkages involved. Thus, the setting up of such advanced functions in affiliates may take much longer than if local enterprises were involved.

To simplify, we can distinguish between two FDI sub-strategies: a passive one of exploiting static wage advantages, and of building new advantages by targeted industrial policies. The first does not automatically lead to the second. A distinct strategic decision (and the creation of the appropriate abilities and institutions) is required; and it is clearly necessary for sustained development. While globalization means that FDI-based strategies have to be used by all countries, it is important to be aware of their inherent limitations. To overcome these and build strong local technology bases, it is vital to build capabilities in local firms as a necessary complement. Most developing countries with TNC-based industrial and export strategies are still at the passive stage, with little policy intervention apart from a welcoming FDI regime, good infrastructure, and a low-cost labour force. Relatively few have moved to the interventionist phase of targeting and upgrading TNC activities and capabilities.

Thus, Sri Lanka, Indonesia, Morocco, Tunisia, China, Jamaica, Honduras, Dominican Republic, and Mauritius are mainly in the first category. Singapore, and to a lesser extent Malaysia, are in the second, with Thailand, Philippines, and Costa Rica, somewhere in transition. This is for countries that have set up export-oriented activities afresh. There are others with TNC export activity in complex activities. As with the automobile industry in Mexico, Argentina, and Brazil, these have developed behind prolonged import-substituting strategies. Their governments have recently used liberalization and regional trade agreements (NAFTA and Mercosur) to induce TNCs to enter exports and upgrade capabilities to world-class levels. The purely market-driven FDI strategy has not led to dynamic upgrading of capabilities or to significant local deepening.

Autonomous strategies: These strategies (with local firms getting foreign technologies at arm's length) are more demanding than FDI-based ones. Developing country entrants not only lack the capabilities to use new technologies at best practice levels, they face greater difficulties than foreign affiliates in mustering the skills, information, facilities, and capital needed to develop them. However, their capability building tends to lead to greater learning and to deeper capabilities (precisely because they cannot call on parent companies) and tends to generate more linkages and externalities. It provides far more autonomy in decision-making on product and market diversification. If local firms are able to enter advanced activities efficiently, over time it creates a broader, more dynamic, innovative base.

'Autonomous' strategies do not mean relying solely on national enterprises to the exclusion of FDI. Autonomy is a matter of degree. All economies have a mixture of local and foreign-owned firms; it is the relative emphasis placed on supporting local enterprises in complex technologies and building up domestic R&D capabilities that defines whether the strategy is autonomous or dependent. Once local capabilities develop, inward FDI feeds into and complements domestic technological effort. Beyond a certain level of development, greater local capabilities induce inward FDI of higher technological 'quality' and lead to outward FDI in technology-based activities. Moreover, as domestic markets and institutions develop, there is less need for government interventions to promote local capabilities. Over time, in other words, the two strategies tend to converge, a tendency greatly strengthened by external pressures to reduce government interventions and provide 'level playing fields' with major trading partners.

Nevertheless, during the critical early stages of building national technology systems, there are important differences between autonomous and FDI-based strategies. The former require more active and pervasive government intervention than the latter, because local enterprises face greater market failures in mastering difficult activities (Lall 1996). It is important, however, to distinguish efficient autonomous strategy from classic import-substitution strategy. While both involve intervention in trade and resource allocation, the design and structure of the interventions differ greatly (Nayyar 1997). Autonomous industrial policy entails the selective (rather than wholesale) promotion of activities and firms, combined with strong incentives (e.g. export orientation) to invest in costly learning to achieve best practice levels of technology and management. It also requires heavy investments in skill and technology systems. Classic import substitution often did neither. Only two countries have managed autonomous strategies effectively: Korea and Taiwan. Others, with sweeping import-substitution policies, have had some elements of capability building, but have not produced the systemic dynamism of these two Tigers.

3.3.2. FDI Flows
FDI in the developing world (that is, *excluding* portfolio investments and lending) has grown rapidly since the mid-1980s (Table 4.2), rising from an annual average of

Table 4.2. *FDI inflows, 1980–97*

	Inflows by year (US$ million)						Inflows (shares) (%)	
	1986–91 average	1990	1992	1994	1996	1997 (prov.)	1986–91	1997
World	159 331	183 835	175 841	242 999	337 550	400 486	100.0	100.0
Developed countries	129 583	151 970	120 294	141 503	195 393	233 115	81.3	58.2
West Europe	66 470	98 941	85 837	78 417	99 954	114 857	41.7	28.7
North America	54 674	43 133	23 662	53 571	82 851	98 994	34.3	24.7
Other	8 439	9 896	10 796	9 515	12 588	19 263	5.3	4.8
Developing countries	29 090	31 766	51 108	95 582	129 813	148 944	18.3	37.2
North Africa	1 196	1 341	1 582	2 364	1 313	1 811	0.8	0.5
Sub-Saharan Africa	1 673	855	1 589	3 329	3 515	2 899	1.1	0.7
Latin America and Caribbean	9 460	10 055	17 611	28 687	43 755	56 138	5.9	14.0
Developing Europe	88	114	214	405	1 029	796	0.1	0.2
West Asia	1 329	1 004	1 827	1 518	303	1 886	0.8	0.5
Central Asia	4		142	896	2 084	2 627	0.0	0.7
South and East Asia	15 135	18 328	27 683	58 265	77 624	82 411	9.5	20.6
Central and Eastern Europe	658	300	4 439	5 914	12 344	18 424	0.4	4.6
Memo item								
Least developed (43)	781	603	1 463	844	1 965	1 813	0.5	0.5

Source: UNCTAD (1998).

$29 billion in 1986–91 to $149 billion in 1997. However, the flows are highly concentrated by region and country.[4] South and East Asia and Latin America together
account for 93 per cent of total flows to developing countries. At the other end, the
forty-three least developed countries receive only half of 1 per cent. The ten leading
host countries raise their shares over the period from 64 to 76 per cent. In 1997, the
bottom fifty recipients accounted for less than 1 per cent of FDI flows to the developing world.

The extent of concentration is increasing with policy liberalization. TNCs are
rationalizing their production systems, concentrating in fewer sites to take advantage
of economies of scale and scope. This means that fewer countries are benefiting from
the resulting larger scales of production, and even fewer from the growing R&D that
supports TNC production.[5]

Table 4.3 shows the share of FDI in capital formation in newly industrializing
countries (the data are for total, not only manufacturing, FDI). The figures for the Asian
Tigers illustrate clearly the different strategic orientation of the different countries.

3.3.3. *Technology Flows*

All developing countries use foreign technology as the primary source of new productive knowledge, and access it in many ways. Apart from FDI, one major form is
licensing. Patchy data are available for royalty and technical fees paid overseas. In 1997
the developing world paid $5.8 billion (14 per cent of the world total of $41 billion), up
from $757.5 million in 1980 (8.4 per cent).[6] The largest single purchaser of foreign
technology in 1997 was Korea ($2.4 billion), accounting for 42 per cent of all devel-
oping countries (up from 8 per cent in 1980). Its dominant position in arm's length
technology imports reflects both its low reliance on internalized (FDI) imports and its
technological dynamism. Korea was followed by Thailand ($804 million), China ($543
million), Mexico ($501 million), Argentina ($241 million), Philippines ($158 million),
and India ($151 million). Data are not available on countries like Taiwan, Singapore,
Brazil, or Malaysia. Sub-Saharan Africa as a whole spent $84 million, 1.4 per cent of the
total for the developing world. The least developed countries together paid $9 million.

The increasing information intensity and transferability of new technologies are
leading innovators to seek stronger intellectual property protection and to extend their
coverage to more forms of knowledge. With the growth of globalized production and

---

[4] A significant and growing proportion of FDI flows (to both developing and developed countries) take
the form of mergers and acquisitions (M&As). M&As may not add immediately to production capacity;
sometimes quite the contrary. However, unless they lead to 'asset stripping' where the acquired enterprises
is dismantled and sold off, they can lead to subsequent investments in new skills and technologies. This
leads to greater flexibility and economic competitiveness, even where the sectors concerned are in
infrastructure and services. M&As are even more concentrated than FDI flows in general, with most going
to Latin America and a few other relatively advanced newly industrializing economies. For evidence and
examples see UNCTAD (1999*f*).

[5] For instance, major pharmaceutical TNCs are now using just two production sites (Egypt and South
Africa) to serve North Africa and East/South Africa, closing down formulation facilities in a large number
of African countries. Information provided by pharmaceutical TNCs in Kenya on a recent trip by the
author.   [6] UNCTAD (1999*f*).

Table 4.3. *Inward FDI flows as percentage of gross domestic investment*

	1985–90	1991	1992	1993	1994	1995
World	5.4	3.1	3.3	4.4	4.5	5.2
All developed	5.5	3.2	3.2	3.7	3.5	4.4
West Europe	8.9	5.3	5.3	5.8	5.1	6.7
North America	5.5	3.4	2.5	3.8	5.5	4.6
All developing	8.0	4.4	5.1	6.6	8.0	8.2
North Africa	2.7	2.2	3.8	4.1	5.7	3.0
Other Africa	9.2	7.3	6.4	8.2	12.5	13.2
Latin America	11.3	7.8	8.1	7.2	10.3	11.0
West Asia	1.2	1.7	1.5	2.2	1.0	−0.6
South and East Asia	9.7	3.8	4.7	7.5	8.3	9.0
Central and East Europe	1.0	0.4	0.8	7.9	5.0	5.2
Hong Kong	12.2	2.3	7.7	7.1	8.2	8.4
Singapore	59.3	33.6	12.4	23.0	23.0	24.6
Korea	1.9	1.0	0.6	0.5	0.6	1.1
Taiwan	5.1	3.1	1.8	1.8	2.5	2.7
China	14.5	3.3	7.8	7.1	8.2	8.4
Indonesia	7.6	3.6	3.9	3.8	3.7	6.5
Malaysia	43.7	23.8	26.0	22.5	16.1	17.9
Thailand	10.2	4.9	4.8	3.4	2.3	2.9
Philippines	13.6	6.0	2.1	9.6	10.5	9.0
India	1.2	0.3	0.4	1.0	2.4	3.6
Argentina	13.0	15.1	25.5	31.0	4.8	11.7
Brazil	3.1	1.4	3.0	1.3	3.0	4.7
Mexico	16.9	8.5	6.4	6.0	14.3	17.1

Source: UNCTAD (1997).

liberalization, access to many forms of technology is only available via direct TNC investment. The ability to exploit technologies in global markets is also increasingly linked to TNC participation. All these factors are raising the cost of accessing new technologies to enterprises from developing countries.

3.3.4. *Technological Effort*
Domestic technological effort is essential to using technologies efficiently. Much of it is informal—learning, incremental improvements, adaptations, and copying—rather than formal R&D effort (Lall 2000). Over time, however, R&D becomes important as countries use complex technologies; it is necessary simply to understand, absorb, and adapt advanced technologies, to increase local content, and to obtain technologies not easily available on licence.

The R&D data show the same differentiation as exports (Table 4.4). Average productive enterprise financed R&D as a percentage of GNP (probably the measure most relevant for production related technology) in the mature Asian NIEs is nearly 400 times higher than in Sub-Saharan Africa. It is around 10 times higher than in the new NIEs and Latin America.

Table 4.4. *Propensities and manpower in major country groups (simple averages, latest year available)*

Countries and regions[a]	Scientists/engineers in R&D		Total R&D % of GNP	Sector of performance (%)		Source of financing			
						% distribution		% of GNP	
	Per million population	Numbers		Productive sector	Higher education	Productive enterprises	Government	Productive enterprises	Productive sector
Industrialized market economies[b]	1 102	2 704 205	1.94	53.7	22.9	53.5	38.0	1.037	1.043
Developing economies[c]	514	1 034 333	0.39	13.7	22.2	10.5	55.0	0.041	0.054
Sub-Saharan Africa (exc. S Africa)	83	3 193	0.28	0.0	38.7	0.6	60.9	0.002	0.000
North Africa	423	29 675	0.40	n/a	n/a	n/a	n/a	n/a	n/a
Latin America and Caribbean	339	107 508	0.45	18.2	23.4	9.0	78.0	0.041	0.082
Asia (excluding Japan)	783	893 957	0.72	32.1	25.8	33.9	57.9	0.244	0.231
NIEs[d]	2 121	189 212	1.50	50.1	36.6	51.2	45.8	0.768	0.751
New NIEs[e]	121	18 492	0.20	27.7	15.0	38.7	46.5	0.077	0.055
South Asia[f]	125	145 919	0.85	13.3	10.5	7.7	91.8	0.065	0.113
Middle East	296	50 528	0.47	9.7	45.9	11.0	51.0	0.051	0.045
China	350	422 700	0.50	31.9	13.7	—			0.160
European transition economies[g]	1 857	946 162	0.77	35.7	21.4	37.3	47.8	0.288	0.275
World (79–84 countries)	1 304	4 684 700	0.92	36.6	24.7	34.5	53.2	0.318	0.337

Notes:

[a] Only including countries with data, and with over 1 million inhabitants in 1995; [b] USA, Canada, West Europe, Japan, Australia, and New Zealand; [c] Including Middle East oil states, Turkey, Israel, South Africa, and formerly socialist economies in Asia; [d] Hong Kong, Korea, Singapore, Taiwan Province; [e] Indonesia, Malaysia, Thailand, Philippines; [f] India, Pakistan, Bangladesh, Nepal; [g] Including Russian Federation; — Not available.

Source: Calculated by author from UNESCO (Statistical Yearbook 1997).

Table 4.5. *Technological effort in major developing countries (ranked by enterprise financed R&D as % GNP)*

Country	Year	Total R&D as % GNP	Enterprise financed R&D as % GNP	R&D per capita 1995 ($)[a]
Korea	1995	2.7	2.27	261.9
Taiwan	1994	1.8	1.00	198.0
Singapore	1994	1.1	0.69	294.0
South Africa	1991	1.0	0.50	31.6
Malaysia	1992	0.4	0.17	15.6
Chile	1994	0.8	0.16	38.6
India	1995	1.1	0.14	3.7
Turkey	1995	0.4	0.12	11.1
China	1993	0.6	0.11	3.7
Mexico	1995	0.4	0.09	13.3
Brazil	1985	0.4	0.08	14.6
Argentina	1996	0.3	0.05	24.1
Peru	1984	0.2	0.05	4.6
Indonesia	1993	0.2	0.04	2.0
Thailand	1991	0.2	0.02	5.5
Sri Lanka	1994	0.2	0.02	1.4
Philippines	1984	0.1	0.02	1.1
Mauritius	1992	0.4	0.01	13.5
Venezuela	1992	0.5	0.00	15.1
Pakistan	1990	0.3	0.00	0.8
Nigeria	1987	0.1	0.00	0.3

Notes: [a]Last available total R&D as percentage of 1995 income ($) using income figures from World Bank (1997).

Source: UNESCO 1995 (Statistical Yearbook 1995); OECD; national sources.

Even these averages conceal the large differences among countries in technological effort (Table 4.5), reflecting their varying industrial strategies. The leader in R&D spending, by far, is Korea, not only in the developing world, but also in the world as a whole. It runs neck and neck with Japan, but is higher than all other industrial countries; until the financial crisis, its R&D was expanding at impressive rates. Taiwan comes next, spending the same proportion as the UK, higher than the Netherlands or Italy. Hong Kong does not publish R&D data, but reports suggest that national R&D is below 0.5 per cent of GNP and enterprise financed R&D is a very small proportion of this. The three mature NIEs are in a clearly different class from the rest of the developing world.

TNCs account for substantial portions of technological effort in countries like Singapore, Malaysia, Brazil, and Mexico.[7] Interestingly, the latter two, while attracting most US TNC affiliated R&D, are poor performers in overall terms; there is little complementarity between TNC and local R&D effort. R&D by TNCs in developing

---

[7] On the share of foreign investors in national R&D in the OECD countries, see OECD (1999*b*).

countries is minuscule compared to their overall research effort. For US TNCs, this constitutes only 1 per cent of the total R&D, under 8 per cent of their overseas R&D spending (UNCTAD 1999*f*). However, the experience of Singapore in raising industrial R&D under the aegis of TNCs suggests that it is possible to induce the transfer of advanced functions to developing countries.[8] This has not evolved as a natural progression from manufacturing activity, however; it has required stringent policies, to target those activities and provide strong incentives and subsidies, along with the creation of high-level technical and scientific manpower.

3.3.5. *Human Capital Formation*

The pattern of skill formation, in particular of high-level technical skills, is similar to that of R&D spending. The mature Tigers lead other developing countries, and also of most of the industrialized world (Table 4.6). The Asian NIEs enrol over 33 times the proportion of their population in technical subjects than in Sub-Saharan Africa (including South Africa). The ratio is 2 times that of industrial countries, nearly 5 times Latin America and the new NIEs, and over 10 times South Asia and China. By all accounts, the quality of their education (dropout rates, relevance of curriculum, knowledge of science and so on) is also much better than that of other developing countries.

3.4. *Implications for Governance*

In this emerging setting of accelerating technical change and policy liberalization, sustained growth necessitates continuous skill and technological upgrading in all countries. In developing countries, in particular, this calls for enormous efforts to improve factor markets, institutions and infrastructure. It also calls for the capacity to undertake and support continuous improvements over time, as the pace of competition intensifies. Some of the necessary improvements may take place under free market conditions, but certainly a *significant portion will not*. Recent experience suggests that development under both autonomous and FDI-based strategies can be enhanced by careful policy intervention to strengthen capabilities as inherited (static) advantages are 'used up'. Such interventions will involve, among other things, targeting future comparative advantage, coordinating interlinked activities, and ensuring that technology and investment inflows support the dynamization of economic activities. While passive policies of 'opening up' and 'getting prices right' can result in bursts of growth—mainly to realize existing comparative advantages—their sustainability is not ensured. The competitive base remains static: intervention is necessary to dynamize this base. There are many possible strategies to do this, depending on the economic and political circumstances. In general, the more rapid the pace of technical change and intensification of competition, the more important the role of the government in shaping an appropriate response. And, the more dynamic and deep the indigenous technological base desired, the more pervasive the interventions required (Lall 1996; Lall and Teubal 1998).

---

[8] For studies of Singapore's strategy on building a semiconductor industry, see Mathews (1999) and the hard disk drive industry, see Wong (1997). On Singapore's general strategy, see Lall (1996).

Table 4.6. *Tertiary level enrolments, total and in technical subjects, 1995 (weighted averages)*

Regions	3rd Level enrolments		Technical enrolments at 3rd level						Total technical subjects	
	Total students		Natural science		Maths and computing		Engineering			
	No.	% of population	No.	% of population	No.	% of population	No.	% of population	No.	% of population
Developing countries	35 345 800	0.82	2 046 566	0.05	780 930	0.02	4 194 433	0.10	7 021 929	0.16
Sub-Saharan Africa	1 542 700	0.28	111 500	0.02	39 330	0.01	69 830	0.01	220 660	0.04
MENA	4 571 900	1.26	209 065	0.06	114 200	0.03	489 302	0.14	812 567	0.22
Latin America	7 677 800	1.64	212 901	0.05	188 800	0.04	1 002 701	0.21	1 404 402	0.30
Asia	21 553 400	0.72	1 513 100	0.05	438 600	0.01	2 632 600	0.09	4 584 300	0.15
NIEs	3 031 400	4.00	195 200	0.26	34 200	0.05	786 100	1.04	1 015 500	1.34
New NIEs	5 547 900	1.61	83 600	0.02	280 700	0.08	591 000	0.17	955 300	0.28
South Asia	6 545 800	0.54	996 200	0.08	7 800	0.00	272 600	0.02	1 276 600	0.10
China	5 826 600	0.60	167 700	0.02	99 400	0.01	971 000	0.10	1 238 100	0.13
Others	601 700	0.46	70 400	0.05	16 500	0.01	11 900	0.01	98 800	0.08
Transition economies	2 025 800	1.95	55 500	0.05	30 600	0.03	354 700	0.34	440 800	0.42
Industrial countries	33 774 800	4.06	1 509 334	0.18	1 053 913	0.13	3 191 172	0.38	5 754 419	0.69
Europe	12 297 400	3.17	876 734	0.23	448 113	0.12	1 363 772	0.35	2 688 619	0.69
North America	16 430 800	5.54	543 600	0.18	577 900	0.19	904 600	0.31	2 026 100	0.68
Japan	3 917 700	0.49		0.00		0.00	805 800	0.10	805 800	0.10
Australia/New Zealand	1 128 900	5.27	89 000	0.42	27 900	0.13	117 000	0.55	233 900	1.09

Source: Calculated from UNESCO (Statistical Yearbook 1997).

How does this relate to international governance of international investment and technology flows? In my view, vitally. The ability of developing countries to tap such flows in their long-term development interest depends directly on international and domestic policy regimes. Both are affected by ruling forms of international governance—the rules, norms, institutions, and enforcement mechanisms that affect trade, investment, and technology transfer. Domestic policies are coming increasingly under the purview of international governance. The question of whether or not such governance is conducive to the effective use of such critical resources (as investment and technology) has serious implications for development. It is argued here that there is a growing risk that it is not. International governance is increasingly driven by an ideologically driven neoliberal agenda. It disregards rigorous economic analysis as well as the experience described above.

4. CURRENT FORMS OF INTERNATIONAL GOVERNANCE

4.1. *'Ideal' International Governance*

In view of the above considerations, we can posit what international governance of technology and FDI flows should look like to promote development. We can consider this at three levels: the general setting, technology transfer, and FDI.

4.1.1. *General Policy Setting*
Import substitution and state-led industrialization are largely accepted as having failed, but it is increasingly accepted that development involves a significant role for government. Since industrial and technological growth faces pervasive market failures, there remains a strong case for selective industrial policy, carefully designed and flexibly implemented (Lall and Teubal 1998). The governance system should encourage, facilitate, and support the new strategic role of government.

4.1.2. *Technology Transfer*
Countries can obtain new technologies at arm's length, by buying capital goods, licensing and so on, or in internalized forms (by FDI). The best way for the government to facilitate technology imports is by giving information and technical support to enterprises, and providing an incentive regime that stimulates the efficient use of technologies. The subsequent steps—for mastery, adaptation, diffusion, and improvement of technologies—need policies to foster learning. This involves a judicious combination of trade, industrial, and factor market policies. The appropriate governance structure is one that promotes access to new technologies and lowers their cost, and allows governments to mount policies to deepen and broaden technological competence and, where necessary, to promote local enterprise.

4.1.3. *FDI*
Countries must provide FDI regimes with stable, transparent, and fair rules for TNCs. This does not imply passive 'open door' policies on FDI or a regime with complete access to TNCs on equal terms with national enterprises. There are two

issues. First, international investors have information and perception deficiencies, and good promotion and incentives can overcome these to attract FDI. In addition, it is possible to raise the 'quality' of FDI and its subsequent impact by targeting investors and using performance requirements (on local content, training, or R&D). A passive open door FDI policy may attract less FDI (unless the country has obvious attractions, like China), and it may attract it mainly to areas of static comparative advantage. 'Using' FDI for development thus calls for good marketing and targeting strategies. Second, a conducive climate for FDI need not entail a 'level playing field' with domestic enterprises in all activities. The two sets of firms often operate in segmented markets for information and capital (foreign affiliates tend to be in much stronger positions), and face different learning processes. There is no valid economic reason why they should face identical policy conditions, since this would accentuate the strengths of foreign entrants.[9] There may be practical reasons, though past experience shows that TNCs are willing to accept restrictions as long as these are stable, clear, and manageable.

This 'ideal' policy scenario provides for much greater openness and reliance on private enterprises and markets than past development strategies. At the same time, it retains a positive role for government in overcoming market deficiencies and dynamizing competitive advantages. In this ideal scenario, the international community facilitates and promotes technological learning and deepening in developing economies, helping governments to devise and implement efficient interventions.

4.2. *New Rules of the Game*

How do the emerging rules of the game compare with this 'ideal' scenario?

The general policy setting for FDI and technology transfer has changed greatly in recent years, from widespread government intervention and participation in economic life to greater free market and private sector orientation. While a significant part of this shift is due to disillusionment with classic import-substitution strategy on the part of national governments, external pressures have also played an important role. The most powerful agencies promoting policy liberalization have been the two Bretton Woods agencies, through their stabilization and structural adjustment programmes, specific operations and general policy advice. Many bilateral aid agencies and regional development banks have supported them. At the level of international agreements, a number of regional trade agreements and, most important, the Uruguay Round of the GATT (now WTO), have set the scene for freer trade and investment flows. The confluence of these various agreements and pressures form the new rules of the game for international trade, investment, and technology transfer.

The WTO summarizes the scene as follows:

The GATT/WTO system has brought about significant progress in the reduction or elimination of border barriers to trade through eight rounds of multilateral trade negotiations. Tariffs in industrial countries have come down from high double digits in the immediate postwar period to less than 10 per cent in the late 1960s, and less than 4 per cent once the Uruguay Round is

---

[9] For analyses of the legal and economic aspects of this argument, see UNCTAD (1999*a–c*).

fully implemented. At the same time, most quantitative restrictions on trade, except those imposed for health, safety, or other public policy reasons, have been removed. Following the Uruguay Round, textiles and clothing and agriculture are being brought within the multilateral framework and subject to progressive liberalization. The Uruguay Round also introduced new disciplines for the protection of trade-related intellectual property rights. Rules on trade and investment in services have been developed under the auspices of the General Agreement on Trade in Services (GATS). Governments have also embarked on services trade liberalization within the GATS framework.   (WTO 1998: 36)

As a distinguished African political scientist remarks on the governance regime,

... [G]lobalization would seem to reinforce the structural adjustment policies that have been followed over the last two decades, especially in the areas of trade, financial and investment liberalization. The establishment of the WTO ... launched and accelerated a process whereby an ever-widening sphere of local policy and decision-making spaces are being further eroded in favour of agreements negotiated at the multilateral level and which are binding on all signatories. Already, African countries are being exposed to a new additional conditionality, that of prior membership of the WTO and adherence to its rules on trade liberalization, in exchange for development cooperation assistance, debt relief and market access. It poses serious questions about the renewal of state capacity to cope with the demands, pressures, and opportunities associated with globalization at a time when structural adjustment has resulted in a near-total erosion of state capacity and the decimation of the morale and coherence of the bureaucracy ... The new global rules governing trade and industrial policy make it impossible for governments, including those of Africa, to pursue the kinds of policies that the East Asian countries were able to get away with as they struggled to industrialize. Such policy measures as industrial protection, trade discrimination, the use of subsidies in trade and industrial promotion, the denial of national treatment to foreign investors, provisions for local value-added, financial repression and outright or concealed disregard for intellectual property rights in the quest for technological development are now ruled out by the existing WTO regime ... [10]

Thus, the new rules constrict many of the policies and tools used in the past (often with spectacular success in the Asian Tigers) to promote national technological development. The most directly affected ones are on FDI entry and operations, public enterprises, infant industry protection, subsidized credit, export subsidies, and local content rules. Even more important is the long-term policy trend. The scope and coverage of the new rules are steadily increasing. Given the underlying reasoning and the ideologies, the objective is to minimize all government influence on resource allocation and to provide completely level playing fields for all international investors and traders.

As far as FDI and technology transfer are concerned, the same underlying principles apply. There are in fact relatively few formal rules affecting FDI and technology flows at the international level, but there are a number of related rules that affect policy-making. National policies on FDI and technology imports have in any event undergone rapid liberalization, to a greater extent than rules on trade and domestic resource allocation. Most liberalization has occurred over the past decade or so, with the pace accelerating in the 1990s.[11] Many of the latest changes are under international

---

[10] Olukoshi (1999). Many of the new rules are noted below.

[11] According to UNCTAD (1998: 57), the number of national regulatory changes on FDI have risen steadily in the 1990s, from 82 in 1991 to 151 in 1997. Of the 650 changes introduced over 1991–97, more

commitments under the Uruguay Round; however, the general trend also reflects a change of attitude on the part of host countries.

Technology transfer: There are practically no policy controls left on formal technology transfer *per se*, in contrast to the 1970s when there were batteries of regulations and interventions by national governments on licensing. The ones that exist are largely indirect: tariffs on capital goods, restrictions on foreign consultants or the setting up of consultancy affiliates, the hiring of expatriates, or the use of national standards to protect local technology suppliers. The remaining international instruments on technology transfer concern intellectual property rights (IPRs) and FDI in services, considered next.

Technology transfer has been subject to long-standing debate at UNCTAD.[12] In the 1970s, UNCTAD launched an initiative on an international code of conduct on the transfer of technology. This aimed to counter the imperfections that existed in international technology markets and the asymmetry in information and bargaining strengths between transnational sellers and developing country buyers. The code sought to contain the use of restrictive business practices by TNCs by providing guidelines on the rights and obligations of parties and dispute settlement procedures. It supported the use of a variety of performance requirements that are now deemed unacceptable. The economic reasoning behind the code was impeccable: there were market failures in technology development and learning that call for remedial interventions, and the experience of many countries testifies to their practicality and usefulness. Many of the statements in the code now seem idealistic and one-sided. For instance, it placed all the weight of action on the technology supplier and did not consider the necessary domestic conditions that would permit performance requirements to be efficient. Nevertheless, its thrust was defensible.

UNCTAD also focused on the imbalances in the patent system, which gave holders monopoly rights that were often not used in production in developing countries. Its target was Article 5A, which gave countries (members of the Paris Convention) the right to use corrective measures to redress abuses arising from the exclusive rights conferred by patents. This initiative also did not bear fruit, and now the pressing desire of TNCs and developed countries to strengthen IPRs has moved the issue to WTO jurisdiction under the TRIPs Agreement. This has greatly strengthened the position of TNCs on the argument that this would benefit developing countries, by facilitating FDI inflows and raising their own innovative output. As we argue below, both arguments have large deficiencies (UNCTAD 1996*a*).

FDI: At the international level, agreements on FDI exist at three levels: bilateral, regional, and international.[13] Most are bilateral. By mid-1996, there were some 1600 bilateral treaties involving 158 countries; the great majority had been concluded in the 1990s. At the international level, arrangements on FDI can be traced back to the rules

than 93 per cent have been favourable to FDI, including measures to reduce control and offer greater incentives to investors.

[12] For a thoughtful and penetrating analysis of this controversy, see Roffe (1999).

[13] One of the most comprehensive and balanced reviews is by UNCTAD (1996*b*). UNCTAD is also producing a technical series of papers on various aspects of TNC related issues (UNCTAD 1999*a–e*). For an earlier review of international regimes on trade and FDI, see Preston and Windsor (1992).

of treaties on commerce developed since the eighteenth century (UNCTAD 1996*b*). In the modern period, the (un-ratified) Havana Charter of 1948 for an international trade organization marks the first attempt to set up multilateral rules for FDI. Since then, there have been over 70 international agreements relating to FDI (UNCTAD 1996*a*: table V.2).

The main issues on FDI currently dealt with by multilateral agreements are as follows:[14]

1. *Services*: The General Agreement on Trade in Services (GATS) covers the supply of markets by foreign firms present in those markets. This is under the WTO, and its general principles are transparency and most-favoured-nation (MFN) treatment (i.e. non-discrimination between foreign firms of different origins). Market access and national treatment (i.e. non-discrimination between foreign and domestic firms) vary by specific commitments by countries. However, the scope of liberal treatment is to be enlarged through further negotiations (and economic pressure).

2. *Performance requirements on TNCs*: This is treated under the Agreement on Trade-Related Investment Measures (TRIMs), under negotiation in WTO. TRIMs are limited in scope: they only affect trade in goods and do not cover such issues as technology transfer. However, within their scope they are important in that they prohibit performance requirements on TNCs. These prohibitions cover instruments used very effectively by NIEs such as local content requirements, trade balancing requirements (extremely effective in promoting the restructuring of the Latin American automobile industry), technology transfer and R&D requirements, and so on.

3. *Intellectual property rights*: The protection of IPRs has moved in effect from the World Intellectual Property Organization to WTO, under the TRIPs (Trade-Related Aspects of Intellectual Property Rights) Agreement. While this agreement contains exhortations to increase technology transfer to the least developed countries, its main objective is to strengthen the protection offered to innovators, largely from industrial countries. It specifies rules on standards for protecting specified IPRs, domestic enforcement procedures and international dispute settlement (UNCTAD 1996*a*; Roffe 1999). The most important point to note about the shift of venue from WIPO to WTO is that trade sanctions can now be applied to countries deemed to be deficient protecting IPRs.[15] This gives it much more 'bite' than before. The implications for the developing world are worrying. While stronger IPRs may benefit the leading innovators in the developed countries, they can inhibit technological development in developing ones. They can raise the cost of formal technology transfers, by allowing technology sellers to impose

---

[14] This draws upon the discussion in UNCTAD (1996*b*: 151–4).

[15] The WTO Agreement on Subsidies and Countervailing Duties may also affect traditional means of supporting technological activity by subsidies. Although the agreement excludes 'fundamental research' from its actionable provisions (i.e. governments may still subsidize research), the text leaves scope for interpreting what the limits of this are. In any case, R&D now comes under WTO scrutiny, and subsidies for research deemed non 'fundamental' could be limited in the future.

stricter restrictions and by preventing copying and 'reverse engineering', the source of much technological learning in newly industrializing countries. The developing countries that are placed to benefit are those that have already built up strong technology bases (often by using lax IPR regimes). The strong protection of brand names lacks the justification of patent protection, in that it does not contribute even to greater innovation.

4. *Insurance coverage*: Political risk insurance at the international level is offered by the Multilateral Investment Guarantee Agency (MIGA) of the World Bank.

5. *Dispute settlement*: The World Bank set up the International Centre on Settlement of Investment Disputes (ICSID) in 1965. This was initially opposed by Latin American countries on the ground that it meant circumventing domestic jurisdiction and giving foreigners privileged treatment. The centre is being increasingly used to settle disputes between TNCs and national governments, again demonstrating the changing nature of international governance.

6. *Employment and labour relations*: The Tripartite Declaration of Principles Concerning Multinational Enterprises and Social Policy contains principles on employment, training and working conditions. It calls upon TNCs to adopt the best standards on these issues but has no enforcement powers. In 1998 the ILO adopted a Declaration on fundamental principles and rights at work, covering freedom of association, elimination of forced or compulsory labour, abolition of child labour, and elimination of discrimination in employment.

7. *Corruption*: The OECD has adopted a Convention on corruption together with some non-members, making the subject an integral part of the international governance process.

8. *General guidelines*: The World Bank published *Guidelines on the Treatment of Direct Foreign Investment* in 1992, but these are illustrative not binding. In a similar vein, the OECD has attempted, but failed to negotiate, a Multilateral Agreement on Investment (MAI). The idea was first to get agreement among OECD member countries (which then included Mexico and the Republic of Korea, with Argentina, Brazil, Chile, and Hong Kong as observers), then invite others to join. While MAI failed in this round, it is possible over the longer-term that a new version will be agreed. MAI embodies existing OECD arrangements, with the following at its core:

- Transparency of rules
- National treatment of investors[16]
- MFN treatment
- Transfer of funds (dividends and equity) freely permitted
- Prohibition of all performance requirements
- Prohibition of expropriation without public purpose or prompt and fair compensation
- Dispute settlement provisions.

---

[16] Foreign firms are to be treated no less favourably than domestic firms, but it is possible for them to be more favourably treated.

The MAI is significant because, despite its present failure, it points the way in which international governance is heading. Some observers regard it as the future benchmark for international governance of FDI, incorporating the provisions of the WTO under the various agreements described above. In many ways it is a logical extension of the other measures launched at the international level by the Bretton Woods institutions and the WTO.[17] However, it cannot be imported *as such* into the WTO. Developing countries will have a large role to play in any future negotiations, and much depends on how they evolve their own FDI regimes. Several are already substantially in conformance with MAI principles, but there are some large countries that do not yet accept its provisions.

The international system—such as it is—is mainly outside the Bretton Woods and UN system, largely under the auspices of the WTO. However, the Bretton Woods institutions have an enormous impact on the broader policy setting in which technology and investment flows occur. By contrast, the UN system has a marginal impact on the broader and more specific policy settings. None of the UN institutions concerned with FDI and technology—UNCTAD and UNIDO in particular—have much influence on international governance. In their practical work, they try to promote understanding of FDI issues and to encourage investment flows, in much the same way as the World Bank.

5. IS THE NEW GOVERNANCE SYSTEM DESIRABLE?

The emerging system of international governance, with its strong neoliberal bias, reflects to some extent the structural changes wrought by the new technological 'paradigm'. The survival and growth of most productive sectors in any economy depends increasingly on competitiveness with other nations: few are insulated from import competition or from direct entry by foreign competing firms. Enterprises are able to organize production across countries in a more rational and integrated manner than was feasible before. The effects on particular economies depend on how well they gear their factors and institutions to cope with new technologies and intensifying competition. The new rules simply recognize the new international order of greater mobility, closeness, and competition, and seek to facilitate its birth. In giving stability, transparency, and legal support to the new order, they provide benefits to those economies that are set to gain from it. They are, however, not simply the objective manifestations of a new technological reality. They also reflect strong economic and political assumptions on *how* countries should behave in the emerging order. The WTO simply extends and strengthens the practice of the international institutions promoting neoliberal policies in the developing world.

We have noted that different assumptions about technological development lead to different 'optimal' rules while promoting the process of integration and investment

---

[17] According to the World Bank (1999), 'Despite the difficulties raised in the MAI negotiations there remains considerable support for international rules on investment. Proposals have been considered by some countries to incorporate certain aspects of the rules governing FDI in the World Trade Organization into the negotiations expected to begin with the November 1999 ministerial meeting' (1999: 49 [Box 3.1]).

flows. Take the broad policy setting. The new rules are based on the explicit or implicit assumption that free markets are the best way to allocate resources and direct economic activities, and that direct government intervention in these should be minimized or removed. The debate on markets *versus* governments is too well known to rehearse here. There is little doubt that many—perhaps most—interventions across the developing world *were* inefficient and that greater liberalization and openness are often better ways of allocating resources in many economies. Often but not always. There is neither theoretical nor empirical evidence that free markets are invariably efficient and governments inefficient. On the contrary, theory suggests pervasive and damaging market failures, and empirical evidence suggests that interventions that target the most critical failures achieve dramatic results. In recent years, rapid and wholesale liberalization in economies that did not prepare themselves strategically has failed to spark a growth process.[18] The issue of which interventions work in what circumstances is an empirical issue, while the new rules opt for universal solutions that do not permit shades of grey.

The new technology paradigm does mean that interventions that worked two decades ago may not work equally well today. The pace and content of technical change are quite different, as is the way in which markets and factors are organized. This does not mean that the underlying issues of learning, skills, externalities, coordination, and institution building have disappeared. On the contrary, they have become more important, if countries are to insert themselves into the global system efficiently. However, the nature of the most efficient policies for less industrialized countries still needs to be fully worked out.

The rules as applied to technology and FDI specifically are subject to the same considerations. These international agreements aim principally at making life easier for TNCs: make policies clear and predictable, remove all obligations apart from maximizing company profits and offer the strongest possible protection for intellectual and commercial property. Their objective is to reduce transaction costs and uncertainty for global operators, by reducing the freedom of action for governments to intervene in the national interest. Thus, they allow little scope for the kind of exclusion, selective targeting and performance requirements that allowed countries like Korea and Taiwan to build up their technology systems. They assume, in effect, that what is good for the TNC (and developed country innovators, the two are often the same) is equally good for a developing host economy, that is, there are no market failures causing divergence between private and social interests. As a logical consequence, they impose no rules on what TNCs can or cannot do, while they constrain the ability of governments to affect market-driven resource allocation. Given their assumptions, all that is needed to extract the maximum welfare benefits from technology and investment flows is to have clear, stable, and 'fair' rules of the game. It is accepted that these rules include strong competition policy within each country, to counter obvious anti-competitive behaviour by all firms. However, this chapter argues that such rules fail to provide policy tools to deal with other forms of market failure apart from anti-competitive behaviour.

---

[18] For recent evidence on Africa, see Lall (1999*b*).

There are many other market and institutional deficiencies on which governments could act to improve welfare and raise their growth potential.

This does not mean that the existing rules close *all* relevant policy options.[19] They still leave scope for a number of actions, such as attracting investments to particular sectors, raising the quality of human capital, subsidizing R&D, or strengthening technology institutions: these now comprise the core of 'competitiveness strategy' in many advanced economies. Developing countries clearly have to explore how much latitude they retain and design strategies that can maximize their growth enhancing effects. However, problems remain. First, some permissible policies may well be constrained in the near future.[20] Second, the scope of currently permissible policies may be too narrow for development needs. They make it impossible to promote infant industries or to discriminate between local and foreign investors. This belies the fact that entry into many complex activities faces high cost, risk, and externalities, or that local firms and TNCs face different factor markets and undergo different learning processes. Providing a 'level playing field' in the presence of such imperfections creates rather than removes distortions. There is no case in economic theory for enforcing such rules. In practice, there may be arguments in favour of adopting simple universal rules, but experience shows that policy interventions do work and that governments can improve their intervention capabilities (Lall and Teubal 1998).

The emerging international rules aim to reduce the transaction costs, uncertainty, and external obligations associated with international business. It is argued that, *ceteris paribus*, they will raise the quantity and quality of FDI in developing countries and provide the investment, skill, and technologies needed for development. However, *ceteris* is not *paribus* where FDI flows are concerned. Given the deficiencies in domestic skills, capabilities, and institutions in 'marginalized' economies, it is not clear that policy liberalization by itself will stimulate significantly larger amounts of direct investment. Will the new policy regime still make things better than they were before? This is far from clear. New FDI does flow to developing economies that are recovering from instability and bad macroeconomic policies, but most of it goes into primary activities or privatized enterprises. Once this tapers off, FDI often does not continue in the productive sectors, even less so in new, high value-added—catalysing this remains the task of national development policies.

The risk, not sufficiently recognized, is that the *new rules can constrict those development policies*. They open countries to international trade and investment flows, but stop them from adopting some policies that can allow them to benefit fully from them. The MAI did envisage some exceptions (Fitzgerald *et al.* 1998). However, these were confined to national or financial security, balance-of-payments crises and other exceptions to be negotiated individually, hardly providing for a systematic use of strategy to build national capabilities and extract greater benefits from

---

[19] On the political options, see Olukoshi (1999).

[20] Note, for instance, the increasing questions being raised in the EU over government grants to TNCs to retain or make investments in member countries. The subsidization of R&D is also likely to be more tightly controlled.

FDI. A level playing field does not make much sense when the players are very unevenly matched and when it actually prevents the weaker players from improving their game.

The rules thus favour countries that have already built up the capabilities to integrate, or are near enough the frontiers to manage without much strategic intervention. However, they may constrain technological upgrading even in more advanced developing countries. For instance, as noted above, after sweeping liberalization much of Latin America has failed to attract high-technology FDI (the exception is Mexico, because of the trade 'distortion' introduced by NAFTA, which discriminates against other, often more efficient, suppliers). At the same time, countries with strong domestic strategies (that do not conform to the MAI ideal) have been able to attract considerable inward FDI. The case of China is so striking that this point hardly needs labouring. Malaysia and Indonesia have not had completely open and liberal regimes. Singapore has provided very welcoming conditions but has used targeting and incentives to influence resource allocation by TNCs. Firms are clearly prepared to live with more exceptions and host country demands that the emerging rules give them credit for. Of course, if all countries are forced to liberalize, the conditions that they find acceptable now may well become onerous. But surely this is getting the economic logic wrong!

On the technology front, there is reason to doubt the benefits of stronger IPRs for developing countries. The new TRIPs regime can promote innovation, providing clear signals to investors that their most valuable assets will be safeguarded. It can also raise the costs of technology purchase and restrict one of the most fruitful sources of learning and competitiveness development: imitation, local diffusion and reverse engineering (UNCTAD 1996*a*). The best way of combining the liberalization of FDI and technology regimes with national development interests in a setting of rapid globalization, thus needs much more thought than it has received. The highly restrictive policies pursued in the past, say by Korea, may now be inappropriate. However, what is economically desirable is unclear and needs analysis. This is something on which the UN system should be working, with the support of the Bretton Woods institutions.

6. CONCLUDING REMARKS

The essential argument of this chapter is that the rapidly changing economic and policy environment in which developing countries face the outside world requires a strong strategic response from their governments to strengthen their competitive capabilities. Yet the governance regime for international investment and technology flows places increasing constraints on their ability to mount such a response, while exposing them more rapidly and indiscriminately to competitive pressures. The Bretton Woods institutions and the WTO are the prime multilateral proponents of the new governance regime, while United Nations agencies are playing an increasingly marginal role (or tamely following the lead of these other institutions).

Yet, there is considerable disquiet on the part of many developing countries on the progress of globalization and liberalization. If the technological processes driving change are irreversible, and globalization a reflection of such processes, the most pressing need now is to reformulate the least desirable rules of the international game. Otherwise, prospects for genuine development, based on reaping and distributing the benefits of the fantastic technological changes under way, are gloomy. What, then, of the way forward?

In an ideal world, the debate on the basic premises of the new rules would be reopened in the United Nations agencies: too much is being left unsaid or simply assumed away. The aim should not be to return to the 'bad old days' of wholesale government intervention, state ownership of means of production, and rigid central planning. It should, instead, be to draw the right lessons of experience and to assist governments in building their capabilities to mount desirable development policies. I believe FDI and technology flows should be far more liberal than in the past, and that they offer an enormous amount to developing countries. However, development calls for careful and selective interventions in these flows: both theory and practice support this. However, the current debate is dominated by the neoliberals, who dismiss any disagreement out of hand not just as economically wrong but also immoral. Only international agencies not wholly committed to the present set of rules can do this: this means essentially the United Nations family.

Within the UN family, there are many possibilities. UNIDO has restructured itself and is ready to tackle afresh the policy needs of manufacturing industry and technology. If it is able to offer new strategic analysis that can improve the conduct of industrial policy, and make a credible case for such policy, it would be an important step forward. However, it is not clear if it can take on basic issues like protecting infant industries or selectively restricting inward direct investment. ILO is addressing emerging issues in the context of labour relations, training, and standards; it is well placed to challenge some of the more egregious initiatives in this area in the WTO. UNCTAD is perhaps the best placed in the UN system to tackle core questions of trade and investment strategy, intellectual property rights, and trade relations. At this time, however, it is not having any noticeable impact on the debate. Perhaps a more basic effort to create a new consensus within the developing world is needed before any of these agencies can move ahead, and this task rests with the UN headquarters.

BIBLIOGRAPHY

Archibugi, Daniele and Jonathan Michie (eds) (1997). *Technology, Globalisation and Economic Performance*. Cambridge University Press, Cambridge.

Baldwin, Richard E., and Philippe Martin (1999). Two waves of globalisation: Superficial similarities, fundamental differences. NBER Working Paper 6904. National Bureau of Economic Research, New York.

Benavente, José M., Gustavo Crispi, Jorge Katz, and Giovanni Stumpo (1997). New problems and opportunities for industrial development in Latin America. *Oxford Development Studies*, 25(3), 261–78.

Best, Michael (1990). *The New Competition: Institutions of Industrial Restructuring*. Polity Press, Cambridge.

Brewer, Thomas L. (1995). Towards a multilateral framework for foreign direct investment: Issues and scenarios. *Transnational Corporations*, 4(1), 69–83.

Cantwell, John and Odile Janne (1998). Globalisation of innovatory capacity: The structure of competence accumulation in European home and host countries. Discussion Paper B253. University of Reading, Dept. of Economics, Reading.

Chudnovsky, Daniel, Andrés Lopez, and Fernando Porta (1997). Market or policy driven? The foreign direct investment boom in Argentina. *Oxford Development Studies*, 25(2), 173–88.

Dunning, John H. (1998). The changing nature of firms and governments in a knowledge-based globalizing economy. Working Paper No. 98.007. Rutgers University, Center for International Business Education and Research, New Jersey.

——(1993). *The Globalization of Business: The Challenge of the 1990s*. Routledge, London.

FitzGerald, E. V. K., R. Cubero-Brealey, and A. Lehmann (1998). The development implications of the multilateral agreement on investment (Draft for the UK Department of International Development). Queen Elizabeth House, Oxford.

Freeman, Christopher and Carlota Perez (1988). Structural crises of adjustment, business cycles and investment behaviour. In G. Dosi, C. Freeman, R. Nelson, G. Silverberg, and L. Soete (eds), *Technical Change and Economic Theory*. Pinter, London.

Kumar, Nagesh (ed.) (1998). *Globalization, Foreign Direct Investment and Technology Transfers*. Routledge, London.

Lall, Sanjaya (1992). Technological capabilities and industrialization. *World Development*, 20(2), 165–86.

——(1993). Transnational corporations and economic development. In S. Lall (ed.), *Transnational Corporations and Economic Development*. The United Nations Library on Transnational Corporations, volume 3. Routledge, London.

——(1995). Industrial strategy and policies on foreign direct investment in East Asia. *Transnational Corporations*, 4(3), 1–26.

——(1996). *Learning from the Asian Tigers: Studies in Technology and Industrial Policy*. Macmillan, London.

——(1998). Exports of manufactures by developing countries: Emerging patterns of trade and location. *Oxford Review of Economic Policy*, 14(2), 54–73.

——(1999a). India's manufactured exports: Comparative structure and prospects. *World Development*, 27(10), 1769–86.

——(ed.) (1999b). *The Technological Response to Import Liberalization in Sub-Saharan Africa*. Macmillan, London.

——(2000). Technological change and industrialization in the Asian NIEs. In Linsu Kim and Richard R. Nelson (eds), *Technology, Learning and Innovation: Experiences of the Newly Industrializing Ecnomies*. Cambridge University Press, Cambridge.

—— and M. Teubal (1998). 'Market Stimulating' technology policies in developing countries: A framework with examples from East Asia. *World Development*, 26(8), 1369–86.

Londero, Elio and Simon Teitel (1998). *Resources, Industrialization and Exports in Latin America*. Macmillan, London.

Mathews, John A. (1999). A silicon island of the East: Creating a semiconductor industry in Singapore. *California Management Review*, 41(2), 55–78.

Mortimore, M. (1997). Dimensions of Latin American integration: The NAFTA and MERCOSUR automobile industries. Mimeo, ECLAC, Santiago.

Nayyar, Deepak (1997). Globalisation: What does it mean for development? RGICS Paper No. 42. Rajiv Gandhi Institute for Contemporary Studies, New Delhi.

—— (ed.) (1997). *Trade and Industrialization*. Oxford University Press, Delhi.

NSF (1996). *Science and Engineering Indicators 1996*. National Science Foundation, Washington, DC.

—— (1998). *Science and Engineering Indicators 1998*. National Science Foundation, Washington, DC.

OECD (1996). *Technology and Industrial Performance*. OECD, Paris.

—— (1998). *Multilateral Agreement on Investment*. OECD, Paris.

—— (1999a). *OECD Science, Technology and Industry Scoreboard 1999: Benchmarking Knowledge-Based Economies*. OECD, Paris.

—— (1999b). *Globalisation of Industrial R&D: Policy Issues*. OECD, Paris.

Olukoshi, A. O. (1999). Democratisation, globalisation and effective policy-making in Africa. Paper prepared for IDRC project on 'Economic policy making and implementation in Africa'. South Centre, Geneva.

Preston, Lee E. and Duane Windsor (1992). *The Rules of the Game in the Global Economy: Policy Regimes for International Business*. Kluwer Academic Publishers, Boston.

Roffe, P. (1999). From the draft code negotiations to the TRIPS agreement: The unfinished agenda. Draft chapter for *Code of Conduct on Transfer of Technology*. UNCTAD, Geneva.

Sauve, Pierre (1994). A first look at investment in the final act of the Uruguay Round. *Journal of World Trade*, 28(3), 5–16.

Stiglitz, Joseph E. (1996). Some lessons from the East Asian miracle. *World Bank Research Observer*, 11(2), 151–77.

UNCTAD (1996a). *The TRIPS Agreement and Developing Countries*. United Nations, New York and Geneva.

—— (1996b). *World Investment Report 1996: Investment, Trade and International Policy Arrangements*. United Nations, New York and Geneva.

—— (1997). *World Investment Report 1997: Transnational Corporations, Market Structure and Competitive Policy*. United Nations, New York and Geneva.

—— (1998). *World Investment Report 1998: Trends and Determinants*. United Nations, New York and Geneva.

—— (1999a). *Admission and Establishment*. UNCTAD Series on Issues in International Investment Agreements. United Nations, New York and Geneva.

—— (1999b). *Scope and Definition*. UNCTAD Series on Issues in International Investment Agreements. United Nations, New York and Geneva.

—— (1999c). *Most-Favoured-Nation Treatment*. UNCTAD Series on Issues in International Investment Agreements. United Nations, New York and Geneva.

—— (1999d). *Investment-Related Trade Measures*. UNCTAD Series on Issues in International Investment Agreements. United Nations, New York and Geneva.

—— (1999e). *Transfer Pricing*. UNCTAD Series on Issues in International Investment Agreements. United Nations, New York and Geneva.

—— (1999f). *World Investment Report 1999: Foreign Direct Investment and the Challenge of Development*. United Nations, New York and Geneva.

Wong, Poh-Kam (1997). Creation of a regional hub for flexible production: The case of the hard disk drive industry in Singapore. *Industry and Innovation*, 4(2), 183–206.

World Bank (1997). *World Development Report 1997: The State in a Changing World*. Oxford University Press for the World Bank, New York.

——(1998). *World Development Report 1998/99: Knowledge for Development*. Oxford University Press for the World Bank, New York.

——(1999). *Global Development Finance 1999*. World Bank, Washington, DC.

WTO (1998). *World Trade Organization, Annual Report 1998*. World Trade Organization, Geneva.

5

Capital Flows to Developing Countries and the Reform of the International Financial System

YILMAZ AKYÜZ AND ANDREW CORNFORD

1. THE INTERNATIONAL INSTITUTIONAL FRAMEWORK AND GOVERNANCE OF CAPITAL FLOWS

The ideas underlying approaches to improving the governance of the international financial system since 1945 have understandably been heavily influenced by the experience of the recent past. Thus the arrangements, which emerged from planning during the Second World War and the negotiations following it reflected the searing impact on thinkers and policy makers of the 1930s—the devastating declines in employment and incomes of the great depression and the associated contraction in international trade, the recourse to competitive devaluations and multiple currency practices, and the proliferation of bilateral trade arrangements and exchange controls. Similarly, much of policy makers' energy, immediately after the war, was focused on the international financing and payments requirements of the economic reconstruction of Western Europe. From the 1950s onwards there was an expansion of the international capital markets, driven partly by the flows of international investment linked to postwar economic recovery but also stimulated by the development of offshore currency markets where financial transactions were subject to much lighter control.[1] Countries were periodically (and from the second half of the 1960s increasingly frequently) subjected to pressures due to surges of short-term capital flows between major currencies, surges which eventually overwhelmed the Bretton Woods system of exchange rates. Henceforth, while problems associated with the financing and payments arrangements of trade and other current account transactions have remained an important concern in consideration of the functioning of the international financial system (a statement

---

[1] Offshore currency markets which, like offshore banking, lack a generally accepted precise definition, refer to financial activities in currencies other than that of the country where they are located or between non-residents of this country (or to activities characterized by both features). Typically they are free of many of the monetary controls and regulations which apply to onshore markets, and benefit from tax advantages.

which for obvious reasons applies *a fortiori* to matters associated with developing countries' participation in this system), increasing attention has been devoted to ways of handling, controlling and responding to capital movements as these have continued to grow in size, unshackled as they increasingly have been owing to the progressive liberalization of capital account transactions in the major industrial countries and to some extent elsewhere.

As is documented in Section 2, this trend in the functioning of the international financial system towards increased importance for private actors was eventually paralleled by an analogous one in the character of developing countries' external financing, with a rapid increase in the importance of private flows during the 1970s and the 1990s (though one which experienced a setback owing to the debt crisis in the 1980s). The progressive integration of developing (and more recently transition) economies into the network of international financial markets has had the consequence that the benefits and costs of this increased 'privatization' of these economies' external financing has become an increasingly important topic in debate concerning the international financial system.

The planning for the postwar world during the Second World War envisaged a set of organizations, which would deal with currency stability and international payments, economic reconstruction and the advancement of less developed economies, and international trade and investment. The negotiations associated with this process eventually gave rise to the IMF, the World Bank, and the GATT.[2] But the triad, which emerged from Bretton Woods and its aftermath are merely the monoliths of a set of about 300 international organizations dealing with economic matters, with memberships varying from the near universal to the purely regional, some of which antedate the Second World War. Of the organizations other than those, which emerged from Bretton Woods, the most important in the context of the governance of international capital flows are the OECD, the EEC/EU, and the BIS. Responsibility for international capital movements is not neatly assigned under this institutional structure. Indeed, the original structure did not include a global regime for capital movements, and no such regime has yet emerged. Instead, at the global level there is a patchwork of rules and agreements bearing directly or indirectly on several aspects of international investment and other financial flows but one which still accommodates a considerable measure of national policy autonomy for the majority of countries. More comprehensive regimes, designed to liberalize international financial flows, have been agreed in arrangements involving limited groups of countries such as the OECD and the EEC/EU.

The only global regime applying to cross-border monetary transactions is that of the IMF but the most important obligations in its Articles of Agreement relate to current and not capital transactions (being set out in Articles VIII and XIV). Concerning

---

[2] In the planning for the postwar world the organizations responsible for global economic governance were linked to the United Nations which would be responsible for the maintenance of peace. The IMF and the World Bank are Specialized Agencies of the United Nations under Article 57 of its Charter. The United Nations has concluded agreements with them under Article 63 recognizing them as independent international organizations.

capital movements Article IV contains the statement that one of the essential purposes of the international monetary system is to provide a framework facilitating the exchange of capital among countries, a statement which is included among general obligations regarding exchange arrangements. The more specific references to capital transfers in Article VI permit recourse to capital controls so long as they do not restrict payments for current transactions, and actually give the Fund the authority to request a member country to impose contracts to prevent the rise of funds from its general Resources Account to finance a large or sustained capital outflow. The World Bank has no direct responsibility for governance of the international financial system. However, it has participated as a source of financing in a number of the international bail-outs put together in response to recent financial crises, and has provided financial and technical assistance (often as a major ingredient of programmes linked to structural adjustment lending) to several countries as part of their efforts to upgrade and reform their financial sectors and their regimes of regulation and supervision. Until 1994, GATT likewise was assigned only very limited responsibility regarding the functioning of the international financial system. The WTO agreement, while not giving the new institution a major role in global financial governance, has nevertheless extended its remit regarding international investment, in particular through the inclusion of the commercial presence of (and thus the FDI of) services suppliers in the GATS. Since the sectors covered by the GATS include financial services, both the pace and the nature of the expansion of the global network of financial markets will henceforth be significantly affected by commitments as to market access and national treatment made in WTO negotiations.

Of the organizations or arrangements with more limited memberships both the OECD and the EEC/EU have established regimes for capital flows.[3] The OECD Code of Liberalization of Capital Movements dates from 1961 and reflects the generally favourable view of its member states concerning the free movement of capital. The code discriminates between two sets (or lists) of capital movement, and member countries authorize transactions in the two lists subject only to reservations listed in an annex to the code, and to derogations granted in certain circumstances such as the onset of serious balance of payments problems.[4] One of the two lists covers transactions generally regarded as more sensitive, owing, for example, to their short-term and potentially more speculative character, and is consequently subject to greater flexibility as to the right to enter reservations. In the EEC/EU a 1988 directive abolished restrictions on capital movements between residents of EEC/EU countries subject only to provisos concerning the right to control short-term movements during periods of financial strain and to take the measures necessary for the proper functioning of systems of taxation, prudential supervision, etc.

---

[3] For more detail, see Akyüz and Cornford (1994).

[4] Derogation from full compliance with the code's obligations is also possible if a country's 'economic and financial situation justifies such a course'. Once surrendered, however, this dispensation is no longer available. The derogation, which, *inter alia*, is intended to cover developing countries, has been used in various cases, for example, by Greece, Iceland, Spain, Turkey, and Portugal (with respect to its overseas territories). See OECD (1990: 21).

The BIS was established in 1930 'to promote the cooperation of central banks and to provide additional facilities for international financial operations; and to act as trustee or agent in regard to international financial settlements entrusted to it'.[5] Since the 1970s the BIS has become the principal forum and provided the secretariat support for a number of bodies established to reduce or manage the risks in cross-border banking transactions. The best known of these bodies is the Basle Committee on Banking Supervision established to promote banking stability through the promotion of strengthened regulation and improved cooperation between national supervisors. Others include the Committee on the Global Financial System (until February 1999 known as the Euro-Currency Standing Committee) established to monitor inter-national banking developments and to disseminate data on the subject from national creditor sources (a source of warnings as early as 1996 concerning the dangers of the increased short-term borrowing of certain East Asian countries), and the Committee on Payment and Settlement Systems, the principal focus of whose work is the timely settlement of large-scale financial transfers but which has also more recently begun to devote attention to the implications of electronic money. While the Basle bodies are not responsible for setting rules for international capital movements as such, their work is designed to strengthen the defences of financial firms both individually and in the aggregate against destabilization due to cross-border transactions and risk expos-ures. In its work on financial firms' involvement in securities transactions, the Basle Committee on Banking Supervision has often collaborated with the International Organization of Securities Commissions (IOSCO), which has a membership consisting of securities regulators and exchanges and which has gradually extended its remit from one concentrating primarily on information sharing to the setting and promulgation of standards for the functioning of exchanges and securities firms and for surveillance of cross-border securities transactions. One other recently established body, the Financial Stability Forum (which is described in more detail later), has a secretariat located in Basle, and is chaired by the general manager of the BIS.

Other regional organizations have remits bearing in various ways on international capital movements: various groups of banking supervisors other than the Basle Com-mittee (both regional and comprising offshore financial centres) deal with regulatory issues affecting their members, typically maintaining close contact in this context with the Basle Committee; and in Asia there are institutions and arrangements, which may eventually come to play roles similar to those of the EEC/EU in the areas of mutual consultation and external payments support, namely the Executive Meeting of East Asia and Pacific Central Banks (EMEAP) (which, *inter alia*, monitors foreign exchange markets in the region), swap mechanisms among ASEAN countries, and a web of bilateral repurchase agreements between monetary authorities of the region under which an authority may exchange its United States Treasury securities for dollars needed to support its currency.

A great many features of the current international financial system have a significant (even if often only indirect) bearing on international capital flows. Thus proposed

---

[5] See Article 3 of the statutes of the Bank for International Settlements.

reforms of this system can generally be expected to affect the scale and character of these flows. Any discussion such as that which follows is necessarily selective, and many readers may feel that important ideas have been only touched upon or completely omitted. The survey here concerns policies which have been at the centre of discussion (particularly concerning economies with emerging financial markets) since the East Asian crisis of 1997 but even so is not comprehensive. Thus Section 2 reviews major features of developing countries' experience of external financing since the 1960s, paying special attention to shifts in the relative importance of private capital inflows and to their volatility. Section 3 contains a schematic account of features of financial instability and crises, which is intended to serve as a backdrop for the policy discussion which follows. This discussion in Section 4 covers a selection of the policies, which have been put forward as ways of helping to prevent and manage financial crises, the policies in question including actions to be taken at both national and international levels as well as combinations of the two. Section 5 then very briefly recapitulates the thrust of the policy discussion and points to certain issues, which the authors believe to be of special importance for developing countries in strategic thinking about capital flows.

Some readers may feel disappointed at the absence of discussion of exchange rate regimes, of proposals for tighter control of international lending and portfolio investment at the source, or of the tax on foreign exchange transactions originally proposed by James Tobin as an instrument for limiting the volatility of currency markets and capital movements. Concerning the latter the authors had expressed their scepticism on a number of occasions before the outbreak of the East Asian crisis, which has not changed their views.[6] Regarding tighter controls on external financial flows at their source, the more ambitious proposals would appear typically to have features which are an obstacle to their adoption, while the ameliorative ones which might face less resistance are unlikely to so reduce financial instability as to eliminate the need for other major changes on the agenda of reform.[7] Regarding exchange rate regimes, for example, for reasons explained at greater length elsewhere, the authors are not convinced, unlike many other commentators, that this crisis furnished decisive arguments against managed flexibility for currencies (so long as it is accompanied by effective management of external liabilities). In conditions of high capital mobility, no exchange rate regime can guarantee stable and competitive rates.[8]

As is implicit in the remarks opening this section, ideas concerning international financial reform have a way of always being provisional owing to their susceptibility to

---

[6] See, for example, the survey of global policy actions in UNCTAD (1996b: Annex, section F) and Cornford (1996) (which is a review article of the book of papers generally more sympathetic to Tobin's proposal, Haq et al. [1996]).

[7] The more ambitious proposals include provision for an International Credit Insurance Corporation which would guarantee international loans for a modest fee, while setting a ceiling on the amount of borrowing by particular countries which it was willing to insure. Of the ameliorative proposals that for raising the costs of international interbank lending is actually discussed below in section D.4(a), and others are designed to achieve objectives such as the slowing of disinvestment in developing-country stocks by mutual funds. For a longer discussion see UNCTAD (1998a: chapter 4 [section C.4]).

[8] For a more extended discussion see UNCTAD (1998a: Part One, chapter 4 [section C.6]) and UNCTAD (1999b: chapter 6 [section B.1]).

being at least partly overtaken by developments on the ground. Cross-border financial transactions—current as well as capital—have been greatly transformed by financial innovation in recent years, and this process can be expected to continue. Derivatives are often cited in this context owing to the way in which they can be used to get around the spirit, if not the letter, of regulation of capital account transactions.[9] In the not too distant future it is possible that new techniques of payment and settlement of cross-border transactions made possible by computer technology will be a source of new challenges to techniques of monetary policy and to tax systems. These challenges will inevitably affect both regimes for international capital movements and the agenda for international financial reform.

2. TRENDS IN EXTERNAL FINANCING FOR DEVELOPING COUNTRIES

As shown in Table 5.1, the size, composition, and distribution of external capital inflows[10] to developing countries have all undergone fundamental shifts during the past three decades. In the period until the early 1970s, the most important source of external financing for developing countries was official loans and aid (though during the period from the 1950s onwards FDI frequently accounted for 20–30 per cent of their external financing and there was also an expansion in the share accounted for by export credits). This was based on the recognition that the ability of developing countries to fill their resource gaps through commercial borrowing on market terms was severely limited. Official financing continued to expand rapidly in the 1970s, but there was also a rapid expansion of private financial flows, primarily in the form of credits by banks in industrial countries, which served to recycle the surpluses of major oil exporters that emerged after the sharp increases in oil prices during 1973–74.

This expansion came to an end in 1982 with a rapid withdrawal of bank lending, resulting in a generalized debt crisis in the third world. During the rest of the 1980s capital inflows to developing countries remained virtually stagnant: while private financing fell sharply, official development assistance increased only moderately compared to the 1970s. Until 1997 the decade of the 1990s witnessed a strong expansion in private capital inflows to developing countries. The increase was sufficiently rapid to more than offset the downward trend in official flows, and was greatly influenced by rapid liberalization of markets and privatization of economic activity in most developing countries. An important proportion of private capital has taken the form of non-debt creating flows, notably but not exclusively FDI.[11]

---

[9] One simple example, pointed out by Robert Merton, is the way in which cross-border swaps of income flows make possible the taking of positions in foreign assets (in Merton's example stocks) by a country's investors without their purchasing the underlying assets involved, which may be prohibited by the country's regime for capital-account transactions. See Mason *et al.* (1995: 4–7).

[10] For the terminology regarding capital flows in this paper, see the notes to Table 5.1.

[11] In this context it should be recalled that FDI includes not only non-debt-creating flows but also intercompany debt transactions.

Table 5.1. *Aggregate net capital inflow to developing countries, by type of flow, and net transfer, 1970–98*

	1970–74	1975–82	1983–89	1990–98
Total net inflow				
Including China	2.60	4.91	2.87	5.00
Excluding China	3.10	5.45	2.97	4.22
Official inflows	1.14	1.58	1.57	1.03
ODA grants	0.46	0.53	0.62	0.56
Other official	0.68	1.05	0.96	0.47
Private inflows	1.46	3.33	1.29	3.97
Non-debt-creating inflows	0.31	0.42	0.55	2.21
FDI	0.31	0.42	0.53	1.67
Portfolio equity	0.00	0.00	0.02	0.54
Bonds	0.02	0.11	0.05	0.52
Bank credit	0.94	2.46	0.44	1.17
Short-term	0.23	1.10	0.10	0.72
Long-term	0.71	1.36	0.34	0.44
Memo item:				
Portfolio inflows	0.02	0.12	0.07	1.06
Interest payments	0.48	1.49	2.58	1.79
Profit remittances	1.08	0.93	0.54	0.56
Net capital transfers	1.04	2.48	−0.26	2.65

Notes: Definition of Different Types of Capital Flows

There is ambiguity in terminology for the different kinds of international capital flows. The same terms used by different institutions or writers often cover different categories of capital transactions, while the same categories are sometimes referred to in different terms. The definitions used throughout this paper are as follows:

Capital inflow: This term refers to the acquisition of *domestic assets* by *non-residents* (plus grants). Sale of domestic assets is defined as a negative capital inflow. Thus, the term *net* capital inflow denotes acquisition minus sales of domestic assets by non-residents. The types of asset included in these flows vary according to the institution publishing the data. The term *net resource flows* used by the World Bank in its *Global Development Finance*, for example, refers to capital transactions by non-residents, but excludes assets that give rise to short-term debt. In the IMF *Balance of Payment Statistics*, capital inflows are the items included in the capital and financial accounts of the balance of payments, comprising mainly credit items (such as debt forgiveness and migrants' transfers) under the heading of 'capital transfers', 'direct investments' in the country concerned, and the liability items under 'portfolio investment' and 'other investment' (which includes both short- and long-term debt in such forms as bank loans, other types of trade credit, and borrowing from IMF).

    Capital outflow: This term refers to the acquisition of *foreign assets by residents*. Sales of foreign assets are defined as a negative capital outflow. Thus the term net capital outflow denotes acquisition minus sales of foreign assets by residents. In the IMF *Balance of Payments Statistics*, capital outflows consist of the debit items under the heading of 'capital transfers', 'direct investment abroad', and the asset items under 'portfolio investment' and 'other investment'.

    Net capital flow: This term refers to total net capital inflow less total net capital outflow as defined above. It is positive when net inflows exceed net outflows.

    Net transfer: This term refers to net capital inflows less net factor payments abroad; the latter include interest payments on external debt as well as profit remittances. Net transfer is thus a broad measure of a country's capacity to finance its trade deficits.

Source: UNCTAD secretariat estimates, based on World Bank (1999).

Net capital inflows to developing countries have risen by more than twentyfold in nominal terms since 1970. In real terms the increase in total net inflows is much less impressive. Measured in relation to the import price index of developing countries (i.e. in terms of its purchasing power over foreign goods), for example, the increase in net capital inflows during the same period is about fivefold. More importantly, measured in terms of the share of output of the recipient countries, the recent surge in capital flows represents only a recovery from the stagnant levels of the 1980s rather than an increase over the levels attained during the years preceding the debt crisis. Excluding China, on average, the total inflow of capital to developing countries as a proportion of their combined GNP was indeed lower during 1990–98 than during 1975–82.

As shown in Fig. 5.1, there has also been a series of major shifts in the composition of capital inflows since the mid-1970s. From 1975 until the early 1980s, private capital accounted for about two-thirds of total inflows, but after 1982 its share fell to less than 50 per cent not so much because of a rise in official finance as because of a collapse in private inflows, notably international bank lending. In the 1990s the surge in private flows and the decline in official financing have meant that private capital has accounted for 80 per cent of total capital inflows to developing countries.[12] As shown in Fig. 5.2, these changes in the composition of capital inflows as between public and private sources have been accompanied by shifts in their distribution among developing countries and regions. In particular, since official flows tend to favour poorer developing countries and regions, their decline relative to that of private capital flows has been a major determinant of the trend in the shares of different groups of developing countries. Moreover, although the share of East Asian countries is shown to have undergone a large increase since 1975 in the chart, it experienced a setback in 1997 owing to the outbreak of the region's financial crisis.

There has also been a considerable shift in the relative importance of different categories of private inflow. From the mid-1970s until the outbreak of the debt crisis of the 1980s, bank credits constituted three-quarters of total private capital inflows to developing countries, while the rest was accounted for by FDI. This pattern changed drastically after the debt crisis when bank loans collapsed and FDI took the highest share in total private inflows. In the 1990s the revival of bank lending has been concentrated mainly on the Asian emerging markets; FDI has accelerated rapidly and portfolio investment has emerged as a major form of private inflow. These changes have also been associated with the increased share of the private sector as borrower.

Net capital inflows received by developing countries from non-residents do not necessarily give the amount available for financing current account deficits and closing resource gaps. Account also needs to be taken of net capital outflows by residents. The importance of capital outflows through acquisition of assets abroad depends, *inter alia*, on the capital account regime adopted by the countries concerned. During the past 10 years, a growing number of developing countries have liberalized outward capital

---

[12] Regarding recent trends and policy issues involving foreign aid, see UNCTAD (2000: Part Two) and the references therein.

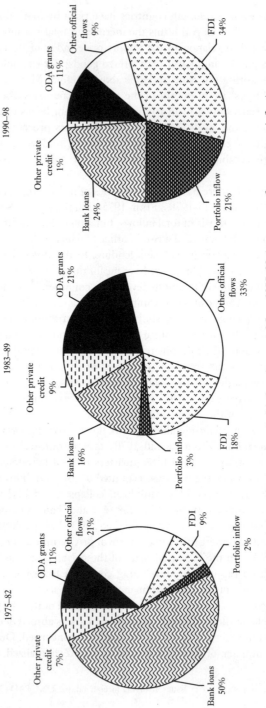

Figure 5.1. *Developing countries: net capital inflows by type of flow, 1975–98 (percentage of aggregate net inflow)*

Source: See Table 5.1 for source and definitions.

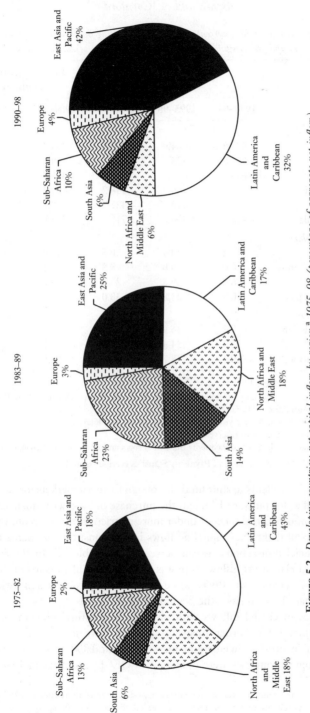

Figure 5.2. *Developing countries: net capital inflow by region,*[a] *1975–98 (percentage of aggregate net inflow)*

Note: [a]Regional classification of the World Bank except for Europe, which comprises Malta and Turkey only.

Source: See Table 5.1 for source and definitions.

Table 5.2. *Net capital inflow, current-account and offsetting financial transactions in developing countries and 16 emerging-market countries*[a] *(Billions of dollars and per cent)*

	All developing countries			Emerging-market countries	
	1990–94	1995–98	1990–98	1980–89[b]	1990–97
Billions of dollars					
Net capital inflow	825.8	1064.9	1890.6	355.3	1083.8
Net capital outflow	−142.0	−435.3	−577.2	−49.6	−256.2
Net capital flow	683.8	629.6	1313.4	305.7	827.6
BoP errors and omissions	−49.9	−106.3	−156.2	−39.5	−53.2
Change in reserves[c]	−221.2	−216.5	−437.7	−10.6	−231.6
Current account balance[d]	−412.7	−306.8	−719.5	−255.6	−542.7
Percentage of net inflow					
Net outflow	17.2	40.9	30.5	14.0	23.6
BoP errors and omissions	6.0	10.0	8.3	11.1	4.9
Change in reserves[c]	26.8	20.3	23.2	3.0	21.4
Current account balance[d]	50.0	28.8	38.0	71.9	50.1
Percentage of net flow					
BoP errors and omissions	7.3	16.9	11.9	12.9	6.4
Change in reserves[c]	32.3	34.4	33.3	3.5	28.0
Current account balance[d]	60.4	48.7	54.8	83.6	65.6

Notes: For definitions see Table 5.1.
[a]Argentina, Brazil, Chile, Colombia, Egypt, India, Indonesia, Malaysia, Mexico, Pakistan, Peru, Philippines, Republic of Korea, South Africa, Thailand, Turkey.
[b]Excluding 1987 and 1988, which were years with current account surpluses.
[c]A minus sign indicates an increase in reserves.
[d]The sum of net capital flow, Balance of Payments Statistics errors and omissions and change in reserves.
Source: World Bank (1999); IMF Balance of Payments Statistics (various issues).

flows, enabling their residents to shift funds to foreign financial markets for short-term investment as well as for outward FDI and the purchase of long-term financial assets. However, such outflows can also occur under more restrictive capital account regimes in the form of capital flight. Net capital outflows in fact constitute an increasing part of offsetting financial transactions, as can be seen from Table 5.2. In the emerging markets, for each dollar of net inflow there was a net outflow of 14 cents in the 1980s and one of almost 24 cents in the 1990s, while for developing countries as a whole this share has more than doubled since the beginning of the 1990s.[13]

The coexistence of capital inflows with outflows is a natural outcome of global financial integration. Cross-border financial activities have increasingly become a feature of financial institutions in emerging markets. Around 300 banking entities from 10 leading developing countries were operating in OECD countries in 1996. Thus,

---

[13] If unrecorded net capital outflows (errors and omissions)—a substantial proportion of which generally consists of residents' purchases of foreign assets—are added to recorded flows, the proportions are even higher.

opening of the capital account in emerging markets presents profitable opportunities for portfolio diversification not only for lenders and investors in industrial countries but also for asset holders in these markets themselves. It also allows businesses to take positions abroad in order to hedge against exchange rate risks. Furthermore, some developing countries have become significant providers of FDI in recent years, with the cumulative outward flow reaching \$52 billion during 1991–96, or 21 per cent of total net capital outflows from developing countries.[14] However, an important part of outflows, as of inflows, also consists of liquid capital driven by short-term arbitrage opportunities. Another important category of offsetting financial transactions is reserve accumulation. During the 1990s more than 20 per cent of total net capital inflows were absorbed by additions to reserves in both developing countries as a whole and in the emerging markets. For the latter there has been a large increase in such additions from a level of only 3 per cent in the 1980s to one similar to the developing country average. This increase would appear to be a response to the instability of private capital flows, especially short-term bank loans and much portfolio investment. The instability is exemplified by major constituents of these two categories of external financing for developing countries which displayed much sharper fluctuations during the 1990s than total net capital inflows, increasing more than 2.5 times more rapidly during 1988–95 but decreasing no less than 83 per cent in 1995–98, while the total net inflow declined only 12 per cent. Such fluctuations reflect the boom–bust cycle of external financing in the 1990s and the impact of the associated financial crises.[15]

3. FINANCIAL INSTABILITY AND CRISES

Since the collapse of the Bretton Woods system, increased global capital mobility has been accompanied by greater frequency of financial crises in both developed and developing countries alike. The episodes of financial instability and crisis in industrial countries include the banking and real estate crises in the United States lasting more than a decade from the late 1970s, the major slumps in the global stock market in 1987 and 1989, several episodes of extreme instability in the currency markets of industrial countries of which an outstanding instance was the currency crisis of the European Monetary System (EMS) in 1992, and the ongoing instability in Japanese financial markets that started with the bursting of the bubble in the early 1990s, whilst those in developing countries include the Southern Cone crisis of the late 1970s and early 1980s, the debt crisis of the 1980s, the Mexican crisis of 1994–95, the East Asian crisis beginning in 1997, the Russian crisis of 1998, the Brazilian crisis of 1999, and a number of other more limited currency and banking crises.[16]

---

[14] See World Bank (1998: table 1.11).

[15] The short-term external financing displaying such higher volatility comprises portfolio investment in equity and short-term debt instruments such as treasury bills, short-term loans other than trade credits, changes in non-residents' domestic-currency holdings and deposits, and changes in other short-term external liabilities of banks. For a more detailed discussion see UNCTAD (1996*b*: chapter 5 [section D]).

[16] For further details concerning some of these crises, see UNCTAD (1998*a*: Part One [Annex to chapter 3]).

There are, however, important differences between industrial and developing countries in the nature and effects of financial instability and crises. Experience shows that in developing countries a reversal of external capital flows and sharp declines in the currency often threaten domestic financial stability. Similarly, domestic financial crises usually translate into currency turmoil, payments difficulties, and even external debt crises. By contrast, currency turmoil in industrial countries since the advent of more flexible exchange rates in the 1970s has frequently involved large movements of rates concentrated into short periods. These movements, which result from buying and selling decisions by economic actors in currency markets often taken with little regard for indicators of countries' fundamentals, generally impose costs on the real economy and can lead to significant misalignments.[17] But such turmoil does not usually spill over into domestic financial markets, nor do domestic financial disruptions necessarily lead to currency and payments crises.

These differences between developing and developed countries stem from a number of factors. First, the size of developing country financial markets is small, so that entry or exit of even medium-size investors from industrial countries is capable of causing considerable price fluctuations, even though their placements in these markets account for a small percentage of their total portfolios. Furthermore, differences in the net foreign asset position and the currency denomination of external debt play a crucial role.[18] Here the vulnerability of developing countries is greater because of their typically higher net external indebtedness and higher shares of their external debt denominated in foreign currencies. The vulnerability of the domestic financial system is increased further when external debt is owed by the private sector rather than by sovereign governments.

A number of common features have marked the history of the post-Bretton Woods crises in developing countries. First, many of them have been preceded by liberalization of the economy, notably the financial sector. Second, all episodes of currency instability have been started by a sharp increase in capital inflows followed by an equally sharp reversal. Such swings in flows are related to internal or external policy changes that produce divergences in domestic financial conditions relative to those of the rest of the world, often initially reflected in interest rate differentials and prospects of capital gains. Reversals of capital flows are frequently, but not always, associated with a deterioration in the macroeconomic conditions of the recipient country. This deterioration often results from the effects of capital inflows themselves (such as overvaluation of the exchange rate, excessively rapid credit expansion, and speculative bubbles in asset prices) but the deterioration is also generally influenced by external developments affecting interest rates and exchange rates in international markets as much as by shortcomings in domestic macroeconomic policies.

---

[17] For two surveys of the voluminous literature on the subject, see 'The exchange rate system' in UNCTAD (1987) and Rosenberg (1996: especially chapters 2 and 12, of which the latter discusses evidence concerning trend-following behaviour of currency traders).

[18] Dollarization adds further to vulnerability since it effectively eliminates the difference between residents and non-residents in the determination of the profitability of their investments and their ease of access to foreign assets.

Financial crises in developing countries are all characterized by a rush of investors and creditors to exit and a consequent financial panic. Indeed, whatever the proximate causes of financial crises or the events that trigger attacks on currencies, international investors and creditors of developing countries tend to manifest herd-like behaviour in exiting as well as in investing or lending. Creditor overreaction to debtors' financial difficulties is often explained in terms of a collective action problem. Even though the creditors as a group are better off if they continue to roll over their maturing claims on a debtor, an individual lender or investor has an incentive to exit. Without access to liquidity a debtor entity is then forced to curtail operations or to resort to distress sales of assets, which in turn lower its income and wealth, thereby further constraining its ability to service debt and hence damaging the interests of creditors as a group.

A generalized debt run by international creditors triggered by a loss of confidence can easily turn a liquidity problem into widespread insolvencies and defaults by altering key asset prices, interest rates and exchange rates. In the absence of a large stock of reserves or access to international liquidity, the ability of a debtor developing country to repay its entire stock of short-term external debt on demand is no greater than the ability of a bank to meet a run by its depositors. In the case of bank lending, withdrawal of loans by foreign creditors is likely to trigger a rush by unhedged private debtors into foreign currency as they seek to pay debt or cover their open positions, and may also lead to speculative selling of the currency by residents. This in turn drives down the foreign exchange value of the domestic currency and raises interest rates, making it more difficult for debtors to service their debt, forcing them to liquidate assets and thereby deepening the debt deflation process. Debt runs by foreign creditors are often also associated with a flight from non-debt instruments held by both residents and non-residents, notably from the equity market.

4. POLICY RESPONSES

Some of the possible lines of defence against financial crises involve action at the national level. These include domestic macroeconomic policies, particularly monetary and interest rate policies, to restore market confidence and halt currency runs, as well as hedging through keeping sufficient foreign exchange reserves and credit lines. Recent experience has pointed to serious weaknesses of macroeconomic policy as a response to currency runs and banking crises. Reliance on foreign exchange reserves and credit lines is likely to be costly and to afford at best partial protection. As a result attention has increasingly turned to structural and institutional weaknesses in the global financial architecture regarding the prevention and management of financial crises, giving rise to an international debate on its reform. Much of this debate has concentrated on five issues, namely (i) transparency, disclosure and early-warning systems, (ii) financial regulation and supervision, (iii) surveillance of national policies, (iv) an international lender of last resort, and (v) orderly debt workouts, and these will be the focus of the discussion which follows. Measures under these headings can help both to prevent and manage financial crises, and a clear distinction cannot always be made between these two objectives.

4.1. *Monetary Policies*

The orthodox policy response to currency turmoil by monetary tightening and high interest rates has not proved effective in recent financial crises. When financial markets panic, the likely effects of such a policy on capital flows tend to be perverse because of the strong adverse influence on credit risk. The withdrawal of foreign lending and flight from the country begin in the first place because lenders and investors do not expect to receive the return on their assets. Higher interest rates simply signal declining creditworthiness and rising default risk, and the expected rate of return adjusted for risk thus tends to fall as interest rates are raised.

If persistently applied, monetary tightening can eventually stabilize the currency by intensifying the difficulties of the debtors and increasing bankruptcies and defaults— that is, by reducing the sales rather than by increasing the purchases of domestic currency. As debt deflation and recession deepen, debtors will become increasingly insolvent and unable to raise funds to purchase foreign exchange to service their debt or to hedge against the exchange rate risk. However, stabilization of markets by monetary tightening will often be a slow process and will eventually be achieved only by depressing the economy and increasing defaults rather than by bringing back foreign capital.

4.2. *Foreign Exchange Reserves and Lines of Credit*

It has been suggested that debtor countries should maintain adequate reserves to meet their short-term obligations in order to avoid currency turmoil in the face of a massive withdrawal of foreign loans and investment. However, the consequences of accumulating reserves by borrowing are quite different from accumulating them through trade surpluses. One way of building up such reserves is to sterilize capital inflows through the issue of domestic public debt. However, there is a certain degree of circularity in such a strategy. In effect, it means that a country should borrow short only when it does not use the proceeds of such loans to finance imports and investment. Such a strategy can be very costly to the economy since the return on foreign reserves generally falls short of the cost of external borrowing. Moreover, the cost of sterilizing private borrowing falls entirely on the public sector whose losses will exceed the foreign exchange cost of carrying such reserves since domestic interest rates on government debt exceed the rates earned on reserves by a larger margin than borrowing rates in international financial markets.[19]

A variant of this proposal is for the public sector fully to cover the external short-term liabilities of the private sector by borrowing at long-term and investing at short-term abroad. However, not all governments have access to long-term foreign borrowing. More importantly, the cost of such an operation can be very high, particularly when the international long-term rates exceed short-term rates by a large

---

[19] For a more schematic account of the incidence of the cost of such borrowing, see UNCTAD (1999*b*: chapter 5 [section C.2]).

margin and the risk premium on long-term sovereign debt is high. Another strategy would be to maintain credit lines with foreign private banks and to use them when faced with an attack, which is tantamount to arranging a private lender of last resort facility. Again, however, this will work only so long as too large a credit line is not sought. Moreover, here too the costs involved can be very large. Finally, there is no guarantee that the funds will actually be available when there is a massive withdrawal of foreign lendings; and even if they are available, the funds so provided may merely offset reduced access to normal credits.

4.3. *Transparency, Disclosure, and Early Warning*

The Asian financial crisis has accelerated initiatives to improve the timeliness and quality of information concerning key macroeconomic variables as well as the financial reporting of banks and non-financial firms.[20] These are viewed as essential for better decision-taking by private lenders and investors, greater market discipline over policy makers, more effective policy surveillance by multilateral financial institutions, and strengthened financial regulation and supervision.

Regarding key macroeconomic variables, an initiative had already been taken after the Mexican crisis when the IMF established the Special Data Dissemination Standard (SDDS) in April 1996 to guide member countries in the public dissemination of economic and financial information in the context of seeking or maintaining access to international financial markets. At the time it was hoped that the new, more stringent rules associated with the SDDS would serve as an early-warning system that would help to prevent future financial crises. However, in any event the rules did not make such a contribution in the case of the East Asian crisis. In April 1998 the Interim Committee proposed a broadening of the SDDS, clearly inspired in part by what it considered to be the role of informational deficiencies in the East Asian crisis, so that the system would also cover additional financial data such as net reserves (after allowance for central banks' liabilities under forward or derivative transactions), private debt (in particular that at short maturities), and other indicators bearing on the stability of the financial sector. At the same time, the Interim Committee also asked the IMF to examine the desirability of a code of good practice on transparency with respect to monetary and financial policies, which was completed in July 1999 and adopted in September 1999 by the Interim Committee.[21] Moreover, initiatives are under way in the Committee on the Global Financial System with the purpose of exploring ways of improving disclosure by the financial intermediaries involved in international capital flows.

While such initiatives are useful, their impact is likely to be gradual since it will depend to a substantial extent on their success in shaping standards and norms not

[20] See, for example, Group of 22 (1998*b*).

[21] This code is to complement one of good practice on fiscal transparency aimed at strengthening the credibility and public understanding of macroeconomic policies and choices regarding fiscal policies. For the main features of the draft code of good practice on transparency in monetary and financial policies and discussion of other multilateral initiatives to strengthen the international financial system, see Drage and Mann (1999).

only of official bodies but also of financial firms, which will frequently require considerable periods of time. Moreover, the potential of such initiatives for preventing financial crises should not be exaggerated. Emphasis on inadequate information as the major reason for failure to forecast the East Asian crisis, for example, appears overdone. What was missing was adequate evaluation by both multilateral financial institutions and market participants of the implications of available information for countries' ability to continue to obtain funding from the international financial markets. A similar unwillingness to be influenced by available data was evident during the Russian crisis. Underlying the emphasis on greater transparency is the implicit assumption that deterioration in a debtor country's position will manifest itself in its external payments, its net external assets, and the growth of domestic credit, allowing gradual adjustment in the behaviour of lenders and investors. But the reality is often that the initial deterioration has little or no effect. However, once the rush to exit has begun, the process itself will lead to a rapid worsening of key indicators and in these circumstances transparency may simply accelerate it.[22]

The East Asian crisis has also focused attention on standards of accounting and financial reporting, particularly those of financial firms.[23] At first sight, recommendations for greater transparency on the part of financial firms have an almost self-evident quality, and the value of improvements in this area seems incontrovertible. Yet, on closer scrutiny the issues become less simple. The quality of information made available to financial supervisors has an important bearing on the effectiveness of their work. However, there is less consensus as to the benefits of disclosure to market participants. Public disclosure of information submitted to supervisors is typically subject to limits resulting from the belief that it could undermine the confidence in the financial system that regulation is intended to promote, complicate the task of banking supervisors in handling the problems of banks in difficulty, and enhance rather than diminish the likelihood of increased volatility and instability confronted by financial firms more generally.[24] Indeed, the Basle Committee on Banking Supervision itself has acknowledged that 'there are certain types of information that should be held confidential by banking supervisors' and that 'the types of information considered sensitive vary from country to country'.[25]

---

[22] The question may be asked, for example, whether disclosure of the rapid accumulation during the spring of 1997 by the Central Bank of Thailand of large forward exchange liabilities that depleted its net foreign exchange reserves would have fostered more orderly adjustment or simply have accelerated its currency crisis.

[23] The improved private-sector transparency for which calls are being made is intended to include not only the reporting of financial firms but also that of non-financial entities. Many of the recommendations under this heading (such as those relating to accounting standards and other disclosures required for shares listed on stock exchanges) refer to both. Financial reporting by several economic sectors is characterized by specificities absent elsewhere, but such specificities are especially important for the financial sector and linked in many ways integrally to its regulation and supervision whose character reflects its central role in economies' functioning and stability. In view of their key position in current reform initiatives the discussion here is limited to the transparency issues involving financial firms.

[24] See, for example, Caouette *et al.* (1998: 409).   [25] See BCBS (1997: 37).

Despite the widespread acknowledgement of the problems which full disclosure by financial firms may cause, there remains an important school of thought among financial regulators which supports the idea that full disclosure's favourable effects, through its strengthening of market discipline, outweigh its costs. However, as in the case of macroeconomic information concerning debtor countries, an implicit assumption of this argument would appear to be that disclosure would make possible the exercise of market discipline in an orderly way, which avoided herd-like or panic stricken reactions on the part of creditors and other counterparties. Such a scenario will undoubtedly apply in some cases. But the outcome will depend on the reactions of different categories of counterparty, some of which have greater access to direct information about a debtor than others, and on different national legal rules and norms. Here, too, experience shows that there is a danger that initial indications of something amiss may have at most a limited effect but once the climate of opinion among creditors changes, disclosure will simply intensify the debtor's difficulties, thus exacerbating the supervisory problems already mentioned (and possibly posing a threat of broader financial destabilization).

Arguments for full disclosure also raise the question of the value of information made available by financial firms for decisions by supervisors as well as by creditors and other counterparties. Financial liberalization and innovation have greatly increased the speed at which financial firms in many countries can now alter the assets and liabilities on their balance sheets as well as their scope for taking off-balance sheet positions of an opaque nature, thereby changing the risks they face in ways which can be difficult for outsiders to identify.[26] These considerations are especially pertinent to banks with substantial trading operations, an increasingly common feature of financial firms.

These limitations of accounting information would apply even if financial firms were fulfilling the requirements of best practice in this area. But, in fact, there is considerable variation even among industrial countries in both the quantity and form of publicly disclosed information: while arrangements for its provision are widely being strengthened, they frequently fall well short of levels corresponding to what is now considered to be best practice.[27] The point emerges from recent surveys of regimes for financial reporting and the regulatory treatment of loan losses. The information in these surveys, some of which is summarized in Table 5.3, is not necessarily fully up-to-date, but although the divergence between accepted best practice and national legal regimes may have narrowed since they were undertaken, in many areas it is still likely to be substantial.[28]

The potential value of the information associated with fuller disclosure for improved surveillance has been a stimulus to econometric analysis of the determinants

---

[26] See, for example, the remarks of William McDonough, president of the Federal Reserve Bank of New York and current chairman of the Basle Committee on Banking Supervision, in Leach *et al.* (1993: 15–16).

[27] For recommendations as to best practice, see BCBS (1998).

[28] In some countries there may also be divergence between the enunciated standards of the regime for accounting and financial reporting and the actual practice of several financial firms.

Table 5.3. *Features of financial reporting and supervision for banks in selected economies, 1992 and 1994*

	Australia	Austria	Bahrain	Belgium	Canada	Denmark	France	Germany	Hong Kong (China)	Ireland	Italy	Japan	Luxembourg	Netherlands	Portugal	Saudi Arabia	Singapore	South Africa	Spain	Switzerland	United Arab Emirates	United Kingdom	United States
I Consolidated accounts required	No	Yes	No	Yes	Yes	Yes	Yes	Yes	Yes	Yes	Yes	Yes	No	Yes	No	Yes	Yes[b]	Yes	Yes	Yes	Yes	Yes	Yes
II Accounting standards fixed by law	No	Yes	No	No	Yes	Yes	Yes	Yes	No	No	Yes	Yes	No	Yes	Yes	Yes	No	No	Yes	Yes	No	No	Yes
III Exemptions from disclosure obligations for banks	Yes	Yes	—	Yes	No	No	No	No	Yes	Yes	Yes[c]	No	No	No	No	No	Yes	Yes	No	No	No	No	No
IV Direct communication between auditors and supervisors in prescribed circumstances	Yes	Yes	Yes	Yes	Yes	Yes	No	Yes	Yes	Yes	No	No	Yes	Yes	No	No	Yes	Yes	Yes	Yes	No	Yes	No
V Segmental reporting required	Yes	No	—	Yes	Yes	Yes	No	No[d]	No	Yes	No	Yes	Yes	Yes	No	Yes	Yes	No	No	No	—	Yes	Yes
VI Criteria for establishment of specific loan-loss provisions	MD	—	—	MD	OR	MD	MD[e]	MD	—	—	MD[f]	MD[g]	MD	MD	—	—	—	—	OR	MD	—	MD	OR[h]
VII Criteria for establishment of general loan-loss provisions	MD	—	—	MD	OR	OR	MD	MD	—	—	MD	OR	MD	OR	—	—	—	—	MD	MD	—	MD	OR[h]
VIII Levels of specific loan-loss provisions	MD	—	—	MD	MD	MD	MD[j]	MD[i]	—	—	MD	OR	MD	MD	—	—	—	—	OR	MD	—	MD	MD[h]
IX Levels of general loan-loss provisions	MD	—	—	OR[j]	OR[j]	OR	OR[j]	OR[k]	—	—	MD	OR[l]	OR[kl]	OR[j]	—	—	—	—	OR[j]	OR[jk]	—	MD	OR[i]
X Valuation of collateral	MD	—	—	MD	MD	MD	MD	MD	—	—	MD	MD[m]	MD	MD	—	—	—	—	OR	MD	—	MD	OR

Notes:

[a]1992: 23 economies (17 industrial, 6 developing); 1994: 14 industrial economies; [b]Subject to exemptions for non-banking subsidiaries; [c]Reflecting flexibility regarding presentation of accounts; [d]Some breakdown of assets and liabilities required; [e]Subject to some guidelines of the French Banking Commission; [f]Subject to general regulatory guidance; [g]Subject to approval of Ministry of Finance; [h]Without distinction between specific and general loan loss provisions; [i]Subject to official guidance as to minimum levels for different categories of loan; [j]For country risk; [k]Including rules for hidden reserves; [l]Including rules set by tax authorities; [m]In consultation with Ministry of Finance.
MD: Management's discretion; OR: Official rules; — not available.

Source: Ernst & Young (1993) for I, II, III, IV, and V; Price Waterhouse (1995) for VI, VII, VIII, IX, and X.

of currency and banking crises. One of the objectives of this work is the development of leading indicators. Analyses of country risk have long been standard features of the operations of firms and other institutions involved in cross-border lending and investment.[29] The new econometric work on currency crises represents an attempt to identify more systematically relations between, and the relative importance of, variables traditionally included in analyses of country risk (but often evaluated more informally, for example, on the basis of scoring systems). Work so far[30] has served to clarify certain issues in international discussion of financial crises but seems more likely to supplement (or serve as an additional input to) pre-existing methods of analysing country risk which, owing to their operational role, must often rely on preliminary, tentative estimates of key variables and inevitably incorporate qualitative evaluation that is specific to particular cases but has an important bearing on the likely actual outbreak of crises. The contribution of econometric work on banking crises can be expected to be similar: here too, the discussion of certain issues can be clarified but it is difficult to foresee a situation where such work replaces first-hand (and sometimes confidential) information about the financial sector available to supervisors (and in some cases also to financial firms), and the rapidly proliferating techniques used by both to analyse different types of financial risk.[31]

4.4. *Financial Regulation and Supervision*

Weak credit evaluation and speculative lending, as well as failure to control currency risk among banks and other financial firms, are often at the origin of financial and currency crises, particularly in emerging markets. There is thus general agreement that regulatory reform is an essential part of the strengthening and restructuring of the financial sector. However, such reform is not a fail-safe way of preventing financial crises, though it can reduce their likelihood and help to contain their effects.

In recent years there has been widespread reform and strengthening of financial regulation at the national level, accompanied by a proliferation of international initiatives to raise regulatory standards and to improve cooperation among supervisors. These processes have been largely driven by concerns raised in relation to financial liberalization and global financial integration. On the one hand, the diversification of their services and the increased competition that are associated with liberalization have exposed financial firms to new levels of risk, which have necessitated an overhaul of financial regulation. On the other hand, global financial integration has brought in its train much greater exposure among countries to each other's financial and macroeconomic conditions and increased possibilities for the cross-border transmission of destabilizing influences, while also exposing weaknesses in banking regulation and in cross-border cooperation among banking supervisors.

---

[29] See, for example, Krayenbuehl (1998: Parts II and III), and Caouette *et al.* (1998: chapter 22).

[30] For brief surveys, see Goldstein (1998) and Eichengreen and Rose (1998/9).

[31] For a highly critical assessment of efforts to develop early-warning indicators of currency and banking crises, see Eichengreen (1999: 13).

The main vehicles for international initiatives in financial regulation and supervision have been the Basle Committee on Banking Supervision and other bodies with close links to the BIS as well as other groups concerned with regulatory and accounting standards discussed above. The initiatives of the Basle Committee have included the adoption of principles designed to ensure that no international bank escapes adequate supervision and the prescription of levels of capital commensurate with the risks that banks run. Agreements under the latter heading were reached concerning credit risks in 1988 (the Basle Capital Accord) and market risks in 1996.[32] More recently, the Basle Committee has enunciated standards for supervisory practice in its statement, *Core Principles for Effective Banking Supervision*, the drafting of which involved cooperation with the supervisory authorities of a number of key emerging markets as well as the IMF and the World Bank.[33] The coverage of these principles includes licensing, various aspects of banks' structure, prudential regulation, the methods and powers of supervisors, information requirements, and issues related to cross-border banking. In time the principles and other international initiatives can be expected to lead to considerable improvements in regimes of regulation and supervision. But there will still be limits to their effectiveness in preventing financial instability and crises owing partly to almost inevitable imperfections in implementation but also to inherent features of financial regulation.

4.4.1. *The Reform of the Basle Capital Accord*

Developments in the past few years have shown that the standards of the Basle Capital Accord are increasingly divorced from the credit risks actually faced by many banks, and are distorting incentives for banks regarding the capital maintained for a given level of risk. Moreover, in the context of preventing and managing financial crisis, there is widespread agreement that better control over international interbank lending in source countries could contribute to greater global financial stability. While the short-term exposure of international banks has been a major feature of recent external debt crises, the Basle Capital Accord attributes a low risk weight for the purpose of calculation of capital requirements to claims on banks outside the OECD area with a residual maturity of up to one year and all claims on banks incorporated in the OECD area.

Such shortcomings have led to pressure for regulatory changes and underlie the new initiative of the Basle Committee on Banking Supervision[34] to reform the Accord. The approach now envisaged rests on 'three pillars': minimum capital requirements, supervisory review of capital adequacy in accordance with specified qualitative principles, and market discipline based on the provision of reliable and timely information. The new proposed capital rules include provision for risk weights for exposure to sovereign entities based on external assessment by rating agencies meeting certain criteria (subject to the country's acceptance of the standards regarding disclosure of

---

[32] Credit risk results from the possibility that a bank's counterparty will default on its obligations, and market risk is that of loss due to changes in the market value of a bank's asset before it can be liquidated or offset in some way.   [33] See BCBS (1997).

[34] See BCBS (1999).

the IMF's SDDS) and two possible approaches to weights for interbank exposures, one linking them to the sovereign risk for the country where the bank is incorporated and the other based directly on external ratings of banks themselves. Under the second approach short-term interbank claims might still receive more favourable treatment than those with longer maturities but either approach would be likely to lead to widespread increases in the capital requirements for interbank lending for entities other than those located in countries with the highest credit ratings or in receipt of such ratings themselves.

4.4.2. *A World Financial Authority*

The increasingly global character of financial markets and growing links between different categories of financial business have given rise to proposals for the creation of a global mega agency for financial regulation and supervision or World Financial Authority (WFA). These proposals would appear to be motivated by two arguments. On one argument, since financial businesses are becoming increasingly interrelated and cross-border, their regulation and supervision should also be carried out on a unified and global basis. The other argument focuses on the stability of capital movements under the present patchwork of regimes which only more globally uniform regulation could be expected to control. Various models for a WFA can be envisaged, spanning the spectrum from an institution built on (and thus involved a limited departure from) existing arrangements to one with more comprehensive responsibilities. The more ambitious variant would involve a body with responsibility for setting regulatory standards for all financial enterprises, off-shore as well as on-shore entities.[35] A less ambitious variant for the WFA might serve simply as an umbrella organization into which existing bodies (in some cases with appropriately expanded mandates) would be brought.[36]

While there is considerable scope for strengthening both national regulatory regimes, eliminating their several, often glaring lacunae, and improving cooperation between national supervisors, it is not clear that the more ambitious variant would be a better instrument for this purpose than improvements in the functioning of institutions and modalities already in existence. Such a WFA would have to confront the problem of reconciling and integrating the different legal and conceptual frameworks under which supervisors concerned with different categories of financial firms work. Furthermore, there are no compelling reasons to believe that such a WFA would be more successful than the IMF in achieving stability in financial markets. The legal

---

[35] See Eatwell and Taylor (1998*a*,*b*).

[36] The recently proposed Financial Stability Forum (mentioned in Section 1) consisting of representatives from the finance ministries, central banks, and senior regulatory authorities of the G-7 countries as well as from the IMF, the World Bank, the Basle Committee on Banking Supervision, IOSCO, the International Association of Insurance Supervisors (IAIS), the Bank for International Settlements, the OECD, the Committee on Payment and Settlement Systems, and the Committee on the Global Financial System (formerly the Euro-money Standing Committee) is arguably of this kind. Objectives include pooling and sharing of information on vulnerability in the international financial system among different bodies, and some kind of monitoring of the implementation of internationally agreed regulatory and supervisory standards and codes of conduct.

instruments on the basis of which the WFA would operate would have to be reconciled with the powers of existing institutions, notably the IMF. There is also the matter of how power would be exercised in the new institution and by whom. It is not realistic to envisage that a global institution like a WFA with genuine clout could be established on the basis of a distribution of power markedly different from that of existing multilateral financial institutions. The alternative to a WFA is not an institutional *tabula rasa*. A network of institutions, albeit imperfect, is already in place, and there can be potential benefits from strengthening it, extending its mandate in certain areas and supplementing it gradually as greater participation is assured and its governance improved.

4.4.3. *The Limits of Prudential Regulation*
The continuing incidence of financial instability and crises in industrial countries suggests that regulatory and supervisory reform is unlikely to provide fail-safe protection in this area. And if this statement is true even of countries with state of the art financial regulation and supervision, it is likely to apply *a fortiori* to most developing and transition economies. These limits to the effectiveness of regulation and supervision have various sources. Firstly, financial regulation is constantly struggling to keep up with financial innovation, and in this struggle it is not always successful. There is thus a continuing danger that new practices or transactions, not yet adequately covered by the regulatory framework, may prove a source of financial instability. Closely related in many ways to financial innovation are growing difficulties regarding the transparency required for regulation and supervision. As described above, the balance sheets and other returns of many financial firms have an increasingly chameleon-like quality, which reduces their value to regulators. But perhaps the most fundamental determinant of the limits of regulation and supervision is the susceptibility of most of banks' assets to changes in their quality resulting from changes in economic conditions. No private sector loan or other asset on a bank's balance sheet should be classified generically as 'good'. However reasonable the original managerial decision to make a loan and however justified its initial classification as low risk by banking supervisors, the loan is vulnerable to the possibility of an eventual deterioration in its status.[37] So long as cycles of financial boom and bust are features of the economic system, so also will be unforeseeable deteriorations in the status of many bank assets.

Some of the consequences of such boom–bust cycles can be described in terms of the concept, 'latent concentration risk', as used in recent literature on credit risk.[38] Concentration risk is traditionally handled in the context of banking regulation and supervision through limits on the size of exposures to particular borrowers. For this purpose 'borrower' is typically defined to include groups of counterparties characterized by links due to common ownership, common directors, cross-guarantees, or forms of short-term commercial interdependency.[39] But boom–bust cycles bring into focus risks due to latent concentration as they lead to deterioration in the economic

---

[37] See UNCTAD (1998a: Part I, chapter 4 [section C.3]).
[38] See Caouette *et al.* (1998: 91 and 240).   [39] See, for example, BCBS (1991: section IV).

positions of counterparties apparently unconnected in other, more normal times. Indeed, a common feature of the boom–bust cycle would appear to be an exacerbation of the risk of latent concentration as lenders move into an area or sector *en masse* prior to attempts to exit similarly.

To some extent the risks of latent concentration can be handled through banks' loan-loss provisions and through higher prudential capital requirements for credit risk. But the financing associated with booms in the value of property and other assets is difficult for supervisors to restrain with the measures at their disposal owing to the size of increases in expected income growth or capital gains which are frequently involved. The limits on the crisis-preventing potential of financial regulation are generally recognized by specialists in the field, so that its primary objectives are regarded as having more to do with reducing financial firms' liquidity and solvency problems, protecting depositors, and preventing or mitigating systemic risks due to contagion.

4.5. *Policy Surveillance*

In view of the growing size and integration of financial markets, every major financial crisis now has global ramifications. Consequently, preventing a crisis is a concern not only for the country immediately affected but also for other countries. Since macro-economic and financial policies have a major role in the build-up of financial fragility and emergence of financial crises, global surveillance of national policies is called for, with a view to ensuring greater stability and sustainability of exchange rates and external payments positions.

The IMF conducts bilateral surveillance of individual countries' policies through annual Article IV consultations and multilateral surveillance through periodic reviews of global economic conditions in the context of the World Economic Outlook. The failure of IMF surveillance in preventing international financial crises reflects, in part, belated, and so far only partial, adaptation of existing procedures to the problems posed by the large autonomous private capital flows. But perhaps more fundamentally it is due to the unbalanced nature of these procedures, which give too little recognition to the disproportionately large global impact of monetary policies of major industrial countries.

Even though the IMF surveillance, as formally defined, is limited to exchange rate policies, its scope has tended to broaden over time, so that it now encompasses 'all the policies that affect trade, capital movements, external adjustment, and the effective functioning of the international monetary system'.[40] Given the degree of global interdependence, a stable system of exchange rates and payments positions calls for a minimum degree of coherence among the macroeconomic policies of major industrial countries subject to the proviso that this quest should not lead to a deflationary bias in policies, since, as stated by IMF Article IV, the ultimate objective of policy is to foster 'orderly economic growth with reasonable price stability'. The existing modalities of IMF surveillance do not include ways of attaining such coherence or dealing with unidirectional impulses resulting from changes in the monetary and exchange rate

---

[40] See Group of Ten (1985: para. 40).

policies of the United States and other major OECD countries. In the absence of incentives and enforcement procedures linked to the process of peer review under IMF surveillance, countries elsewhere in the world economy lack mechanisms under the existing system of global economic governance for redress or dispute settlement regarding these impulses. In this respect governance in macroeconomic and financial policies lags behind that for international trade, where such mechanisms are part of the WTO regime. Nor does the Group of 7 provide an effective forum for policy surveillance. Multilateral financial institutions remain the only legitimate and appropriate forums for securing policy consistency and coherence among major industrial countries with a view to their effects on global growth and stability. But if such a function is to be performed effectively, it is necessary to reform not only surveillance but also the governance of these institutions.

The need for strengthening IMF surveillance in response to conditions produced by greater global financial integration and recurrent crises has been recognized by the Interim Committee in April 1998.[41] However, despite the reference to interdependence, it is not evident that these proposals extend to weaknesses arising from the lack of balance in existing procedures. Moreover, even within the current limits of surveillance, the IMF does not have a satisfactory record of diagnosis of build-up of financial fragility and external vulnerability. An important reason is that bilateral surveillance has concentrated on macroeconomic policies, paying little attention to sustainability of private capital inflows and financial sector weaknesses associated with surges in such inflows, in large part because of the faith in financial liberalization and the infallibility of market forces. After the Mexican crisis, the list of developments that may trigger discussions between the Fund and a member country under IMF surveillance of exchange rate policies was extended to include 'unsustainable flows of private capital',[42] but this did not prevent the East Asian crisis.

In future surveillance will need to pay greater attention to unsustainable exchange rate and payments developments caused by capital inflows, and the Fund's recommendations should include, where needed, control over such inflows. This is quite consistent with the original IMF mandate on surveillance over exchange rate policies, and it is in this context that IMF could be given a mandate over exchange rate policies. Given the difficulties in identifying factors likely to cause financial crises, it may indeed be more prudent to place greater reliance as a matter of course on capital controls and other measures at the national level directed at external assets and liabilities. The effectiveness of IMF surveillance will also depend on the reform of the Fund and its governance structures. Such reform must ensure transparency, accountability, and participation (in particular of developing countries). One possibility in this context would be to subject the Fund's prescriptions to independent review, and the proposal that the United Nations should constitute an IMF External Review Commission is worth pursuing.[43]

[41] Interim Committee Communiqué of 16 April 1998.
[42] IMF Executive Board Decision No. 10950-(95/37) of 10 April 1995 (amending Decision No. 5392-[77/63] of 29 April 1977).   [43] See Sachs (1998*b*: 17).

4.6. *An International Lender of Last Resort*

There have been calls to establish an international lender of last resort facility in order to provide international liquidity to countries facing financial panic and to support their currencies. Provision of liquidity to pre-empt large currency swings has not been the international policy response to currency crises in developing countries. Rather assistance coordinated by the IMF has usually come after the collapse of the currency, in the form of bail-out operations designed to meet the demands of creditors, to maintain capital account convertibility, and to prevent default. Moreover, availability of such financing has been associated with policy conditionality that went at times beyond macroeconomic adjustment. Such bail-out operations pose a number of problems. First, they protect creditors from bearing the full costs of poor lending decisions, thereby putting the burden entirely on debtors. Moreover, they create moral hazard for international lenders and investors, encouraging imprudent lending practices. Finally, they require increasingly large amounts of financing that have been difficult to raise. Such problems could not be evaded in the creation of a genuine international lender of last resort. The effective functioning of such a lender depends on two conditions: it should have the discretion to create its own liquidity (or to have unconstrained access to international liquidity), and there should be reasonably well defined rules and conditions that the borrower must meet. Strictly speaking, the IMF does not satisfy either of these conditions.[44] Moreover, as described in Section 1, the Fund was originally conceived as an instrument for handling external financing problems originating in imbalances in the current account of the balance of payments. None the less on the eve of the Mexican crisis, the IMF explored the possibility of creating a new 'short-term financing facility' (STFF) to be used by countries with close integration with international capital markets which were faced with large capital outflows, including industrial countries and emerging markets. Although it was not put into practice, discussions concerning the scheme pointed to various problems involved (which were subsequently highlighted during the bail-out operations in response to the Mexican and East Asian crises). Of special importance in this context was the sheer scale of the financing required (although it was not envisaged that the facility would fully offset financial shocks) and the difficulty of deciding on the terms on which money would be made available.[45]

The SDR might play a key role in the creation of a lender of last resort facility as part of a process of making it a true fiduciary asset and enhancing its role in global reserves. Recently, proposals have been made to allow the Fund to issue reversible SDRs to itself for use in lender of last resort operations, that is to say the allocated SDRs would be repurchased when the crisis was over.[46] But either approach would

[44] For a more optimistic appraisal of the IMF's potential here, see Fischer (1999).

[45] This idea actually goes back to the Committee of Twenty. It was revived by the IMF in 1994, and elaborated in a paper by the management (IMF 1994). For discussions of the issues raised therein, see Fitzgerald (1996) and Williamson (1995).

[46] See Ezekiel (1998); United Nations (1999); and Ahluwalia (1999).

probably require an amendment of the Articles of Agreement and could face opposition from some major industrial countries. If one were to agree that the IMF could act as an international lender of last resort but without such a capability to create its own liquidity, the Fund would require access to adequate resources. Since there is agreement that the IMF should remain largely a quota-based institution, funding through bond issues is ruled out. This leaves the Fund's own resources and borrowing facilities (both the GAB and the NAB) as the only potential sources of funding. However, they alone could not provide financing on the scale made available by the IMF and other sources during the Mexican and East Asian crises. Moreover, even if mechanisms could be put in place to allow the IMF to have rapid access to bilateral funds at times of crisis, it is highly questionable whether the Fund could really act as an impartial lender of last resort in accordance with rules analogous to such operations by national central banks, since its decisions and resources would depend on the consent of its major shareholders who are typically creditors of those countries experiencing external financial difficulties.

The terms of access to such a facility pose additional problems. The conditions of lender of last resort financing, namely lending in unlimited amounts and without conditions except for penalty rates, would require much tightened global supervision over borrowers to ensure their solvency, an unlikely development. While automatic access would ensure a timely response to market pressures, it would also create moral hazard for international borrowers and lenders and considerable risk for the IMF.

One way of avoiding these problems might be through pre-qualification: countries meeting certain *ex ante* conditions would be eligible for lender of last resort financing, with eligibility being determined during Article IV consultations. Access to the lender of last resort facility on a pre-qualification basis could be subject to limits, but after a crisis occurred, the country might have access to additional funds subject to its commitment to undertake certain actions. However, pre-qualification involves its own set of problems. First, IMF would have to act like a credit rating agency. Second, the result could be a further segmentation of the Fund's membership, with attendant consequences for its governance. Third, lending at penalty rates might not be enough to avoid moral hazard. Finally, it would be necessary constantly to monitor the fulfilment of the terms of the financing, adjusting them as necessary in response to changes in conditions. In these respects difficulties may emerge in relations between the Fund and the member concerned.

The IMF has recently taken steps to strengthen its capacity to provide financing in response to crises, though this capacity still falls short of that of a genuine international lender of last resort and the terms associated with the new financing are likely to be subject to the shortcomings discussed above. The Supplemental Reserve Facility (SRF) approved by the IMF's executive board in response to the deepening of the East Asian crisis in December 1997 provides financing without limit to countries experiencing exceptional payments difficulties but under a highly conditional standby or extended arrangement. However, the SRF would depend on the existing resources of the Fund which, recent experience suggests, are likely to be inadequate on their own to meet the costs of bail-outs.[47] The creation of the Contingency Credit Line (CCL) in April is intended to provide a precautionary line of defence in the form of short-term financing which would be available to meet balance of payments problems arising from international financial contagion.[48] The pressures on the capital account and international reserves of a qualifying country must result from a sudden loss of confidence amongst investors triggered largely by external factors. Its availability is subject to the country's compliance with conditions related to macroeconomic and external financial indicators and with international standards in areas such as transparency, banking supervision, and the quality of its relations and financing arrangements with the private sector. The hope is that the precautionary nature of the CCL will restrict the level of actual drawings, but the danger is that countries will avoid recourse to it, even in the circumstances for which it is intended, owing to fears that it will have the effect of a tocsin in international financial markets, thus stifling access to credit. Moreover, although no limits on the scale of available funds are specified, like the SRF, the CCL will depend on the existing resources of the Fund.

Perhaps a more critical issue is that establishing a genuine international lender of last resort would imply a fundamental departure from the underlying premises of the Bretton Woods system which provided for the use of capital controls to deal with capital flows. In discussion of such a facility, its introduction is frequently linked to concomitant arrangements regarding rights and obligations with respect to international capital transactions together with a basic commitment to capital account liberalization. Thus, even if a properly functioning international lender of last resort could be put in place, it is not clear that this would be the right course of action for developing countries.

4.7. *Orderly Debt Workouts*

Commenting on the debt crisis of the 1980s more than a decade ago, UNCTAD pointed to the circumstance that debtor countries often had to face and at the same time 'the financial and economic stigma of being judged *de facto* bankrupt, with all the consequences that this entails as regards creditworthiness and future access to financing, [while also largely lacking] the benefits of receiving the financial relief and financial reorganization that would accompany a *de jure* bankruptcy handled in a manner similar to chapter 11 of the United States Bankruptcy Code'.[49]

Chapter 11 procedures are especially relevant to international debt crises resulting from liquidity problems. Debtors are usually left in possession of their property, and the aim of the procedures is to facilitate orderly workouts in three stages. At the outset procedures allow for an automatic standstill on debt servicing in order to provide the debtors in possession with a breathing space from their creditors. This prevents a 'grab race' for assets by the creditors and allows the debtor the opportunity to formulate a reorganization plan, and ensures that creditors are treated equally. Secondly, the code

---

[47] See *IMF Survey*, 12 January 1998: 7.   [48] See IMF Press Release No. 99/14, 25 April 1999.
[49] See UNCTAD (1986: annex to chapter 5).

provides the debtor with access to working capital needed to carry out its operations. The final stage is the reorganization of assets and liabilities of the debtor and its operations. The code discourages holdouts by a certain class of creditors. For solvent but illiquid firms, automatic stay and access to new financing may need to be supplemented with an extension of debt maturities. Insolvent firms, on the other hand, would require debt write-downs and conversions, financial and managerial reorganization, and where solvency cannot be restored through such means, liquidation. These procedures are used not only for private debt. Chapter 9 of the code deals with public debtors (municipalities) and applies the same principles. Similar arrangements exist in most other industrial countries.[50]

Naturally, the application of such principles to cross-border debt involves a number of complex issues. What is under consideration here is not the resolution of individual cases of cross-border claims, but systemic illiquidity problems associated with a generalized rush to exit and a run on the currency. Individual debtors may enjoy insolvency protection subject to provisions in their contracts with the creditors. However, while helpful, under generalized debt runs such provisions do not offer much relief to the country concerned, even if the bulk of the external debt is owed by private banks and firms. When there are numerous debtors, it is very difficult to activate appropriate procedures simultaneously for all so as to halt the run on the currency. More importantly, as in East Asia, most private debtors may indeed be solvent, but the country may not have the reserves to meet the demand for foreign exchange. However, as noted above, debt runs can make such debtors insolvent.

Current judicial practices and government policies in the major industrial countries do not allow debtor governments to benefit from standstill provisions regarding their external debt. In practice governments are reluctant to resort to unilateral suspension of debt servicing and exchange controls even in the extreme event of financial panic. In view of the deficiencies of current institutional arrangements for dealing with debt crises, and the increased capacity of financial markets to inflict serious damage, there is now a growing recognition of the need for reform. One proposal is to create an international bankruptcy court in order to apply an international version of chapter 11 (or chapter 9) drawn up in the form of an international treaty ratified by all members of the United Nations.[51] A less ambitious and perhaps more feasible option would be to establish a framework for the application to international debtors of key insolvency principles mentioned above.

On one view, under such a framework, standstills would need to be sanctioned by the IMF. The Canadian government has gone further, proposing an emergency standstill clause to be mandated by IMF members.[52] However, it would be difficult to avoid delays and panics in any procedure requiring prior consultations with the Fund. Moreover, there is a problem of conflict of interest. The executive board of the IMF is not a neutral body which could be expected to act as an independent arbiter, because

---

[50] For a comparison between the United States, the United Kingdom, and German bankruptcy codes, see Eichengreen and Portes (1995); and Franks (1995).   [51] See Raffer (1990).

[52] See Department of Finance (Canada) (1998).

countries affected by its decisions are also among its shareholders. Besides the Fund itself is a creditor and a source of new money. An alternative procedure would be to allow countries meeting certain *ex ante* criteria during Article IV consultations to have the right to impose standstills should their currencies come under attack. This would be similar to pre-qualification in lender of last resort financing discussed above, and while such a procedure would suffer from the same drawbacks, it would certainly be superior to a procedure requiring *ex post* negotiations with the IMF.

Under another alternative, which is free of the objections to procedures involving sanction by the IMF, the decision for a standstill could be taken unilaterally by the debtor country and then submitted to an independent panel for approval within a specified period. The ruling of the panel would need to have legal force in national courts for the debtor to enjoy insolvency protection. Such a procedure would help to avoid inciting a panic, and is in important respects similar to WTO safeguard provisions allowing countries to take emergency actions. In recognition of the difficulties in establishing internationally agreed standstill provisions, emphasis has been placed, notably in the Group of 22 Working Group,[53] on voluntary mechanisms. The dilemma here is that the need for mandatory provisions has arisen precisely because voluntary approaches have not worked in stemming debt runs. On the other hand, while a number of proposals have been made to introduce mechanisms to provide automatic triggers such as comprehensive bond convenants or debt roll-over options designed to enable debtors to suspend payments, these are unlikely to be introduced voluntarily and would thus need an international mandate.[54] Indeed, in the absence of a genuine lender of last resort, an internationally agreed standstill of this kind would appear to be the only effective mechanism to stop self-fulfilling debt runs.

If they are to have the desired effect on currency stability, debt standstills should be accompanied by temporary exchange controls over all capital account transactions by residents and non-residents alike. There would also be a need to combine debt standstills with debtor in possession financing in order to replenish the reserves of the debtor country and provide working capital. This would mean IMF 'lending into arrears'. Legally sanctioned standstills would facilitate debt-restructuring negotiations. For sovereign debt to private creditors, reorganization could be carried out through negotiations with the creditors, and the IMF could be expected to continue to play an important role by providing a forum for negotiations between creditors and debtor governments. For private debtors, government involvement in negotiations would be inevitable when the stability of the domestic banking system was at stake. In past episodes of crisis negotiated settlements often resulted in the socialization of private debt when the governments of developing countries were forced to assume loan losses. Such practices are not consistent with bankruptcy principles. The introduction of

---

[53] See Group of 22 (1998*a*: section 4.4).
[54] Concerning the difficulty of achieving changes in this area voluntarily, see Eichengreen (1999: 66–9). For the proposal that all lending in foreign currencies include a 'universal debt roll-over option with a penalty' to enable the borrower at his own discretion to roll over such debt for a specified period, see Buiter and Silbert (1998).

an internationally sanctioned automatic stay, together with debtor in possession financing, could help to relieve such pressures. Judicial procedures could be applied to individual debtors according to the law and the forum governing the contracts at issue.

Writing such a standstill mechanism into the rules and conditions governing international financial contracts would mean that lenders and investors knew in advance that they might be locked in, should a financial panic develop and a country's currency come under attack. This should promote a better assessment of risks, eliminate moral hazard, and reduce purely speculative short-term capital flows to emerging markets. It would also eliminate the need for large-scale bail-outs. Together with IMF lending into arrears, it would prevent an unnecessary squeeze on the economy and collateral damage for firms and other economic agents bearing no responsibility for the financial crises, while allowing the country breathing space to design and negotiate an orderly debt reorganization plan.

5. CONCLUSIONS

Given the inherent instability of international capital movements, recent experience shows that any country closely integrated into the global financial system is susceptible to financial crises and currency turmoil. Developing countries are particularly vulnerable owing to their dependence on foreign capital and their net external indebtedness. Indeed, the recent bouts of crisis in emerging financial markets have pointed to the limits of national macroeconomic policy responses for dealing with such crises and have provoked widespread agreement that there are structural and institutional weaknesses regarding their prevention and management.

In an ideal world, global arrangements designed for the prevention and management of financial instability and crises would include (i) some combination of disclosure and transparency by both public and private institutions, (ii) effective surveillance over national macroeconomic and financial policies, perhaps eventually making possible improved global macroeconomic coordination, (iii) globally agreed but nationally implemented rules for the control of capital flows through oversight of international lenders and borrowers, (iv) a lender of last resort with discretion to create its own liquidity, and (v) orderly debt workout procedures in international finance.

However, the changes required for the achievement of this agenda would require extensive reform of the institutional framework described in Section 1, so that such global arrangements are still a remote prospect. So far efforts to redesign the financial architecture have been hostage to disagreements among the Group of 7 countries. The case for improved disclosure and transparency is now widely accepted, as is that for strengthened financial regulation and supervision. Indeed, in both cases the potential benefits, while real, are often exaggerated. But there is more resistance to reform of multilateral surveillance over monetary and exchange rate policies of the major industrial countries, and prospects for curbing financial instability through global rules and controls over international capital movements are equally bleak. There is also unwillingness to establish a genuine international lender of last resort. Instead, the tendency is to introduce solutions involving limited increases in the availability of external financing designed to impose discipline on debtor countries and to keep them on a short leash. By contrast, political support is growing in the major industrial countries for more orderly debt workout procedures, and for involving the private sector in the resolution of financial crises.

Thus, in the current political environment a feasible strategy offering considerable potential benefits to developing countries in their search for greater financial stability would involve preservation of the principle of national control over capital flows together with internationally agreed arrangements for debt standstills and lending into arrears. This national control would, hopefully, be exercised in a context that would include policy measures at the international level in areas such as improved transparency, stronger and more even-handed multilateral surveillance, and better coordinated financial supervision which were supported in earlier sections of this chapter. The emphasis on the importance of continuing national policy autonomy is linked to various features of the earlier discussion of this chapter. Ways have not yet been found at a global level to eliminate the cross-border transmission of financial shocks associated with greater global financial integration or other pressures connected with capital movements, which are capable of triggering financial crises. And the international financial system will continue to be affected in unpredictable ways by ongoing technological and transactional innovation, so that any international regime involving substantial constraints on policy autonomy regarding the capital account of the balance of payments risks being overtaken by changes requiring new policy responses. The need for this autonomy is an argument against international agreements on capital account convertibility, international investment, or wholesale liberalization of financial services. It also points to caution regarding the attribution of additional powers over international capital movements to existing global financial institutions (or to possible new ones which can be envisaged) owing to domination by countries with strong vested interests in further financial liberalization.

REFERENCES

Ahluwalia, Montek S. (1999). The IMF and the World Bank: Are overlapping roles a problem? *International Monetary and Financial Issues for the 1990s*, vol. XI. United Nations, New York and Geneva.

Akyüz, Yilmaz and Andrew Cornford (1994). Regimes for international capital movements and proposals for reform. UNCTAD Discussion Paper No. 83 reprinted as 'International Capital Movements: Some Proposals for Reform', in J. Michie and J. Grieve Smith (eds), *Managing the Global Economy*. Oxford University Press, Oxford.

Bank for International Settlements (BIS) (1994). Public disclosure of market and credit risk by financial intermediaries. A discussion paper proposed by a Working Group of the Eurocurrency Standing Committee of the Group of Ten Countries (Basle).

Basle Committee on Banking Supervision (BCBS) (1991). *Measuring and Controlling Large Credit Exposures*. BCBS, Basle.

Basle Committee on Banking Supervision (BCBS) (1997). *Core Principles for Effective Banking Supervision.* BCBS, Basle.

——(1998). *Enhancing Bank Transparency: Public Disclosure and Supervisory Information that Promote Safety and Soundness in Banking Systems.* BCBS, Basle.

——(1999). A new capital adequacy framework. Consultative paper. BCBS, Basle.

—— and IOSCO (1998). Trading and derivatives disclosures of banks and securities firms. Joint Report by the BCBS and the Technical Committee of the International Organizations of Securities Commissions (IOSCO). London and Washington, DC.

Beattie, Vivien A., Peter D. Casson, Richard S. Dale, George W. McKenzie, Charles M. S. Sutcliffe, and M. J. Turner (1995). *Banks and Bad Debts: Accounting for Loan Losses in International Banking.* John Wiley & Sons, Chichester, etc.

Buiter, Willem and Anne Silbert (1998). UDROP or you drop: A small contribution to the new international financial architecture. November. Mimeo.

Calvo, Guillermo (1994). The management of capital flows: Domestic policy and international cooperation. *International Monetary and Financial Issues for the 1990s*, vol. IV. United Nations, New York and Geneva.

Caouette, John B., Edward I. Altman, and Paul Narayanan (1998). *Managing Credit Risk: The Next Great Financial Challenge.* John Wiley & Sons, New York.

Cornford, Andrew (1996). The Tobin tax: A silver bullet for financial volatility, global cash cow or both? *UNCTAD Review.*

—— and Jim Brandon (1999). The WTO agreement on financial services: Problems of financial globalization in practice. *International Monetary and Financial Issues for the 1990s*, vol. X. United Nations, New York and Geneva.

D'Arista, Jane W. (1994). *The Evolution of U.S. Finance. Volume II: Restructuring Institutions and Markets.* M. E. Sharpe, Armonk, NY.

Department of Finance (Canada) (1998). Canada's six point plan to restore confidence and sustain growth. September. Mimeo.

Díaz-Alejandro, Carlos (1985). Good-bye financial repression, hello financial crash. *Journal of Development Economic*, 19(1/2) (September–October).

Drage, John and Fiona Mann (1999). Improving the stability of the international financial system. *Financial Stability Review*, 6 (June).

Eatwell, John and Lance Taylor (1998a). The case for a world financial authority. Mimeo.

——————(1998b). International capital markets and the future of economic policy. CEPA Working Paper Series III, Working Paper No. 9. Center for Economic Policy Analysis, New York (September).

Edwards, Richard W. (1985). *International Monetary Collaboration.* Transnational Publishers, Dobbs Ferry, NY.

Eichengreen, Barry (1999). *Towards a New Financial Architecture: A Practical Post-Asia Agenda.* Institute for International Economics, Washington, DC.

—— and A. K. Rose (1998/9). The empirics of currency and banking crises. *NBER Reporter*, Winter.

—— and R. Portes (1995). *What Crises? Orderly Workouts for Sovereign Debtors.* Centre for Economic Policy Research, London.

Ernst and Young (1993). *International Bank Accounting*, 3rd edn. Euromoney Publications, London.

Ezekiel, Hannan (1998). The role of special drawing rights in the international monetary system. *International Monetary and Financial Issues for the 1990s*, vol. IX. United Nations, New York and Geneva.

Feldstein, Martin (1998). Refocusing the IMF. *Foreign Affairs*, 77(2), 20–33.

Fischer, Stanley (1999). On the need for an international lender of last resort. Available on http://www.inf.org/external/np/speeches/1999.

FitzGerald, E. V. K. (1996). Intervention vs regulation: The role of the IMF in crisis management and prevention. *UNCTAD Review*.

Franks, J. (1995). Some issues in sovereign debt and distressed reorganization. In B. Eichengreen and R. Portes (eds), *What Crises? Orderly Workouts for Sovereign Debtors*. CEPR, London.

Goldstein, M. (1998). Early-warning indicators of currency and banking crises in emerging economies. *Financial Crises and Asia*. CEPR Conference Report No. 6. CEPR, London.

Graham, Benjamin (1944). *World Commodities and World Currencies*. McGraw-Hill Book Company, New York and London.

Group of 10 (1985). The functioning of the international monetary system. A report to the Ministers and Governors by the Group of Deputies. Washington, DC.

Group of 22 (1998a). Report of the working group on international financial crises. Washington, DC. Mimeo.

——(1998b). Report of the working group on transparency and accountability. Washington, DC. Mimeo.

Haq, Mahbub-ul, Inge Kaul, and Isabelle Grunberg (1996). *The Tobin Tax: Coping with Financial Volatility*. Oxford University Press, New York and Oxford.

IMF (1994). A short-term financing facility. September. IMF, Washington, DC.

——(1995). *International Capital Markets: Developments, Prospects and Policy Issues*. World Economic and Financial Surveys. IMF, Washington, DC.

——(1998). *World Economic Outlook*. October. IMF, Washington, DC.

——(1999). *Involving the Private Sector in Forestalling and Resolving Financial Crises*. IMF, Washington, DC.

——(various issues). *Balance of Payments Statistics*. IMF, Washington, DC.

Jackson, John H. (1997). *The World Trading System: Law and Policy of International Economic Relations*, 2nd edn. The MIT Press, Cambridge, MA and London.

Kaldor, Nicholas (1964). *Essays on Economic Policy*, vol. II. Gerald Duckworth, London.

——A. G. Hart, and J. Tinbergen (1964). The case for an international commodity reserve currency. In N. Kaldor (ed.), *Essays on Economic Policy*, vol. II. Gerald Duckworth, London.

Krayenbuehl, Thomas (1988). *Country Risk: Assessment and Monitoring*. Woodhead-Faulkner, Cambridge.

Leach, James A., W. J. McDonough, D. W. Mullins, and B. Quinn (1993). Global derivatives: public sector responses. Occasional Paper No. 44. Group of Thirty, Washington, DC.

Mason, Scot P., Robert C. Merton, Andre F. Perold, and Peter Tufano (1995). *Cases in Financial Engineering: Applied Studies of Financial Innovation*. Prentice Hall, Englewood Cliffs.

Michie, Jonathan and John Grieve Smith (eds) (1995). *Managing the Global Economy*. Oxford University Press, Oxford.

OECD (1990). *Liberalization of Capital Movements and Financial Services in the OECD Area*. OECD, Paris.

Price Waterhouse (1995). Price Waterhouse survey of bank provisioning. In Vivien A. Beattie et al. (eds), *Banks and Bad Debts: Accounting for Loan Losses in International Banking*. John Wiley & Sons, Chichester, etc.

Radelet, Steven (1999). Orderly workouts for cross-border private debt. In *International Monetary and Financial Issues for the 1990s*, vol. XI. United Nations, New York and Geneva.

——and Jeffrey Sachs (1998). The East Asian financial crisis: Diagnosis, remedies and prospects. *Brookings Papers on Economic Activity*, 1, 1–74.

Raffer, Kuniber (1990). Applying Chapter 9 insolvency to international debts: An economically efficient solution with a human face. *World Development*, 18(2).

Rosenberg, Michael R. (1996). *Currency Forecasting: A Guide to Fundamental and Technical Models of Exchange Rate Determination*. Irwin, Chicago, etc.

Sachs, Jeffrey (1995). Do we need an international lender of last resort? Frank Graham Memorial Lecture. Princeton University, Princeton.

——(1998a). External debt, structural adjustment and economic growth. *International Monetary and Financial Issues for the 1990s*, vol. IX. United Nations, New York and Geneva.

——(1998b). Proposals for reform of the global financial infrastructure. Paper presented to the UNDP meeting on the Reform of the Global Financial Infrastructure, December. New York.

Sassoon, David M. and Daniel D. Bradlow (eds) (1987). *Judicial Enforcement of International Debt Obligations*. International Law Institute, Washington, DC.

UNCTAD (1986). *Trade and Development Report 1986*. United Nations, New York and Geneva.

——(1987). *International Monetary and Financial Issues for Developing Countries*. United Nations, New York and Geneva.

——(1994) *International Monetary and Financial Issues for the 1990s*, vol. IV. United Nations, New York and Geneva.

——(1995). *International Monetary and Financial Issues for the 1990s*, vol. V. United Nations, New York and Geneva.

——(1996a). *UNCTAD Review*. United Nations, New York and Geneva.

——(1996b). *Trade and Development Report 1996*. United Nations, New York and Geneva.

——(1998a). *Trade and Development Report 1998*. United Nations, New York and Geneva.

——(1998b). *International Monetary and Financial Issues for the 1990s*, vol. IX. United Nations, New York and Geneva.

——(1999a). *International Monetary and Financial Issues for the 1990s*, vol. X. United Nations, New York and Geneva.

——(1999b). *Trade and Development Report 1999*. United Nations, New York and Geneva.

——(1999c). *International Monetary and Financial Issues for the 1990s*, vol. XI. United Nations, New York and Geneva.

——(2000). *The Least Developed Countries 2000 Report*. United Nations, New York and Geneva.

United Nations Task Force (of the Executive Committee on Economic and Social Affairs of the United Nations) (1999). Towards a New International Financial Architecture. ECLAC, Santiago.

Williamson, John (1977). *The Failure of World Monetary Reform, 1971–1974*. Thomas Nelson, Sunbury-on-Thames.

——(1995). A New Facility for the IMF. *International Monetary and Financial Issues for the 1990s*, vol. V. United Nations, New York and Geneva.

Woods, Ngaire (1998). Governance in international organizations: The case for reform in the Bretton Woods Institutions. *International Monetary and Financial Issues for the 1990s*, vol. IX. United Nations, New York and Geneva.

World Bank (1998). *Global Development Finance 1998*. World Bank, Washington, DC.

—— (1999). *Global Development Finance 1999*. (CD-Rom). World Bank, Washington, DC.

6

Cross-border Movements of People

DEEPAK NAYYAR

1. INTRODUCTION

The movement of people across national boundaries, which began a long time ago, is a matter of interest and an issue of concern as we enter the twenty-first century. The attention is not just a function of the present conjuncture. It is attributable to the fact that the pressures for international migration are considerable and appear to be mounting despite restrictive immigration laws. This is not surprising in a world where income disparities and population imbalances between countries are vast, while the spread of education combined with the revolution in transport has led to a significant increase in the mobility of labour. Yet, this remains a relatively unexplored, almost neglected, theme in the extensive literature on the world economy. The object of this chapter is to focus on cross-border movements of people so as to outline the contours, examine the underlying factors, analyse the implications of globalization, explore the future prospects, and consider issues and problems of governance.

The structure of the chapter is as follows. Section 2 sketches a profile of international labour migration over the past fifty years and situates it in historical perspective to highlight the contrast between the old and the new. It also draws a distinction between different categories of labour flows in the contemporary world economy. Section 3 examines the underlying factors with an emphasis on structural determinants at a macrolevel. Section 4 attempts to explain why the gathering momentum of globalization has coincided with a discernible slowdown in migration during the last quarter of the twentieth century, to analyse how globalization might influence emigration pressures on the supply side and immigration needs on the demand side. Section 5 explores the future prospects of labour flows in the context of the forces set in motion by the process of globalization and the nature of demographic change. Section 6 reflects upon the necessity of formulating international rules or creating international institutions for the governance of cross-border movements of people.

I would like to thank Amit Bhaduri, Andrea Cornia, Bhagirath Lal Das, Vijay Joshi, Eddy Lee, and Adrian Wood for valuable suggestions on a preliminary draft. For helpful comments, when the paper was presented at a meeting of contributors, I am grateful to the participants in the discussion at Helsinki in May 1999. I would also like to thank Ananya Ghosh-Dastidar for useful comments on an earlier draft and valuable assistance in the search for information.

2. A HISTORICAL PERSPECTIVE

International migration goes back a long time. Indeed, the migration of people is as old as humankind. And migration across borders and oceans is at least as old as nation states. There were, of course, invaders and conquerors such as the Mongols, the Romans, and the Crusaders. There were also adventurers and merchants. Migration, however, is different, for it is associated with the movement of people from countries where there is a labour surplus to countries where there is a labour shortage. Even such movement, which constituted the beginnings of an international labour market, started almost five centuries ago. It would thus be worthwhile to situate the labour flows associated with international migration in historical perspective.

It began, in a substantive sense, with slavery. The slave trade started in the mid-sixteenth century. The markets for slaves developed along the African coastline from Senegal in the north to Angola in the south. Britain, Portugal, and France were the main countries involved. This trade in slaves continued until the early nineteenth century when it was brought to an end. It is believed that, over two centuries, more than 15 million people were taken from Africa to Europe, North America, and the Caribbean, to work in households and on plantations. The slave trade was the largest, enforced, mass migration of labour in human history. Slavery was ultimately abolished in the British Empire in 1833 and in the United States of America in 1865.

The abolition of slavery in the British Empire was followed by the movement of indentured labour, which was yet another form of servitude. Starting around the mid-1830s, for a period of fifty years, about 50 million people left India and China to work as indentured labour on mines, plantations, and construction in the Americas, the Caribbean, Southern Africa, South East Asia, and other distant lands.[1] This was probably close to 10 per cent of the total population of India and China *c.*1880. The destinations were mostly British, Dutch, French, and German colonies. But the United States was another important destination where indentured labour also came from Japan.

There was some movement of people from Europe during these periods of slavery and indentured labour. English convicts were deported to Australia. People from Portugal and Spain moved to South America, while people from England, Holland, and France moved to North America. Most of them, however, were adventurers or refugees rather than migrants. The real exodus from Europe came later. Between 1870 and 1914, international labour migration was enormous. During this period, more than 50 million people left Europe, of whom two-thirds went to the United States while the remaining one-third went to Canada, Australia, New Zealand, South Africa, Argentina, and Brazil.[2] These people were essentially labour displaced from the agricultural sector, who could not find industrial employment. The migration was, in effect, driven by the push of land-scarce Europe and the pull of land-abundant Americas as also other new lands with temperate climates that attracted white settlers. This mass emigration from Europe amounted to one-eighth its total population in 1900. For

---

[1] See Tinker (1974) and Lewis (1977).   [2] Cf. Lewis (1978).

some countries such as Britain, Italy, Spain, and Portugal, such migration constituted as much as 20–40 per cent of their population.[3]

International labour movements on this massive scale came to an end with the First World War. In the period from 1919 to 1939, migration continued but at much lower levels as immigration laws were put in place and passports came to be needed. In Europe, to begin with, passport controls were introduced to prevent the enemy from entering national territory but, soon thereafter, immigration controls were also shaped by labour market interests. In the United States, however, restrictive immigration laws were the outcome of a combination of economic, social, and political factors, which had been in the making for more than two decades. The timing may have been determined by short-term influences such as an economic downturn, a war, or a rash of labour unrest.[4] The great depression of the 1930s further dampened migration flows as unemployment levels rose sharply everywhere in the industrialized world. The end of the Second World War led to a massive movement of people within Europe, an estimated 15 million, most of whom were refugees seeking to settle. But the aftermath of the war also witnessed emigration on a significant scale from Europe to the United States and Latin America.

In the second half of the twentieth century, it is possible to discern two phases of international labour migration: from the late 1940s to the early 1970s and from the early 1970s to the late 1990s.

During the first phase, from the late 1940s to the early 1970s, there were two distinct streams of international migration. First, people migrated from Europe to the United States, Canada, Australia, and New Zealand. This movement was driven by a search for economic opportunities on the part of the migrants. It was also shaped by the nature of immigration laws in the countries of destination which, with the exception of the United States, restricted immigration largely to Europeans. In the period from 1950 to 1970, the total immigration was almost 6 million into the United States and 3 million into Canada.[5] Second, people moved from the developing world in Asia,

---

[3] For evidence on the magnitudes of emigration from Europe during this period, see Massey (1988). See also, Stalker (1994).

[4] The political economy of immigration restriction in the United States, as it evolved in the period from 1890 to 1921, is analysed at some length by Goldin (1994). It is worth noting that restrictive immigration legislation almost became law in 1897. But shifting political interests and favourable economic times kept the door open for two decades. Yet, a regime change, many economic historians believe, was almost inevitable. And it was only a matter of time before some exogenous force triggered a change that would close the door. In fact, the era of open immigration to the United States came to an abrupt end with the final passage of the Literacy Test in February 1917. The next step was the passage of the Emergency Quota Act in May 1921, which introduced a quota system that was to last, virtually unchanged, until 1965. It has been argued that changes in immigration policies in the United States and Canada, prior to the 1930s, were shaped by long-run fundamentals rather than short-term influences (Timmer and Williamson 1998). Thus, governments sought to protect the economic position of unskilled workers, with whom the immigrants competed, and to stop any absolute decline in their wages. The increase in income disparities between skilled and unskilled workers in these economies, during the late nineteenth and early twentieth centuries, accentuated political pressures and compounded social sensitivities.

[5] The figures cited here are obtained from immigration statistics published by the United States Immigration and Naturalization Service and the Canadian Employment and Immigration Centre. For

North Africa, and the Caribbean to Western Europe where economic growth combined with full employment created labour shortages and led to labour imports. To begin with, this demand was met from the labour-surplus countries in Southern Europe, and Italy was perhaps the most important source of such labour. But these sources were not sufficient for long. And, by the late 1950s, the labour-scarce countries of Europe were searching elsewhere for labour, mostly unskilled or semiskilled workers for employment in the manufacturing sector or the services sector. Britain imported workers from the Indian subcontinent and the Caribbean islands. France imported workers from North Africa. Germany imported workers from Yugoslavia and Turkey. Available evidence suggests that total immigration into Western Europe, from 1950 to 1970, was about 10 million.[6]

During the second phase, from the early 1970s to the late 1990s, migration to Europe almost came to a stop. It was the end of the era of rapid economic growth combined with full employment. And immigration laws became restrictive almost everywhere in Western Europe.[7] But there were, once again, two different streams of migration. First, there was a permanent emigration of people not only from Europe but also from the developing world to the United States and, on a smaller scale, to Canada. These were mostly persons with professional qualifications or technical skills. This was made possible, in part, by a change in immigration laws in the United States, which meant that entry was related to skill levels rather than country-of-origin, thereby providing more access to people from developing countries.[8] And, in the period from 1970 to 1995, total immigration into the United States was 17 million while total immigration

details, see Nayyar (1994). During much of this period, even in the United States, more than half the immigrants were of European origin. The Immigration and Nationality Act of 1952 eliminated previous racial exclusions, but it retained the national origins formula which allocated visas according to quotas based on nationalities already represented in the US population.

[6] The evidence is not definitive and is possibly based on estimates. Stalker (1994) reports that, between 1950 and 1973, net immigration into Western Europe was nearly 10 million.

[7] These changes in immigration policies are described in UN (1998). Evidence available for the period 1986–96 also shows that the proportion of foreign or foreign-born population in the total population in most countries of Western Europe was remarkably stable. See OECD (1998: 224). Even in countries, such as Germany, where it rose modestly, it was probably attributable to the slower growth in the native population rather than to more immigration. It is worth noting, however, that the disintegration of the former Soviet Union and the opening of borders in Eastern Europe has increased pressures for migration to Western Europe, particularly from refugees.

[8] The Immigration Act of 1965 abolished national origins quotas, fixed a ceiling on western hemisphere immigration and devised a preference system that favoured relatives of United States citizens and residents, those with needed occupational skills, abilities or training, and refugees. Immigrant visas were allocated on a first-come-first-served basis, subject to seven categories of immigrants in order of preference and without any numerical limit on spouses, parents, or children of US citizens. This led to a rapid shift in the countries-of-origin of immigrants. Consequently, in the stock of foreign-born population in the United States, the proportion of European immigrants fell from 32.2 per cent in 1970 to 19.7 per cent in 1980 and 11.7 per cent in 1990, while the proportion of Asian immigrants rose from 5.2 per cent in 1970 to 10.8 per cent in 1980 and 15.2 per cent in 1990. These proportions have been calculated from OECD (1998: 249). The Immigration Act was amended in 1990. It revised the numerical limits and the preference system. Reunification of families continued to be the most important criterion, but the number of employment-based visas was almost tripled, from 54 000 to 140 000 per annum, and distributed among five main categories of preferences primarily for those with professional, managerial, or technical qualifications.

into Canada was about 4 million.[9] Second, there was a temporary migration of people from labour-surplus developing countries, mostly unskilled workers and semiskilled, or skilled workers in manual or clerical occupations. There were three sets of destinations for such labour flows. Some went to the industrialized countries. Some went to the high-income, labour-scarce, oil-exporting countries. Some went to the middle-income newly industrializing countries which attained near full employment. The guest workers in Western Europe, the seasonal import of Mexican labour in the United States, the export of workers from South Asia, South East Asia, and North Africa to the oil-exporting countries of the Middle East, and the more recent import of temporary workers by labour-scarce countries in East Asia, are all components of these temporary labour flows.

The second half of the twentieth century has also witnessed a movement of people, as refugees rather than migrants, across national boundaries. Refugees, as much as migrants, go back a long time. But such cross-border movements during the past fifty years have been on a different, much larger, scale. This process began life in the late 1940s, at the end of the Second World War, as displaced people, who could not or did not wish to return to their homes, sought to resettle elsewhere. The onset of the cold war was the next impetus for refugees as people, experiencing or claiming political persecution, fled from East to West seeking asylum. The de-colonization struggles in Africa, during the 1960s, were another new source of refugee flows. Such labour flows remained within manageable proportions until the early 1970s. During the last quarter of the twentieth century, however, the phenomenon of migration in distress has been on an altogether different scale. The geographical spread is far greater. The reasons are many more. And the number of people affected is much larger. The reasons have ranged from the internationalization of liberation struggles, civil wars, ethnic strife, religious violence, political persecution, and xenophobic nationalism to famines and natural disasters. The geographical spread has ranged from Angola, Mozambique, Ethiopia, Sudan, and Somalia through Afghanistan, Cambodia, and Laos to Central America and, most recently, former Yugoslavia. It is estimated that the number of people seeking asylum has gone up from about 30 000 per annum in the early 1970s to more than 800 000 per annum in the early 1990s.[10] And, over this period, the world-wide population of refugees, driven from their homes by natural disasters or the search for political asylum, rose from 8 to 20 million.[11]

It is clear that international labour migration during the past fifty years has been at relatively modest levels compared with the past. And, in sharp contrast with the earlier magnitudes, it has slowed down during the last quarter of the twentieth century. But

---

[9] The primary sources of data are immigration statistics published by the United States and Canada. For the period 1970–90, see Nayyar (1994). For the period 1991–95, see OECD (1998).

[10] If anything, the problem intensified during the 1990s as there was a dramatic increase in the absolute numbers of asylum seekers in OECD countries. Between 1987 and 1996, for example, the inflow of asylum seekers rose from 26 100 to 128 200 in the United States, from 57 400 to 116 400 in Germany, from 5900 to 41 500 in the United Kingdom (OECD 1998: 223).

[11] For evidence on, and a discussion of, the refugee problem, see Bohning and Schloeter-Paredes (1994) and Stalker (1994).

the dimensions remain significant. There are, however, different forms of labour flows across national boundaries.[12] Thus, new distinctions can be drawn between voluntary migration and distress migration, permanent emigration and temporary migration, or legal migration and illegal migration. In the contemporary world economy, it is then possible to distinguish between five categories of labour flows, of which two are old and three are new.

The old labour flows are made up of emigrants and refugees. *Emigrants* are people who move to a country and settle there permanently. The principal destinations now are the United States, Canada, and Australia. Most such people are admitted for their professional qualifications or for reunification of families. Such emigration is estimated to be in the range of 1 million people per annum. *Refugees* are people who leave their homes because of famine, ethnic strife, civil war, or political persecution, to seek a home or asylum so as to take up permanent residence in other countries. It is estimated that such distress migration, which is involuntary, leads to the movement of about 1 million people across borders every year.

The new forms of labour flows are guest workers, illegal immigrants, and professionals. *Guest workers* are people who move to a country, on a temporary basis, for a specified purpose and a limited duration. Most of them are unskilled or semiskilled workers. The largest number, estimated at more than 5 million, is in the Middle East.[13] And there are now some in Malaysia and Singapore. But they are also to be found in Western Europe. This category includes seasonal workers employed in agriculture or tourism, particularly in the United States and Canada.[14] *Illegal immigrants* are people who enter a country without a visa, take up employment on a tourist visa or simply stay on after their visa has expired. The largest number of such persons are in the United States (about 3 million), Western Europe (at least 3 million), and Japan (perhaps 1 million).[15] However, there are also a significant number in Latin America and East Asia. *Professionals* are people with high levels of education, experience and qualifications, whose skills are in demand everywhere and can move from country to country, temporarily or permanently, as immigration laws are not restrictive for them. Most of them are employed by transnational corporations. But some of them circulate in their professional capacities or through systems of education and research.

It needs to be said that these categories are not mutually exclusive or exhaustive. Nor do they define a once-and-for-all status. After a time, it is difficult to distinguish between emigrants and refugees in their countries of settlement. Guest workers who acquire a right-of-residence are, in effect, not very different from emigrants. Illegal

---

[12] Cf. Stalker (1994).   [13] See Amjad (1989) and Abella (1994).

[14] In this context, it is worth noting that in the United States the annual inflow of temporary workers far exceeded the annual inflow of permanent settlers throughout the period 1986–96. For instance, in 1986, the inflow of temporary workers was 85 400 as compared with an inflow of 56 600 permanent settlers. Similarly, in 1996, the inflow of temporary workers was 254 400 as compared with an inflow of 117 500 permanent settlers (OECD 1998: 226).

[15] It is exceedingly difficult to obtain reliable evidence on the number of illegal immigrants. Much of it is essentially conjecture, or casual empiricism, often based on reports in newspapers. The figures cited here are reported in Stalker (1994). See also, UN (1998).

immigrants who benefit from amnesties, which come from time to time, attain a legal status. The distinction between professionals and emigrants is in any case somewhat diffused, for the former are often a subset of the latter in the industrialized countries. Yet, these categories serve an analytical purpose in so far as the distinctions are clear at the time that the cross-border movements of people take place.

3. THE UNDERLYING FACTORS

The available literature on the economics of international labour migration is rich in terms of microtheoretic analysis but somewhat sparse in terms of macroeconomic analysis. Some of the earlier literature was concerned with the effect of migration on economic welfare so that the focus was on costs and benefits for migrant workers or their families.[16] Subsequent contributions extended the analysis to factors underlying the decision to migrate.[17] Theoretical constructs sought to emphasize the sensitivity of migrant flows, both internal and international, to economic rewards. And, the more recent theoretical developments stress the importance of the household as a decision-making unit in which it is argued that migration is a risk-reducing strategy for the household.[18] It is clear that migrant workers and migrant households have been the prime concern of theoretical analysis both in its normative aspects and in its positive aspects. This approach seeks to explain migration in terms of individual decisions. It is necessary but not sufficient.[19] For movements of people are also shaped and influenced by structural determinants at a macrolevel. Therefore, the individual approach and structural explanations should be seen as complements rather than substitutes in attempting to understand the factors underlying migration. However, if we wish to analyse labour flows across national boundaries, to understand patterns and determinants, it is essential to consider structural explanations of migration at a macrolevel.

The process of industrialization and development is associated with a structural transformation of economies. In a long-term perspective, the most important dimension of such transformations is a structural change in the composition of output and employment over time.[20] To begin with, the share of the agricultural sector in both output and employment is overwhelmingly large. As industrialization proceeds, the share of the manufacturing sector, and later the services sector, in output and employment rises, while that of the agricultural sectors falls. The absorption of surplus labour is reflected in the migration of unemployed or under-employed workers from rural hinterlands to urban settlements. Given the enormous differences in employment probabilities and wage levels, wherever possible, migration of workers across national boundaries also absorbs a part of the labour surplus. Over time, the process of economic development is associated with a migration transition. Rural–urban migration

---

[16] See, for instance, Berry and Soligo (1969).

[17] For a survey of this literature, see Krugman and Bhagwati (1976).   [18] See Stark (1991).

[19] The macroeconomic implications and consequences of international labour migration, whether for labour exporting countries or for labour importing countries, are also neglected in the extensive literature on the subject. There are some exceptions. See, for example, Paine (1974), Piore (1979), and Nayyar (1994).

[20] Cf. Kuznets (1966).

comes to an end when the surplus of labour in the subsistence sector is exhausted. Emigration flows are also significantly reduced in part because surplus labour is not readily available, and in part because economic development provides more employment, higher wages, and better living conditions at home, even if differences in the level of income or the quality of life persist *vis-à-vis* the world outside. In some economies, rapid industrialization and sustained growth, which create full employment, may open up the possibilities of a turn-around in migration flows as labour imports begin.[21] Late industrializers in southern Europe and East Asia have indeed experienced such a transition during the second half of the twentieth century.

During the early stages of industrialization, labour exports from surplus-labour economies are a common occurrence. There are both push-factors and pull-factors underlying emigration pressures. On the supply side, demographic factors combined with unemployment and poverty obviously create pressures for internal migration, mostly rural–urban but also rural–rural, in surplus-labour economies. The same push-factors probably lead to a spillover of migration across national boundaries. The pull-factor is also significant as a determinant of international migration, just as it is for rural–urban migration within countries. It is attributable not only to the actual differences in wage levels and employment probabilities at a point in time, between labour-exporting countries and labour-importing countries, but also to the perceived differences in the stream of income and the quality of life over a period of time. In this context, it is worth noting that the emigration of educated people with professional qualifications, technical expertise or managerial talents from poor countries to rich countries, described as the brain drain, is attributable almost entirely to this pull-factor. It is not attributable to the push-factor as these people are not only employed but also at the upper end of the income spectrum before emigration. Clearly, labour markets are segmented. The push-factor is dominant in some while the pull-factor is dominant in others.

Given the massive differences in income levels and living conditions between countries, actual or perceived, international labour movements would be much larger in an unconstrained world. In fact, they are not. In labour-exporting countries, the desire to migrate, arising from both push- and pull-factors, is constrained by the ability to migrate which depends on the endowments of skills, education, or savings among the potential migrants. There are, also, transaction costs of migration across borders which are significant. The ability to migrate is constrained further by the patterns of demand for labour in labour-importing countries. And the story cannot be complete without considering the demand side. Emigration pressures surface, or emerge stronger, once destinations for migrants are opened up by a demand in labour-scarce countries.

Labour shortages in economies are the fundamental reason for labour imports on the demand side. For analytical purposes, it would be instructive to consider the conditions under which industrialized countries seek to import labour from developing

---

[21] For a discussion on migration transitions which, over time, transform labour-exporting countries into labour-importing countries, see Nayyar (1994*a*).

countries, or elsewhere, in the form of permanent emigration. As an economy reaches full employment, labour shortages surface at the lower end of the spectrum of skills, whether in the agricultural sector, the manufacturing sector, or the services sector. Those who employ wage labour either face or anticipate a substantial increase in real wages, as a consequence of the actual excess demand or the emerging scarcities. The response of producers or employers takes three forms. These responses are not, in general, simultaneous but often proceed in sequence. First, producers attempt to substitute capital for labour through technological choice, by acquiring technologies that economize on labour use or augment labour productivity. Second, firms endeavour to use trade flows as a substitute for labour, either by importing goods that embody scarce labour or by exporting capital which employs scarce labour abroad to provide such goods through an international relocation of production. Third, producers or firms seek to import labour, but this is a last resort in so far as immigration laws in most countries tend to be restrictive for social and political reasons.

It must be recognized that the possibilities of replacing labour by capital, within an economy, through technological choice are not unlimited. The possibilities of substituting trade flows for labour movements, across national boundaries, are much larger. Yet, there are reasons why it may not be possible to do without imports of labour altogether. In the manufacturing sector, trade flows and capital exports can be a substitute for labour imports for quite some time. However, the same is not true for the agricultural sector or the services sector. It is not true for the agricultural sector simply because, unlike capital, land cannot be exported, and once an economy reaches full employment it is exceedingly difficult, if not impossible, to reverse the initial flow of labour from the urban sector to the rural sector. It is not true for the services sector simply because services are not quite as tradable as goods and even international trade in services often requires physical proximity between the producer and the consumer for the service to be delivered, because these are services which cannot be stored and transported across national boundaries in the same way as goods.[22] It is not surprising, then, that labour imports often begin with unskilled or semiskilled labour for employment in the agricultural sector or the services sector. In general, whenever such labour shortages surface, countries begin to import unskilled or semiskilled workers for manual or clerical occupations. Until the early 1970s, such labour imports in the industrialized countries were possible within limits and consistent with immigration laws. Since then, however, such labour imports have been in the form of either guest workers for a specified purpose and a limited duration or illegal immigrants who enter in collusion with employers.

It should be obvious that the factors underlying international labour migration are manifold and complex. Nevertheless, it is possible and necessary to highlight some structural explanations of migration at a macrolevel. The most important among them, of course, is disparities in income levels and employment opportunities between countries. The population imbalances between labour-scarce and labour-abundant

---

[22] The distinction between goods and services, as also that between trade in goods and trade in services, is analysed in Nayyar (1988).

countries also play an important role.[23] In this context, it is worth noting that, a century earlier, differences in natural endowments between countries, particularly land, played a similar role as people moved from land-scarce to land-abundant countries. The process of economic development, too, exercises an important influence. Interestingly enough, it can both dampen and stimulate international migration. As economic development provides more employment, higher wages, and better living conditions at home, it reduces the significance of the push-factor even if differences in the level of income and the quality of life persist *vis-à-vis* the world outside. This is because people do not wish to leave their homes. Yet, even if economic development reduces the need to migrate, improved levels of education and higher levels of aspiration increase both the desire and the ability to migrate.

Such structural factors at a macrolevel explain the fact of migration, but do not help us understand the link between the origin and the destination of international labour movements. For this purpose, we need to go beyond economics to history, geography, or even sociology. There are links between labour-exporting and labour-importing countries in each of these spheres. Post-colonial ties, a common language, or cultural similarities are often embedded in history and have shaped the direction of labour flows. The emigration from developing countries in Asia, Africa, or the Caribbean to western Europe provides an example. The movement of people from the Indian subcontinent and the Caribbean Islands to the United Kingdom, from Algeria to France, or from Indonesia to the Netherlands was shaped by such history embedded in post-colonial ties.[24] Geographical proximity is another important determinant. The movement of people from Mexico to the United States, from eastern Europe to western Europe, or from Indonesia to Malaysia and Singapore provides examples.[25] There is also a sociological dimension. Migrants follow trails charted by pioneers. And the notion of diaspora now extends much beyond Jews in exile. For the existence of an

---

[23] It is perhaps important to make the distinction between labour-scarce and labour-abundant countries clearer. The most plausible reference point, or denominator, is land. Historically, it is the land–labour ratio that has mattered. Even today, it is not irrelevant. Indeed, it is no coincidence that the United States, which is *inter alia* land-abundant, was for a long time (and still remains possibly for different reasons) the single biggest destination for migrants. If the denominator has all other inputs (quality-adjusted), rather than just land, then the distinction between labour-scarce and labour-surplus countries conforms closely to the distinction between high-wage and low-wage countries.

[24] The significance of such cross-border movements of people is borne out by available evidence. Even in 1990, two decades after these migrant flows tapered off, Indians constituted 9 per cent of the total stock of foreign population in the United Kingdom, preceded by the Irish and followed by Americans (OECD 1998: 256). Similarly, in 1990, Algerians and Moroccans together constituted 33 per cent of the total stock of foreign population in France (OECD 1998: 251). And, it is no surprise that, in 1990, Indonesians constituted the largest proportion, 15 per cent, of the total foreign-born population in the Netherlands (OECD 1998: 247).

[25] Evidence available from the United States Census shows that Mexicans constituted the largest proportion, 15.6 per cent in 1980 and 21.7 per cent in 1990, of the total foreign-born population in the United States (OECD 1998: 249). The importance of geographical proximity as an underlying factor is also borne out by the fact that, in 1990, Irish workers constituted 30 per cent of the total stock of the foreign labour force in the United Kingdom. The latter, of course, is also strongly influenced by historical ties, a common language and, more recently, the European Union which provides complete freedom for labour mobility between member countries.

immigrant community, with which the migrant shares a language, nationality, or culture in the country of destination, becomes a source of cumulative causation that continues to shape the direction of labour flows. The movement of people from Turkey to Germany, from India to the United States, or from China to Canada provide examples.[26] Interestingly enough, the same sociological nexus explains why such migrants come from a particular region (rather than from anywhere else or for that matter everywhere) in the country of origin and move to a particular region, sometimes even specific cities in specific activities (instead of a more uniform distribution across geographical space) in the country of destination.[27]

It should be obvious why it is difficult to understand international migration in terms of economic analysis alone. There are two, other, important reasons. For one, non-economic factors are significant determinants of cross-border labour flows even where the underlying reasons are economic. For another, there are cross-border labour flows where the underlying factors are not economic. Consider each in turn.

International labour movements are, of course, influenced by forces of supply and demand but are also constrained by non-economic factors such as explicit immigration laws or implicit consular practices. Thus, in labour-importing countries, it is not only the pattern of demand for labour but also the barriers to entry that determine the magnitude and the composition of labour inflows. Such barriers to entry can be explained, in part, by economic factors where government intervention seeks to pre-empt the possible adverse effect of immigration on employment and wages, particularly for unskilled or semiskilled workers. But non-economic factors in the realm of polity and society also shape attitudes and policies in the sphere of immigration. These barriers to entry, irrespective of the underlying reasons, constrain market-driven movements of people across borders so that actual outcomes are not shaped by economic factors alone.

There are, also, movements of people across national boundaries on a significant scale, almost as large as migration, which represent neither voluntary decisions nor economic decisions. To begin with, this was essentially a search for political asylum on the part of people who were driven from their homes by political persecution or just political repression. But things have changed with the passage of time. Migration in distress is now attributable to a much wider range of underlying factors. It is attributable, in large part, to man-made conflict situations such as civil war, ethnic strife, religious violence, or xenophobic nationalism often associated with the violation of human rights. It is also attributable to natural disasters such as recurring famines or

---

[26] Data on inflows of foreign population to Germany, for the period 1986–96 when such migration was not as large as earlier, suggest that Turkey ranked second in importance as a country-of-origin (OECD 1998: 231). And, in 1990, Turkish workers constituted as much as 33 per cent of the total stock of foreign labour in Germany (OECD 1998: 266). There is a similar story, albeit on a much smaller scale, about Indians in the United States. In 1970, Indians constituted only 0.5 per cent of the total foreign-born population in the United States but, by 1990, this proportion was 2.3 per cent (OECD 1998: 249).

[27] There is an interesting example of this phenomenon at a microlevel. A significant proportion of the taxi drivers in New York city are migrants from a few districts of the state of Punjab in India.

environmental degradation. The relative importance of these factors, obviously, varies across space and over time.

The preceding discussion in this section has sought to focus on the determinants of cross-border movements of people. There are, of course, important consequences of migration across national boundaries, with benefits and costs for the migrant at a microlevel as also for the country of origin and for the country of destination at a macrolevel. The distribution of benefits and costs between individuals and economies raises one set of issues. The divergence between private and social benefits or costs raises another set of issues. The movement of educated people with professional expertise, technical qualifications, or managerial talents, from developing countries to industrialized countries, raises the entire range of issues which are analysed at some length in the literature on the brain drain. Such cross-border movements may have significant implications for development in the changed context of globalization. But it would mean too much of a digression to enter into a discussion about the economic consequences of international migration, which is a subject in itself and beyond the scope of this chapter.[28]

4. GLOBALIZATION AND MIGRATION

The world economy has experienced a progressive international economic integration since 1950. However, there has been a marked acceleration in this process of globalization during the last quarter of the twentieth century. This phenomenon has three manifestations—international trade, international investment, and international finance—which also constitute its cutting edge. An increasing proportion of world output is entering into world trade. There is a surge in international investment flows. The growth in international finance has been explosive. The economic factors underlying the process, which have enabled it to gather momentum, are the dismantling of barriers to international economic transactions and the development of enabling technologies. Globalization has followed the sequence of liberalization and deregulation in the world economy from trade flows, through investment flows to financial flows. The technological revolution in transport and communications has pushed aside geographical barriers, as the time needed and the cost incurred are a tiny fraction of what they were earlier. But this is not new. There was a similar phase of globalization from 1870 to 1914. In many ways, the world economy in the late twentieth century resembled the world economy in the late nineteenth century.[29] The parallels between the two periods are striking in terms of the characteristics and underlying factors. And there is much that we can learn from history, for there is the past in our present. Yet, there is a fundamental difference between these two phases of globalization. It is

---

[28] The economic implications and consequences of international migration are discussed, at length, in Nayyar (1994). The literature on the brain drain is not recent but is extensive. See, for example, Sen (1973), UNCTAD (1975), and Bhagwati (1976).

[29] For an analysis of this historical parallel between globalization in the late nineteenth century and in the late twentieth century, see Nayyar (1995).

in the sphere of labour flows. In the late nineteenth century, there were no restrictions on the movement of people across national boundaries. Passports were seldom needed. Immigrants were granted citizenship with ease. And international labour migration was enormous then. In sharp contrast, now, the cross-border movement of people is closely regulated and highly restricted.

Yet, over the past fifty years, international labour movements have been significant in absolute terms, even if much less than in the nineteenth century and much smaller as a proportion of total populations. Indeed, despite the immigration laws and the consular practices, the average inflows of foreign population into the industrialized world were 3 million people per annum during the first half of the 1990s.[30] The inflows of foreign population into the developing world were probably at least as large. The latter came entirely from developing countries, whereas two-thirds of the former originated in developing countries. In the mid-1990s, worldwide migrants' remittances were in the range of $75 billion per annum. Of these, remittances to developing countries were about $45 billion per annum, compared with inflows of foreign direct investment at $100 billion per annum and foreign portfolio investment at $63 billion per annum.[31]

These magnitudes are significant, but are no match for the other manifestations of globalization. The share of world exports in world GDP, for example, rose from one-eighth in the early 1970s to almost one-fifth in the late 1990s, just as the stock of direct foreign investment in the world economy as a proportion of world output rose from less than 5 per cent in 1980 to more than 10 per cent in 1996.[32] Although comparable evidence is not available, it is clear that international migration lagged far behind international trade and international investment in the process of globalization. In fact, the number of new immigrants per 1000 inhabitants in the world as a whole in 1990 was lower than it was in 1970.[33] It is clear that the spread of globalization and its gathering momentum during the last quarter of the twentieth century have not led to any substantial increase in cross-border movements of people. Migration is more intra-regional than inter-regional. And there is no globalization of labour. This is neither an accident nor a coincidence. It is the outcome of the ideology, the interests, and the institutions associated with the process of globalization.

Ideology: Recent years have witnessed the formulation of an intellectual rationale for globalization that is almost prescriptive. It is perceived as a means of ensuring not only efficiency and equity but also growth and development in the world economy. The analytical foundations of this belief are provided by the neoliberal model. Orthodox

---

[30] During the period 1990–95, the annual average inflows of foreign population into selected OECD countries were as follows: United States (1 128 000), Germany (920 000), Japan (239 000), Canada (232 000), Australia (97 000), and France (92 000). The total inflows were 3.1 million people per annum. Of these, 2 million people per annum came from developing countries, 0.5 million people per annum came from transition economies and 0.6 million people per annum came from OECD countries. These figures for average annual flows have been calculated from the data in OECD (1997) and OECD (1998).

[31] For the data on remittances, see World Bank (1995) and UNDP (1999). For the data on direct investment and portfolio investment, see UNCTAD (1998).   [32] Cf. Nayyar (2000).

[33] See World Bank (1995).

neoclassical economics suggest that intervention in markets is inefficient. Neoliberal political economy argues that governments are incapable of intervening efficiently. In conformity with this world view, governments everywhere, particularly in the developing countries and the former communist countries, are being urged or pushed into a comprehensive agenda of privatization (to minimize the role of the state) and liberalization (of trade flows, capital flows, and financial flows). It is suggested that such policy regimes would provide the foundations for a global economic system characterized by free trade, unrestricted capital mobility, open markets, and harmonized institutions. And the ideologues believe that such globalization promises economic prosperity for countries that join the system and economic deprivation for countries that do not.[34] This normative and prescriptive view of globalization is not validated by either theory or history. Nor is it borne out by development experience.[35] The dominant conception of globalization, which has become a 'virtual ideology' in our times does not consider international migration as necessary, conducive, or beneficial. It is based on the belief that the liberalization of trade flows and capital flows is a substitute for labour flows. Indeed, the present phase of globalization seeks to substitute for labour mobility in the form of trade flows and investment flows. For one thing, industrialized countries now import manufactured goods that embody scarce labour. For another, industrialized countries export capital which employs scarce labour abroad to provide such goods.

Interests: The ideology is not abstract. It reflects economic, political, and social interests of the industrialized world. In the economic sphere, it is argued that the high level of unemployment among unskilled and semiskilled workers, as also the stagnation or decline in their real wages, in the industrialized countries is already attributable to the import of goods and the export of capital to developing countries.[36] Such arguments are obviously exaggerated and have been treated with scepticism by most economists. In refuting such arguments, it is important to recognize that the stagnation in real wages and the high level of unemployment in the industrialized countries are attributable to the nature of technical progress, which is replacing several unskilled workers with a few skilled workers, and the impact of macroeconomic policies, which have sought to maintain price stability at the expense of full employment. Yet, political considerations overrule economic reasons. And populist politics finds it convenient to blame trade with the developing world for problems of unemployment, particularly among unskilled workers, in the industrialized countries. In this milieu, where an

---

[34] See, for example, Sachs and Warner (1995).

[35] The implications of globalization for development, as also this issue, are discussed at some length in Nayyar (1997, 2000).

[36] It is difficult to find conclusive evidence that would validate or refute such hypotheses. In his work, however, Wood (1994) provides evidence to show that competition from the developing world, in the form of trade has led to dislocation in the industrialized countries in low skill manufacturing activities. He also makes an attempt to assess how much of labour-saving technical progress in the industrialized world was a response to competition from developing country trade. But this sort of analysis invariably ignores the possibility that unemployment is attributable to a lack of effective demand. What is more, such an approach does not sufficiently recognize the impact of macroeconomic policies and the nature of technical progress on employment levels in the industrialized economies.

engagement with globalization even in terms of trade and investment is a cause for concern, a freer movement of labour is a distant prospect. What is more, attitudes towards immigration in the industrialized world are also shaped in the political and social spheres. It is feared that more immigration can only erode the political hegemony of the native population, just as it is believed that more immigration would undermine social cohesion and cultural solidarity. There are, in addition, perceptions, which may be objectively false but are exploited by xenophobic politicians, that immigrants have displaced citizens from jobs or become a burden in terms of social security expenditures.

Institutions: Immigration laws impose explicit restrictions, while consular practices constitute implicit curbs, on the cross-border movement of people. But that is not all. The industrialized countries also seek to protect their interests through institutions and rules. The multilateral framework of the WTO is perhaps the most important medium. The new international regime of discipline provides for a progressive dismantling of barriers to international trade in goods. This is associated with a strict regime for the protection of intellectual property rights. The agreement on trade in services also caters to the interests of rich countries, which have a revealed comparative advantage in capital-intensive or technology-intensive services, but makes little allowance for labour-intensive services in which poor countries have a potential comparative advantage. There is now an attempt to create a multilateral agreement on investment in the WTO, which seeks free access and national treatment for foreign investors, combined with provisions to enforce commitments and obligations to foreign investors. It would seem that the institutional framework for globalization is characterized by a striking asymmetry. National boundaries should not matter for trade flows and capital flows but should be clearly demarcated for technology flows and labour flows. It follows that the developing countries would provide access to their markets without a corresponding access to technology and would accept capital mobility without a corresponding provision for labour mobility. This asymmetry, particularly that between the free movement of capital and the unfree movement of labour across national boundaries, lies at the heart of inequality in the rules of the game for globalization in the late twentieth century.[37]

It is clear that in the sphere of international labour movements actual outcomes are not shaped by economic factors alone. Yet, we must also recognize that the process of globalization is driven by economic forces in the market, whether the lure of profit or the threat of competition. Thus, it is worth reflecting on the implications and consequences of globalization for the prospects of migration across borders, by analysing emigration pressures on the supply side and the need for labour imports on the demand side.

4.1. *Emigration Pressures: The Supply Side*

The process of globalization is bound to exercise a significant influence on the push-factors underlying international migration. It would decrease emigration pressures if it

---

[37] For a more detailed discussion, see Nayyar (1996, 1997).

leads to a convergence of levels of income between the industrialized countries and the developing countries. But it would increase emigration pressures if it leads to a divergence in levels of income between the industrialized countries and the developing countries. Similarly, it would decrease emigration pressures if it leads to a reduction in poverty, an expansion of employment opportunities and an improvement in the quality of life for people in developing countries. But it would increase emigration pressures if it leads to rising poverty, growing inequality, worsening employment prospects, and a deterioration in the quality of life of people in developing countries. It is difficult to provide conclusive evidence. For some, the verdict may not be clear as the experience with globalization is not long enough. For others, it may be difficult to attribute cause and effect. In my judgement, however, development experience over the past twenty-five years, which could be termed *the age of globalization*, provides cause for concern.

Available evidence suggests that the past twenty-five years have witnessed a divergence, rather than convergence, in levels of income between countries and between people. Economic inequalities have increased during the last quarter of a century as the income gap between rich and poor countries, between rich and poor people within countries, as also between the rich and the poor in the world's population, has widened.[38] And income distribution has worsened. The incidence of poverty increased in most countries of Latin America and Sub-Saharan Africa during the 1980s and in much of Eastern Europe during the 1990s. Some countries in East Asia, Southeast Asia, and South Asia, which experienced a steady decline in the incidence of poverty, constitute the exception. However, the recent financial meltdown and economic crisis in Southeast Asia has led to a marked deterioration in the situation. There are, also, some other features of recent development experience in the wake of economic liberalization, which are a cause for concern in most developing countries, as also in the erstwhile socialist economies.[39] Inequality in terms of wages and incomes has registered an increase. Employment creation in the organized sector continues to lag behind the growth in the labour force, so that an increasing proportion of workers are dependent upon low productivity and insecure casual employment in the informal sector. The competition for export markets and foreign investment has intensified, so that there is some deterioration of labour standards in what is termed a 'race to the bottom'. There is little progress in creating social safety nets or social protection systems, which are now more necessary than earlier, because the openness, interdependence, and integration associated with globalization have created new forms of vulnerability for economies in general and for poorer segments of their population in particular. It is obviously not possible to attribute cause-and-effect simply to coincidence in time. But there are several mechanisms through which globalization may have accentuated inequalities.[40]

---

[38] For evidence in support of this proposition, see UNCTAD (1997) and UNDP (1999).
[39] See Lee (1998).
[40] For a discussion on these mechanisms, see Nayyar (2000). See also, Lee (1998).

Globalization has created opportunities for some people, regions, and countries that were not even dreamed of three decades ago. But it has also introduced new risks, if not threats, for many others. It has been associated with a deepening of poverty and an accentuation of inequalities. There are some winners: more in the industrialized world than in the developing world. There are many losers: numerous both in the industrialized world and in the developing world. It is, perhaps, necessary to identify, in broad categories, the winners and the losers.[41] If we think of people, asset-owners, profit-earners, rentiers, the educated, the mobile and those with professional, managerial, or technical skills are the winners, whereas the asset-less, wage-earners, debtors, the uneducated, the immobile and the semiskilled or the unskilled are the losers. If we think of firms, large, international, global, risk-takers and technology-leaders are the winners, whereas small, domestic, local, risk-averse and technology-followers are the losers. If we think of economies, capital-exporters, technology-exporters, net lenders, those with a strong physical and human infrastructure, and those endowed with structural flexibilities are the winners, whereas capital-importers, technology-importers, net borrowers, those with a weak physical and human infrastructure, and those characterized by structural rigidities are the losers. It needs to be said that this classification is suggestive rather than definitive, for it paints a broad-brush picture of a more nuanced situation. But it does convey the simultaneous inclusion and exclusion that characterize the process of globalization. In a world of inclusion and exclusion, the excluded do not simply suffer in silence. They seek shortcuts to the consumerist paradise through crime or violence. Sometimes, this also leads to reaction or backlash as ethnic identities or cultural chauvinism assert themselves. Such assertion of traditional or indigenous values is often the only thing that poor people can assert, for it brings an identity, continuity, and meaning to their lives. In some instances, then, global integration can provoke national disintegration as ethnic, cultural, or religious passions fragment society. Distress migration in the form of refugees and asylum seekers is a possible outcome. Similarly, in a world of winners and losers, the losers do not simply disappear. They seek somewhere else to go. In view of these realities and possibilities, it would be reasonable to infer that globalization is not likely to reduce emigration pressures on the supply side. It may even accentuate them.

4.2. *Labour Imports: The Demand Side*

Given the nature of ideology, interests, and institutions in the industrialized world, it should come as no surprise that globalization has not, in general, stimulated the demand for labour imports. In fact, the reality that has unfolded could have led to the opposite. The period from the early 1970s to the late 1990s, *the age of globalization*, has witnessed a profound change in the economies of the major industrialized countries. The Keynesian consensus has vanished. So has full employment. The rise of monetarism has meant that macroeconomic policies have sought to maintain price stability

---

[41] Cf. Streeten (1996), who draws up a balance sheet of globalization based on a rough approximation of what is good and what is bad.

at the expense of full employment. Thus, unemployment in the industrialized countries has increased substantially since the early 1970s and has remained at high levels since then, except in the United States, while there has been almost no increase in the real wages of a significant proportion of the workforce in many parts of the industrialized world. Inequalities, in terms of wages and incomes, have registered an increase almost everywhere. Over the same period, the rate of growth of output in these economies has slowed down. Under normal circumstances, this change should have shut out labour imports altogether.[42] But it has not. The reason is that there are unpleasant or menial jobs, particularly in the agricultural sector and the services sector, which nationals or citizens are not willing to do. And, the existence of social security means that they can afford this luxury even in a situation of unemployment. It is because of this that the demand for guest workers and illegal immigrants continues, albeit at modest levels, despite high unemployment in the industrialized world. Such migration will continue until technical progress does away with such jobs or employers improve the working conditions in such jobs. A return to full employment could, of course, revive the demand for labour imports on a modest scale. But there is another crucial factor that could revive the demand for labour imports in the industrialized countries on a significant scale. The ageing of the population in these countries, which is a consequence of increased life expectancy and near zero population growth, carries an enormous potential for immigration needs on the demand side.

The demand for labour, which may reinforce the pull-factor underlying international migration, is not confined to the major industrialized countries, essentially the United States, Canada, and Western Europe, which have been the prime destinations for permanent emigration until now. There is, of course, Japan, where immigration has been limited so far to overseas Japanese who went to Latin America as migrants a century earlier, but the import of labour in the form of illegal immigrants is large. In addition, there are two sets of countries in the developing world which would continue to be, or emerge as, destinations for migrants from poor surplus-labour economies. For one, there are the labour-scarce, high-income, oil-exporting countries in the Middle East which are characterized by significant labour shortages, insufficient skills among some segments of the local population and a wide range of unwanted jobs which nationals are simply unwilling to do. For another, there are the newly industrializing, middle-income countries in East and Southeast Asia, such as Korea, Hong Kong, Taiwan, Singapore, Malaysia and, to a limited extent, even Thailand, which are increasingly labour-scarce at the lower end of the spectrum of skills. This demand for labour imports is met in small part through temporary migrants who are guest workers but in much larger part through illegal immigrants.[43] The latter is possible because

---

[42] It has been argued by Timmer and Williamson (1998) that the increase in economic inequalities in the industrialized countries, experienced since the early 1970s, manifested especially by a rising income gap between unskilled and skilled workers, is bound to create pressures in the United States and Europe to reduce inflows of migrants, just as it did in the New World economies in the late nineteenth century.

[43] The literature on migration to the Middle East and the East Asian economies suggests that such imports of labour are often necessitated by shortages of labour in certain sectors or occupations where employment is dirty, demanding, or dangerous. These are described as '3D jobs' which nationals or citizens

there is collusion on the part of employers who pay much lower wages to such workers and because governments conveniently turn a blind eye, as such migrants do not have to be provided with any social security benefits. In the short term, this process may slow down because of the recent financial crisis in these Asian economies but, in the long term, the demand for labour imports will revive and grow. Of course, most of these countries will be characterized by simultaneous imports of unskilled or semi-skilled workers and exports of highly skilled persons with technical or professional qualifications.

5. LABOUR FLOWS: FUTURE PROSPECTS

There are both push-factors and pull-factors underlying international migration. The discussion in the preceding section analysed how globalization might or might not influence these factors. This is necessary but not sufficient, for it is possible that globalization, in itself, may create conditions and unleash forces that could become an impetus for the movement of labour across national boundaries. The evidence is limited yet suggestive. And it leads me to set out two possible mechanisms, which are plausible hypotheses. The first hypothesis is that there are some attributes of globalization, which are conducive to, and helpful for, people who seek to cross borders in search of work. The second hypothesis is that globalization has set in motion forces which are creating a demand for labour mobility across borders, some old forms and some new forms, as also developing institutions on the supply side to meet this demand. Consider each in turn.

There are three migrant-friendly attributes of globalization, which are supportive of cross-border labour flows.

First, the revolution in *transport and communications* has slashed geographical barriers, in terms of time and cost, not only for the movement of goods, services, technology, and finance, but also for the movement of people across national boundaries. Communication between people across countries is also much easier and far cheaper. In 1990, air transport costs per passenger mile were less than one-half of what they were in 1960 and not even one-sixth of what they were in 1930. Similarly, in 1990, international phone charges were less than one-tenth of what they were in 1970. The price of computers in 1990 was just about one-twentieth of what it was in 1970.[44] Thus, potential or actual migrants are no longer deterred by the cost of travel or the cost of speaking to their families, for it is now only a modest fraction of their incomes. And, in most countries, airlines and telephone companies aggressively compete with each other in terms of prices to capture the large market for their services provided by immigrants. The advent of Internet with its array of web sites, combined with the remarkable speed and the negligible cost of e-mail, makes it that much easier for people to live away from their homes temporarily or even permanently.

are unwilling to do and are taken up by migrant workers. See Amjad (1996). Much the same is true in the industrialized countries particularly in sectors or occupations that employ illegal immigrants.

[44] These comparisons are in terms of 1990 US dollars. For details of the evidence cited here, see UNDP (1999: 30).

Second, *market institutions* have developed which make it much easier for people to move across borders. For one thing, there are intermediaries in the labour-exporting countries, mostly brokers and agents who recruit and place people abroad for a price. For another, given the substantial demand for illegal immigrants, as also the enormous profits associated with it, there are brokers in both labour-importing and labour-exporting countries who are engaged in illegal trafficking of people. In this milieu, the cross-border movement of people is no longer dependent upon the ability of individuals alone as it was until not so long ago. The process of migration is now facilitated by institutional arrangements that have emerged in response to needs perceived by the market. Consequently, transaction costs are probably lower. These market institutions are reinforced by social networks of migrants in the labour-importing countries. Such networks, which have evolved with the passage of time and become stronger with globalization, provide their compatriots with information on immigration procedures and employment possibilities. This help often extends to legal advice on visa procedures and immigration laws. But that is not all. The networks also find temporary homes and extend financial support to the new arrivals. The word diaspora has acquired a generic meaning.

Third, the reach of the *electronic media* is enormous. And so is the power of television as a medium. For one thing, it has led to the global spread of cultural impulses. The culture of the young in metropolitan cities everywhere—north or south, east or west—is globalized: jeans, T-shirts, sneakers, jogging, fast-foods, pop music, Hollywood movies, satellite TV, and so on. Consumerism is global. Even corruption has become similar everywhere. So that distant lands with an alien culture and a different language are neither strange nor unexpected for the potential migrant. For another, the same media creates a home away from home for the actual migrant. Immigrant communities have their own TV channels, their own newspapers and their own entertainment.

The process of globalization is creating a demand for new forms and institutionalizing the demand for old forms of labour mobility. In this process, there is an inherent coordination between the demand side and the supply side. There are three important manifestations that are worth noting.

First, the reach and the spread of *transnational corporations* is worldwide. In the past, they moved goods, services, technology, capital, and finance across national boundaries. Increasingly, however, they have also become transnational employers of people.[45] They place expatriate managers in industrialized and developing host countries. They recruit professionals not only from industrialized countries but also from developing countries for placement in corporate headquarters or affiliates elsewhere. They engage local staff in developing countries who acquire skills and experience that make them employable abroad after a time. They move immigrant professionals of foreign origin, permanently settled in the industrialized world, to run subsidiaries or affiliates in their countries of origin. They engage professionals from low-income countries, particularly

---

[45] In 1992, for example, total employment in transnational corporations was 73 million, of which 44 million were employed in the home countries while 17 million were employed in affiliates in industrialized countries and 12 million were employed in affiliates in developing countries. The share of developing countries in such employment rose from one-tenth in 1985 to one-sixth in 1992. See UNCTAD (1994).

in software but also in engineering or health care, to work on a contract basis on special non-immigrant status visas, which has come to be known as 'body-shopping'. This intra-firm mobility across borders easily spills over into other forms of international labour mobility.

Second, the *mobility of professionals* has registered a phenomenal increase in the age of globalization. It began with the brain drain. It was facilitated by immigration laws in the United States, Canada, and Australia, which encouraged people with high skills or professional qualifications. This process has intensified and diversified. It is, of course, still possible for scientists, doctors, engineers, and academics to emigrate. But there are more and more professionals such as lawyers, architects, accountants, managers, bankers, or those specializing in computer software and information technology, who can emigrate permanently, live abroad temporarily, or stay at home and travel frequently for business. These people are almost as mobile as capital across borders.

Third, the *globalization of education* has gathered momentum. This has two dimensions. The proportion of foreign students studying for professional degrees or doctorates in the university systems of the major industrialized countries, in particular the United States, is large and more than two-thirds simply stay on.[46] The situation is similar in Europe albeit on a smaller scale. At the same time, centres of excellence in higher education in labour-exporting developing countries are increasingly adopting curricula that conform to international patterns and standards. Given the facility of language, such people are employable almost anywhere.

It is, thus, plausible to argue that globalization, in itself, has set in motion forces which are creating a demand for labour mobility across borders and are, at the same time, developing institutions on the supply side to meet this demand. The basic reason is simple. The factors which make it easier to move goods, services, capital, technology, and information across borders, but for explicit immigration laws and implicit consular practices that are barriers to entry, also make it easier to move people across borders. Earlier, I made a distinction between five categories of labour flows across national boundaries. It would seem that the process of globalization is going to increase labour mobility in three categories. The professionals, at the top of the ladder of skills, will be almost as mobile as capital. Indeed, we can think of them as globalized people who are employable almost anywhere in the world. Similarly, where it is not feasible to import goods or export capital as a substitute for labour imports, or is less profitable, the use of guest workers, who move across borders on a temporary basis for a specified purpose and a limited duration, is bound to increase. And, despite the political reality of immigration laws, the market-driven conditions and institutions being created by globalization, will sustain, perhaps even increase, illegal immigration and the associated cross-border labour flows.

The process of globalization may, thus, influence cross-border movements of people in the world economy. But the prospects for labour flows in the first quarter of the twenty-first century are also bound to be shaped by demographic change and population imbalances. It is expected that, between 2000 and 2025, the population of

---

[46] See Bhagwati and Rao (1996).

industrialized countries will remain almost unchanged at about 1.25 billion while the population of developing countries will increase from 4 to 7.5 billion. But that is not all. The zero population growth in the industrialized world, combined with increased life expectancy, is expected to lead to a rapid ageing of the population in these countries. Consequently, dependency ratios (the proportion of the population aged 65 years or more) are projected to rise sharply from about one-fifth to more than one-third.[47] This means that a shrinking working population, made up of producers and earners, would have to support an expanding elderly population, made up of consumers and pensioners. Notwithstanding technical progress, labour shortages are inevitable. This, in itself, will create a demand for immigrants. The ageing of industrial societies, however, will also generate a demand for labour imports to provide services, such as health care and home care, so as to maintain the quality of life among the aged or the elderly in the population. Such service providers, whether permanent emigrants, guest workers or illegal immigrants, would have to come from the developing world. Therefore, even if globalization creates more employment and better living conditions in surplus labour countries, the demographic factor may accentuate both emigration pressures and immigration needs to shape labour flows in the future.

In sum, it would be reasonable to infer that there is a potential conflict between the laws of nations that restrict the movement of people across borders and the economics of globalization that induces the movement of people across borders. And, within limits, markets are adept at circumventing regulations. As we enter the twenty-first century, this process may be reinforced by demographic change. The ageing of the population in the industrialized countries, which is a consequence of increased life expectancy and zero population growth, carries an enormous potential for reviving labour flows across national boundaries. If such movements of labour become an economic necessity, it could even lead to selective relaxation of immigration laws and consular practices. History, probably, will not repeat itself. But it would be wise to learn from history.

---

[47] Simulations of population scenarios suggest that large scale labour imports, much greater than immigrant inflows in the recent past, would be required to compensate entirely for the impact of the ageing process on the working population in OECD countries. There are some projections of old-age-dependency ratios (ODR), defined as the ratio of persons aged 65 years or more to persons in the age group 15–64 years and expressed as a percentage, in OECD countries for 2010 and 2020, based on the medium-variant projections in United Nations, *World Population Prospects, 1996*. These show that the ODR would register a significant increase, everywhere, between 2010 and 2020. It is possible to estimate the number of additional persons of working age required for the ODR in 2020 to remain unchanged at the 2010 level. Such a calculation shows that, in the United States, an additional 66 million people of working age would be required in 2020 for the ODR to remain unchanged at its 2010 level. This number is 11.5 times the actual net migration of 5.8 million people into the United States during the ten year period from 1985 to 1995. The striking conclusion is that, even if migration were used only to increase the working age population, the immigration needed to keep the ODR unchanged between 2010 and 2020 would be several times the immigration levels in the recent past. This multiple works out at 17.4 for France, 10.6 for the United Kingdom, 7.9 for Italy and so on. For Japan, it is estimated that an additional 22 million people of working age would be required in 2020, for the ODR to remain at its 2010 level, compared with a net migration that was negative during the period from 1985 to 1995! The projections and estimates cited in this note are obtained from OECD (1998: 29).

6. ISSUES, PROBLEMS, AND GOVERNANCE

There are hardly any international rules or international institutions that govern cross-border movements of people. The solitary exception, perhaps, is the UNHCR. Its statutes, which were adopted by the General Assembly of the United Nations in 1950, provided for the protection of refugees. These also set out criteria for voluntary repatriation, local settlement in the country of asylum and resettlement in third countries. Repatriation, settlement, and resettlement were thought of as durable solutions that the international community should pursue. This institutional framework has evolved with the passage of time in response to changes in the nature and the dimensions of the refugee problem. The original object was to provide relief and resettlement. Relief provided a temporary safe haven for refugees, while resettlement meant a recognition that those who had fled from their homes were unlikely to return. The end of the cold war and the geographical spread of the refugee problem have led to emphasis on an old object and the introduction of a new object. The former seeks to encourage voluntary repatriation after conflicts end through economic assistance for reconstruction and development. The latter seeks to address the root causes of the problem in an endeavour to prevent such occurrences. The refugee problem, of course, is a subject in itself, which is beyond the scope of this chapter.[48] For the cross-border movement of people other than refugees, however, there are no international institutions or rules, let alone governance. Such cross-border movements are governed entirely by national immigration laws and consular practices.

In this context, the fundamental question arises from the asymmetry between the free movement of capital and the unfree movement of labour across national boundaries. In the contemporary world economy, economic openness is not simply confined to trade flows, investment flows, and financial flows. It also extends to flows of services, technology, information, and ideas across borders. But the cross-border movement of people is closely regulated and highly restricted. A perfect symmetry between labour and capital may not be a plausible idea in the context of political reality. In the abstract world of orthodox economic theory, however, the symmetry between labour and capital, as factors of production, is only logical. After all, international labour movements create efficiency gains in a neoclassical sense, as much as international capital movements, when workers move to where they are more productive. In this mode, the case for unrestricted labour mobility is as compelling as the case for unrestricted capital mobility or the case for free trade. It would contribute as much to optimizing resource allocation and maximizing economic welfare for the world as a whole. Yet, this is not part of conventional wisdom. Economic theory, it would seem, is also shaped by political reality.

Nevertheless, it is plausible to suggest that if there is almost complete freedom of capital mobility across national boundaries, the draconian restrictions on labour mobility across national boundaries should at least be reduced, if not eliminated.

---

[48] There is an extensive literature on the refugee problem. See, for example, Widgren (1993). See also Bohning and Schloeter-Paredes (1994).

Similarly, it is reasonable to argue that any provision for commercial presence of corporate entities (capital) should correspond to provisions for temporary migration of workers (labour), just as the right-of-establishment for corporate entities (capital) has an analogue in the right-of-residence for persons (labour).[49] Indeed, if such a perspective is carried to its logical conclusion, the movement of labour across borders must be just as free as the movement of capital. It is not surprising that the two views on this matter are polar opposites.[50] On the one hand, there is a rights-based argument that the freedom of movement within countries is a basic human right and there is no reason why it should not extend across countries. What is more, in so far as the citizenship of industrialized countries is the modern equivalent of feudal privilege, such freedom of movement would reduce international economic inequalities.[51] On the other hand, there is a community-based argument that nations have a right to self-determination in terms of social cohesion and cultural solidarity. What is more, unrestricted immigration is bound to have serious economic and social implications for citizens. It is worth noting that the United Nations Charter incorporates both perspectives. For one, it accepts the human right of freedom of movement as a universal principle. For another, it recognizes that sovereign states have a right of self-determination. There is clearly an inherent tension between these perspectives, which can readily turn into a contradiction.

Irrespective of how any person chooses between these two extreme positions, the political reality is clear. A significant relaxation of immigration laws is simply not in the realm of the feasible. An international acceptance of universal moral obligations is perhaps out of the question. At least for the present. There is, of course, a strong concern about mounting pressures for international migration, which surface almost everywhere. National interests and liberal concerns appear to coincide in the response that has gathered momentum as an idea in recent times. The prescription is to, somehow, reduce emigration pressures.[52] In the economic sphere, it is believed that economic development which improves the material living conditions of people in poor countries would dampen the pressures for voluntary migration that is motivated by economic factors. Development assistance from rich to the poor countries is meant to facilitate this process. In the political sphere, it is believed that the spread of political democracy which protects the human rights of people in poor countries with authoritarian regimes would dampen the surge of distress migration that is driven by political repression or social exclusion. Humanitarian assistance from rich to poor countries, which seeks to assist in rehabilitation and reconstruction, is meant to facilitate this process. These are statements of good intentions, which are sometimes long on words and short on substance. And there is often a mismatch between what is said and what is done. Even without such problems, it must be recognized that the reach of economic development and the spread of political democracy require much more than development assistance or humanitarian assistance. Thus, such endeavours, which are most desirable, may or may not reduce pressures for labour exports, for even

---

[49] This argument is developed, at some length, in Nayyar (1989).   [50] Cf. Lee (1998).
[51] See Carens (1996).   [52] This is the central theme in Bohning and Schloeter-Paredes (1994).

if the need to migrate decreases the ability to migrate increases. What is more, this cannot reduce the emerging needs for labour imports in the rich industrialized countries or even in the middle-income industrializing countries.

International migration is a reality. It cannot be wished away. Thus, the almost complete absence of international institutions, or rules, that govern the cross-border movement of people is a cause for concern. And it is essential to reflect upon this need which has grown with the passage of time. As we enter the twenty-first century, it is necessary to highlight two dimensions of governance needs in this sphere. First, we have to think of the actual migrants so as to ensure rights and to eliminate abuse in their countries of residence after they have moved. Second, we have to think of the potential migrants before they have moved so that the cross-border movement of people is governed at least in part by transparent and uniform multilateral rules rather than by diverse national laws and non-transparent consular practices alone. Consider each of these in turn.

Among the actual migrants, it is necessary to make a distinction between legal immigrants and illegal immigrants. There are some similarities in the problems faced by them. But there are also important differences. For the former, the essential objective should be to ensure a respect for their rights. For the latter, the fundamental objective should be to eliminate exploitation and abuse. Thus, the institutional solutions would need to be somewhat different.

There are some genuine causes for concern even about the working and living conditions of legal migrants.[53] In the industrialized countries, the problems of immigrant workers are accentuated by: (i) high levels of unemployment among unskilled workers; (ii) flexibility in labour markets with much weaker trade unions; and (iii) reforms in social security systems associated with the retreat of the welfare state. Even without xenophobic attitudes, which are beginning to surface in many countries, each of these developments has a more pronounced effect on migrants than on nationals. In the high-income or middle-income developing countries, which import labour, the problems of immigrant workers are much more acute and are exacerbated by: (i) the distinctly inferior status of contract workers who have no legal claim to permanent settlement, let alone citizenship; (ii) rudimentary or minimal systems of social protection; and (iii) the near absence of trade union movements or mandated labour standards. It is not surprising that the living conditions of immigrant workers in developing countries are discernibly worse, while their rights are much weaker, than in the industrialized countries. What needs to be done is clear. First, there must be social protection for migrants which is on a par with that for nationals. Second, there must be a discipline on employers who exploit migrant workers in terms of wages paid or hours worked. Third, everything must be done to combat the physical and sexual abuse of migrants, particularly women migrant workers. In other words, there must be some equivalent of the concept of 'national treatment' for migrant workers who have been admitted to their countries of destination in accordance with the laws of the land. The importance of such 'national treatment' cannot be stressed enough. In this context, it is

---

[53] For a more detailed discussion, see Lee (1998). See also Amjad (1996).

essential to draw attention to a striking asymmetry. There is so much emphasis on labour standards, which are sought to be lodged in the WTO. There is so little concern about rights of migrant workers, which are written into obscure ILO conventions that have been ratified mostly by labour-exporting countries rather than by labour-importing countries. Yet, it should be clear that labour standards and migrants' rights are two sides of the same coin. The former is the focus of attention because labour standards are to be imposed mostly on poor countries, while the latter is the object of neglect because migrants' rights are to be implemented in large part by rich countries. There is an obvious need to redress the balance. The rights of migrant workers can only be protected through an understanding between, and a commitment on the part of, sovereign nation states. This, in turn, requires a universal acceptance and ratification of ILO conventions on migrant workers.[54] The issue of labour standards, of course, is simply not in the domain of the WTO and should remain in the ILO where the rights of workers are a fundamental concern.

The labour flows associated with illegal migration, attributable to market forces despite immigration laws, are also a reality.[55] And it is possible that such labour flows may increase in the future. Yet, the plight of illegal immigrants, everywhere, is a cause for serious concern. The working conditions are exploitative, the living conditions are abysmal, the risk of capture and repatriation is ever present, and the stranglehold of international criminal syndicates is common enough. This is not simply a matter of enforcing the law. In many countries, which experience labour shortages in selected occupations, sectors, or activities, intermediaries who act in collusion with employers are responsible for the illegal immigration while governments turn a blind eye to this reality. This neglect is not without purpose. For one thing, it means that labour shortages can be met without relaxing immigration laws and providing such workers with a legal right of residence. For another, governments have no obligation to provide social security for such illegal immigrant workers. There is a clear need for transparency rather than ambivalence in the attitude of governments towards illegal immigrants. Such tacit approval of illegal migration to meet labour shortages must be replaced by an explicit recognition of the need for labour imports, which should be met through legal channels even if such imports are seasonal or temporary. At the same time, there is a clear need for concerted action to curb the trafficking in people that is organized by international criminal and smuggling syndicates. In the hope of reaching new havens, migrants often provide such syndicates with large sums of money. They are passed down a chain of agents, smugglers, ships, safe houses, and corrupt officials. There are risks at most points in transit. Sometimes, however, the aspiring migrants are simply abandoned in transit to fend for themselves in countries where they do not speak the language, without money or passports, to end up in prison and await

---

[54] In this context, it is worth noting that the International Convention on the Protection of the Rights of All Migrants and Their Families, which was formulated with the technical assistance of the ILO and adopted by the United Nations General Assembly in 1990, has so far been ratified by less than ten countries all of which are labour-exporting economies.

[55] For a discussion on the causes and consequences of what is described as undocumented migration, see UN (1998).

repatriation. Such trafficking in people is a gross violation of human rights. It is a telling example of international 'public bads' which need to be regulated through concerted joint action by labour-exporting and labour-importing countries both at a regional level and at the global level. In this task, there is a critical institutional role for the ILO.

For the potential migrants, it is necessary to develop institutions, or rules, that govern the cross-border movement of guest workers, who move temporarily for a limited duration, as also professionals or service providers who move temporarily for a specified purpose. Labour flows in these categories have increased significantly during the last quarter of the twentieth century and are likely to increase further during the first quarter of the twenty-first century. Thus, it has become necessary to develop some rules or institutions that would govern such flows. The temporary migration associated with guest workers is market driven. It is often based on an *ad hoc* relaxation of, or accommodation in, immigration laws. It is, inevitably, a unilateral act on the part of labour-importing countries, as and when the need arises, influenced by employers or firms interested in importing such workers on a temporary or seasonal basis. For professionals, as we have seen, there are almost no barriers to entry. But for other service providers, who do not have the high skills or the professional qualifi- cations, the cross-border movement of people is largely subject to discretionary regimes. It is not an integral part of the multilateral framework of the General Agreement on Trade in Services. It is often based on an *ad hoc* modification of consular practices to grant visas more easily, say, for 'body-shopping'. Once again, it is a uni- lateral act on the part of labour-importing countries, in response to pressures from employers without any commitment to, or assurance of continuation. It is, therefore, important to develop a set of transparent and uniform rules for the temporary movement of guest workers or service providers across national boundaries. In doing so, the equivalent of the 'most-favoured-nation principle', which makes for uncon- ditional non-discrimination, could provide a basic foundation.

The preceding discussion suggests that the issues and problems associated with labour flows across borders cannot be addressed by single countries acting in isolation or on an unilateral basis. There is a clear need for a dialogue between countries where there are outflows or inflows of labour from or to each other. The dialogue could begin on a bilateral or plurilateral basis, for labour flows are unevenly distributed in geo- graphical space and are shaped by links between countries of origin and destination. But it should extend to the regional level, where such labour flows are essentially intra- regional, as also to the global level, for a significant proportion of labour flows are inter- regional. It should, perhaps, begin with an exchange of information on surpluses and shortages between labour-exporting and labour-importing countries, which might ultimately provide the basis for the creation of an International Labour Exchange. It should seek to develop a coordination of policies among labour-exporting countries. It should endeavour to create some harmonization of policies among labour-importing countries. It should work towards a regime of discipline to be imposed on intermedi- aries. It should build a system for the regulation of international 'public bads'.

The fundamental objective of such a dialogue, which would be a preparatory process, should be to work towards a new institutional framework that would govern labour flows across national boundaries. At one level, this means rules for those who are already migrants, possibly through a strengthening of ILO conventions on the rights of migrants, with some provision for national obligations to create enforcement mechanisms. At another level, this means a transparent and uniform system, based on rules rather than discretion, for those who may wish to move across borders. To begin with, regional arrangements such as the EU, which build on other forms of economic integration, could yield feasible solutions. But regional arrangements are difficult to replicate and do not always constitute building blocks. Sooner rather than later, therefore, it is worth contemplating a multilateral framework for immigration laws and consular practices that govern the cross-border movement of people, similar to multilateral frameworks that exist, or are sought to be created, for the governance of national laws, or rules, about the movement of goods, services, technology, investment, finance, and information across national boundaries. This may seem somewhat far fetched at present and perhaps not in the realm of the feasible. But it is no more implausible than the thought of a general agreement on trade in services, an international regime of discipline for the protection of intellectual property rights, or a multilateral agreement on investment would have appeared a quarter of a century ago. Indeed, suggesting international rules or an international institution, say a world financial authority, to regulate or govern international financial flows would have sounded just as implausible even a decade ago.

REFERENCES

Abella, Manolo (1994). International migration in the Middle East: Patterns and implications for sending countries. In *International Migration: Regional Processes and Responses*. UN Economic Commission for Europe, Geneva.

Amjad, Rashid (1989). *To the Gulf and Back: Studies on the Economic Impact of Asian Labour Migration*. ILO-ARTEP, New Delhi.

——(1996). International labour migration and its implications in the APEC Region. *Journal of Philippine Development*, 23, 45–78.

Berry, R. A. and R. Soligo (1969). Some welfare effects of international migration. *Journal of Political Economy*, 77, 778–94.

Bhagwati, Jagdish (ed.) (1976). *The Brain Drain and Taxation: Theory and Empirical Analysis*. North Holland, Amsterdam.

——and M. Rao (1996). The US brain gain: At the expense of Blacks? *Challenge*, 39(2), 50–4.

Bohning, W. R. and M. L. Schloeter-Paredes (eds) (1994). *Aid in Place of Migration?* International Labour Office, Geneva.

Carens, Joseph H. (1996). Aliens and citizens: The case for open borders. In R. Cohen (ed.), *Theories of Migration*. Edward Elgar, Cheltenham.

Goldin, Claudia (1994). The political economy of immigration restriction in the United States, 1890 to 1921. In C. Goldin and G. Libecap (eds), *The Regulated Economy: A Historical Approach to Political Economy*. University of Chicago Press, Chicago.

Krugman, Paul and Jagdish Bhagwati (1976). The decision to migrate: A survey. In J. Bhagwati (ed.), *The Brain Drain and Taxation: Theory and Empirical Analysis*. North Holland, Amsterdam.

Kuznets, Simon (1966). *Modern Economic Growth: Rate, Structure and Spread*. Yale University Press, New Haven.

Lee, Eddy (1998). The migrant in an era of globalization. Paper presented at the World Congress on the Pastoral Care of Migrants and Refugees, 5–10 October. Vatican City. Mimeo.

Lewis, William A. (1977). *The Evolution of the International Economic Order*. Princeton University Press, Princeton.

——(1978). *Growth and Fluctuations: 1870–1913*. Allen and Unwin, London.

Massey, Douglas (1988). Economic development and international migration in comparative perspective. *Population and Development Review*, 14(2).

Nayyar, Deepak (1988). The political economy of international trade in services. *Cambridge Journal of Economics*, 12(2), 279–98.

——(1989). Towards a possible multilateral framework for trade in services: Some issues and concepts. In *Technology, Trade Policy and the Uruguay Round*. United Nations, New York.

——(1994). *Migration, Remittances and Capital Flows*. Oxford University Press, Delhi.

——(1994*a*). International labour movements, trade flows and migration transitions: A theoretical perspective. *Asian and Pacific Migration Journal*, 3, 31–47.

——(1995). Globalization: The past in our present. *Indian Economic Journal*, 43(3), 1–18.

——(1996). Free trade: Why, when and for whom? *Banca Nazionale del Lavoro Quarterly Review*, 49(198), 333–50.

——(1997). Themes in trade and industrialization. In D. Nayyar (ed.), *Trade and Industrialization*. Oxford University Press, New Delhi.

——(2000). Globalization and development strategies. *High-Level Roundtable on Trade and Development at UNCTAD X*. TD X/RT.1/4. United Nations, New York and Geneva.

OECD (1997). *SOPEMI: International Migration Statistics*, 1997 edition (available on diskette) OECD, Paris.

——(1998). *SOPEMI: Trends in International Migration: Continuous Reporting System on Migration, Annual Report 1998*. OECD, Paris.

Paine, Suzanne (1974). *Exporting Workers: The Turkish Case*. Cambridge University Press, Cambridge.

Piore, Michael J. (1979). *Birds of Passage: Migrant Labor in Industrial Societies*. Cambridge University Press, Cambridge.

Sachs, Jeffrey and Andrew Warner (1995). Economic reform and the process of global integration. *Brookings Papers on Economic Activity*, 1, 1–118.

Sen, Amartya K. (1973). Brain drain: Causes and effects. In B. R. Williams (ed.), *Science and Technology in Economic Growth*. Macmillan, London.

Stalker, Peter (1994). *The Work of Strangers: A Survey of International Labour Migration*. ILO, Geneva.

Stark, Oded (1991). *The Migration of Labor*. Basil Blackwell, Oxford.

Streeten, Paul P. (1996). Governance of the global economy. Paper presented at a conference on Globalization and Citizenship, 9–11 December. UNRISD, Geneva. Mimeo.

Timmer, Ashley S. and Jeffrey S. Williamson (1998). Immigration policy prior to the 1930s: Labor markets, policy interaction and globalization backlash. *Population and Development Review*, 24(4), 739–71.

Tinker, Hugh (1974). *A New System of Slavery: The Export of Indian Labor Overseas: 1830–1920*. Oxford University Press, Oxford.

UNCTAD (1975). *The Reverse Transfer of Technology: Economic Effects of the Outflow of Trained Personnel from Developing Countries*. United Nations, New York and Geneva.

——(1994). *World Investment Report 1994*. United Nations, New York and Geneva.

——(1997). *Trade and Development Report 1997*. United Nations, New York and Geneva.

——(1998). *World Investment Report 1998: Trends and Determinants*. United Nations, New York and Geneva.

UNDP (1999). *Human Development Report 1999*. Oxford University Press, New York.

United Nations (1998). *International Migration Policies*. UN, New York.

Widgren, Jonas (1993). Movements of refugees and asylum seekers. In *The Changing Course of International Migration*. OECD, Paris.

Wood, Adrian (1994). *North-South Trade, Employment, and Inequality*. Clarendon Press, Oxford.

World Bank (1995). *World Development Report 1995: Workers in an Integrating World*. Oxford University Press, New York.

PART III

INSTITUTIONS

7

The United Nations System: Prospects for Renewal

RICHARD FALK

The undertaking of this chapter is to consider the record of the United Nations system since its inception, with an eye focused on prospects for renewal and reform at the present time. The main criteria relied upon for assessment are considerations of effectiveness and legitimacy in relation to the operations of the United Nations (UN).

The chapter begins with a discussion of why the present global setting is resistant to renewal and reform, but with the qualification that such a climate of resistance could change rapidly. And that over time, the sheer complexity of international life and the salience of global scale problems is likely to exert pressures to strengthen the UN.

From matters of context, the chapter moves on to discuss the historical origins of the UN, and the extent to which the experiences with global security prior to 1945 shaped the character of the UN in relation to the all-important peace and security agenda. This look backwards is then followed by an analysis of the evolution of the Organization, especially in relation to the two most influential contextual factors, namely, the decolonization process and the cold war. In these regards, the UN system as a whole has over the years emerged as a site of struggle in relation to both the East–West conflict, largely superseded since 1989, and the still persisting North–South encounter. The chapter also considers the creative role played by the UN with respect to arranging conferences on global challenges on a range of issues including the environment, women, population, and human rights. These conferences were not only important substantively, but they gave considerable access to transnational social forces as represented by non-governmental organizations.

The chapter concludes with sections devoted to prospects for enhancing UN effectiveness and legitimacy. In this regard, emphasis is placed on geopolitical factors as creating the most difficult obstacle to reform. Also, several concrete proposals for reform are sketched to provide examples of practical, non-Utopian steps that would both strengthen the UN and serve the cause of human well-being. At the same time, to underscore the dysfunction of geopolitical influences, it is made clear that the short-term prospects for achieving needed and desirable reforms are rather grim. It would seem that the UN will not be fundamentally reformable until the movement for global democracy gains far greater leverage than it presently possesses.

1. POINTS OF DEPARTURE

It needs to be acknowledged at the outset, for reasons to be explained later, that the global setting is not currently favourable to moves designed to strengthen most key activities of the UN system. Such an assessment is sharply at odds with the case for new roles and functions based on the changing world order agenda. It also reflects the missed opportunities of the historical situation to promote peace, justice, development, democracy, and sustainability provided by the ending of the cold war and the associated muting of strategic conflict among leading states. Such opportunities were also provided by the mood after the Gulf War in 1991 and again in 1995 on the occasion of the 50th anniversary of the UN. Somehow these moments of seeming opportunity for major UN reform and evolution came and went without a single notable achievement.

This pessimistic mood, as well, expresses the institutional frustration arising from the apparent inability in this period for UN members to reach any agreement on a formula for an expansion of the permanent membership of the Security Council. It is generally accepted by all shades of opinion that some Security Council expansion would be important, at least, to take account of the fundamental changes in the composition of international society since 1945, especially the far greater role being played by non-Western countries. The failure to make progress on this symbolic issue has tinged with doubt the whole project of UN reform.

But there are some additional factors that have also had a negative impact. The failure of the United States to meet its financial obligations in recent years has acted as a depressant throughout the UN system. Because the United States shoulders the biggest financial burden, being responsible as of now for 25 per cent of the budget, its non-payment produces considerable pressure throughout the UN system and puts the bureaucracy constantly on a crisis footing that distracts energies from its substantive duties. Furthermore, the recent American theme song of 'downsizing', while justified with respect to aspects of the UN, generally works against efforts to strengthen the Organization.

Even more to the point, the UN is judged by the public mainly in relation to peace and security issues, and although the criteria for assessment vary in different parts of the world, there is a general sense that the UN has not fared well in the 1990s. The UN performance in Bosnia and Rwanda were widely perceived as dismal failures, associated with inept and insufficient responses in the setting of genocidal behaviour. In light of these experiences, the bypassing of the UN Charter requirements of Security Council authorization in the launch of the NATO War over Kosovo in early 1999 reinforced the impression that the UN peace and security role was being eclipsed in dangerous ways that left the way open for unregulated geopolitical initiatives.

It should be appreciated that the UN does not deserve most of the blame for these developments. It was expected to address complex humanitarian emergencies without the necessary resources and guidelines to ensure successful outcomes. The membership of the Security Council often lacked sufficient political will to generate effective action in response to the challenges of the last decade, and irresponsibly designated the UN to take action. It needs to be remembered that the UN is essentially 'a club of sovereign states', with the Permanent Members of the Security Council being given a privileged status. As such, especially in the area of peacekeeping, it is an extension of the state system rather than an alternative to it. It also needs to be appreciated that aside from the Gulf War, the challenges directed at the UN derived from catastrophic circumstances *internal* to sovereign states. The status of these challenges was somewhat questionable constitutionally and logistically, given the understanding that the defining mandate of the UN was deliberately confined to *international* conflict situations.[1] In fact, the last three secretary-generals of the Organization have in various ways argued that the evolution of international human rights norms has eroded the domestic jurisdiction limitation. These leaders insisted that the UN was now available in the event of humanitarian catastrophes even if situated entirely within a state.

It would be a great mistake to confuse this present conjuncture of disappointments and setbacks with a more durable assessment of the prospects of the Organization for reform and adaptation. The climate of relevant opinion can change rapidly. The complexity of international life, combined with the reluctance of leading states to act where their national interests are not at risk, will create many occasions when the UN provides the only arena within which an acceptable pattern of response can be fashioned. Despite the disillusionment with the peacekeeping efforts of the 1990s, the major states continue to turn to the UN. This was again evident late in 1999. Emergency arrangements for East Timor and Sierra Leone were fashioned, although belatedly, in view of the human carnage, as responses to humanitarian catastrophes that had been experienced by each of these countries.

It is also a serious error, although commonly made, to reduce the actuality of the UN to its efforts in the realm of peace and security. True, this is the litmus test relied upon by the media and the public, particularly in the North, to assess whether the UN is working or not. A more adequate assessment would also consider the relevance of the UN to a spectrum of issues, including development, human rights, environment, health, labour, and global economic policy. Arguably, for most of the peoples in the world, who are located in the South, the role of the UN outside the area of peace and security is what makes the Organization affect their lives and improve life circumstances, as when UNICEF or UNDP are active and visible on the local scene. In contrast, for the countries of the North, their awareness of the UN role is largely confined to media reports relating to the peace and security agenda.

Overall, the UN has proved to be resilient. The complexity of international society, as well as multiple forms of interdependence, has established the Organization as indispensable for the practical implementation of many aspects of the global policy agenda. As well, the range of activities that proceed in the specialized agencies of the

---

[1] According to the UN Charter, Article 2(7), the Organization was prohibited from intervening in matters 'essentially within the domestic jurisdiction of states'. This was understood to mean civil strife and conditions of oppressive government. The only qualification of this principle was the caveat that such a restriction of UN authority 'shall not prejudice the application of enforcement measures under Chapter VII'.

UN perform a myriad of useful, even indispensable, information-gathering and law-making functions.[2]

Furthermore, it is quite likely that the currently obstructive approach of the United States will swing back in more internationalist and positive directions in the years ahead. Such a policy shift in Washington would alter the overall climate of opinion, being far more appreciative of the contributions of the UN and supportive of needed reforms, including selective support for institutional expansion to take better account of various global developments. The present phase of American foreign policy, characterized by President Clinton as newly 'isolationist', reflects a temporary conservative turn toward domestic politics, which may well be soon replaced by a new phase of internationalist engagement. Such an American readjustment would likely have many favourable ramifications for the future role of the UN system.

It is also important not to take due account of some long-term trends that have been evident in the course of the UN experience that now stretches over more than five decades. The UN survived the fissures of both the cold war and the turbulent dynamics of decolonization without producing any significant withdrawal from participation. Such a record is in contrast to the experience of the League of Nations. Several important countries never participated and others withdrew in disgust. The UN has achieved near universality of membership that now extends to about 99 per cent of the people living on the planet. Its solid footing in world politics is almost beyond question at this point.

Despite ups and downs in perception and performance, the UN is here to stay. The increasingly global scope and complexity of policy issues, as well as the diminished territoriality of economic relationships, suggest a potentiality for expanding governance roles for the UN. At the same time, difficulties, as noted, are apparent. At their core is a concern as to whether the richer, more powerful, countries of the North will be wise and generous enough to allow the UN to act on behalf of all the peoples of the world in a manner that is both effective and legitimate. At issue is the extent of willingness to endow the UN with the capabilities to uphold the global public goods of the planet as a whole, and to serve as an agent for the promotion of human development.[3]

2. THE ORIGINAL DESIGN

The mixture of global circumstances and short-term historical memory conditioned the original conception of the UN. In 1945, the Second World War had ended and the Atlantic Alliance of victorious powers was intent on preserving the peace in the world ahead. The UN was formed predominantly to avoid the recurrence of a major war, but there was a tension at the outset between sceptics and true believers. The sceptics doubted that the wartime alliance would hold or that collective security would work.

---

[2] For useful introductory overviews of the UN system, see Ziring *et al.* (2000); Mingst and Karns (1995). Also Alagappa and Inoguchi (1999) for a wide ranging interpretation of the UN's role in a changing global setting.

[3] See Haq (1995); see also the annual volumes since 1991 containing the *Human Development Report* of UNDP, published under the imprint of Oxford University Press.

They were convinced that only countervailing power organized to deter potential adversaries could increase the chances for the avoidance of major warfare in the future. The so-called 'lessons of Munich' were uppermost in their minds, that appeasement and disarmament do not bring peace, but on the contrary, nurture an appetite for aggression.

The true believers in the UN idea take a longer view of history. They thought that any reversion to balance of power geopolitics would culminate in World War III, which would be catastrophic in the nuclear age. For them the only path to peace and stability was by way of a strong UN. They hoped that the UN would gradually induce the leading sovereign states to disarm by stages, building up in the process an independent enforcement capability within the UN, and producing over time a world order premised on respect for the Rule of Law. Such a maximalist view of the UN rested on the belief that the peaceful evolution of international society depended on establishing some form of limited world government that would eliminate war as a social institution.[4]

The war/peace preoccupation surrounding the establishment of the UN needs to be understood in relation to several additional formative factors. To begin with, the Westphalian idea of a world of sovereign, territorially based, states as the sole significant political actor on the global stage was so widely accepted as to be presupposed. At the same time, there was an appreciation, especially by the victorious powers in the Second World War, that the prospects for collective security depended on sustaining their wartime alliance against the defeated Axis powers. It was this geopolitical argument that was translated into a constitutional arrangement by establishing a Security Council with five permanent members, each given a veto power over substantive decisions. Here was the central gamble with respect to the UN role on the essential goal of keeping world peace: if the P-5 could agree, there was no further obstacle to creating within the framework of the UN an effective response, and the institutional skeleton for doing so was set forth in Chapter VII of the Charter; contrariwise, in the face of disagreement between the five permanent members, the Organization encoded its inability to act at all in response to a world crisis, however serious.

This submission to geopolitical realism has persisted throughout the entire lifetime of the UN. It raises two sorts of questions: first, are the geopolitical premises of 1945 still valid in 2000? If not, should there be changes made in the character of permanent membership to reflect shifts in power relations? So far, to the extent that shifts have been seriously contemplated at all by leading members, they have been in the direction of expanding the P-5 to P-7 or even P-11, but not of substituting, say, India for Britain or Japan for France. Nor have serious proposals been made to consider 'Europe' as a consolidated representative that would break the statist monopoly over formal participation and membership, or, more radically, to create a permanent rotating seat for economically disadvantaged states or for a roster of the ten governments with the best human rights records.

---

[4] See proposals to convert the UN into a form of limited world government in Clark and Sohn (1966); for general theoretical inquiry see Murphy (1999).

The second more fundamental question is the whole idea of conditioning UN response on a geopolitical consensus. Such a notion takes account of the concentration of military power and diplomatic leverage in the hands of several predominant states. By so doing, it contradicts the premise of a law-governed world community, and tends to invite selective enforcement of the UN Charter. This raises serious questions about *legitimacy* as well as *effectiveness*, issues that have dogged the Organization since its inception.

Moving in a quite opposite direction was the lower profile agenda of the UN as reflected in the wider ambit of the UN system. It was recognized that the *complexity* and *interrelatedness* of international life meant that the Organization needed to coordinate policy and dissemination of information across a broad range of specialized concerns: food, children, culture, labour, health, communications, monetary stability, and developmental finance. This set of functional undertakings has been in the form of a large number of specialized agencies and programmes that together comprise the UN system. Their activities have been almost always backgrounded in relation to the overall work of the UN, and are knowledgeably perceived by only a handful of specialists. On occasion, in the face of a political encounter, this or that specialized agency or substantive programme becomes controversial. The role of the IMF/World Bank is difficult to categorize in these respects. These Bretton Woods agencies are technically part of the UN functional landscape, but operationally and psychologically they operate autonomously, outside the UN system, with influence concentrated in a few governments representing the world's richest states.

Leaving aside the Bretton Woods dimension, it is widely agreed that these functional activities of the UN have contributed greatly, although unevenly, to the governance of human affairs over the course of the last century. Over the years, as the global agenda shifts and policy priorities change, innovations have been made, adding and adapting programmes, commissions, and institutional arenas. Especially prominent have been a variety of important initiatives associated with the developmental priorities of the countries of the South, as well as the establishment of UNEP in recognition of a global environmental dimension and the steady expansion of human rights activities in response to rising interest and support for a global approach to their implementation. Within these functional settings of the UN system much more of a spirit of technical cooperation prevails. There is far less allowance made for a privileged status for leading states, partly because fundamental questions of sovereign rights and ideological identity are not often at stake. At the same time, especially when East/West and North/South tensions became acute, these agencies and activities could come under sharp attack from one or another perspective because their functional objectivity was allegedly being subordinated to partisan concerns. For instance, the United States withdrew from UNESCO almost 20 years ago, and remains unrepresented.

As a preliminary assessment, it can be concluded that the central UN mission to provide peace and security for countries confronting aggression, has had a generally disappointing history. The geopolitical consensus that existed in 1945 was soon replaced by the gridlock of the cold war. When the UN was able to act at all, it was either a matter of fortuitous circumstance (as in the Korean War) or exceptional geopolitical conditions of superpower convergence (as in the Suez Campaign of 1956). Otherwise, the UN role was either to provide a kind of geopolitical cover (as in the Gulf War) or to act in a neutral peacekeeping role based on consent of adversary parties (the essential innovation of Dag Hammarskjöld). In neither setting, did the UN demonstrate the political will or capability to protect potential and actual victims of aggression, and in this central respect did not overcome the self-help character of global security based on the military might of particular states as augmented by alliance relationships.

The UN peace and security role should then be understood as *facilitative* of traditional diplomacy, but in no way *superseding* a statist form of world order. As such, the promise of the Charter has not been fulfilled in practice, and the decade since the end of the cold war confirms that the resistance to collective security is deeper than had been widely supposed, namely, as merely a reflection of strategic conflict and ideological antagonism. Unlike in relation to world trade arrangements, or in the setting of European regionalism, the member states of the UN have not been prepared to transfer sovereign authority and capabilities to the Security Council with respect to matters of peace and security. Leading states, the geopolitical actors, obviously prefer to rely upon traditional methods of unilateral action or by way of a coalition of the like-minded. The UN Security Council has been invoked on occasion to legitimize or even to disguise recourse to war in the event that a consensus exists among the P-5, as occurred to some extent during the Gulf Crisis of 1990–91. But if such legitimation is not forthcoming or might be seen as an impediment to effective action, then the UN is evaded as occurred during superpower actions in the cold war (e.g. Vietnam, Afghanistan) or subsequently, as in the war waged by NATO early in 1999 against former Yugoslavia in relation to the fate of Kosovo.

With respect to the functional side of UN activities, the overall picture is much more favourable. The UN has fulfilled, or in some cases exceeded, what seemed to be expectations in 1945. The budgets of specialized agencies and commissions have risen over the years, and the work being done has been generally respected and useful, although some of it has been controversial. The functional dimension of the UN system has demonstrated an impressive capacity to provide niches for new undertakings within the existing framework (as with providing a forum for indigenous peoples) or to establish entirely new institutional arenas (as with UNEP and UNDP). Of course, there are complicating features that qualify enthusiasm for the functional work of the UN. Some agencies declined in prestige due to changes in the social structure, such as the ILO. Others became embroiled in one way or another, often arbitrarily, in a variety of reformist or backlash reactions associated with dogmatic neoliberalism, as was the case with respect to UNESCO and to some extent the ILO. More could certainly have been usefully done by the UN in relation to this functional agenda, but overall the functional side of the UN system seems to be well-established on a basis that does not disappoint UN supporters or greatly antagonize UN critics. Such a generalization needs to be qualified to take account of the general downsizing mandate of the last several years of budgetary austerity, which itself may reflect some wider tendencies associated with downward pressures on expenditures on public goods, particularly on global public goods.[5] This latter development seems connected with the drift in all areas of finance in the direction of privatization, a reflection of the view that market discipline is more efficient than bureaucratic management of a public sector character.

3. THE RELEVANCE OF THE GLOBAL SETTING

The history of the UN is very much entwined with two fissures in international society that has preoccupied the political imagination for more than fifty years. The first of these fissures was the East/West divide that spiralled out of the unresolved aftermath of the Second World War. It assumed the character of a war-threatening rivalry that affected all regions of the world and made plausible the possibility of an apocalyptic world war fought with nuclear weaponry. The second fissure was the North/South divide that came to the fore as a sequel to decolonization. These two conflict configurations were overlapped at many points, including the efforts of both superpowers to find as many ideological friends as possible among the newly independent countries in the South. These efforts gave governments leverage to obtain foreign economic assistance. But the superpower rivalry also produced ghastly competitive interventions that resulted in prolonged warfare, especially in relation to divided countries such as Vietnam and Korea, but also in borderland areas such as Afghanistan.

The UN was one arena in which these two defining struggles were waged, but in differing modes, with confusing and variable effects. The East/West rivalry was most evident in its tendency to paralyse the Security Council in relation to issues of peace and security. At times, this stalemate was broken. At the start of the Korean War in 1950, the Soviet Union was boycotting the Security Council. With an irony that became evident only after the Sino/Soviet break years later, Moscow was absent to protest the refusal of the Security Council to acknowledge the outcome of the Chinese Revolution by allowing the most populous country to be represented by Beijing. As a result of the Soviet absence, the UN Security Council was not paralysed by the veto, and was able to authorize an American-led UN response to the North Korean invasion of South Korea. The Soviet Union never again made such an institutional mistake, and was thus able to block subsequent Security Council action with which it disagreed.

On a few other occasions, the superpowers were in agreement, usually for differing reasons. In 1956 they both opposed in the Security Council the attack on Egypt by the combined military forces of Israel, France, and Britain, and successfully induced these countries to withdraw from occupied Egyptian territory. There was also a much contested effort to cooperate in the newly independent Belgian Congo (later Zaire) in 1960 to prevent civil war and secession, but the end result was to bring the East/West struggle to the fore with contradictory views about what should have been the UN mission. And again in the early 1980s, both superpowers encouraged a non-response by the Security Council to Iraq's invasion of Iran because both welcomed the efforts to

[5] See Kaul *et al.* (1999).

weaken, if not destroy, the Islamic Republic that Iran had become since the Shah's overthrow in 1979. Finally, during the Gorbachev period of leadership, the Soviet Union adopted a cooperative attitude that enabled the UN to play an important facilitative diplomatic role in bringing to an end violent regional conflicts in the Iran/Iraq War, Afghanistan, El Salvador, Angola, and elsewhere.

What seems clear is that the East/West conflict pervaded all aspects of UN activity during the cold war years. It was particularly evident whenever global security issues were raised, and in relation to the activities of the Security Council. The ideologically grounded gridlock was widely accepted as the explanation for the relative ineffectiveness of the UN with respect to peace and security questions. In actuality, the cold war tensions affected all aspects of the work of the UN, requiring compromises to be reached so as to permit activity of any sort. From the outset, the Soviet side adopted a defensive posture, recognizing that it was outnumbered if issues were resolved on a straight majority basis. At one point in the 1960s, Nikita Khrushchev proposed a troika arrangement for UN governance, including the creation of three secretary-generals to represent the differing perspectives of the East, the West, and the Non-Aligned Movement. Such an initiative was angrily rebuffed by the West, and led nowhere. Similarly, the Western-led effort in the same period to deprive the Soviet Union of its vote in the General Assembly due to its refusal to pay for peacekeeping operations that it opposed was eventually abandoned as futile. The Organization lived with the cold war after these failed efforts to exert control; limping along, but managing to remain useful, at least as a talking shop, in relation to its less visible humanitarian activities, and as support for the priorities of the South.

Of course, by the 1990s, the cold war came to an abrupt end, the Soviet Union collapsed into its constituent republics, and the disruptive effects of a pervasive geo-political rivalry, reinforced by ideological antagonism, disappeared. This change of atmosphere allowed the Security Council to act cohesively in 1990–91 in response to Iraq's conquest and annexation of Kuwait, authorizing a major military response to aggression as an expression of collective security. President George Bush even pro-claimed the emergence of 'a new world order' as premised upon fulfilling this promise of cooperation under UN auspices in meeting threats of international aggression.

The Gulf War 'succeeded' to the extent of restoring Kuwaiti sovereignty and independence, but it left controversy in its wake that persists to this day. Many observers within and without the UN believed that the Security Council had give the American-led coalition a blank check to conduct warfare without fully exhausting diplomatic remedies, thereby giving rise to the criticism that the Security Council had itself been 'hijacked' by the Americans. In this respect, the legitimacy of the Organization depends on its gaining greater distance from the control mechanisms of geo-politics, but the manner of UN financing, Security Council voting, and backroom diplomacy make this prospect now seem remote.

In any event, as the prior section suggests, the end of the cold war did not bring the UN into a golden age in the peacekeeping area. China and Russia, as do many lesser states, remain sceptical about using the Organization for undertakings that infringe on territorial sovereignty. The United States seems reluctant to support the UN unless it can exert virtually unilateral control over the definition of the mission and its operational implementation. Such an attitude induced leading Western governments to bypass UN authority in fashioning a Kosovo strategy that relied on the more hospitable arena of NATO to carry out a response to Serbian ethnic cleansing. Such an experience damaged the reputation of the UN, but only briefly, as the Organization was brought back into the Kosovo picture in the post-conflict setting, as well as almost immediately being given central responsibility for difficult new peacekeeping missions in East Timor and Sierra Leone.

The other great configuration affecting the UN has been the North/South divide. Because of a differing agenda and a lack of influence on the Security Council, this divide has been most evident within the one state/one vote General Assembly. It was in this setting that the newly independent states from non-Western countries mounted their various attacks on the way in which international society was organized, especially its economic dimensions. This attack reached its climax in the 1970s with the demand by the non-aligned bloc of countries for 'a new international economic order'. This demand for restructuring was backed up in this period by the formidable 'oil weapon' being wielded by OPEC, and by a generally accommodating West worried about alienating leaders of the South in the overriding struggle with the East for global pre-eminence. The South achieved a kind of pyrrhic victory in 1974, taking the form of a Charter for the New International Economic Order and an accompanying Programme of Action. It achieved some tangible results by establishing and expanding some arenas within the UN system that were responsive to its demands for assistance in the process of development, including UNCTAD and UNDP, but also in other organizational settings as well. The normative momentum culminated in the articulation of a Right to Development that remains a relevant influence in efforts to implement the International Covenant on Economic, Social, and Cultural Rights, and underpins the now well-known support of UNDP for an orientation toward global trade and investment policy that rests on 'human security', a deliberate challenge to a capital-driven preoccupation that assesses 'development' and economic performance by exclusive reference to growth and efficiency trends.

But then came the 1980s with their ideological backlash led by the Thatcher/Reagan governments of Britain and the United States that included attacks on socialist thinking, non-market approaches, and 'the irresponsible majorities' mobilized in the General Assembly. This backlash was the beginning of the neoliberal consensus that took hold of world society in the 1990s, greatly strengthened by the collapse from within of the Soviet bloc and by the extraordinary developmental achievements of market-oriented countries with strong private sectors in the South, especially in the Asia-Pacific region. The North became more ideologically united around the neoliberal approach, including an effort to curtail UN activities oriented toward the normative outlooks of the South, which had been funded and established during earlier periods of cooptation by the 1980s; the South was so deeply divided that it could not mount any kind of effective resistance.

In this atmosphere, the role of the UN in promoting equitable development was eclipsed, and all efforts at criticism of capitalist approaches to growth were sidelined, if not abandoned. Symbolic was the abolition of the UN Centre on Transnational Corporations, which was targeted by Washington in the early 1990s, as potentially hostile to private sector approaches to the world economic development. Despite this general trend to downplay normative concerns in the setting of the world economy, some minor rearguard efforts went forward, but with only minimal impact. Undoubtedly, the most interesting of these counter-moves was the 1995 Copenhagen 'Social Summit' that did its best to put back on the UN agenda concerns of the peoples of the South with such social issues as unemployment, poverty, and personal insecurity. The leading UN members of the North gave this initiative only the most grudging nominal support, and so far, this challenge to neoliberalism has not amounted to much.

In conclusion, as the UN enters the twenty-first century neither of the two large defining cleavages so central to its activities over the last half of the twentieth century remain, at least not in their earlier, coherent form. The prevailing ideas are dominated by a fairly bland ideological agreement that has resulted in the ascendancy of the Bretton Woods approach to development and *ad hoc* opportunism in the context of peace and security. Whether greater concern with the social dimensions of development and a more principled approach to global security will emerge in the years ahead are among the most salient issues confronting the UN at this time.

The 1997 Asian financial crisis, and its wider reverberations in Japan, Russia, and Latin America, did create some apparent exercises in rethinking by advocates of neoliberalism, including by those who led the Bretton Woods institutions. Many attempts were made to assess what had generated the collapse, as well as to criticize economistic prescriptions for recovery that caused disastrous short-term human consequences, as in Indonesia where many millions were abruptly pushed back below the poverty line. This experience led to soul searching by neoliberals, and to looking for policy alternatives. Calls for 'a new financial architecture' and 'responsible globality' were frequently uttered to call attention to the need for more governance associated with the workings of financial markets and to emphasize the relevance of social dimensions to public sector policies. The idea of 'globalization with a human face' was put forward as a new orientation toward economic policy, and seemed to guide the World Bank and IMF leadership toward the adopting of more flexible approaches to matters of conditionality, debt repayment, and structural adjustment. With the apparent Asian recovery process now underway, this reformist mood seems to be have been dissipated before any serious substantive adjustments were made. The neoliberal consensus seems in control once more, at least until the next crisis!

4. A NOTE ON GOVERNANCE WITHIN THE UN SYSTEM

The placement of the Bretton Woods institutions within the organizational frame of the UN is deeply misleading, an ambiguity that was not repeated in relation to the World Trade Organization, which enjoys a formally autonomous status. Such a status was insisted upon by the US government to reinforce its resolve to detach the management of the world economy, as far as possible, from the domain of the UN influence. For all practical purposes, the IMF and World Bank are also autonomous international actors, governed by their distinct institutional structures and accountable to their managerial boards composed of country representatives weighted to reflect proportionate capital contributions. Not surprisingly, the orientation of the Bretton Woods/WTO has tended to reflect the neoliberal outlook in its purest Northern forms, raising many questions of representativeness from the perspectives of the South. These actors have been the focus of grassroots protest activities for many years, being seen as virtual conduits for the allegedly heartless policies and priorities of private sector banks and corporations. They have also been accused of being environmentally insensitive in their endorsement of mega-projects in the name of growth-oriented development.[6]

Any deep reform of the UN system as a whole would have to extend to these hitherto nearly autonomous actors, creating a more organic link to ideas of human development favoured by other arenas within the UN, especially UNDP. Such reforms would include representation on a basis that gave some managerial voice to officials confronting massive poverty and other forms of social and environmental devastation, as well as some voice from global civil society directly accountable to the peoples of the world.

This issue of representation is accentuated by the degree to which countries in the North and private sector actors deliberately structure global economic governance in a manner that avoids accountability to or participation by the UN with its more avowedly *normative* or *value-oriented* agendas associated with equity and responses to human suffering arising from growing economic disparities. The annual meetings of the G-7 leaders and the gatherings of the World Economic Forum at Davos lend credibility to the view that global economic governance is fashioned by a coalition of leading private sector advocates and of ideologically passive political leaders from the world's most prosperous countries that seek to guide the global policy agenda on the basis of *technocratic* criteria.

It is evident that the significance of the Bretton Woods institutions plus the WTO is not acknowledged adequately in most formal presentations of the UN system. There are two ways to approach this. One would be to portray these global economic institutions as having moved to the centre of the UN scheme, displacing earlier ideas of the Organization as centred around the General Assembly or Security Council. The other way to conceive of this relationship is to treat these institutions as outside the UN, and linked to states in the North and to such private sector arenas as the World Economic Forum. Such a conceptualization would admit the autonomous character of these actors—being non-accountable in the UN—and avoid an artificial inclusion arising from a nominal, formal link by way of UN flow charts. Either portrayal contains a partial truth, which will be explored in the next section that considers the different 'images' of the UN system that derive from three principal ways of depicting the hierarchy of institutions that make up the Organization.

[6] E.g. Rich (1994) and Broad with Cavanagh (1993).

5. FOUR IMAGES OF THE UN SYSTEM

In most organizational presentations of the UN system, the General Assembly is depicted as the central organ, with the Security Council, Trusteeship Council, International Court of Justice, Economic and Social Council, and Secretariat as the five subsidiary organs comprising the core operation of the UN (see Fig. 7.1). Radiating from this core, by way of the Economic and Social Council, are the specialized agencies and several commissions, while other subsidiary bodies are attached directly to the General Assembly. It is true that the General Assembly is the UN organ with the widest substantive mandate, with all members represented, and with annual sessions that attract heads of state and prominent officials. When the Security Council has been deadlocked, or when the agenda has been dominated by issues other than peace and security, then the General Assembly has been in the limelight.

At the same time, such a depiction of the system seems misleading in some fundamental respects. For one thing, the overall rationale for the UN and the continuing perception of its success and failure is very much related to the roles assigned to the Security Council. For another, by deliberate design, only the Security Council can make 'decisions' binding on the entire membership, and it is only in the Security Council that the geopolitical actors are given permanent membership and a veto. By contrast, the General Assembly has only recommendatory authority, which can be obtained by a two-thirds majority vote, that might be composed of states representing a very small percentage of either the world's population, its GDP, and its financial contribution to the UN. Especially during the late 1960s and the 1970s when newly independent states were active in coalition, assertive in their demands directed at the market economies of the North, and the Security Council was paralysed by superpower rivalry, the General Assembly did seem to epitomize the UN.

Such majoritarian developments occasioned a backlash among leading countries in the North that started in the 1980s, and has continued until the present. It was partly motivated by an ideological response to the demands of the South for economic restructuring based on countervailing power (OPEC in the 1970s) and equitable arguments for reform (Non-Aligned Movement and the campaign to establish a New International Economic Order). With the collapse of the Soviet Union and the end of the cold war, the spread of market-oriented constitutionalism among the countries of the South, and the rise of neoliberal economic globalization, the General Assembly has been again eclipsed.

The Security Council re-emerged in the late 1980s and 1990s as the lynchpin of the UN, with great media attention given to a large expansion of UN peacekeeping activities in many countries, and a deliberate effort spearheaded by the P-5 to focus UN budgetary and administrative reform on 'downsizing' organizational commitments to the developmental priorities of the South (see Fig. 7.2).

It is also possible to conceive of the Bretton Woods institutions, with the addition of the WTO, as the central player in the UN system (see Fig. 7.3). Although normally portrayed as part of the periphery occupied by specialized agencies, the IMF/World

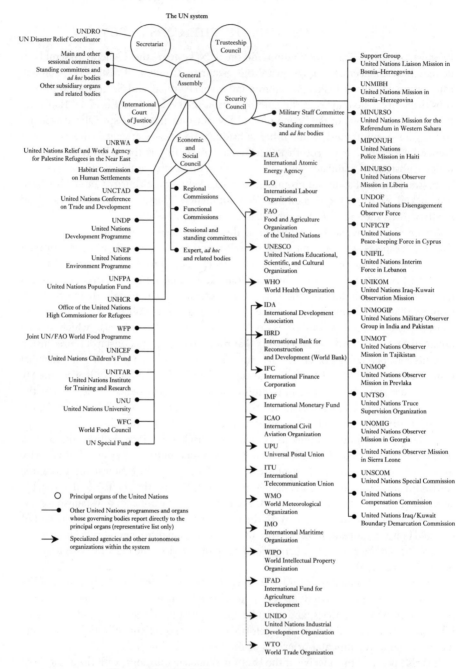

Figure 7.1. *Official image of the United Nations system*

Figure 7.2. *Geopolitical and media view of the core United Nations system*

Figure 7.3. *Image of the United Nations system as global economic governance*

Bank are arguably the most influential and consequential part of the Organization. Their influence is felt by many governments, and their policy and authority are supported by financial leverage, geopolitical authority, and ideological consensus. Such a view of the UN system is admittedly idiosyncratic, especially as the Bretton

Woods actors operate so autonomously in relation to the rest of the UN, as to be often perceived as actually *outside* the system.

The final image is partly futuristic, taking account of possible institutional reforms (global peoples assembly; economic security council) and of the importance of economic global governance (IMF, World Bank, and WTO). It conceives of the UN system as significantly renewed by incorporating both the democratizing demands of transnational social forces and the marketizing requirement of globalization.

Each of these four images reveals a partial reality, and none is entirely satisfactory on its own. On balance, the second image, based on the peace and security agenda, with the Security Council as the presiding organ, seems to be the most accurate of the three. After all, the establishment of the UN, as was the case with its predecessor, the League of Nations, was overwhelmingly a response to war and a quest for a more peaceful world. Also, as a matter of public perception, the success and failure of the UN seems principally connected with its ability to keep the peace and protect its members from aggression. As well, the constitutional arrangements of the Charter do seem to be far more sensitive to power configurations and organizational responsibilities in relation to the Security Council than anywhere else in the system. Thus, while a combination of the three images is helpful, it seems correct to view the second image as the most consistently illuminating, especially, as in this project, since the Bretton Woods actors are viewed as distinct from the UN. Further, the current climate of opinion in the Organization seems to be in favour of minimizing the UN role in the promotion of human development and global social priorities.

6. THE UN AS A CONTESTED POLITICAL ARENA

As mentioned earlier, in 1945 the structure of world order was very much dominated by sovereign states, and by Western ideas and arrangements, including vast overseas colonial empires. At first, the only important tension within the UN was between the socialism of the Soviet bloc and the market constitutionalism of the Atlantic Alliance. No doubt, partly because the Soviet group of UN members was much smaller than its Atlanticist rivals, Moscow was particularly insistent on respect for sovereign rights and the non-intervention norm. In this respect, the UN from the outset was a creation and creature of the state system of diplomacy, an instrument of statecraft, and a club of states that limited full access to states.

Membership in the UN resulted in some significant formal abridgements of sovereignty, especially for 'normal states', that is, other than the P-5. For these normal states, decisions could be made in the Security Council that affected their vital interests, despite the absence of their agreement or even participation. And even the General Assembly, as the conscience of the world community, could mobilize pressures that exerted influence on matters about which important states felt deeply, as seemed to be the case in relation to Chinese representation or during the latter stages of the anti-apartheid campaign. Yet, by and large, the UN was and remains a bastion of statism, even more so in some respects than at the time of its creation. It now incorporates the former colonies from Africa and Asia, extending its statist reach to embrace virtually the entirety of the planet. The formal proceedings of all parts of the UN system are restricted in their participation to states, and only states.

This statist model of organization is confronting three important challenges as a result of the emergence of new actors and organizational claims. These challenges have been widely interpreted as resulting in the decline (or at least the change in the role) of the state, and have cast doubt on the legitimacy and adequacy of a UN based on a membership that is strictly limited to states.

The first set of challenges are associated with the great and growing influence exerted by international NGOs and generally by transnational voluntary associations of various sorts.[7] There is much writing evaluating these initiatives, and whether there is in gestation a new political reality that can be described as 'global civil society' or alternatively, as 'globalization-from-below'.[8] The Charter makes a minimal gesture of acknowledgement in the extremely limited setting of the Economic and Social Council with respect to NGOs in Article 71, proposing 'suitable arrangements for consultation with non-governmental organizations which are concerned with matters within its competence'. Informally, civil society actors have been effectively active in a variety of UN arenas, especially in relation to the great global conferences of the early 1990s on policy issues and in lawmaking settings, particularly on environment and human rights. At the same time, given the importance widely attributed to these transnational civic initiatives and the growing support for global democracy, the UN is seen as not providing sufficient formal and effective access to this dimension of international political life.[9]

The second important area of formal exclusion involves the direct representation in some form of global market forces, the business and finance actors that have given shape and direction to economic globalization, capital-driven 'globalization-from-above'. Arguably, given the orientation of many governments and of the Bretton Woods institutions, these perspectives have sufficient access and influence by way of indirect representation and influence, and do not need, or even desire, any more direct form of participation in the UN system. At the 1992 Rio Conference on Environment and Development part of the budget was covered by a Business Council composed of CEOs from world corporations, which was active at the conference and has continued to operate in relation to the Commission on Sustainable Development. Also, there have been discussions about financing part of the UNDP budget on the basis of voluntary contributions from the private sector.

In a widely publicized initiative, the media billionaire, Ted Turner, pledged $1 billion a few years ago to cover a selected group of issues involving UN human-itarian activities. The financing crisis of the UN, arising from non-payment of dues and arrears by leading members, has encouraged options involving various strategies of 'privatization', an aspect of a broader trend toward transferring responsibility from the public sector to the private sector. Most controversially, there are privatizing initiatives of a mercenary character in the peacekeeping field, especially in Africa

---

[7] See Keck and Sikkink (1998); Risse-Kappen (1995), and Smith *et al.* (1997).
[8] Falk (1995).   [9] Held (1995); Wapner (1996); also Falk and Strauss (1999).

where private companies, such as Executive Outcomes, have taken on peace-keeping roles as profit-making ventures in the face of internal strife. Such a disturbing development has occurred partly to re-employ the security operatives from the apartheid regime in South Africa and partly to fill the vacuum created by the decline of great power interest in Sub-Saharan Africa.

There is also the matter of taking account of arenas that have been formed by private sector initiative to exert influence on global policy. The Global Economic Forum that meets annually at Davos, Switzerland, is currently the most prominent of these arenas. Presumably, in recognition of its relevance, the UN Secretary-General Kofi Annan has addressed the Forum each year prior to 2000. The main burden of his remarks has been the need of the UN to find ways to take account of the less statist character of international society. In 1998 Mr Annan proposed a double 'partnership', first between the UN on one side and the business community on the other, and secondly, between the UN and civil society. He did not go into specifics, but strongly suggested that such partnership was necessary to ensure continued UN relevance. In 1999 Mr Annan moved in a complementary direction, urging business actors to comply voluntarily with international standards applicable to environmental, labour, and human rights even when not obliged to do so by states within which operations were occurring. He pledged UN collaboration in such efforts, and seemed to be proposing such action as a move toward the negotiation of a global social contract based on a novel idea of private sector 'global citizenship'.

One expression of the potency of global market forces involves the establishment of the WTO, involving important transfers of sovereignty by states for the sake of promoting freer trade. If the logic and dynamics of globalization support institutional innovation at the global (and regional) level, then opposition will recede. It is worth comparing the obstacles to institutionalization with respect to the environment, an area where market forces prefer to rely on the self-organizing features of markets to the establishment of a coercive regime promoting 'free trade'.

A third area of significance involves the growth of regionalism, especially in Europe over the course of the last half century. The Charter seeks to accommodate regional actors in Chapter X, especially with respect to their role in peace and security based on the primacy of the Security Council. Whether the NATO initiatives in Kosovo permanently disrupt this relationship is uncertain at this point, but at least suggest the need to rethink coordination between the Security Council and enforcement under the aegis of regional organizations. The issue has arisen before on several occasions during the cold war when the Soviet Union used the Warsaw Pact to validate interventions in Eastern Europe and the United States relied on SEATO authorization for Vietnam and other regional mandates for Caribbean interventionary activities.

Perhaps, the more consequential issue arising from regionalism is one of representation and restructuring. In some sense, if the European Union were to occupy a permanent seat in the Security Council, it would pave the way for expanded non-Western representation, as well as giving non-represented 'nations' in Europe a sense that their identities were less violated than by way of statist patterns of representation. If regionalism evolves further in other parts of the world, then it would seem desirable to find ways to enable their formal participation *as regions* in a wide range of UN activities.

As far as I know, Kofi Annan has yet to include regional actors in his speculations about the necessary outreach of a revitalized UN. A better incorporation of regionalism within the UN system would fit with his general appreciation that it is important to take organizational account of the rise of international actors other than states in this period since the founding of the UN. Of course, there is a certain degree of ambivalence in UN circles about the merits of mega-regionalism as it could be understood as a rival approach to global governance rather than as an aspect of a UN-led world order. A world of regions could evolve either as a complement or as an alternative to an augmented UN, but the regional dimension cannot be any longer neglected in analysing prospects for global governance.

There is no assurance that regionalism would operate in a more democratic manner than the UN. Indeed, there have been complaints about the democratic deficit in Europe and the non-accountability and non-transparency of the European Commission in Brussels. At the same time, the future of regionalism is tied closely to the European experience, and this experience clearly emphasizes the importance of a shared commitment to democracy as a foundation for further integrative steps. By democracy, the main emphasis has been upon democracy in state/society relations, but there are glimmerings of a growing acceptance of democratic practices in relations between member states and the European Union. The evolution of the European Parliament and the acceptance by members of external accountability with respect to economic disputes and human rights suggest the democratization of regionalism in a manner and depth that remains inconceivable for the UN.

It is also unclear as to whether regionalism will displace or complement the UN in the years ahead. The most likely expectation is that the relationship will vary with the subject matter. In peacekeeping there seems to have been a complementary relationship in Africa, but a somewhat competitive one in relation to Balkans peacekeeping in the 1990s. In more functional areas, such as environment and economic relations, the prospects remain good for cooperative relations between the UN and regional actors.

7. RECONSIDERING COLD WAR GRIDLOCK

The generally disappointing UN performance on peace and security was explained and excused by reference to the cold war. After all, the original understanding of the UN rested on an acceptance of the idea that collective security could only operate on the basis of a P-5 consensus. Accordingly, with the end of the cold war, there was the hope that the UN could finally fulfil this more ambitious role contemplated by the UN Charter. Such an expectation seemed confirmed when the Gulf crisis of 1990 gave way to a political consensus that was translated in the Gulf War into a recovery of Kuwaiti sovereignty. It then seemed natural to believe that the UN was finally entering a golden age of P-5 cooperation, which would feature the flourishing of collective security. And then when the Security Council proceeded to endorse humanitarian missions to overcome internal conflicts in several countries in the early 1990s, this sense of an emergent strong UN peaked.

Unfortunately, it soon became clear that such optimism about the UN was ill-founded and premature. The Gulf War quickly came to be seen as a job half done, and carried out in a manner that contained disturbing implications. It was soon evident that despite the Security Council mandate, the war itself amounted to an exercise in traditional alliance diplomacy, with only the most nominal participation by the UN. There was little or no reliance on a collaborative process of the sort contemplated by Chapter VII of the Charter. Once the UN mandate was given, it functioned virtually as a signal for the American-led coalition to embark on a war, control its parameters, define its goals, and negotiate its termination.

The Security Council moves in the direction of humanitarian intervention also ran into formidable obstacles. These undertakings were UN ventures bearing on situations of *intranational* strife or emergency. By conception, such undertakings were constitutionally controversial due to the domestic jurisdiction provision of Article 2(7) of the Charter, and the attachment to its strict interpretation by a sovereignty-oriented group of states led by China. This limitation on UN authority written into the Charter was a pledge given particularly to weaker states, but also at the time to large states likely to be outvoted, such as the Soviet Union, that their territorial sovereignty would not, under *any* circumstances, be subject to challenge as a result of becoming members of the UN. The counter-argument also seemed strong: given the evolution of international human rights in the course of several decades, governments had effectively accepted over time an erosion of this limitation on UN authority, and had submitted themselves to the possibility of humanitarian intervention in the event of gross and massive violation of fundamental human rights or in situations of chaos in which large portions of the citizens found that their basic rights, including the right to life, were in jeopardy. Such a reinterpretation of the Security Council role, while generally endorsed by the West and successive secretary-generals (Perez de Cueller, Boutros Boutros-Ghali, and Kofi Annan) remains controversial. It has never been accepted in Asia, where there existed the contrary view that human rights violations and humanitarian emergencies, even of an acute variety, could never justify a UN intervention in internal affairs. In Asia, suspicion abounds about the renewal of Northern dominance of the region under the aegis of 'human rights' and 'humanitarian intervention'. The riposte of the North has been that such concerns are but a diversionary move to hide the refusal to uphold international human rights standards. As with many such disputes, both sides seem to be right. The fundamental matter remains in a condition of constitutional flux.

Additionally, decisive political problems arose that have mooted the constitutional controversy, at least for the present. It became obvious first in relation to Somalia, and then more blatantly with respect to Bosnia and Rwanda, that the P-5, and especially the United States, did not possess the political will to engage in effective forms of humanitarian intervention. As Kosovo in 1999 shows, such will for a variety of reasons seems abundantly present when NATO acts, because the credibility of this prince of alliances is a strategic interest for geopolitical actors that must be upheld at all costs. But even here, it is upheld in a manner that has deepened the tragedy of those for whom the intervention is supposedly being undertaken. NATO bombed extensively for 78 days without committing ground forces, thereby insulating vicious patterns of retaliation against the Kosovar community. Beyond this, NATO focused its initial bombing almost exclusively on anti-aircraft capabilities rather than Serb military forces, conveying the impression that the safety of NATO flight crews was given clear priority over the fate of Kosovars.

And of course, by shifting humanitarian intervention from the collective frame of the Security Council to that of NATO, the undertaking evades vetoes by China and Russia, but at a constitutional and political cost. It is evident, that such a path contravenes the Charter idea clearly expressed in Article 53 that regional enforcement activity is never legally permissible without Security Council approval. As such, the UN has been bypassed by this NATO operation, as rarely so blatantly before in the course of its history. Such a sidelining of the UN is only partly explained by the fact that China and Russia deeply opposed recourse to the use of force against Yugoslavia. The West was also convinced that NATO was more capable than the UN of bringing force to bear effectively based on earlier experiences in Bosnia. Also, it seemed geopolitically advantageous to give the mandate to NATO, which was in any event casting about for a role since it had lost its *raison d'être* after the collapse of any Soviet threat to Europe. Of course, in defence of evading the Security Council was the perception of urgency based on Belgrade's repressive policies in Kosovo that were assuming genocidal proportions. In such a setting, some sort of humanitarian response, regardless of constitutional niceties, had become a moral and political imperative.

Despite this discouraging picture of UN marginalization, it still seems useful to consider the case for adjustments of the UN system that would make the Organization more effective in the early twenty-first century. The balance of opinion as to the UN could shift quickly, especially if the traditional non-UN approaches to peace and security come to be regarded as self-destructive and policy failures. It is also possible that a surge of public support could at some point induce political leaders to engage more fully and creatively with the UN, including the provision of more independent financing and peacekeeping arrangements.

8. CHALLENGES AND RESPONSES: TWO EXAMPLES

Of course, in the history of the UN, there have been many challenges directed at institutional style, capacity, and orientation. Some of the most complex and difficult challenges have been produced by changes in the global setting, particularly in relation to geopolitical alignment. The onset and then the termination of the cold war were undoubtedly the most decisive changes associated with the UN system, especially as conceived from the perspective of the second image of Security Council dominance. The cold war involved a deep geopolitical cleavage that interfered with the capacity of the UN to achieve consensus on a wide range of issues, especially those involving contest, peace and security questions. The difficulty of injecting UN peacekeeping into an East/West contested situation became evident in relation to the Congo crisis of 1960, and its aftermath.

The end of the cold war did not mean the end of geopolitical disputes and divergencies, but it did make many previously gridlocked issues available for potential UN response. The Gulf War manifested the potential for consensus, but it also served as a warning sign that seems to have made many states more reluctant to give a blank check to UN action of an enforcement nature. Also, the problems of political will associated with the proposed humanitarian operations under UN auspices in relation to Somalia, Bosnia, and Rwanda made it clear that consensus was not enough to ensure an effective UN response. It was also important to have sufficient resolve to mobilize the means or capabilities required to have a reasonable prospect of attaining the desired goal. It became clear in the 1990s that the P-5 were not prepared to satisfy this condition in humanitarian settings even if a consensus could be obtained in support of a UN undertaking.

But other challenges to the UN system derived from other sources, especially from the various effects of decolonization and from the appearance of new concerns on the global policy agenda. With decolonization came a new focus on the concerns of the South. These took a variety of forms, including an emphasis on development and economic assistance. By the 1970s these concerns became increasingly militant, representing not only an effort not to be drawn into the cold war, but also to reform the terms of trade between North and South, and generally establish what was claimed to be a more equitable set of relations affecting global economic policy. This campaign was crystallized around the call for a 'new international economic order' (NIEO), an effort reinforced by the use of OPEC influence to raise world oil prices, moves that caused petrol queues in the West and created the novel impression that the North might be vulnerable to initiatives taken by way of the coordinated action of the South. 'The oil weapon' was wielded within the halls of the UN, especially at the Sixth Special Session of the General Assembly, devoted to the call for a NIEO. The result was a series of normative instruments purporting to set a new framework for North/South relations based on greater fairness and mutuality than in the past, weakening international legal protection of foreign investment, but mainly dealing with tone and atmospherics. There was little of a substantive nature in this normative assault, enabling most countries in the North to go along with these pronouncements without feeling that their present conduct was being questioned or that they had undertaken to act differently in the future.[10]

The fact that a new normative architecture is set forth without any prospect of substantive results is not by itself discrediting of a UN initiative, or evidence that the General Assembly is a toothless giant. I think such an assessment could be made of the early efforts of the UN to internationalize the subject-matter of human rights, and yet over time this undertaking has to be ranked with leading UN achievements.[11] But the campaign to create the NIEO must be assessed as a disabling failure. It prompted an ideological/geopolitical backlash led by Reagan/Thatcher forces during the 1980s. It overstated the solidarity of the South and did not take account of the degree to which

---

[10] See Declaration on the Establishment of a NIEO and Charter of Economic Rights and Duties of States in Weston *et al.* (1997: 705–16).   [11] Falk (1998: 255–72).

socialism and state-directed economies were in retreat all over the world. And most of all, unlike with human rights, there was neither civil society reinforcement of the inter-governmental momentum nor some degree of geopolitical opportunism at work (as had helped give human rights degrees of potency in various settings such as in relation to mounting Western pressure against the oppressive regimes of Eastern Europe). And so the NIEO seemed like empty confrontational rhetoric that was not related to any viable political project. When the oil weapon disappeared and OPEC disunity sur-faced, the final nail was hammered into the NIEO coffin. The NIEO experience does show how the UN General Assembly can be mobilized for sweeping reform, but also how such efforts can end in frustration if there is either a political backlash or an absence of follow-through.

This failure to reform the world economy as such should not detract from the success of the South with respect to the enactment of supportive normative guidelines by way of a series of General Assembly initiatives. As early as 1962, the General Assembly adopted a resolution on 'permanent sovereignty over natural resources' that was supposed to put the rights of a people ahead of those of foreign investors, regardless of contractual arrangements.[12] The International Covenant on Economic, Social and Cultural Rights also affirms the importance of ensuring each person in every country basic human needs.[13] And perhaps most relevant of all was the adoption in 1986 of a comprehensive Declaration on the Right of Development.[14] The success of the South, at a normative level of discourse, was to establish the goal of development as a policy imperative that could not be trumped even by invoking market efficiency factors. This must be counted as a limited victory, as it was not possible to move from the right to development to specific reforms that might facilitate what the UNDP called 'pro-growth development' in its *Human Development Reports* or what Chile claimed to be 'growth with equity'.

The UN story pertaining to the new agenda of environment, population, and resources tells a different, generally more positive, story about the creative capacity of the General Assembly to respond to the felt needs of the peoples of the world. The idea of organizing a global inter-governmental conference on a broad policy concern under UN auspices was an expansion of activities explicitly foreseen. The 1972 Stockholm Conference on the Human Environment, despite a variety of difficulties, was a major contribution in several respects. It greatly raised environmental awareness among the governments and peoples of the world, and was thus an invaluable learning experience. Such learning occurred in the preparatory process, at the conference itself, and in its aftermath. Many governments established ministries of environmental affairs or bureaucratic units devoted to environmental policy. The UN itself established UNEP as an expression of continuing concern, which was less than what environ-mentalists hoped for, but more than what had existed. The transnational environmental movement made its debut at Stockholm, capturing the imagination of many among the

---

[12] GA Res. 1803, 14 December 1962; see also GA Res. 3171, 17 December 1973.
[13] See Article 25, 28 of Universal Declaration and Covenant, 16 December 1966.
[14] 4 December 1986.

assembled media, and suggesting the presence of new non-state actors as real social forces. And the UN displayed a capacity to promote consciousness-raising with respect to emergent global challenges. The Stockholm Declaration on the Human Environment, although non-binding in a legal sense, was an immense contribution to the creation of a normative architecture for environmental protection, and has served as a building block for subsequent international law efforts.

The Stockholm conference also disclosed problems. It became evident that organizers had not addressed the North/South dimension of environmentalism in a reconciling manner. Many from the South believed that the stress on environmental dangers, especially those associated with industrialism, were being invoked intentionally or unwittingly, to inhibit the drive to develop poor countries as rapidly as possible. Governments confronted by massive poverty and capital scarcity did not want to accept responsibility for expensive restrictions on industrial and agricultural activities. The insensitive militancy of environmental activists from Northern voluntary organizations also contributed to an atmosphere of North/South tensions. Also, much of the citizen activism in relation to the governmental undertakings seemed overly confrontational. Finally, the geopolitical dimension was evident at Stockholm, especially in view of the exclusion of environmental harm caused by war from the agenda, given the sensitivities surrounding this concern that arose from some of the tactics relied upon by the United States in the Vietnam War.

But the idea of UN-sponsored global conferences took off. Other conferences in the 1970s and 1980s were held on population policy, on food, on human habitat, and on women. Although somewhat less visible than the Stockholm event, these conferences exhibited the virtues associated with Stockholm and avoided some of the weaknesses, making a special effort to take account of developmental priorities of the South. And then came the 1990s, and a series of highly orchestrated UN conferences were arranged, with strong provision for participation by global civil society. The Rio Conference on Environment and Development held in 1992, twenty years after Stockholm, was the most elaborate world conference ever held, and managed to attract both more heads of state than any prior international event and more civil society activists. It also gave an explicit role to business leaders, recognizing the relevance and importance of market forces to environmental protection. Benefiting from the report of the Brundtland Commission that had been widely distributed within the UN system, the North/South divide was significantly lessened. This was signalled by adopting the name 'environment and development' for the conference as compared to the Stockholm name of 'human environment'.[15] The reconciling idea of 'sustainable development' was widely endorsed as the guiding concept, and it was understood that 'poverty' would be treated as a form of 'pollution'.

A new normative framework was adopted in the form of the Rio Declaration on Environment and Development, and some progress was made on such broad issues as climate change, biodiversity, and the protection of forests. The Declaration, in comparison with that adopted in Stockholm, does contain explicit reference to indigenous

[15] WCED (1987).

peoples, women, and youth as constituencies with special concerns and potential contributions relative to environmental process. Also, Rio was sensitive to the importance of follow-through, formulating an elaborate action programme in the form of Agenda 21 that included cost estimates for each recommended course of action, as well as establishing a 'commission for sustainable development' with periodic meetings to monitor implementation of the programme of action.

But again there were problems. At Rio it was the rich countries of the North that seemed most worried, fearing that either their life style would be cramped or criticized, or that they would be asked to pay most of the costs for environmental clean-up. There was also the feeling that civil society perspectives were being 'handled' rather than 'addressed', and that arrangements for participation were designed for 'cooption' rather than 'dialogue'. Yet again the main impression was one of learning and policy impact, especially by media attentiveness. The UN organized and sponsored several other mega-conferences in the succeeding years: human rights in Vienna (1993); population in Cairo (1994); social summit in Copenhagen (1995); women in Beijing (1995); and habitat in Istanbul (1996). All of these conferences linked their efforts explicitly to development, and each attracted major civil society inputs. Indeed, the impact of civil society initiatives at Cairo and Copenhagen challenged many governmental perspectives both substantively and in terms of process. As a result, there has been a backlash. UN conferences on broad issues of global policy are not likely to occur in the near future. The official explanation will be that such conferences were 'expensive jamborees' that accomplished little, and were thus good targets for the budget-slashers. My own interpretation of the backlash is different, and stresses the extent to which the UN conference arenas were losing their statist character, and becoming 'dangerous' experiments in global democracy.

Whether such conferences will be held in the future, and whether they will be inclusive of civil society and market perspectives, is an important uncertainty about the UN role early in the twenty-first century. Surely the need persists for consciousness-raising and the provision of broad normative frameworks useful for resolving more specific controversies. And surely, the democratic spirit of the times is not likely to exempt UN activities indefinitely. But whether the present downsizing approach can be effectively challenged in relation to the UN role in providing the auspices for global conference diplomacy is not at all clear at this point.

9. TOWARD A MORE LEGITIMATE AND EFFECTIVE UN

To simplify matters, reformist energies need to be understood in relation to two overriding goals: a more legitimate UN and a more effective UN. The Organization, in general, will operate more legitimately and appear to be doing so in relation to three standards of assessment: (1) acting in accordance with the United Nations Charter, including its broad constitutional principles and objectives; (2) achieving representativeness in relation to the peoples of the world, particularly on the Security Council, and operating in a manner that embodies democratic practices of participation, transparency, and accountability; (3) moving toward political independence in relation to the most powerful geopolitical actors in the world, which will depend on the avoidance of 'double standards' in responding to circumstances of conflict and emergency and on staffing its bureaucracy with international civil servants who possess integrity and competence.

The quest for UN effectiveness is a matter of ensuring that the Organization has the capabilities and political will to carry out its various missions.[16] At times, as arguably in the Gulf War, effectiveness is achieved at the expense of legitimacy. UN effectiveness is partly a matter of money, but it is mainly a matter of achieving the requisite degree of support from its members, especially the permanent members of the Security Council. The UN can only hope to be effective to the extent that these members are in substantial agreement about specific undertakings and overall organizational role, although there are various opportunities for bargaining and compromises if there is a commitment to effectiveness and to the goals of humane global governance.

It is increasingly important in achieving legitimacy and effectiveness for the UN to be strongly supported by relevant sectors of global civil society and the most influential media commentary and coverage. There is no doubt that 'the CNN factor' shapes perceptions of legitimacy and effectiveness, not only for large parts of the public, but also for many leaders. It is a subtle matter as various political tendencies also use the media to advance their particular agendas.

As stressed earlier, the outlook for significant institutional reform does not appear to be bright at present. Yet, the future potential of the UN system cannot begin to be realized without some significant adjustment to changing global realities. In brief, a UN created in 1945 to serve the interests of the then largely Western group of states that continued to govern many peoples by colonial title. This world order has been significantly transformed by the universality of participation by independent sovereign states, by policy agendas shaped in response to multiple forms of global interconnectedness, and by the emergence of global civil society and of global market forces that often manage to elude the regulatory mechanisms of the state system.

Accordingly, it seems appropriate to offer a few recommended institutional modifications despite an appreciation that their attainment is not likely within the short run. At the same time, it is important not to be captive of projective thinking that measures future possibilities by the present outlook. From such a projective perspective, the movement against colonialism would never have been entertained, nor the emancipation of the countries of East Europe from Soviet dominion, nor the dismantling of apartheid in South Africa, nor the political independence of East Timor. Defining what the UN needs, as well as taking account of the current set of circumstances, guides the following set of illustrative recommendations.[17]

---

[16] For comprehensive proposals, see report of the Commission on Global Governance (1995: esp. 225–302); Childers and Urquhart (1994).

[17] Note that the most ambitious orientation toward reform, the establishment of a world government, is not even considered here. Such an exclusion is justified on practical grounds. There is no significant support for such a transformative move either at the level of grassroots or among elite opinion. At the same time, there are visionaries who continue to believe that the integrative trends of world society and the disintegrative dangers of a total ecological or geopolitical collapse make world government possible,

9.1. *Independent Financing*

The idea of separating UN funding to some extent from government contributions has been around for a long time. Whether to tax transnational financial transactions or some use of the global commons or arms sales has also been debated for years. The financing pressures on the UN in recent years as a result of the non-payment of dues and assessments provide an additional rationale for restructuring UN financing arrangements at this time. Also, the weakness of political will in humanitarian settings suggests that an enhanced UN role in the future depends in part on a financing structure that is independent of P-5 control.

For these reasons, it is important to renew the recommendation to seriously explore the prospect for various alternative modes of partial independent financing. Success here would both contribute to the overall effectiveness of the UN system but would also be understood as a loosening of the reins of political control now exercised by the strongest member states. Precisely for this reason, it is important to realize that the issue of financing is less about money than political control. Once this is realized, it makes plain why the resistance of some governments is so intense, and why only a mobilization of even stronger counter-pressures from civil society in those same countries is likely to make independent financing a feasible project.

9.2. *Volunteer Peace Force*

To enable more reliable Security Council responses, especially in the setting of humanitarian challenges of small or medium scale, the establishment of a high quality UN volunteer peace force would be of great benefit. It would allow the Organization to respond without expecting member states to expose their citizens to loss of life. It would tend to depoliticize such undertakings, and yet provide the UN Security Council with a mechanism to extend rapidly collective security responses to situations of severe humanitarian emergency.

The character of such a force, and its administrative relation to the UN system, would have to be worked out in great detail. It would be an expensive undertaking if done in a professionally responsible manner. The coordination of control between the Security Council and the secretary-general would be an important concern of members if such an initiative moved beyond the proposal stage. Again, major sovereign states are reluctant to allow to come into existence peacekeeping capabilities that might not be subject to their political control. And as with financing, the pressures from civil society will be crucial to shape a setting in which sympathetic leaders can accept some loss of sovereign authority. Of course, the payoff for such states is a shift of responsibility away from themselves in situations where the pressure to act is great, but the absence of strategic interests makes any substantial commitment difficult to justify.

necessary, and desirable. One such carefully presented proposal is that of Yunker (1993); see also a range of views on these issues in Harris and Yunker (1999); for the more influential ideas favouring 'global governance' as a functional and normative goal that avoids the feasibility and bureaucratic pitfalls of 'world government', see Rosenau and Czempiel (1992) and the range of contributions to Paul and Hall (1999).

Despite practical obstacles, the case for a UN volunteer force drawn from many countries seems strong at this point. Resistance from P-5 governments, reluctant to give up their current measure of control over UN peacekeeping, is likely to persist, but it might dissipate in due course, given disenchantment with alternative approaches.

9.3. *Global Peoples Assembly*

Modelled somewhat on the European Parliament, and designed to give the peoples of the world more meaningful opportunities for participation in the UN system, it is proposed that a 'peoples assembly' would help to diminish the so-called 'democratic deficit' in the UN.[18] This new organ could be structured to be a parallel body to that of the General Assembly.[19] It would be the voice of global civil society, providing a great testing ground for the practice of global democracy.

Here, too, problems of organization and conception are complex and opposition can be expected to be formidable. The current secretary-general, Kofi Annan, supported the convening of a 'peoples millennium assembly' in the year 2000. It was a low-priority project, to meet only on a single occasion, but its advocacy expressed the desirability of having the peoples of the world participate more directly and democratically in the work of the UN. At this point, it is uncertain whether such an assembly will spark a movement to achieve some more regular institutionalization, and if so, on what basis.

There are some experiments along these lines that suggest the operational feasibility of the idea. There have been three Assemblies of the Peoples of the UN held in alternate years in Perugia, Italy. Delegates come from as many as 140 countries, their participation financed by a coalition of municipalities in Italy, each of which takes responsibility for paying the travel and accommodation costs of one or more delegate from a non-Western country. The result is a stimulating confirmation of the extent to which such a democratizing initiative brings to the surface a different set of grievances and aspirations from those deriving from inter-governmental or even NGO circles.

9.4. *Economic Security Council*

One proposal that has received prominent endorsement is the idea of establishing an 'economic security council'.[20] Such a new organ for the UN would acknowledge the

---

[18] See Falk and Strauss (2000, 1999, and 1997) and also Commission on Global Governance (1995).

[19] The GPA would be started on an informal, experimental basis, with an annual session of one month. One approach would be to allow each member of the UN, on the basis of population, to establish a democratic procedure for selecting 1–10 delegates. Another approach would be to ask the Nobel Prize Committee to convene a panel of Nobel Peace Prize winners to designate a corporate body of 300 delegates representing the peoples of the world. Funding could be arranged on a decentralized basis taking account of income levels. As with the European Parliament, the early activities of the GPA would not have lawmaking effects, but as the experiment proceeded, a gradual accretion of functions and powers could be expected to occur.

[20] Jacques Delors elaborated his support for this new UN organ during his keynote address to the UN seminar on 'Values and Market Economies'.

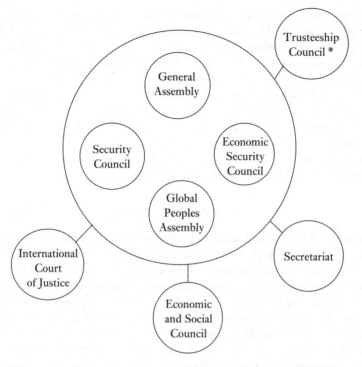

Figure 7.4. *Reformed image from a global political governance perspective*

*This organ of the United Nations was associated with the colonial era. To keep the Trusteeship Council functional in the twenty-first century would require that its trust focus be shifted to upholding the rights of future generations and of indigenous peoples, and to protecting 'the common heritage' of humanity against encroachment.

increasing importance of the economic dimensions of world order, as well as the current insufficiency of institutional arrangements for economic governance at the global level. In part, such a proposal seeks to ensure that the UN possesses an arena suitable for the formation of global economic policy and capable of providing regulatory authority as needed (Fig. 7.4).

Perhaps, the most compelling rationale for an economic security council relates to security dimensions of the world economy. The Asian financial crisis of 1997 disclosed how abruptly the economic vulnerability of countries in the South can result in massive suffering for large proportions of the population. Indonesia, probably the hardest hit of the Asian countries, was confronted with a humanitarian catastrophe, with some 50 per cent of its population being pushed well below subsistence in the months after the brunt of the Asian financial crisis and the prescribed IMF medicine were felt. An economic security council would be tasked with addressing the social and environmental effects of world economic developments.

Of course, the prospects for establishing an economic security council are not currently favourable. Rich countries favour addressing global economic issues outside the UN, and have established their own arenas, including the Annual Economic Summit (G-7), the World Economic Forum, and the WTO, among others. It is likely that the permanent members of the Security Council would regard the idea of an economic security council as a threat to their institutional primacy. Also, the bargaining to construct an economic security council that took account of varying levels of influence and yet was representative of the peoples of the world would undoubtedly strain diplomatic capabilities to their limits. Such strain would be greater still if efforts were made to eliminate the veto and ensure access for certain NGOs and private sector representatives in the formal workings of the new organ.

But the existence of practical and political obstacles is no reason to bury an idea, whose realization could bring great benefit to the global public good.

10. CONCLUSION

The full range of institutional adjustments that would strengthen the capacity of the UN system to respond to the range of challenges is beyond the scope of this chapter. The proposals sketched were chosen for illustrative purposes, and because they seemed responsive to the most salient current weaknesses. Omitted was the much discussed reform of the Security Council, both in relation to membership and the exercise of the veto. Until the Security Council incorporates the changes in the composition of international society wrought by the collapse of colonialism and the rise of non-Western civilizations, the entire Organization will remain under a shadow of anachronistic Euro-centrism. And yet the Charter is difficult to amend, making it easier for countries with entrenched advantages to oppose needed adjustments. In a sense, the inability to reform the Security Council despite the magnitude of change in the global setting is symbolic of the extent to which the Charter framework reflecting the realities of 1945 hampers the effectiveness and legitimacy of the UN at the start of the twenty-first century.

But the Charter has proved flexible in some respects, and the overall role of the Organization has proved invaluable for all members of international society. It is notable that the UN membership now represents over 99 per cent of the people living in the world, and that no government currently conceives of its interests as better served by withdrawing from the UN. Such universality of participation (leaving aside the special case of Switzerland) is in contrast with selective membership and withdrawal that undermined the League of Nations from its inception in 1920.

No one knows what will prove feasible by way of reform, as it becomes evident that the impact of globalization is profoundly changing perceptions, influence patterns, and aspirational priorities, as well as altering the perspectives and role of the sovereign state. The 1999 'Battle of Seattle', although directed at the WTO, was directed against the overall pattern of global governance associated with economic globalization. Whether such protest was a flash in the pan of global consciousness or an expression of a rising challenge to the manner by which the world is now organized, cannot yet be foretold. Certainly one possibility is to bring greater transparency and accountability into all aspects of UN operations. In this regard, the effectiveness and legitimacy of the

UN seems likely to depend on whether it funds suitable ways to incorporate representatives of both global civil society and global market forces into its everyday operations. In an important sense, the challenge of the first fifty years was centred on the incorporation of non-Western states. For the next fifty years the challenge will be to incorporate non-state actors. The UN must meet this challenge, or it will find its potential and actual influence ebbing away to other policymaking arenas. Such an outlook should encourage a boldness of imagination as a way of engaging world citizenry, the media, and private and public sector leaders in discussion about building a sustainable and satisfying future for the peoples of the world as we embark on a new century. Such a discussion is more necessary than ever given the rise of non-Western civilizations, making a dialogue of civilizations the only viable alternative to a clash of civilization. And what better focus for such an undertaking than building the sort of UN that can be of benefit to all peoples in the world.

REFERENCES

Alagappa, Muthiah and Takashi Inoguchi (eds) (1999). *International Security Management and the United Nations*. United Nations University, Tokyo.

Broad, Robin (with John Cavanagh) (1993). *Plundering Paradise: The Struggle for the Environment in the Philippines*. University of California Press, Berkeley, CA.

Childers, Erskine and Brian Urquhart (1994). *Renewing the United Nations System*. Dag Hammarskjöld Foundation, Uppsala, Sweden.

Clark, Grenville and Louis B. Sohn (1966). *World Peace Through World Law*, 3rd rev. edn. Harvard University Press, Cambridge, MA.

Commission on Global Governance (1995). *Our Global Neighborhood*. The Report of the Commission on Global Governance. Oxford University Press, Oxford. 225–302.

Delors, Jacques (2000). Keynote address presented at the UN seminar on 'Values and Market Economies', 19–20 January. Centre de Conférence Internationales, Paris, France.

Falk, Richard (1995). *On Humane Governance: Toward a New Global Politics*. Polity Press, Cambridge, UK.

——(1998). A half century of human rights. *Australian Journal of International Affairs*, 52, 255–72.

——and Andrew Strauss (1997). For a global peoples assembly. *International Herald Tribune*. 14 November, 8.

————(1999). Globalization needs a dose of democracy. *International Herald Tribune*. 5 October, 8.

————(2000). On the creation of a global peoples assembly: Legitimacy and the power of popular sovereignty. *Stanford Journal of International Law*, 36, 191–220.

Haq, Mahbub-ul (1995). *Reflections on Human Development*. Oxford University Press, New York.

Harris, Errol E. and James A. Yunker (eds) (1999). *Toward Genuine Global Governance: Critical Reactions, 'Our Global Neighborhood'*. Praeger, Westport, CT.

Held, David (1995). *Democracy and the Global Order: From the Modern State to Cosmopolitan Governance*. Stanford University Press, Stanford, CA.

Kaul, Inge, Isabelle Grunberg, and Marc A. Stern (eds) (1999). *Global Public Goods: International Cooperation in the 21st Century*. Oxford University Press, New York and Oxford.

Keck, Margaret and Kathryn Sikkink (1998). *Activists Beyond Borders: Advocacy Networks in International Politics*. Cornell University Press, Ithaca, NY.

Mingst, Karen A. and Margaret P. Karns (1995). *The United Nations in the Post-Cold War Era*. Westview, Boulder, CO.

Murphy, Cornelius F. Jr. (1999). *Theories of World Governance*. Catholic University of America Press, Washington, DC.

Paul, T. V. and John A. Hall (1999). *International Order and the Future of World Politics*. Cambridge University Press, Cambridge.

Rich, Bruce Rich (1994). *Mortgaging the Future: The World Bank, Environmental Impoverishment, and the Crisis of Development*. Beacon Press, Boston.

Risse-Kappen, Thomas (ed.) (1995). *Bringing Transnational Relations Back In: Non-State Actors, Domestic Structures, and International Institutions*. Cambridge University Press, Cambridge.

Rosenau, James N. and Ernst-Otto Czempiel (eds) (1992). *Governance Without Government: Order and Change in World Politics*. Cambridge University Press, Cambridge.

Smith, Jackie, Charles Chatfield, and Ron Pagnucco (eds) (1997). *Transnational Social Movements and Global Politics: Solidarity beyond the State*. Syracuse University Press, Syracuse, NY.

Wapner, Paul (1996). *Environmental Activism and World Civic Politics*. SUNY Press.

WCED (World Commission on Environment and Development) (1987). *Our Common Future*. Oxford University Press, New York.

Weston, Burns H., Richard Falk, and Hilary Charlesworth (eds) (1997). *Supplement of Basic Documents to International Law and World Order*, 3rd rev. edn. West Publishing Company, St. Paul, MN, 705–16.

Yunker, James A. (1993). *World Union on the Horizon: The Case for Supranational Federation*. University Press of America, Lanham, MD.

Ziring, Lawrence, Robert Riggs, and Jack Plano (2000). *The United Nations: International Organization and World Politics*, 3rd edn. Harcourt College Publishers, Orlando, FL.

8

The Bretton Woods Institutions: Evolution, Reform, and Change

JONG-IL YOU

1. INTRODUCTION

The Bretton Woods institutions (BWIs), the International Monetary Fund (IMF) and the World Bank were created to bring about orderly development of the world economy in the post-Second World War era. The IMF was to oversee the new international monetary system of an adjustable peg linked to gold, and the World Bank to provide financing for reconstruction and development projects. Over the course of half a century, their roles have undergone drastic changes in response to changes in the economic realities and the dominant economic thinking. They have, at the same time, been key players in shaping the world of today. Reforming the BWIs will be a critical part of any effort to reform global economic governance in the new millennium.

On the occasion of the fiftieth anniversary of the Bretton Woods conference, a number of forums examined these institutions and proposed various reforms.[1] Momentum for serious reform of the BWIs, however, developed only after the Asian financial crisis in 1997 and its repercussions in Russia in 1998, which brought the world economy to the brink of collapse. It was the devastation of the great depression and the disastrous breakdown of the international monetary and trading system in the 1930s that led world leaders to create the BWIs in the belief that stable economic growth requires active economic management by government in both the domestic and international spheres. In the wake of the recent financial turmoil, the world is once again debating a new 'international financial architecture'.[2]

I am thankful to the comments and encouragement from Deepak Nayyar. I have also benefited greatly from discussions with Devish Kapur, Andrea Cornia, Robert Brenner, and other participants at the project meeting held in June 1999 in Helsinki. Anonymous referees also provided valuable suggestions. Needless to say, remaining inadequacies are solely mine.

[1] Prominent among these forums were the Bretton Woods Committee (Bretton Woods Commission 1994), the North–South Roundtable (Haq *et al.* 1995), the G-24 developing countries (Helleiner 1996), the Institute for International Economics (Kenen 1994) and the Bretton Woods institutions themselves (Boughton and Lateef 1995).

[2] See articles in the *Journal of Economic Perspectives* (fall 1999), the *Economic Journal* (Nov. 1999), and Ahluwalia (1999), Eichengreen (1999) and Sachs (1998). For official views, see Camdessus (1998), IMF

Devising a new and safer international financial architecture is not the only major challenge to the BWIs. Although capital flow volatility concerns mainly a couple of dozen middle-income developing countries and transition economies (the so-called emerging markets), its potential threat to the entire international financial system makes it a grave problem indeed. The persistent hunger and poverty of two billion people around the world and the lack of development in the poorest countries also pose a grave challenge. Amidst cheers for the highly efficient globalized markets, the poor of the world are losing ground further. More than half of the low-income economies saw a decline in living standards and a significant widening of the disparity between rich and poor countries over the past few decades (World Bank 1999*a*). The BWIs must ensure that the world economy provides opportunities for poor countries to sidestep the poverty trap and to start catching up with developed countries.

The acute financial crisis that threatens the middle-income countries and the chronic development crisis that grips most of the low-income countries call for a radical reform of the BWIs. This chapter is an attempt to suggest broad directions of reform. It employs historical and institutional approaches in trying to understand the sources of failures and limitations of the BWIs. A detailed blueprint for reform would require much technical and analytical work on specific issues, but at this stage, it is more important to forge a consensus on the direction of reform.

The rest of the chapter is organized as follows. The following section reviews the evolution of the BWIs, identifying the main driving forces behind the changes in the role and functions of the system. Section 3 discusses institutional reform, including reform of governance and conditionality. Section 4 discusses how to redefine the roles of the BWIs. A brief conclusion follows.

2. EVOLUTION OF THE BWIs

The BWIs were established in 1944 at the New Hampshire Conference where major governments negotiated the institutional set-up for the postwar world economic order. These institutions have made continuous adaptations to reflect the changing economic circumstances and have become quite different from the original concept. The single most important factor in this process of change has been the enormous growth of capital markets with increasing mobility of capital across borders.

2.1. *Original Design and the Golden Age*

The Bretton Woods system consisted of three elements. An adjustable peg system in which the US dollar played a key role was introduced. Rates of other currencies were pegged to the dollar that was to maintain a fixed parity to gold with infrequent changes in the pegged rates. Capital controls introduced during the wartime were to remain in place in an effort to prevent similar disruptive capital flows that occurred during the

(1999), UN (1999), Hills *et al.* (1999) which is a report of the Council on Foreign Relations and the Meltzer Commission (2000).

inter-war years. To oversee this new monetary approach, the IMF was created and endowed with financial resources and powers of surveillance. Exchange rates were to be adjusted only with the IMF's approval when 'fundamental disequilibria' occurred. In the event of temporary disequilibria, the IMF provided financing to member countries experiencing balance-of-payments difficulties in order to allow adjustments to be made without having to resort to excessively deflationary policies or import restrictions. This monetary and financial arrangement was to provide the basis for a liberal trading system. The International Trade Organization originally proposed to oversee international trade did not materialize, but GATT became its substitute.

While the IMF was designed to provide short-term balance of payments relief, the IBRD was to allocate longer-term funds for investment in productive endeavours. The IBRD has added new affiliates to the World Bank Group: IFC in 1956, IDA in 1960, ICSID in 1966, and MIGA in 1988. Even though the World Bank was almost an afterthought at the time of its creation, it has grown in importance to match the IMF. The Bank's mission was to mediate between the capital market and governments needing financial support for reconstruction and development projects. Backed by the uncalled portion of capital committed by member governments, the Bank offers funds at favourable rates to countries which would have difficulties acquiring loans on the market or which would have to borrow at considerably higher interest. The International Development Association (IDA), created in 1960, provides concessional loans to poor developing countries with funds made available through grants from rich capital-exporting member governments.

The quarter century following the creation of the BWIs is deservingly dubbed the 'golden age', an era when the world, except for Africa and parts of Asia, witnessed the greatest period of prosperity in its history. This era also coincided with the period of the Bretton Woods monetary system that ended with the transition to floating exchange rates among major currencies in 1973. It would, however, be misleading to ascribe the achievements of the golden age mainly to the successful functioning of the Bretton Woods system.

At the conclusion of the Second World War, the conditions for rapid growth were in place since the follower countries possessed advanced social capabilities needed to bridge the vast technological gap between the leader country (the US) and themselves (Abramovitz 1986). To realize the potential offered by the technological gap, domestic institutions for capital accumulation and international institutions for financial stability and trade expansion were required. Domestic institutions provided a social compromise between capital and labour based on collective bargaining and the welfare state, and the BWIs, aided by the hegemonic leadership of the US, and other institutions like the European Payment Union (EPU), filled the need for international institutions. The BWIs, therefore, constituted only one aspect of the golden age. Moreover, the relatively smooth operation of these institutions owed a great deal to the stability of the economic environment of that period (Eichengreen 1992). We should nonetheless note that the BWIs were successful in promoting financial stability and liberal trade among the advanced countries, and giving the opportunity to developing countries to latch on to a growing world economy.

One reason for the success of the Bretton Woods system was its institutional flexibility as exhibited, for example, by the Marshall Plan and the EPU created to complement BWI functions. After the successful currency convertibility of the European countries, achieved with the help of EPU, the IMF began to turn its attention increasingly to the developing countries in the 1960s. Another important innovation was the creation of SDRs in 1969 to respond to the shortage of international liquidity. However, one of the inherent difficulties of the Bretton Woods system, stemming from the asymmetry between the US dollar and other currencies, was the conflict between adequate provision of international liquidity and US balance-of-payments stability, known as the Triffin's dilemma. The creation of SDRs was to be the solution to this problem, but because of disputes over distribution, it was 'too little, too late' to prevent the eventual fall of the Bretton Woods system.

The IBRD also shifted its attention from reconstruction to development. In 1960, the IDA was established to provide concessional loans to poor countries with limited creditworthiness. It was an attempt to answer the needs of the newly independent countries in Africa and elsewhere and, at the same time, a measure to meet the demand of the developing countries for a soft loan or grant agency under the auspices of the UN. There was also an important shift in the activities of the World Bank. Initially, the Bank funded mainly infrastructure, with two-thirds of its assistance going to electric power and transportation projects during the first two decades of its operations, but later diversified into social projects and funding for policy reform.

2.2. *Adaptations in the World of Increasing Capital Mobility*

As a result of the shift to the floating rates system in 1973, the relatively tranquil Bretton Woods approach of fixed exchange rates with infrequent adjustments gave way to much greater exchange rate variability. The two oil shocks in the 1970s shook the world economy. These were followed by the debt crisis of the 1980s, a 'lost' decade for the majority of the developing world. In the 1990s, the world economy was faced with the challenge of transforming the former socialist planned economies into capitalist market economies. It was also severely tested by the volatility of capital flows that produced a new form of financial crisis originating from capital, rather than current, account.

Underlying much of this turbulence was the increasingly free and massive movement of capital. The demise of the Bretton Woods 'fixed-but-adjustable' rate system itself owes a great deal to this. The very success of the BWIs meant that countries had become more integrated through increased trade and capital flows as exchange restrictions and capital controls were replaced with convertibility and increasing capital mobility. While these helped to fuel international trade and investment, they also became the force to unhinge the par value system because any hint of an impending devaluation within this system would invite speculative attacks, making it impossible for governments to make low-key exchange rates adjustments, as changes in economic fundamentals would have necessitated. Devaluations were, therefore, effected only in crisis conditions and at severe political cost. These difficulties were accentuated by the gradual liberalization of capital movements; that is, increasing capital mobility compounded the difficulty of balancing flexibility and commitment inherent in the fixed-but-adjustable exchange rate system.

The debt crisis, originating from recycled oil dollars in the aftermath of the first oil shock, was triggered by a steep rise in interest rates and the ensuing world recession of the early 1980s. The commercial bank-centred recycling of oil dollars dragged many developing countries into excessive indebtedness, creating systemic risks. The Fund failed to recognize the risks of, or to intervene in, this process. Even after the outbreak of the debt crisis, IMF response was slow, weak and inadequate, and resolution of the crisis had to wait for an initiative of the US Treasury, the Brady Plan of 1989. Similar failures were repeated in the 1990s. The Fund failed to focus on the growing risks of the large capital inflows into Mexico before the 1994–95 crisis, or those of Asian countries before the 1997–98 crisis.

The shift from the par value system to floating exchange rates seemed to diminish the Fund's role as the guarantor of exchange rate stability and regulator of international liquidity, and the Fund responded by intensifying its 'surveillance' role in monitoring domestic policies. The argument was that, since the exchange rate was going to be determined in the market, the Fund needed to monitor not only exchange rate policy, but also domestic, fiscal, and monetary policies that affected exchange rates. But the Fund's surveillance proved to be inadequate in securing exchange rate stability. The floating rate system was characterized by excessive volatility in the 1970s under managed floating and by large misalignments in the 1980s when the US and Japanese governments became more liberal towards exchange rates. Liberalization of capital accounts led to a rapid increase in gross capital flows, making exchange rates more susceptible to changes in sentiment and short-term movements of capital than changes in economic fundamentals.

While many saw the need for effective coordination of macroeconomic and exchange rate policies of major industrial countries, the Fund shied away from taking an active role, leaving the task of policy coordination to the squabbling G-7 governments.[3] Instead, Fund surveillance was confined to the role of 'limiting the likelihood and severity of difficulties calling for [its] support' (Masson and Mussa 1997). The IMF's uneasiness in dealing with the exchange rate issue is also reflected in its country programmes, in which recommendations wavered between fixed and floating rates. Contrary to what its name and mandate suggest, the Fund remained less concerned about exchange rate policy than fiscal policy and inflation.

After the abandonment of the Bretton Woods system, the Fund and the Bank evolved into agents of structural reform for debt-ridden developing countries, with loans as inducements and conditionality as the weapon. With the transfer to floating exchange rates and the growth of capital markets, the Fund became irrelevant as a source of finance for the developed countries and began to concentrate on developing, and later transition, countries. The Fund was thus moving closer to development financing

---

[3] The Bretton Woods Commission (1994) suggested that the IMF take over the responsibility of policy coordination from the G-7 countries in order to reduce exchange rate volatility and misalignments, and eventually to introduce a system of flexible exchange rate bands.

with the creation of such new longer-term loan facilities as the Extended Fund Facility in 1974 and Structural Adjustment Facility in 1986. In doing so, the Fund began to promote structural reforms in the borrowing countries, stretching its mandate by arguing that these reforms would strengthen the countries' prospects for growth and thereby reduce exchange rate instability and the need for IMF assistance. While this shift started as a response to the first oil crisis and the ensuing balance-of-payments difficulties in many oil-importing countries, full-blown focus on structural reforms was motivated by the debt crisis of the 1980s. This move has led to widening the scope for loan conditions. As chief architect of adjustment programmes, the Fund now incorporated a whole range of structural reforms on its agenda.

The Bank, on the other hand, began to grant loans for balance-of-payments support as many developing countries experienced severe macroeconomic imbalances and accumulating external debts after the oil crises. The Bank introduced structural adjustment lending in 1979, but it was in the early 1980s that the Bank, in an effort to tackle the deepening economic problems of developing countries, launched in earnest its programme of reforms to eliminate structural rigidities and improve incentives.[4] The structural adjustment loans differed from past lending modalities in their focus on balance-of-payments problems rather than on specific projects or sector reforms, and in the introduction of explicit and detailed conditionalities, as well as greater commitment on the part of the Bank to enforce these (Kapur 1997).

With the Fund moving closer to development financing and structural reform and the Bank increasing its role for balance-of-payment support and policy reform, their activities started to overlap (Ahluwalia 1999). At the same time, the views of the two institutions converged greatly, producing the so-called 'Washington consensus' that underpinned their operations in developing and transition economies in the 1980s and 1990s.

2.3. *Washington Consensus*

The Washington consensus refers to the development approach, which arose from the integration of traditional IMF concerns for macroeconomic stability (anti-inflation, anti-deficit policies) and the Bank's agenda of efficiency-enhancing reforms (openness, competition, deregulation, privatization). A typical package of IMF stabilization and World Bank adjustment includes fiscal and monetary austerity, devaluation, trade liberalization, financial liberalization and banking system restructuring, price liberalization, privatization, labour market deregulation, tax reform, and subsidy cuts (Williamson 1990).

The birth of the Washington consensus reflected a shift in ideology toward neoliberalism that emerged after the erosion of the golden age. The golden age growth regime had been based on a social compromise on income distribution and Keynesian management of domestic demand and international liquidity. The reason for the

---

[4] Adjustment lending increased rapidly, accounting for about 25 per cent of the Bank's total lending during the second half of the 1980s.

demise of the golden age is debatable, but problems arose in both areas (Marglin 1990; Schor and You 1995). Renewed capital–labour conflicts and mounting difficulties since the late 1960s in the monetary system, in addition to such exogenous disturbances as the oil shocks, led to a profit squeeze, productivity slowdown, and rising inflation in the 1970s. Neoliberalism emerged in this context as the offensive from capital, with the aim to repudiate the deal with labour and to reduce the role of the state in economic management. The conservative governments of Thatcher and Reagan at the beginning of the 1980s ushered in the era of neoliberalism.

As ideology shifted toward neoliberalism, Keynesianism and structuralism were discredited by economics professionals. These changes in the dominant thinking formed the background for the rise of the Washington consensus. While many of the policies in the Washington package could have been useful if applied pragmatically, they were typically implemented with excessive zeal in an effort to achieve the textbook ideal, and without due consideration to institutional, political, and other local factors. As a result, they often created such unexpected pressures as demand overkill, financial instability, increased corruption, and deterioration in income distribution (Taylor 1997). These have been particularly acute in the case of transition economies where 'big bang' reforms have taken place. This is not the forum for a comprehensive evaluation of Fund–Bank structural adjustment programmes. Suffice it to note that most studies, including those by BWI staff, find no systematic effects on growth, inflation, and income distribution, although individual country episodes of disaster or success are common.[5] The studies report only moderate improvement in the balance of payments but at the cost of declining aggregate investment.

The problems of the Washington consensus may be summarized as follows. Growth-related dialogue takes issue with the short-term orientation of adjustment programmes. Compression of aggregate demand being the preferred means of adjustment, these programmes were blamed for the lack of concern for improvement in growth prospects and often for actual damage to growth prospects by implementing cuts in public investment (Taylor 1988). Equity-oriented criticism, on the other hand, reflects the adverse effects of adjustment programmes on poverty and income distribution. Indeed, such adverse effects were apparent in most Latin American and African countries, although not in Asia (Stewart 1995). The sustainability-oriented dialogue criticizes the BWIs not only for their insensitivity to the environmental impact of their programmes, but also criticizes the institutions for their single-minded pursuit of liberalization policies on the ground that 'Illiberal policies, which do not damage overall macro stability are preferable to liberal policies, which are inherently unsustainable or endanger macro instability' (Rodrik 1990: 933).[6] On a more specific level, the drive to

---

[5] See Schadler *et al.* (1995) and Fischer (1997) for the views of IMF staff. Killick's analysis (1995*a*: 157) contains a review of many studies, and he concludes that the adjustment programmes have 'rather limited revealed effects on developing country economies'.

[6] These critiques are encapsulated in a report by the Group of Twenty-Four (G-24 1987: 9): 'The experience of developing countries that have undertaken Fund supported adjustment programmes has not generally been satisfactory. The Fund approach to adjustment has had severe economic costs for many of these countries in terms of declines in the levels of output and growth rates, reductions in employment and

promote financial and capital account liberalization in developing and transition economies has proven to be dangerous.

2.4. *Two Neoliberal Crises*

The structural reforms and liberalization measures of the Washington consensus that were introduced in the 1980s and 1990s could not prevent the general decline of growth in most parts of world, with Sub-Saharan Africa and the former Soviet Union experiencing disastrous falls in standards of living. Until 1997, East Asia was the notable exception, but has since then gone through a serious financial crisis and setback. The neoliberal world economy has exhibited two kinds of crises: the acute financial crisis, which has hit many emerging-market economies and the chronic development crisis that has gripped much of the poor developing world.

The incredible rise in the mobility of capital—with about two trillion dollars currently crossing borders every day, and 80 per cent of which is purely speculative—has become a major threat to economic stability. Indeed, the 1990s witnessed a series of major crises—Mexico in 1994, East Asia in 1997, Russia in 1998 and Brazil in 1999—all of which shared the common element that these problems originated in the capital account, unlike earlier payment crises, which arose in the current account (Ahluwalia 1999). After the premature and hasty liberalization of capital movements, developing and transition economies became vulnerable to periods of rapid expansion of capital flows and their abrupt reversals, a problem aggravated by fragile domestic financial structures, and weak financial regulation and supervision. Capital account liberalization, by exposing a country to the ebbs and flows of capital that are regulated by the judgement and opinions of international bankers and fund managers, turned an entire range of economic and social policies into a popularity contest. Losers in this contest, which may not necessarily be fair because of imperfections in information flows, suffer crises of confidence. Such crises have often been quite contagious, increasing the systemic risks of the global financial structure.

Having helped generate the financial crises by urging capital account liberalization in developing and transition economies, the Fund took on the role of firefighters, enlisting the Bank for a supporting role. The quick recoveries of Mexico and Asia are taken by some as vindication of the Fund's role in crisis management. These quick recoveries, however, may simply have been a consequence of the fact that the crises were mainly panic-driven. In fact, the patent failure of the Fund's initial rescue operations in the wake of the Asian financial crisis underscored the fact that it was ill-equipped to deal with this new form of crisis (Radelet and Sachs 1998). Troubled countries, faced with a large sudden capital flow reversal, would have needed sufficient up-front support or swift debt rescheduling rather than phased-funding that comes

---

adverse effects on income distribution. A typical Fund programme prescribes measures that require excessive compression of domestic demand, cuts in real wages, and reductions in government expenditures; these are frequently accompanied by sharp exchange rate depreciation and import liberalization measures, without due regard to their potentially disruptive effects on the domestic economy'.

with high conditionality. Stricken Asian countries began to show signs of stabilization and recovery only after debt rescheduling and a relaxation of the belt-tightening measures initially imposed by the Fund. The recent financial crises have necessitated a rethinking of the global financial system and the role of the Fund.

While the Fund must redefine its role so as to meet the challenges of the new financial reality with primary focus on prevention and management of acute financial crises in the emerging market economies, the Bank needs to confront the other failure of the neoliberal era, chronic development crisis. The poorest countries of the world have fared badly in the neoliberal era. Between 1980 and 1997, out of the 37 low-income economies for which data are available, per capita private consumption fell in 20 countries and stagnated in 2.[7] In contrast, it fell in only 13 out of 40 middle-income economies and in none of the 21 high-income economies. Regionally, Sub-Saharan Africa suffered the most, with 22 out of 33 countries recording a negative or zero growth in per capita consumption. Many of these countries saw disastrous declines in living standards.

The dismal economic performance of the poorest countries translates into increasing disparity between rich and poor nations. Between 1970 and 1995, average per capita GDP of the poorest third of all countries dropped from 3.1 to 1.9 per cent of the richest third, a relative income decline of 39 per cent (World Bank 1999a). The result is devastating: globally, 20 per cent of the world's people in the poorest countries account for a minuscule 1.3 per cent of total private consumption (UNDP 1998). These people live in such abject poverty that their calorie intake is inadequate to support active life.

Many of the countries in the grip of a development crisis have followed the neo-liberal prescriptions of the Washington consensus. At the same time, China and India among the low-income economies and the East Asian countries among the middle-income economies have been able to register spectacular success in development by diverging from the standard prescription. The Bank needs to acknowledge its past failures and to find new and more effective ways to address the persistent poverty currently affecting two billion people and the chronic development crisis of the poorest countries.

3. INSTITUTIONAL REFORM OF THE BWIs

The importance of institutional reform of the BWIs cannot be overemphasized. Since they are monopolists or near-monopolists, they cannot be disciplined by external competition or the 'exit' option (Stiglitz 1999). The alternative, the 'voice' mechanism, has not worked well because of poor governance in terms of representation and participation, accountability, and transparency. As a result, many flaws and failures have persisted, including conditionality which, in spite of theoretical controversies and practical difficulties, continues to proliferate and to become increasingly intrusive.

---

[7] See World Bank (1999a: 232, table 2) for growth of per capita private consumption and World Bank (1999a: 290) for classification of economies by income and region.

3.1. *Governance in the BWIs*

A defining characteristic of the governance of the BWIs is that major shareholders, the rich industrial countries, control decision-making and that the borrowing countries have little say. Although BWIs are formally cooperative agencies, which member countries own and which they voluntarily join, real ownership belongs to select powerful countries. This ownership is ensured by a quota-based voting system.[8] In order to maintain their identities as universal and public organizations, the BWIs allocated equally to all members a certain share of votes, namely the basic votes, but never to such an extent as to threaten the control of the major shareholders. In fact, the proportion of basic votes has been dramatically reduced, from a peak of 14 per cent in 1955 at the Fund to around 3 per cent at both the Fund and the Bank, to ensure that control remains invested with the wealthy countries even after decolonization led to an increasing, and eventually almost universal, membership at the BWIs (Woods 1998).

The quota-based voting system meant that perspectives and interests of rich capital-exporting countries pervaded the BWIs. Combined with the fact that no country would commit large amounts of resources for international purposes without trying to advance its own power and interests, the voting system produced major problems.

First, there has been a tendency to advocate financial restraint over Keynesian expansion, particularly in the Fund. Reflecting the dominant economic thinking and the political currents of the time, there was definitely a Keynesian, social democratic and internationalist spirit in the original design of the BWIs.[9] But, compared to ideas contained in the 'clearing union' proposal by Keynes himself, the IMF came to be decidedly less Keynesian (Singer 1995). As a result, the Fund's programmes have been perennially accused of a bias toward demand overkill—an ironic situation, given that the very rationale of IMF loans is to avoid unnecessary deflationary adjustments. It is only natural that lenders advocate financial conservatism, because borrowers may be inclined toward financial irresponsibility. Initially, it was the capital-exporting US that vetoed the more expansionary British Plan and the commodity price stabilization scheme. It was the US that insisted, over objections by the Europeans, on the introduction of conditionality. But as European countries became donors, their stand on loan conditionality and financial discipline for borrowing countries came to resemble that of the US. German and Japanese reluctance to expand their economies in the 1980s also point to inherent difficulties of international Keynesianism without political integration.

Second, as a result of undue influence from large shareholders, there have been too many politically motivated loan decisions. Dominance by the United States, the largest shareholder, meant a frequent injection of US politics and foreign policy into loan

---

[8] The quotas are to reflect the relative economic strength of member countries, but quota adjustments are highly political and do not reflect a coherent principle.

[9] The purpose of the IMF as set out in Article 1 of the Articles of Agreement includes 'the promotion and maintenance of high levels of employment and real income' and 'providing opportunity to correct maladjustments in [the] balance of payments without resorting to measures destructive of national or international prosperity' in addition to international monetary cooperation, exchange stability, expansion of trade, and convertibility.

decisions by the BWIs, violating the principle of political neutrality.[10] But the US was not alone in its attempts to manipulate loan decisions for advancing its own economic and political objectives. The EU—in what is perhaps the most egregious lending in IMF's history, the loans to Russia—has been at least as guilty as the US. Other notable examples include the role of France in francophone Africa and Japan in Asia in pressuring the BWIs to lend in a manner that bolsters the interests of these countries.

Third, excluding borrowing countries from the decision-making processes provided the institutional conditions for the proliferation of increasingly intrusive conditionality and lack of ownership in the adjustment programmes. Greater participation by countries directly affected by BWI decisions would have ameliorated the situation. It must be added that participation is not entirely a matter of formal governance structure. Notable exceptions notwithstanding, representatives of borrowing countries were often more interested in enjoying their stay in Washington than in articulating their views at executive meetings.

Flaws in the governance of the Bretton Woods institutions are also evident in the lack of accountability and transparency of their operations. Even in the formal set-up, the BWIs are accountable to the finance ministers of member countries who may not necessarily be impartial representatives of the people (Stiglitz 1999). In practice, such accountability means little. Risks of IMF programmes have been disproportionately borne by borrowing countries, with little risk to IMF or its major shareholders (Kapur 1997). The World Bank situation is no different. Controversy has risen over various Bank-financed projects that resulted in poor performance or the destruction of indigenous people's livelihoods and environment, again with little responsibility borne by the Bank.[11] It even objected to independent project evaluations before being forced by US Congress pressure to introduce these (van de Laar 1980). The Fund has acquiesced to external evaluations only recently.

Accountability suffers when information on decisions and operations of institutions are not subject to public scrutiny. Even though the Fund and Bank both publish copious volumes of operational information, the public does not have access to the most sensitive facts regarding actual decision-making process. Tens of billions of dollars have been committed during confidential telephone conversations between the managing director of the Fund and the finance ministers of a few key countries. The BWIs are justly accused of preaching—but not practising—transparency (Sachs 1997).

The lack of transparency and accountability has allowed the expansion of programmes and objectives. As economic conditions and policy objectives evolved, new

---

[10] Examples of how the IMF and the Bank were used to promote the US foreign policy agenda include, among others, rejection of the loans to Poland and Czechoslovakia in 1949, cessation of lending to Chile during the Allende years and to Vietnam and Afghanistan in 1979, and support for Turkey in the mid-1950s and El Salvador in the 1980s despite European objections (Payer 1982).

[11] Some of the infamous projects include the Sardar Sarovar dam project in India, the Polonoroeste frontier development scheme in Brazil and the Pak Mun dam project in Thailand. While Bank policies recommend adequate compensation for people forcibly displaced by its projects, a Bank review could not point to a single example of a Bank-financed resettlement plan in Latin America or Africa where the Bank's guidelines had been implemented properly (World Bank 1994).

agendas have been added, but without a clear demarcation of the roles or a refocus of the programmes. More serious still, limited accountability has enabled failed practices and flawed doctrines to continue, as the persistent practice of conditionality and the continuing influence of the Washington consensus exemplify.

3.2. *Conditionality*

Conditionality, due to opposition from European members, was not embodied in the original IMF Articles of Agreement. The Fund was in fact considered 'a sort of automatic machine selling foreign exchange to members within certain limits and on certain terms' as Mr Gutt, the managing director, put it in a 1946 statement to the executive board (Dell 1981). The Fund began to apply conditionality in 1952.[12] With the successive introduction of standby agreements, phasing and binding performance criteria over the 1950s, conditionality steadily became more onerous. As the Fund began to promote structural reform in the 1970s, performance criteria per programme were increased by 50 per cent over the 1970s to the 1980s (Killick 1995*a*).

The World Bank followed the IMF's lead in this. While Bank loans had always implied project-level conditionality in the form of loan covenants, the introduction of structural adjustment lending resulted in conditionality becoming highly formal, explicit and detailed. As the Bank devoted increasing resources to structural adjustment, the scope of loan conditions also expanded. From an initial focus on fiscal and trade policies and price liberalization, increasing emphasis was given to privatization and deregulation, and public and financial sector reforms. In addition to these purely economic conditionalities, the Bank's agenda expanded further in the 1990s to include environment, governance, and public expenditures on its agenda (Kapur 1997). The proliferation of conditionalities and interference with domestic politics inevitably followed. For instance, the average number of Bank conditions per adjustment loan increased from 39 in 1980–88 to 56 in 1989–91 (Killick 1995*b*).

The proliferation of conditionality occurred as developing countries replaced European countries as principal borrowers. Initially, Europe's abhorrence of interference with its domestic policies prevented the inclusion of conditionality in the Fund's Articles of Agreement.[13] Even when conditionality was firmly established, a large standby arrangement was approved for the United Kingdom in 1967 with a minimum of conditions. This provoked developing country executive directors to demand equal treatment, and it became apparent that performance criteria for loans to Latin American and Asian members were, on average, far greater than for Europeans (Dell 1981).

---

[12] Introduced initially as a matter of a Board policy decision, it was not until 1969 that the principle of conditionality was given explicit legal sanction through an amendment of the Articles of Agreement.

[13] Interference by Bretton Woods institutions staff in the economic affairs of their members 'would have surprised the American delegation to Bretton Woods and would probably have infuriated the British, who regarded national economic sovereignty as an absolute, whatever might be agreed about plans for a Fund and a Bank' (Oliver 1985: 41).

As European countries stopped borrowing from the Fund and the Bank, their objection to conditionality faded and the BWIs, without complaints from Europe, developed increasingly intrusive programmes as they focused on structural adjustment and reform in developing countries. They came to see themselves as the catalyst for change rather than mere financial institutions. Their experience with structural reform during the debt crisis was utilized in the 1990s after the collapse of the Soviet Union and the liberation of its former Eastern European satellites. Entrusted by the G-7, the BWIs directed the transition experiment, implementing far-reaching stabilization and reform measures. They also attempted a similar transformation exercise in Asia during the financial crisis of 1997, by trying to convert non-orthodox market economies into orthodox ones. This provoked Feldstein (1998: 27) to ask, 'If the policies to be changed are also practised in the major industrial economies of Europe, would the IMF think it appropriate to force similar changes in those countries if they were subject to a fund programme?'

On a conceptual level, we can identify four separate conditionality problems. First, there is the conditionality content problem. Many critics have objected to the monetarist aspect and the neoliberal zeal that conditionality frequently embodies. Moreover, the so-called 'one-size-fits-all' approach of the BWIs in designing and implementing programmes has often neglected both the economic and socio-political circumstances of specific countries.

Second, conditionality—expanding into areas, which have no direct bearing on loan repayment, including wide-ranging structural reform issues—has become an infringement on national sovereignty (Collier and Gunning 1999). And the recent tendency of donor governments, responding to pressures from single-issue NGOs, to impose non-economic conditions on human rights, social policy, and the environment is making its way to the BWIs. Regardless of how desirable the changes sought by these international financial institutions may be, they should not be forced on crisis-stricken governments.

Third, conditionality subverts the democratic process when it goes beyond the essential macroeconomic adjustments needed to restore balance of payments (Stiglitz 1999). In the name of efficiency and good economics, the BWIs tend to impose policies on more or less reluctant governments desperate for money that should rightfully be decided by domestic politics, for instance central bank independence or labour market rules. 'This process . . . has undermined political legitimacy in dozens of developing countries, especially since the IMF is often happy to conspire with governments to make end runs around parliaments in the interests of "reform". . . . [We should aim] to restore legitimacy to local politics, and abandon the misguided belief that the IMF and World Bank can micro-manage the process of economic reform' (Sachs 1998).

Fourth, conditionality is an ineffective tool for changing the policies of recipient governments, not to mention, improving economic performance.[14] Externally

---

[14] See Mosley *et al.* (1995). Indirect evidence on the ineffectiveness of conditionality is provided by Bank staff, who show that Bank supervision had no significant effect on success, after controlling for political economy variables (Dollar and Svensson 1997).

imposed conditionality undermines local 'ownership', the extent to which a borrowing government would regard a programme as its own. It also invites a lack of commitment to carry out programmes, undermines the legitimacy of programmes, and strengthens opposition to reform. It can even drive reform-minded governments to oppose reform in order to maximize the price at which reform can be sold (Gilbert *et al.* 1999). The proliferation of conditionality has thus produced a high incidence of non-compliance in both Fund and Bank programmes. Non-compliance, in turn, has induced 'paper conditionality': the introduction of programmes, which, as all parties recognize, will not be implemented but merely satisfy the need to keep money moving (Martin 1991). These incentive problems render conditionality rather ineffective.

3.3. *Directions for Institutional Reform*

It is vital that the BWIs, in order to continue as the central institutions for governing global economy, reform their structures of governance and modes of operation. First, they must devise ways in which developing country concerns can be better rep-resented, because shared stewardship is needed more than ever. Transforming the Interim Committee and the Development Committee, currently ceremonial advisory agents, into decision-making bodies with better representation of the developing and transition countries would be one such option.[15] At the same time, the voting system must be reformed to give greater representation to the developing countries. This is not to suggest an equal vote for countries of different size and capabilities, because an equal vote would not only be unworkable due to the superpowers' reluctance to participate, but it would also imply a highly distorted representation among peoples. Some combination of quota-based votes and basic votes would seem to offer a rea-sonable solution. Although this is precisely the system used by the BWIs, the share of basic votes at present is so minimal that these have little impact. Perhaps an arrangement of a 'double-majority' rule, requiring a majority in both quota-based votes and basic votes is needed.[16]

Second, transparency and accountability need to be strengthened. While there have been recent efforts to provide more information and to acknowledge external evaluations, they fall short of what is needed. External evaluation of individual programmes must be strengthened, with representatives from relevant countries included in the appraisal teams, and the staff in charge held accountable for failed programmes. All relevant information should be made available, and the practice of decision by consensus, which keeps genuine decisions, negotiations, and arm-twisting behind the scenes should be replaced with open discussions and voting procedures (Woods 1998).

---

[15] I am persuaded by the view of Ahluwalia (1999) on this issue. At the annual meeting of 1999, the IMF board of governors approved the transformation of the Interim Committee into the International Monetary and Financial Committee. In addition to the name change, more substantive discussions are expected as there is now an explicit provision for preparatory meetings. But there is no change in the composition of the committee or in its status as an advisory body.

[16] See Woods (1998) for a good discussion on this issue.

Third, the practice of conditionality should be reformed. As a remedy to conditionality ineffectiveness, some scholars have argued for simpler terms and stronger penalties for countries that renege (Mosley *et al.* 1995; Hills *et al.* 1999). Having the government of the recipient country formulate its adjustment programmes in order to strengthen ownership is also an option. A more drastic reform proposal is to make conditionality *ex post*—that is, to direct loans to only those countries that have good policies in place and thus simply make conditionality obsolete (Gilbert *et al.* 1999). The majority opinion of the International Financial Institution Advisory Commission, popularly known as the Meltzer Commission and which was established in 1998 by the US Congress as part of the legislation authorizing additional funding by the US for the IMF, takes a similar approach by proposing 'pre-conditions for liquidity assistance' (Meltzer Commission 2000).

These reform proposals are not without certain drawbacks. Simpler conditionality may reduce—but not eliminate—the ownership/incentive aspect. The Fund, in loans to support balance of payments, could take this approach, but with a built-in modification option, in case demand compression exceeds target. Programmes formulated by recipient countries can succeed only if the governments concerned are committed to reform, and the BWIs are prepared to approve the programmes with minimal BWI input. Otherwise, it would simply be a cosmetic change. Therefore, this idea may best be put into practice in conjunction with *ex post* conditionality. As far as 'good policy' countries are concerned, it makes eminent sense for the BWI to provide automatic approval of a programme prepared by the recipient country and thus eliminate conditionality, as we know it. The issue here is determining the criteria to be used for evaluating the recipient as a 'good policy' or a 'poor policy' country. These stipulations, however indirect, could still infringe on sovereignty and undermine the democratic political process. In order to minimize this problem, the criteria must be restricted to a small set of policy variables.[17]

Another problem with *ex post* conditionality is that it will steer resources away from 'poor policy' countries, often the most needy. These countries have been turning to the Fund programme after programme, creating the Fund trend of approving programmes for a permanent group of developing countries (Bird 1996). As there is not much point in keeping these countries in a debt trap, the Fund should get out by simply forgiving these countries their debts and leave the task to the Bank. The Bank, on the other hand, should not simply sustain aid to these recipients, but increase it, albeit in a totally different manner as is discussed in the next section.

Fourth, efforts should be made to decentralize as much as possible the decision-making process and research activities of the BWIs that are currently concentrated in their Washington headquarters. Without such a move, it will be difficult to achieve true ownership and involvement of the people and to devise policies that fully

---

[17] The Meltzer Commission (2000) recommends four pre-conditions: freedom of entry and operation for foreign financial institutions, publication of the maturity structure of the outstanding sovereign and guaranteed debt and off-balance sheet liabilities, adequate capitalization of commercial banks, and a proper fiscal requirement. Financial market opening and commercial bank capitalization seem overly restrictive conditions, and the fiscal requirement needs to be made simple and explicit.

acknowledge special local conditions. Transferring more research and decision-making activities to the local offices is essential for enhancing ownership, and the Bank fully realizes the importance of ownership.[18] Rhetorical change aside, however, there is little change in ground operations. Meetings are being held with local NGOs and labour unions, but these constitute mere cosmetic touches rather than serious consensus building.

Decentralization of research in the BWIs would also be an effective way of injecting a greater dose of pragmatism to programmes and greater diversity to the intellectual and political perspectives of institutional thinking. Because of the screening effect of the hiring process and the later socialization effect, the staff community in Washington is apt to become more or less homogeneous in its outlook and to assume doctrinaire positions without much regard to the specificities of local contexts. This has to change. The size of staff at the Washington headquarters should be cut radically, and more research projects should be conducted within recipient countries. This would also enable a substantial increase in hiring local economists who are knowledgeable about specific local conditions and the subtle political implications. At the same time, it will help build up local capacity in policy research.

4. REDEFINING THE ROLES OF THE BWIs

Capital flow volatility and the contagious nature of recent financial crises prove that the current international financial system is unable to safeguard the world economy and that a new, safer international financial architecture is needed. At the same time, the persistent development crisis calls for a major rethinking of the options available to help accelerate growth in poor countries. It is in the context of these challenges that we must redefine the roles of the BWIs.

4.1. *New International Financial Architecture and the Fund*

The recent crises provoked impassioned calls for a fundamental overhaul of global financial governance. There emerged a shared sense of crisis and a broad agreement on the need for serious reforms in the summer of 1998, when the crisis-stricken East Asia was plunging into the depths of recession and, particularly after the Russian crisis, the contagion effect was threatening a global deflation. However, the BWIs and G-7 are once again retreating into complacency and business as usual. The 1999 Bank–Fund annual meeting was a big disappointment. The dominant feeling was that the crisis has passed, that lessons have been learned and that more intelligent *ad hoc* action is a better bet than grand systemic reforms. The Meltzer Commission (2000) came up with a surprisingly far-reaching reform proposal. Despite the political weight it carries, however, its main proposals—that the Fund must reduce its role by focusing

---

[18] A report by its Evaluations Department found a highly significant relationship between borrower ownership and programme success (Johnston and Wasty 1993). The IMF was more reluctant to acknowledge the importance of this issue, but has recently come around to advocate greater ownership.

on short-term liquidity crisis assistance and eliminating long-term loans for structural reform, and that the Bank must be transformed from capital-intensive lenders to a development agency that provides poverty alleviation grants to poor countries without capital market access—have met with a strong opposition from the US Treasury (Summers 2000) and failed to gather effective support from the Congress.

So far, the IMF's response to the calls for reform has resulted in relatively marginal actions in the areas of surveillance and transparency and some modifications in financing facilities such as replacing ESAF with the Poverty Reduction and Growth Facility (PRGF), creating the Supplemental Reserve Facility (SRF) and the Contingent Credit Lines (CCL) and eliminating a few unused facilities. These changes amount to little in terms of addressing the 'enormous discrepancy that exists between an increasingly sophisticated and dynamic international financial world, with rapid globalization of financial portfolios, and the lack of a proper institutional framework to regulate it' (UN 1999). This state of affairs did not evolve out of the blue. As indicated in the historical review, the Fund has been increasingly marginalized in managing capital flows and exchange rates even as they become more and more volatile. Rather, the Fund has been drawn into clearing up the financial mess left behind by volatile capital flows. Many of the proposals for strengthening international financial architecture concern measures that individual countries, both recipient and originating countries, should do, or the creation of new international institutions. As worthy as these may be, it is of central importance that the Fund plays a constructive role in stabilizing global finance through crisis prevention, not just crisis management.

First, the Fund, along with the Bank, should help strengthen the financial systems of individual countries through such measures as greater transparency, better regulation and supervision, and improved corporate governance and bankruptcy laws.[19] There are two caveats, however. For one thing, it would be difficult and probably unwise to apply universal global standards, given the diversity of economic conditions and institutional capacity. Instead of imposing universal standards, the emphasis should be on helping countries improve laws and regulations in order to minimize systemic risks and develop the expertise to back up national laws. For another, insofar as common minimum standards are advisable, there are disagreements on the proper institution to take charge of setting up and implementing them. While many seem content to leave the task to the BWIs or other existing institutions like the Basle Committee and the International Organization of Securities Commissions, others see the importance of creating a global financial regulator (Eatwell and Taylor 1998; Kaufman 1998). In any case, with a multiplicity of accumulated country experience at their disposal, the BWIs are well positioned to play a constructive role in this regard.

Second, the Fund should review its position on capital account liberalization. The BWIs were created at a time when capital controls were almost the universal practice.

---

[19] While this is commonly recognized as something that capital-recipient countries must do, it is also important for capital-originating countries to take some measures in this area. Chief among them are strengthening the regulation of highly-leveraged financial institutions and the introduction of 'collective action clauses' in their sovereign bond contracts so that developing countries could do the same without being stigmatized in the market (Hills *et al.* 1999).

While these agencies were instrumental in promoting financial market integration and free capital mobility, they are not adequately prepared to deal with the volatility and contingency problems. Therefore, unless the international financial system is radically improved, it is vital that developing and transition economies retain their autonomy in managing capital accounts.[20]

In fact, the Fund should go one step further and officially sanction and encourage certain types of measures to curb excessive inflows of short-term capital in developing and transition economies that are affected by weak financial supervision and regulation (see, for instance, Hills *et al.* 1999). While the benefits of free capital flows are yet to be established, it is clear that capital account liberalization has created difficulties in macroeconomic management and vulnerabilities in financial systems (Bhagwati 1998; Furman and Stiglitz 1998). The fact that China and India in Asia and Chile in Latin America were able to avoid severe financial gyrations or sharp output contractions during recent regional crises should not be overlooked.[21] In a sense, capital controls, particularly with regard to inflows, are a form of prudential policy operating at the macro level. It seems illogical for those who advocate tightening prudential regulation on financial institutions to be hostile toward any measures to control capital flows.

Third, in the interest of more rational management of global demand, the Fund should assume responsibility for macroeconomic policy coordination and exchange rate stabilization, instead of leaving the task to the G-7 (or G-3 after the monetary unification in EU). Currency fluctuations among the G-3 can have serious repercussions on smaller economies, generating macroeconomic imbalances and financial instabilities. Unfortunately, the Fund remains non-committed on the issue of exchange rate management, and suggests further study as the only answer (IMF 1999). As more and more developing economies choose to float their currencies in thin exchange markets, the Fund needs to pay greater attention to exchange rate stability.

Fourth, the Fund should reconsider its lending policy by moving away from long-term lending and focusing on its role as global lender of last resort. The Fund has not been effective in helping poor countries through its concessional long-term loans, and the overlap with the Bank activities is better removed. It must be noted that the Fund, together with the G-7 governments, has already assumed the role of lender of last resort by providing emergency rescue financing to countries facing liquidity crises. In order to strengthen this role, the Fund recently created new facilities: the Supplemental Reserve Facility and the Contingent Credit Lines. However, in spite of increased resources through the New Arrangements to Borrow in 1998 and increased

---

[20] The IMF Articles of Agreement (Article VI, section 3) authorize member countries to 'exercise such controls as are necessary to regulate international capital movements'. However, the Fund, prodded by the US Treasury, had been pushing to broaden its mandate to include capital account convertibility before the Asian financial crisis. While the Fund has, since then, tempered its position to advocate 'cautious' liberalization of capital account, it is still committed to the goal of capital account liberalization (Camdessus 1999).

[21] This is not to say that capital controls are without problems and costs. But they seem minor compared to the big danger of free capital mobility. Opponents of capital controls point to the fact that Chile has recently removed taxes on capital inflows. But the rationale of the Chilean system is precisely to be able to adjust tax rates according to economic conditions. Chile removed the taxes as the current account went into deficit and consequently there was need to attract more foreign capital.

quota in 1999, these measures are inadequate to counter major swings in capital flows.[22] Reliance on supplementary funds from G-7 governments has at times resulted in the inclusion of unnecessary loan conditions.[23] If the Fund were to be a true global lender of last resort, it would have to be empowered to issue SDRs to itself, subject to a limit, which would be eliminated on repurchase by the borrowing country (UN 1999). This move would ease the Fund's problem of resource shortage as well as relieve some of the pressure exerted by contributing governments.

Making the IMF a true global lender of last resort would empower the Fund with greater authority and resources, and understandably it looks favourably on this role (Fischer 1999*a*). However, the financial bureaucrats of the Fund should not be allowed to wield even greater power over crisis economies or emasculate local political systems more than they already do. Thus, a set of criteria should be developed so that last resort financing would be available without any conditionality only if a crisis clearly is driven by panic or contagion. In case of other payment crises in 'good policy' countries, conditionality should cover only the minimum macroeconomic adjustments needed for balance-of-payments improvement, and be subject to automatic modification in case demand compression exceeds target. The Fund should refrain from lending to 'poor policy' countries except in the case of panic or contagion.[24]

Finally, the Fund needs to develop a 'bail-in' programme, which would promote greater private sector involvement in forestalling and resolving crises (Fischer 1999*b*). Strengthening the Fund's role as lender of last resort raises the concern of moral hazard in international lending. For borrowing countries, the problem can be minimized by linking availability and borrowing costs of the emergency-rescue financing to their crisis prevention measures. But the problem can become serious with respect to creditors who will be tempted to downplay the risks of lending to developing and transition economies if they are bailed out repeatedly from the effects of reckless lending. This is morally and politically unacceptable, as well as being economically inefficient.

The bail-in option can take alternative forms. The Fund can encourage the utilization of such market-based incentives as private contingency credit lines *a la* Argentina in order to keep the private sector involved. This is a useful defence, but similar to building up large reserves, is costly. The Fund could provide guarantees, thus reducing the costs of such arrangements. Another method used, for instance in

---

[22] The total amount of resources available to the Fund under the NAB and the General Arrangements to Borrow rose to SDR 34 billion, double the amount under the GAB alone. And the quota increase of 1999 raised overall quotas from SDR 146 billion to SDR 212 billion, vastly improving the Fund's liquidity position (IMF 1999*b*).

[23] A blatant example of this occurred when the Japanese government succeeded in including the removal of the import diversification policy—restrictions on the importation of certain Japanese manufactured products—in the letter of intent for the Korea loan of 1997.

[24] A possible objection to this arises when strategically important countries, which do not qualify as 'good-policy' ones, are in trouble. But these troubled countries should be the responsibility of those governments that have strategic interests in them, rather than the responsibility of IMF. At the same time, the criteria for 'good policy' should not be overly restrictive as in the proposal by the Meltzer Commission, which would disqualify most member countries from receiving IMF assistance.

the framework of the Paris Club or more recently in the Korean case, is to encourage—and to intervene in—debt restructuring negotiations. However, this process is frequently adopted *ad hoc* and *ex post* and often entails the conversion of private debt into public debt with little loss-sharing. A more fundamental reform is the introduction of collective-action clauses in sovereign bond contracts and the formation of creditor clubs for bank loans so as to make quick rescheduling possible in the event of a crisis. This may introduce increased borrowing costs by forestalling the creditors' exit option, but the certainty of orderly rescheduling may also be an attractive alternative to creditors. Such arrangements would be helpful for crisis prevention and resolution, but are difficult for developing countries to institute on their own, thus making an active role by the Fund and support by the G-7 countries necessary. One of the more radical proposals for bailing-in the private sector calls for the creation of an international bankruptcy court whereby an orderly debt workout can take place under a debt standstill (Sachs 1995; UNCTAD 1998). This proposal, however, has certain difficulties. For instance, the court would need to function according to pre-arranged criteria in order to ensure that decisions on debt standstill can be given quickly, or the court may encounter problems with the enforcement of debt workout programmes (Rogoff 1999). These difficulties should not, however, prevent further investigation of the possibilities of an international bankruptcy court.

4.2. *Development Crisis and the Bank*

Unlike the acute financial crises in emerging economies, the chronic development crisis has failed to advance any bold proposals. Politicians give frequent lip service to the urgent need to eradicate the abject poverty faced by a third of the world's population, but there is little action on the ground. There is also a paucity of action plans from the BWIs to fight the dilemma.

It would seem that the BWIs have always lacked coherent development strategies. First, the BWIs failed to introduce a commodity price stabilization scheme despite the fact that large fluctuations in these prices were causing difficulties in managing developing country economies.[25] Second, there was initially no plan for orderly and adequate capital flows, not to mention transfer of technology, to the developing countries. Although the Bank later took up this issue, it was only on a limited scale. Third, the difficult question of promoting the political and institutional changes vital for sustainable development without compromising sovereignty was never faced squarely and was left to be moulded in practice by the financially powerful.

Since the 1980s the BWIs supported the 'market-friendly' development strategy based on the Washington consensus. However, it was not a genuine global strategy for development as the BWIs frequently failed to consider the overall effect of their actions in individual countries, producing a fallacy of composition (Stewart and

---

[25] The IMF responded to this problem by creating the Compensatory Financing Facility, but it is not an *ex ante* but *ex post* measure available only after a fall in commodity prices has created balance-of-payments difficulties.

FitzGerald 1997). A classic example is the episode in the 1980s, when individual countries with balance-of-payment difficulties resulting from falling commodity prices were advised to encourage commodity production and export, which subsequently precipitated further declines in commodity prices. Moreover, the Washington consensus failed to generate sustained growth in most poor countries, often exacerbating income distribution and policy sustainability.

It is true that the BWIs have gradually shifted their emphases and objectives. The distributional impact of programmes receives greater attention and, in the case of the Bank, environmental consequences are acknowledged. There has also been some change in the underlying economics and subsequently in the policy stance of the BWIs. The importance of certain public interventions such as prudential regulation of financial institutions and the establishment of social safety nets are recognized. The need to provide supporting revenue is also now recognized. The Fund's doctrine of higher interest rate stimulating saving and therefore growth is no longer maintained, and it has been realized that controls on external capital movements can help contain financial fragility. The World Bank is now developing a 'comprehensive development framework' that purports to seek 'broader goals' with 'more instruments'.[26]

However, doubts remain with regard to the degree of actual change in the position of the Fund. Its 1997 programmes for Thailand, Indonesia, and South Korea were heavily criticized for stipulating a fiscal tightening when no chronic deficit problem existed, for imposing a high interest rate policy where it could cause serious damage because of the high leverage ratio of firms, and for advocating all-out capital market liberalization when an earlier liberalization attempt had precipitated the crisis. The Bank has certainly changed a great deal in terms of its rhetoric, but so far there has been little noticeable change in its country operations and in its capacity to accommodate dissenting views.

In any case, a shift from the Washington consensus to 'comprehensive development framework' is not enough. What is needed is a truly global approach, in which the Bank becomes a staunch advocate of a system of international trade and finance that supports rapid growth in poor countries and allows a degree of freedom in choosing development strategy. This will include commodity price stabilization as well as the reform of international finance discussed above. Before internal changes can be effected in developing countries, the patronizing attitude of 'We know what is best for you' needs to be replaced by extending a helping hand to domestic forces of change. Instead of endeavouring to teach good economics or micromanage economies through conditionality, the Bank should provide assistance in the field in terms of resources and technical support.

The legacy of past mistakes, which resulted in the hopeless indebtedness of poor countries must be expunged. The Heavily Indebted Poor Countries (HIPC) Initiative, proposed by the World Bank and IMF and agreed by governments around the world in 1996, was the first international response to provide comprehensive debt relief to the world's poorest, most heavily indebted countries that are engaged in endless debt

---

[26] See Wolfensohn (1999) and Stiglitz (1998) for elaboration of this idea.

restructuring. Prompted by the criticisms from the NGOs and other quarters, the Bank and the Fund undertook a major review in 1999 and endorsed three key enhancements: deeper and broader debt relief, faster debt relief and a stronger link between debt relief and poverty reduction.[27] But there is widespread scepticism about the effectiveness of the initiative, which adopts a gradualist approach to achieve 'debt sustainability'. Given that much of the debt of HIPC countries cannot be repaid under any foreseeable future developments, the 'market value' of the debt write-off provided by the initiative is only a fraction of the face value—one-tenth according to Cohen (2000). Furthermore, since debt repayment capacity is defined in terms of the debt-to-export ratio, some countries will face increased debt servicing or gain only limited benefits under the initiative (Oxfam 2000). Slow implementation continues to be a problem, partly because of unrealistic conditions that eligible countries must comply with.

The gradualist and conditional approach of the HIPC initiative only prolongs the debt overhang of poor countries. It is time to eliminate the indebtedness problem with a one-shot write-off, after which the Fund should refrain from providing long-term development loans, and the Bank should take primary responsibility for tackling the development crisis. The Meltzer Commission also recommended that HIPC debt be written off in its entirety conditional on the debtor countries implementing 'institutional reforms and an effective development strategy'. However, rather than subjecting HIPCs to IMF conditionality, as the dissenting commissioner Jerome Levinson argues, 'it makes more sense to accept the implications of the majority observation that the debt cannot be repaid; unconditionally forgive the HIPC debt, and let the debtor countries start over with a clean slate' (Meltzer Commission 2000: 168). The conditionality principle can be used in determining future assistance by linking it to an assessment of how well they have used resources freed up by unconditional debt relief.

What should be the main functions of the Bank? Obviously, the Bank needs to concentrate its efforts on the poor IDA countries, and its aid should clearly be focused on the provision of public goods that generate little interest among private capital.[28] The Bank could promote development of the poor countries by contributing to investments in health, education, environmental protection, and technology transfer. Infrastructure should be financed by private capital as much as possible, and only critically important but privately non-fundable projects should be considered for support by the Bank. Instead of formal conditionality for these projects, the primary means of ensuring quality management could be the noticeable presence of Bank staff in the recipient countries.

---

[27] Under the new initiative, external debt servicing will be cut by approximately $50 billion, more than twice the relief provided under the original framework. And its implementation will be accelerated by providing debt relief beginning immediately or soon after at the decision point. Finally, freed-up resources will be used to support poverty reduction strategies, developed with civil society participation.

[28] The Meltzer Commission (2000), for instance, accuses the Bank of directing much of its non-aid resources to countries that enjoy access to capital markets which have a relatively high income and recommends that these countries be excluded from the Bank assistance. However, since a majority of the world's poor live in these countries, the Bank's focus on poverty reduction should not result in exclusion of these countries from receiving assistance for projects that are specifically designed to help the poor.

To support social projects, the Bank should adopt the principle of fewer loans and more grants. Lest the move away from loans toward grants reduce the total amount of aid flows, the rich governments must reverse the trend of declining bi-lateral aid and significantly increase their contribution to the multilateral aid agencies. Loans for social investment may be useful in 'good policy' countries but in 'poor policy' countries, these may ultimately create debt problems without achieving much good. In the beginning, Bank activities were motivated by imperfections in the capital market that denied developing countries access to foreign capital. But since then, there has been considerable development in capital markets and it should not be difficult to have good investment projects financed privately. It is a fact that, despite the expanding capital markets, poor developing countries are still by and large shut off from private capital inflows. But this stems mostly from the fact that economic and political conditions in these countries make potentially good projects commercially unattractive. Given these circumstances, it is no longer as compelling to justify Bank activities in terms of correcting capital market failures.

Recently, under the leadership of President James Wolfensohn, the Bank announced its intention to expand from a 'loan bank' to a 'knowledge bank'. It is argued that as knowledge is a public good, the Bank can contribute to international development by producing and disseminating knowledge on development policies. Its loan operations will also improve if this knowledge is used to identify suitable projects and programmes. The modality of a 'knowledge bank' contrasts with the 'conditionality bank' (Gilbert *et al.* 1999). According to conventional views, the Bank, because of conditionality, has better prospects of repayment and returns on investment and can subsequently lend profitably to projects and programmes which private capital would not risk. While both interpretations highlight loans as the key activity of the Bank, they deviate only in what other activities—imposing conditionality and monitoring or producing and applying development knowledge—would enable the Bank to do better than private lending institutions. Such an interpretation of the 'knowledge bank' is not sufficiently far-reaching: the Bank should not restrict its mission to making commercially feasible loans, had the capital market been perfect. Instead, it should redefine its role to become a development agency, offering not only policy advice, but also providing the field with 'development soldiers' gifted with skills, expertise and dedication while maximizing the hiring of local people.

4.3. *The Bank–Fund Relations*

Since the mid-1970s and more extensively in the 1980s, the Fund and the Bank experienced a large degree of overlap in their activities. The 1966 guidelines for Fund–Bank collaboration demarcated the areas of primary responsibility for each institution: macroeconomic issues such as exchange rates, balance of payments and stabilization for the Fund, and development programmes and project evaluation for the Bank. But the increasing overlap created two major problems—the possibility of conflict between the two and the possibility of each institution losing sight of its core mission.

By and large, collaboration rather than conflict has prevailed between the Fund and the Bank for three reasons.[29] First, there was pressure for more effective collaboration from the rich countries on the two institutions (Junguito 1996). Second, the Fund was in the driver's seat, with its adjustment programme giving the seal of approval sought by the market.[30] And finally, the two institutions converged greatly in their policy views.

But this is no cause for celebration. While collaboration and coordination to enhance the effectiveness of the overlapping and interconnected agenda is one thing, suppression of differences of opinion and healthy debate is another matter. It is a known fact that in matters of economic policy, consensus is rare. Maintaining the pretence of consensus precludes possibility of correcting flawed policies and undermines legitimacy of the programmes. The BWIs need to discard the bureaucratic instinct for maintaining an identical voice in favour of freer discussions on controversial issues.

This, on the other hand, does not imply that they should continue to converge in activity.[31] A sharper division of labour is needed, with the Fund focusing on short-term and systemic problems of international finance and the Bank on the long-term development needs of poor countries. Since issues of international finance are closely linked to the interests of rich and powerful countries while development needs are not, the Bank's scarce resources and activities are easily diverted away from their target. The Bank's approval of the Emergency Structural Adjustment Lending procedure that enables it to allocate funds to supplement IMF financing during crises is causing serious concern, and the Bank should resist providing extra funds for IMF rescue financing. Instead, the Bank's resources and capacities must be deployed to confront the persistent development crisis.

Clearer division of labour between the Fund and the Bank does not eliminate the need for mutual collaboration and their joint efforts to strengthen financial systems through the newly created Financial Sector Liaison Committee are indeed justified. The Bank has also assisted in crisis management by emphasizing the social aspects of adjustment and by providing technical assistance for financial restructuring. It is making efforts to promote better policy responses to the social repercussions of financial crises (World Bank 1999b). Strengthening social policy is now an integral part of the new financial system.

---

[29] See Junguito (1996) for a review of the Fund–Bank collaboration. The most celebrated case of overt conflict between the Fund and the Bank was the Argentina fiasco in 1988, when the Bank decided to go ahead with adjustment lending despite the collapse of EEF negotiations with the Fund. It led to the Bank–Fund Concordat of 1989, which superseded earlier guidelines and elaborated procedures to enhance coordination between the two institutions (Ahluwalia 1999). More recently, in handling the Asian financial crisis, the Bank expressed its disagreement with such Fund policies as bank closure, fiscal restraint and raising the interest rate.

[30] The Bank's Structural Adjustment Loans were expected to be used in cases where a Fund programme was already in place, thus giving Fund staff the final say in mutually formulated policy framework papers for SAF and ESAF programmes.

[31] The increasing overlap in the activities of the Fund and the Bank prompted some to suggest a merger to avoid duplication of work and conflicting advice (Crook 1991). But the recent crises highlight the Fund's need to focus increasing attention on short-term market factors and systemic issues. This implies greater emphasis on the distinctive role of the Fund versus that of the Bank (Ahluwalia 1999).

5. CONCLUSION: THE BWIs FOR THE TWENTY-FIRST CENTURY

Reforming the Bretton Woods institutions is an important part of redesigning the governance of world economy in the twenty-first century. Based on historical and institutional analyses, this chapter has suggested the various reform measures. First, measures for institutional reform include (i) reforming the voting system to give greater voice to developing countries; (ii) enhancing transparency and accountability; (iii) radically downsizing or eliminating conditionality, and (iv) decentralizing research and the decision-making process.

Changes in the roles and policies of the Fund should include (i) contributing to strengthening national financial systems; (ii) encouraging measures to curb excessive inflows of short-term capital; (iii) coordinating macroeconomic policy and stabilizing exchange rates; (iv) discontinuing long-term lending and focusing on the lender of last resort function; and (v) developing a mechanism for orderly debt workout.

New roles suggested for the Bank include (i) advocating global economic governance conducive to development of poor countries; (ii) giving up attempts to micromanage recipient economies; (iii) focusing on provision of public goods in poor countries; and (iv) shifting away from loans toward grants.

In addition, a clearer division of labour, which would be based on the Fund focusing on short-term and systemic problems of international finance and the Bank on the long-term development needs of poor countries, has been recommended.

These are tall orders, and many technical details have to be elaborated. Political constraints also need to be considered in devising a practical reform strategy, but before any realistic reform proposal is possible, advanced countries need to be fully engaged in the process and the concerns of developing countries must be well represented. To ensure the involvement of developing countries in the new international financial architecture dialogue, the US government created the G-22, which was later expanded to G-33 and then was succeeded by G-20. This kind of *ad hoc* consultation should be replaced with an institutionalized forum for reaching a consensus on the governance of global finance and development.

In order to maximize opportunities for genuine reform, we have to maximize the forces that favour reform by utilizing both the 'voice' mechanism and the 'exit' mechanism. The voice mechanism must be strengthened by a more effective formulation of the mutual interests of developing countries. On certain issues, the NGO community may be able to provide support, as exemplified by the Jubilee 2000 movement and the Tobin Tax movement. The 'exit' mechanism here does not imply closure of the economy or withdrawal from the world market. Rather, it refers to the possibility of developing countries having alternative sources of official support for funding and technical assistance when the private capital market is effectively beyond reach.

The BWIs have been so powerful and resistant to reform, precisely because of their unique monopoly position. This would imply that competitive pressure on these institutions could prove beneficial. Subjecting their research to open competition may be a good way to increase the competitive pressure (Mellor 1996). A more significant step would be to design a network of regional and sub-regional organizations, including the regional and sub-regional development banks and reserve funds, to support the management of monetary and financial issues (UN 1999). This would not only play a useful role itself in both crisis management and development financing, but would also bring competitive pressure on the Washington-based BWIs to improve their performance. A starting point for this road would be the establishment of an Asian Monetary Fund, which was proposed by Japan and gained support from countries like Malaysia and Korea in 1997 when the Asian crisis began to unfold. The AMF proposal, quickly shot down by the US Treasury, faces political difficulties, but its economic merits seem sufficient to overcome such difficulties (see, for instance, Mathews and Weiss 1999).

A related issue is whether it is better for global financial governance to have a consolidated institutional framework, that is, the BWIs with enhanced powers, or to have a multiplicity of institutions with overlapping and competing jurisdictions. Indeed, there are calls for the creation of new institutions such as a global financial regulator, an international bankruptcy court and an international deposit insurance system. From the perspective of using competitive pressure to discipline the powerful institutions, such proposals should be considered favourably even at the risk of duplicating similar functions. After all, all of these institutions co-exist along with a lender of last resort in domestic financial systems. Just as the national financial markets came to acquire a measure of stability after the establishment of banking and securities regulations, deposit insurance and lenders of last resort, stabilizing today's globalized financial markets will require similar functions at a worldwide level. And it is preferable to have alternative institutions available than to have a single super-agency. This is not to say that it is unimportant to strengthen the roles and functions of the BWIs in ways that can best meet the challenges of the next century.

REFERENCES

Abramovitz, Moses (1986). Catching up, forging ahead, and falling behind. *Journal of Economic History*, 46, 385–406.

Ahluwalia, Montek S. (1999). The IMF and the World Bank in the new financial architecture. Mimeo.

Bhagwati, Jagdish (1998). The capital myth, the difference between trade in widgets and dollars. *Foreign Affairs*, 77(3), 7–12.

Bird, Graham (1996). Borrowing from the IMF: The policy implications of recent empirical research. *World Development*, 24(11), 1753–60.

Boughton, James M. and K. Sarwar Lateef (eds) (1995). *Fifty Years After Bretton Woods: The Future of the IMF and the World Bank*. IMF and World Bank Group, Washington, DC.

Bretton Woods Commission (1994). *Bretton Woods: Looking to the Future*. Bretton Woods Committee, Washington, DC.

Camdessus, Michel (1998). Toward a new financial architecture for a globalized world. Address at the Royal Institute of International Affairs, London.

—— (1999). Global financial reform: The evolving agenda. Address at the Council on Foreign Relations, New York.

Cohen, Daniel (2000). The HIPC initiative: True and false promises. Technical Papers No. 166. OECD Development Centre, Paris.

Collier, Paul and Jan Willem Gunning (1999). The IMF's role in structural adjustment. *Economic Journal*, 109, F634–F651.

Crook, Clive (1991). The IMF and the World Bank. *The Economist*, 12 October.

Dell, Sidney (1981). On being grandmotherly: The evolution of IMF conditionality. Essays in International Finance, No. 144. Princeton University, Princeton.

Dollar, David and Jakob Svensson (1997). What explains the success or failure of structural adjustment programmes? Mimeo, World Bank, Washington, DC.

Eatwell, John and Lance Taylor (1998). The performance of liberalized capital markets. Working Paper Series III No. 8. Center for Economic Policy Analysis, New School University, New York.

Edwards, Sebastian (1999). How effective are capital controls? *Journal of Economic Perspectives*, 13(4), 65–84.

Eichengreen, Barry (1992). Three perspectives on the Bretton Woods System. NBER Working Paper, 4141. National Bureau of Economic Research, Cambridge, MA.

—— (1998). *Globalizing Capital: A History of the International Monetary System*. Princeton University Press, Princeton.

—— (1999). *Toward a New International Financial Architecture*. Institute for International Economics, Washington, DC.

Feldstein, Martin (1998). Refocusing the IMF. *Foreign Affairs*, 77(2), 20–33.

Fischer, Stanley (1997). Applied economics in action: IMF programmes. *American Economic Review Papers and Proceedings*, 87(2), 23–7.

—— (1999a). On the need for an international lender of last resort. *Journal of Economic Perspectives*, 13(4), 85–104.

—— (1999b). Reforming the international financial system. *Economic Journal*, 109, F557–F576.

Furman, Jason and Joseph E. Stiglitz (1998). Economic crises: Evidence and insights from East Asia. *Brookings Papers on Economic Activity*, 2, 1–114. Brookings Institution, Washington, DC.

Gilbert, Christopher, Andrew Powell, and David Vines (1999). Positioning the World Bank. *Economic Journal*, 109, F598–F633.

Group of 24 (1987). *The Role of the IMF in Adjustment with Growth*. Report of a Working Group. Group of 24, Washington, DC.

Haq, Mahbub-ul, Richard Jolly, and Paul Streeten (eds) (1995). *The United Nations and the Bretton Woods Institutions: New Challenges for the 21st Century*. St. Martin's Press, New York.

Helleiner, G. K. (ed.) (1996). *The International Monetary and Financial System*. St. Martin's Press, New York.

Hills, Carla A., Peter G. Peterson, and Morris Goldstein (1999). Safeguarding prosperity in a global financial system: The future international financial architecture. Report of an Independent Task Force Sponsored by the Council on Foreign Relations. Institute for International Economics, Washington, DC.

IMF (1999). Report of the managing director to the interim committee on progress in strengthening the architecture of the international financial system. IMF, Washington, DC.

Johnston, John H. and Sulaiman S. Wasty (1993). Borrower ownership of adjustment programmes and the political economy of reform. WB Discussion Paper 199. World Bank, Washington, DC.

Junguito, Roberto (1996). IMF-World Bank policy advice: The coordination/cross-conditionality question. In G. K. Helleiner (ed.), *The International Monetary and Financial System*. St. Martin's Press, New York.

Kapur, Devesh (1997). The new conditionalities of the international financial institutions. *International Monetary and Financial Issues for the 1990s*, vol. VIII. United Nations, New York and Geneva.

——(1998). The IMF: A cure or a curse? *Foreign Policy*, Summer.

Kaufman, Henry (1998). Preventing the next global financial crisis. *Washington Post*, 28 January: A17.

Kenen, Peter B. (ed.) (1994). *Managing the World Economy: Fifty Years after Bretton Woods*. Institute for International Economics, Washington, DC.

Killick, Tony (1995a). *IMF Programmes in Developing Countries*. Routledge, London and New York.

——(1995b). Adjustment and economic growth. In J. M. Boughton and K. S. Lateef (eds), *Fifty Years After Bretton Woods: The Future of the IMF and the World Bank*. IMF and World Bank Group, Washington, DC.

Marglin, Stephen A. (1990). Lessons of the Golden Age. In S. A. Marglin and J. B. Schor (eds), *The Golden Age of Capitalism*. Clarendon Press, Oxford.

Martin, Matthew (1991). *The Crumbling Façade of African Debt Negotiations*. Macmillan and St. Martin's, London and New York.

Masson, Paul R. and Michael Mussa (1997). *The Role of the IMF: Financing and Its Interactions with Adjustment and Surveillance*. IMF, Washington, DC.

Mathews, John A. and Linda Weiss (1999). The case for an Asian monetary fund. Working Paper No. 55, Japan Policy Research Institute.

Meller, Patricio (1996). The roles of international financial institutions: A Latin American reassessment. In G. K. Helleiner (ed.), *The International Monetary and Financial System*. St. Martin's Press, New York.

Meltzer Commission (2000). *Report of the International Financial Institution Advisory Commission*.

Mosley, Paul, Jane Harrigan, and J. F. J. Toye (1995). *Aid and Power: The World Bank and Policy-Based Lending: Analysis and Policy Proposals*, 2nd edn. Routledge, London.

Oliver, Robert W. (1985). Bretton Woods: A retrospective essay. *The California Seminar of International Security and Foreign Policy*, June.

Oxfam (2000). HIPC leaves poor countries heavily in debt: New analysis. Available on http://www.caa.org.au/oxfam/advocacy/debt/enhanced_hipc.

Payer, Cheryl (1982). The World Bank: A critical analysis. *Monthly Review Press*. New York.

Radelet, Steven and Jeffrey Sachs (1998). The East Asian financial crisis: Diagnosis, remedies and prospects. *Brookings Papers on Economic Activity*, 1, 1–74.

Rodrik, Dani (1990). How should structural adjustment programmes be designed? *World Development*, 18(7), 933–47.

Rogoff, Kenneth (1999). International institutions for reducing global financial instability. *Journal of Economic Perspectives*, 13(4), 21–42.

Sachs, Jeffrey (1995). Do we need an international lender of last resort? Frank Graham Memorial Lecture. Princeton University, Princeton.

——(1997). IMF is a power unto itself. *The Economist*, 11 December.

——(1998). Global capitalism: Making it work. *The Economist*, 12 September.

Schadler, Susan, Adam Bennett, Maria Carkovic, Louis Dicks-Mireaux, Mauro Mecagni, James Morsink, and Miguel Savastano (1995). IMF conditionality: experience under stand-by and extended arrangements. IMF Occasional Paper No. 128. IMF, Washington, DC.

Schor, Juliet B. and Jong-Il You (1995). After the Golden Age. In J. B. Schor and J.-I. You (eds), *Capital, the State and Labour*. Edward Elgar, Aldershot.

Singer, H. W. (1995). An historical perspective. In Mahbub-ul Haq, Richard Jolly and Paul Streeten (eds), *The United Nations and the Bretton Woods Institutions: New Challenges for the 21st Century*. St. Martin's Press, New York.

Stewart, Frances (1995). *Adjustment and Poverty*. Routledge, London and New York.

——and Valpy FitzGerald (1997). The IMF and the global economy: Implications for developing countries. QEH Working Paper Series, QEHWPSO3. Queen Elizabeth House, University of Oxford, Oxford.

Stiglitz, Joseph E. (1998). More instruments and broader goals: Moving toward the Post-Washington consensus. *WIDER Annual Lectures* 2. UNU/WIDER, Helsinki.

——(1999). The World Bank at the millennium. *Economic Journal*, 109, F577–F597.

Summers, Lawrence H. (2000). Testimony before the House Banking Committee, March 23. Available on http://www.treas.gov/press/releases/ps480.htm.

Taylor, Lance (1988). *Varieties of Stabilization Experience. Towards Sensible Macroeconomics in the Third World*. Clarendon Press, Oxford.

——(1997). Editorial: The revival of the liberal creed—the IMF and the World Bank in a globalized economy. *World Development*, 25(2), 145–52.

UNCTAD (1998). *Trade and Development Report 1998*. United Nations, New York and Geneva.

UNDP (1998). *Human Development Report 1998*. Oxford University Press, New York and Oxford.

United Nations Task Force (of the Executive Committee on Economic and Social Affairs of the United Nations) (1999). Towards a new international financial architecture. ECLAC, Santiago.

van de Laar, Aart (1980). *The World Bank and the Poor*. Martinus Nijhoff, The Hague.

Williamson, John (1990). *Latin American Adjustment: How Much Has Happened?* Institute for International Economics, Washington, DC.

Wolfensohn, James (1999). A proposal for a comprehensive development framework. Available on http://www.worldbank.org/cdf/cdf-text.htm.

Woods, Ngaire (1998). Governance in international organizations: The case for reform in the Bretton Woods Institutions. *International Monetary and Financial Issues for the 1990s*, vol. IX. United Nations, New York and Geneva.

World Bank (1994). *Resettlement and Development: The Bankwide Review of Projects Involving Involuntary Resettlement 1986–1993*. Environment Department, World Bank, Washington, DC.

——(1999a). *World Development Report 1999/2000: Entering the 21st Century*. Oxford University Press for the World Bank, New York.

——(1999b). *Principles of Good Practice in Social Policy: A Draft Outline for Discussion and Guidance*. World Bank, Washington, DC.

9

Globalization and the Logic of International Collective Action: Re-examining the Bretton Woods Institutions

JOSEPH E. STIGLITZ

1. INTRODUCTION

The Bretton Woods institutions were established just over fifty years ago, at the conclusion of the Second World War and in the aftermath of the great depression, to aid in the reconstruction of Europe and to make it less likely that another global calamity such as the great depression would occur again. As an afterthought, the World Bank was also charged with promoting the development of the third world countries, most of which at that time remained under the yoke of colonialism.

Much has happened in the world since then. The cold war came and went. Colonialism has ended, but the end of colonialism has failed to bring with it prosperity to the ex-colonies as many had hoped. The dependence of so many countries on assistance from abroad—and the dependence of countries that have generally been doing well on external assistance in times of crisis—have brought worries of a new form of economic colonialism. Though different from nineteenth century colonialism, the new economic colonialism is perhaps equally insidious: the nascent democracies have economic policies dictated to them by the international organizations, whose policies in turn are largely driven by the G-7, and some would say by financial interests in the 'G-1'.[1]

The global economy has changed dramatically as well. Trade has increased enormously as transportation and communications costs have decreased. Multinational firms have taken on an increasingly large role, both in disseminating technology, creating a global market place, and moving capital.[2] One of the primary rationales for the World Bank was to direct an official flow of capital to less developed countries, but in the early 1990s, private flows increased enormously—sixfold between 1990 and 1996. Though the global financial crisis demonstrated that private flows were highly

---

[1] The G-1 is the euphemism for the largest shareholder in both of the Bretton Woods institutions, the United States, which actually has veto power in the many decisions of the IMF that require a super-majority vote.   [2] See World Bank (1998a).

unstable, their sheer magnitude came to dwarf official aid flows. In some circles, questions were raised about whether the World Bank was really needed. But a closer look at where the money went—disproportionately going to relatively few countries (almost none of it to Africa) and little of it going to such vital sectors as education and health—suggested to most observers that there was still a need for the World Bank. It did become clear that World Bank aid had to be more targeted, focusing on areas where the private sector was less likely to go. Increasing attention also focused on the role of the World Bank in expanding knowledge: facilitating the flow of knowledge and helping countries to design a policy environment that would attract capital was recognized to be every bit as important as, and an important complement to, the provision of capital.

Back in 1971, the fixed exchange rate system had been abandoned, raising questions at that time about the role of the International Monetary Fund. But the abandonment of the fixed exchange rate system did not mark an end to crises; rather, they seemed to become both more frequent and of greater depth. Some argued that there was an even greater role for the IMF in this increasingly unstable global environment.

At the same time that the world was changing in so many ways, our understanding of the world was also changing. When the Bretton Woods institutions were founded, there was a less well-developed theory of *collective action* that outlined the circumstances under which public, as opposed to private, action was desirable. There was, in particular, a less well-developed theory of *market failure*, of the circumstances under which markets by themselves did not yield efficient (or otherwise desirable) outcomes. For Keynes and the other founders of the Bretton Woods institutions, the great depression was evidence itself that markets sometimes did not work well, and that there was a role for government intervention.

2. GLOBAL PUBLIC GOODS AND THE LOGIC OF COLLECTIVE ACTION

Today, we have a well-developed theory of market failure. Market failure may occur when any of the following is present: *public goods*, items that are difficult to exclude people from enjoying and whose cost to an additional individual enjoying it is zero, or very low (such as a public park or the air we breathe); *externalities*, situations in which the action of an individual has repercussions on others for which the individual neither pays nor is compensated; *incomplete markets*, situations in which certain markets are absent, especially risk markets and markets for intertemporal trades; and *imperfect markets*, and especially *markets with imperfect competition*. Perfect competition is necessary (though not sufficient) to achieve economic efficiency. Yet, there are a variety of circumstances in which firms attempt to monopolize markets or otherwise restrain trade. The theory that shows free markets leading to efficiency also assumes that information and knowledge (e.g. about production processes) is fixed; yet today, the production and dissemination of information and knowledge is a central economic activity. In general, whenever information is imperfect (or markets incomplete) the economy is not Pareto efficient.

Perhaps the most important market failure is that occasionally the economy fails to use resources fully—and especially labour. Whether this should be treated as a separate market failure, or as a particularly dramatic manifestation of one or more of the other market failures, need not detain us here.

The various market imperfections interact: the costs associated with the production of information and knowledge often lead to imperfections of competition; that the returns to knowledge can almost never be perfectly appropriated implies that there are spillovers (externalities) associated with the generation of information and knowledge.

In addition to these circumstances in which markets fail to produce (Pareto) efficient outcomes, there may be a desire for collective action as a result of dissatisfaction with the distribution of income generated by market processes. Some individuals, for instance, may have an income so low that they cannot survive, and this may be viewed to be 'socially unacceptable'.

The discussion of market failures has helped clarify the circumstances under which collective action *might* be desirable (I say might, because it has to be demonstrated that there is some form of collective action that can actually, or is likely to, improve upon the market). Analyses over the past quarter of a century have also clarified *where* it is most appropriate for collective action to occur, that is, at the local, national, or global level. Earlier literature focused on showing that there exist some public goods (or externalities) that affect only those living within a particular geographic area, and that these public goods and externalities should be handled by public bodies embracing that particular area. Such goods were referred to as *local public goods*. More recently, some economists have identified a set of public goods the benefits of which are not limited to a particular country, but are global in nature.[3] They are, quite naturally, referred to as *global public goods*. Six areas have been identified in particular: (i) global security; (ii) global economic stability; (iii) knowledge; (iv) global environment; (v) humanitarian assistance (e.g. for famines); and (vi) global health (especially contagious diseases). The provision of global public goods provides a central part of the logic of global collective action, but the rationale for global collective action goes further: potentially, it can address any of the market failures. Just as there are global public goods, there are global externalities. In the past sixty years, global institutions have been established to address, in part, each of the areas identified above. And many of the international institutions play a role in the provision of several of these public goods, or the regulation of several of the global externalities.

In this chapter, I want to explore the role of the Bretton Woods institutions from the perspective of global public goods and externalities.

2.1. *The International Monetary Fund*

I begin my discussion by focusing on the IMF, simply because there was, in its establishment, a clear vision of a global market failure that it was supposed to address. The great depression was widely viewed as having resulted from, or at least been

---

[3] See, for example, Stiglitz (1995).

exacerbated by, negative interactions among countries. As each country's GDP fell, it cut back on its imports, and that reduced the demand for its neighbours' products, reducing its neighbours' (or trading partners') GDP. The depression itself was, of course, a manifestation of a massive market failure, but it did not provide the rationale for collective action at the global level. Each country had an incentive to undertake expansionary monetary and fiscal policies to restore its economy to full employment. It was when countries tried to restore their own economic strength at the expense of their trading partners' that collective action was needed.

Because, in the event of a global recession, some of the benefits of expansionary policies accrue to neighbours, if there is a cost to these expansionary policies (in terms of, say, a future debt burden), then countries will pursue expansionary policies less far than they should. There is thus a rationale for global collective action to induce each country to pursue expansionary policies further than it would pursue them of its own accord.

These concerns were particularly paramount at the time of the founding of the IMF, when there were real worries that in the aftermath of the War the world would return to a situation in which there was insufficient aggregate demand. In particular, people worried that some countries might try to pursue a mercantilist-style policy (though not necessarily with mercantilist methods) of running trade surpluses. Since the sum of the world surpluses and deficits has to be zero, if some countries run surpluses, other countries are forced to run deficits, importing more than they are exporting, reducing those countries' aggregate demand from what it otherwise would have been, and thereby threatening those countries with a greater chance of unemployment.

The running of sustained surpluses by some countries forces sustained deficits on the rest of the world, thus imposing certain risks on them. Though 'crises' were perhaps less on their mind than they are today, the maintenance of surpluses by some countries over an extended period of time leads to indebtedness abroad that may be unsustainable. More precisely, high indebtedness leaves a country open to the risk of a sudden change of foreign investor sentiment about the credit worthiness of the country or the firms within the country. The resulting attempt to pull money out of the country (or the increase in interest rates intended to encourage money to stay in the country) can have enormous disruptive effects.

Policies such as fiscal expansion and choosing to run a trade surplus are both examples of activities with global externalities, and it would seem quite appropriate to create an international institution to help address these concerns. The argument for doing so is strengthened by another set of market failures (which arguably has been somewhat reduced over time)—that associated with the functioning of capital markets. Capital markets work very differently from the way in which they are depicted in simplistic models of perfect competition. For example, there may be credit rationing, and limitations in equity markets imply that there is far from perfect risk sharing. Research in the economics of information has laid out the theoretical reasons why we should expect such imperfections, and empirical research over the past two decades has provided ample documentation. The macroeconomic consequences are particularly important in developing countries. Many face credit rationing, at least at some times, and many countries seem to follow pro-cyclical fiscal policies, because in times of crisis they cannot borrow, and accordingly have to cut back on expenditure (or risk costly inflationary pressures). Keynes worried that in many countries, monetary policy would be ineffective in stimulating aggregate demand, and countries with limited capital markets, and without access to international capital, might not be able to pursue expansionary fiscal policies. In recessions, countries faced *liquidity constraints*.

Global collective action might help relax those liquidity constraints, enabling countries to pursue more expansionary policies, with positive externalities to their trading partners. Because countries did not have sufficient incentives to pursue strong expansionary policies to the extent needed (or at least desirable) globally on their own, the international community needed to 'persuade' countries to be more expansionary than they otherwise would be. One way of doing so was to make access to the loans conditional on countries pursuing a sufficiently expansionary policy. Similarly, since running a trade surplus posed a negative externality on others, either surpluses should be taxed, or not running a surplus (or running a smaller surplus) should be made a condition for access to any liquidity provided by the international financial institutions.

Today, Keynes must be turning over in his grave! The major thrust of IMF conditionality is that countries cut back on their fiscal expenditures, increase taxes, and reduce their trade deficits. The kinds of conditionalities that were implicit in the original rationale for the establishment of a collective global institution seem to have been turned on their head. Beggar-thy-neighbour policies have been replaced by even worse beggar-thyself policies, in which each country, to restore its trade balance, is forced to cut back on its GDP. The resulting reduction in imports—other countries' exports—has exactly the same impact on them that the beggar-thy-neighbour policies had. Other countries do not care why their exports are no longer selling—whether it is competitive devaluations, tariffs or trade restrictions, or reduced GDP—all they know is that their exports have decreased. Arguably, IMF policies have thus served to exacerbate, rather than reduce, negative global externalities.

How could such a state of affairs have come about? There are several possible explanations. One is that the Fund has focused on another set of market failures or externalities. If countries follow imprudent macropolicies, they are more likely to have to default on their debts to the IMF, and the costs of non-repayment are borne by others. But this is an unconvincing explanation: the conditionalities imposed by the IMF go well beyond those that have a significant effect on the probability of repayment. Indeed, given the IMF's status as a senior creditor, the probability of default, at least in many cases, is so low that it can be ignored. If anything, the contractionary policies foisted on countries arguably actually impair their ability to repay.

At times the IMF has argued that it worries about contagion, that a fall in the exchange rate in one country can lead to a destabilization of exchange rates more generally. Though anecdotal in nature, the recent global crisis suggests that this explanation too is unpersuasive. Brazil's massive devaluation (which the IMF attempted to prevent) did not set off any significant 'contagion' effects. On the other hand, the IMF's attempts at stabilization in East Asia proved ineffective at containing the damage to the countries first affected. Indeed, one can argue that the policies imposed by the IMF actually exacerbated global 'contagion' effects: their policies exacerbated economic downturns that had global effects, not only directly (through reduced imports) but also indirectly, as commodity prices (e.g. for oil) plummeted. More generally, there is little theoretical basis either for the hypothesis that contagion (other than through trade effects) would be a serious problem without intervention (though to be sure it might produce momentary instability in markets—which can experience volatility for a myriad of causes) or that the IMF's interventions would be effective in stemming it.[4] The IMF has shown little ability to identify the correct equilibrium exchange rates—and thus to know whether there is a threat of overshooting. And the mistakes it has made on that count have had enormous costs to the affected countries. The notion of competitive devaluations, and the set of interventions designed to stop them, is more appropriate for a gold standard system than for a system of market-determined flexible exchange rates.

There is another possible hypothesis: the IMF's governance structure makes it accountable to finance ministries and central banks, with close connections to the financial community. It would, accordingly, be unsurprising if the institution came to reflect the interests of that community. Forcing countries to eliminate trade deficits—encouraging them to run surpluses—may increase the probability of creditors being repaid (regardless of whether the creditors engaged in due diligence when making the loans, and regardless of the adverse impact that the policy has on workers and others within the borrowing economy). The irony, of course, is that when contractionary policies are pursued in an inappropriate way, they may so weaken the economy that the probability of repayment will be reduced; in some cases, however, the IMF's provision of money *to the government* has encouraged, or at least enabled, the nationalization of private liabilities, thereby increasing, overall, the probability of repayment of private debts. This process has occurred in numerous countries.

In this interpretation, the IMF has pursued the *collective interests* of a subset of the international community, rather than serving the broader collective interests for which it was originally created.[5] There are further examples that are consistent with this interpretation. The IMF has been a strong supporter of capital and financial market liberalization, paying insufficient attention to whether countries have the appropriate regulatory risk management, and risk absorption capacities in place. One could argue that international institutions should limit themselves to areas of global public goods and externalities. At the time the IMF pushed these policies of liberalization, there was little evidence that such policies had positive global externalities in general—though they might indeed bring benefits to the financial interests in the more advanced industrial countries. By contrast, there was evidence that they increased the risk of economic instability within countries adopting those policies—and if one worried about contagion (as the IMF allegedly did), it should have accordingly *opposed* those

---

[4] See Furman and Stiglitz (1998) and Stiglitz (1998).

[5] It should be clear: many of the policies advocated by the IMF are those about which there is a broad agreement among economists and that are almost surely in the broad national interest. The issue is that the IMF sometimes—often—goes well beyond these policies.

policies. More generally, there was no evidence that such liberalization increased economic growth or investment in developing countries, and some arguments were even put forward as to why they might have adverse effects.[6]

Special interests in the advanced industrial countries interact with special interests in the developing countries, often to the detriment of the general interest. The IMF interacts with a country's finance ministry, which all too often largely reflects the interests of that country's financial community, or more broad élites. The interaction enhances the strength of the finance ministry—which is often already out of proportion. Critics are labelled as populists, and other members of government are told that if they resist the demands of the finance ministry, it will jeopardize the Fund programme, forcing the country's budget into disarray, and risking the country's standing in international financial markets. Since typically only the finance ministry deals directly with the IMF, and the dealings are in secret, other ministries have to take the threats seriously: the IMF, in effect, enlarges the bargaining power of the finance ministry. To the extent that the agenda advanced by the finance ministry is in accord with broad national interests based on principles—such as sound budgeting—about which there is general consensus, this may be all to the good. To the extent that it advances special interests, the shift in bargaining power is far more dubious.

The changes in the world referred to at the beginning of this chapter suggest a rationale for re-examining the role of the IMF as an institution providing global action directed at enhancing global stability. But as compelling as those changes are, arguably, the institution has not only failed to live up to its original mission but has actually undertaken counterproductive policies. That makes such a re-examination compelling. Our analysis suggests that the re-examination must be fundamental in nature, addressing not only what the institution does, but how it does it, its governance structure and its modes of operation. Otherwise, there is a real risk that what so often happens within national governments—that power is used not to advance general interests but to further special interests—will happen at the international level. One might argue that the problems at the international level are even more severe, for the electoral process provides at least a partial check on abuses of these powers within countries. The international financial institutions and the IMF in particular are sufficiently far removed from systems of direct electoral accountability that there is no effective check on abuses of this kind.

The absence of such direct accountability makes it necessary that other control mechanisms be put in place to ensure that broad, global international interests are promoted, rather than special interests of particular countries, or of particular groups within those countries. As I suggested, a change in the formal governance structure may be the key. But there are other changes necessary in the *modes* of operation and the *span* of activities. The secrecy with which the IMF has traditionally operated—including the absence of broad public debate in adopting IMF programmes, where in some cases not all the terms of the agreement are even made public—removes an important set of disciplines on the institution. (Back in Washington, there is no more

---

[6] For a review of these arguments, see Stiglitz (1996); and Hellmann *et al.* (2000).

love of openness and transparency than there is in the countries themselves.) This liberty—this absence of public scrutiny—has given it scope to undertake the policies that it has pursued.[7]

That there is no competition in the services it provides—it is a monopoly—enhances its powers. To be sure, it is difficult to conceive of there being competition for some of the services it provides—for instance, crisis lending. But one of the most important advances in the theory of industrial organization is the recognition that many of the old-style natural monopolies (industries in which competition is impractical) can be broken down, and there can be active competition in many of the key segments. While the World Bank and the Fund have both been strong advocates of competition and the industrial restructuring that has facilitated competition in these former natural monopolies, they have been less than enthusiastic in applying the lessons to themselves. (This is not surprising; most businesses argue for competition and no subsidies in general, but are quick to recognize the special circumstances in their own industries that warrant subsidies and limitations in competition.) In particular, bundled up with the provision of funds is the provision of advice, review of the performance of the economy as a whole and various segments of the economy, and the collection of statistics. There can be far more effective competition in several segments. To be sure, there are economies of scope that provide a partial explanation of why these activities are bundled together—just as there are some economies of scope in some of the natural monopolies that have been broken up. But there is increasing recognition that the value of competition more than offsets the slight inefficiencies that might arise from the inability to exploit fully the economies of scope.

In particular, the Fund has resisted public debates concerning the efficacy and appropriateness of its policies; it has resisted the provision of alternative views. It has, for instance, resisted the notion that countries have outside 'counsel'—independent economists—in their negotiating team, and has discouraged governments from engaging in consultations with economists who oppose their views. During the Asian crisis, it even refused to engage in closed discussions with the World Bank and outside experts about the appropriateness of the policies. And while it made much to-do over its own retrospective of the policies, the Bank's analyses, which were more critical, were not only unwelcome, but also the US Treasury tried to suppress the Bank's normal dissemination programme for such studies (and partially succeeded). The US Treasury has played a key role in the formulation of these policies, so it is not surprising that it has been quite unenthusiastic about such public discussions. Given the dominant role it played in policy-making at the IMF, it worried that criticism of the

---

[7] The IMF often tries to shift blame—it is perfectly willing to disclose more, but can only do so with the agreement of the country. There are some instances in which there are good reasons for maintaining some degree of secrecy: an analysis of a banking system that shows that it is about to collapse would precipitate a run—precisely the event that the authorities are trying to avoid. But these instances are more the exception than the rule. The IMF has shown little hesitation in imposing conditions on countries that go well beyond the situation or crisis that is its immediate concern. Is there a reason that it could not require much broader transparency as a condition of funds—thus removing one of its major excuses for non-disclosure, at least with regard to countries receiving assistance?

IMF was tantamount to a criticism of the Treasury. The Treasury has even used the considerable political weight of the US to try to suppress such discussions when they arise from international institutions such as the World Bank or the Asian Development Bank. I believe that one of the global public goods is the promotion not just of development, but of *democratic* development, and the suppression of public debate on key issues of public policy undermines democracy.[8] In short, rather than attempting to suppress alternative views, the Bank and the Fund should be encouraging them, and some of the assistance provided to developing countries by the international community should be devoted to establishing independent and competing sources of advice. Competition in the marketplace of ideas is every bit as important as competition in the marketplace for goods and services.

Another practice that undermines democracy is the imposition of 'conditionality' on a country. Countries are forced to accept a wide array of conditions in order to receive assistance. Many of the conditions have nothing to do with the crisis at hand; some even go into areas that are highly political in nature. Few of the conditions are directly related to the fiduciary responsibility of a lender to ensure a high likelihood of repayment. In some cases, in fact, the policies, by pushing a country into deep recession, may actually reduce the probability of repayment.[9]

When an institution (in this case, the IMF) has a monopoly or market power in one area, without enforced competition (in this case, in the marketplace of ideas), it can leverage its monopoly power in that area to extend it to another. Its market power in the realm of crisis lending enables it to leverage its power to impose conditions that extend well beyond those directly germane to the crisis.

The IMF's market power, however, is even greater than might be indicated by its role in crisis lending. The consequences of the IMF denouncing a country's economic policy is not just that the country will lose funding from the IMF, but will also lose funding from other public and private sources. The IMF has managed to persuade other public authorities to make their lending to a given country (partially or totally) contingent on the Fund's approval of that country's macroeconomic policies.

---

[8] Some argue that my raising the issue of democracy is beside the point: the Articles of Agreement of the Fund and the Bank explicitly preclude the institutions' engaging in political matters—and the focus on economics rather than politics has in fact been one of the great sources of strength of the Bretton Woods institutions. While this may be true, two points should be made in reply: first, what I am discussing here is not the imposition of political conditionality, but the recognition that the way that the Fund interacts with the country affects political processes—it affects whether democratic processes are strengthened or weakened. The way it operates should take these consequences into account. Secondly, in fact the Fund (and the Bank) always enter into political arenas; indeed, one of my criticisms is that they do so more than is necessary for the accomplishment of their economic objectives. I have already referred to the fact that the conditions imposed in times of crisis reach out into political areas. (See also Feldstein 1998). Judgements about whether to privatize public pension systems, or attempts to improve the performance of the public programmes, rest largely on political economy arguments. More broadly, political judgements are pervasive in Fund programmes.

[9] There is also considerable evidence that conditionality is actually ineffective in achieving 'better' policies. See, for example, World Bank (1998*b*). For a fuller discussion of the role, effectiveness, and consequences of conditionality, see Collier (1999).

In some cases, the Fund has suspended programmes to a country not because the country's macro-performance is weak, but for other reasons. Ethiopia is a case in point, where the Fund's programme was suspended even though that country had no inflation, and by most economists' reckoning, was pursuing good fiscal policies, with expenditures limited to tax revenues and foreign aid receipts. The IMF was pushing reforms in Ethiopia's financial market that many economists argued were inappropriate for a country at that stage of development. (As an example, in Kenya, financial market liberalization had led to an increase in interest rates paid by borrowers, not a decrease as had been predicted.) The failure of the policies to achieve the predicted effects did not impede the Fund from pushing them, but these failures played an important role in the Ethiopian government's resistance—it did not want its already desperately poor farmers to be further impoverished as a result of higher borrowing costs.[10]

That the Fund can have such a powerful effect on other suppliers of funds gives the Fund enormous power, of course. It is a kind of leverage that every monopolist seeks, but few achieve. In other arenas, enormous thought has been put into the question of how to reduce that kind of power. One way is to force competition in areas where that is possible—as in the area of advice—and the other way is to restrict its activities in other areas that may enhance its power.

For instance, the Fund is engaged in 'surveillance', an annual review of economies' performance. The surveillance represents an example of 'mission creep'. The Article 4 reviews are named after the section of the IMF's Articles of Agreement that mandates supervision by the Fund of member countries' exchange rate policies to ensure that countries are complying with the Article 1. Today, that particular topic is a minuscule part of the overall review. If the Fund is to carry out its stabilization mission, it must monitor countries, but the annual review is an inefficient way of gathering the relevant information. Too many resources are allocated to countries such as the United States where the probability of a crisis is very low and where the value added by the review to information available elsewhere is almost surely zero. (My own experience while I was chairman of the Council of Economic Advisers was that the review added nothing to our understanding of the economy. Its assessments lacked the depth of insight that was available from a multitude of other sources, and its policy recommendations were often misguided.) By the same token, more resources could have been added to learning about and monitoring countries that were more likely to have crises. The surveillance function could easily be performed by others at least as effectively, for example, by regional or other groupings of countries (such as is currently done by the OECD) through processes of peer monitoring.

One could argue that the data gathering services provided by a variety of international organizations, including the UN, the World Bank, and the IMF, represents an

---

[10] Other, more nefarious, reasons have been suggested for the suspension of the IMF programme. Ethiopia repaid a high interest loan to an American bank early, without asking 'permission' of the IMF. Some suspected that it was no surprise that the US was particularly critical of this action (though few disagreed that it was a reasonable action, in terms of strengthening the country's financial position—what it was earning on the reserves used to repay the loan was far less than what it ended up paying to the American bank).

international public good. Such data can be viewed as part of 'knowledge' and is thus clearly a global public good, one that, in turn, contributes to other global public goods, such as improved international economic stability. But a general principle that has emerged from observing data collection activities within governments is that there are real dangers when these activities are entrusted to an operating agency; conflicts of interest too easily arise.[11] That is why many countries have established independent central statistical organizations.

In the case of the IMF, these concerns take on a concrete manifestation: its growth projections of countries with IMF programmes do not represent the best estimate of the future course of the economy, but are the numbers negotiated in the midst of the implementation of an IMF programme. All too often, there are significant gaps between those numbers and reality. An IMF programme, to hang together, must show, for instance, a certain level of tax revenues, that would in turn require a certain rate of growth. If the most accurate growth projection entailed a smaller growth projection, the deficit would be too large to be 'acceptable'. The Fund, rather than showing flexibility in what is acceptable as a budget deficit, has demonstrated at least in some instances more flexibility in what is accepted as a reasonable estimate of growth.

Separating out the surveillance and data collection functions from the Fund would potentially not only increase the efficacy with which these functions are performed, but also reduce the monopoly power of the IMF.

I have argued in this section that there is an argument for international collective action in enhancing global economic stability, but the IMF, the institution created for that purpose, has often not only failed in advancing that objective, but may have been counterproductive—and acted in ways that undermine other basic global values such as democracy. I have also suggested that what is required is basic reforms in account-ability and in some of its basic modes of operation, for instance, its degree of openness and transparency.

There is an interesting debate about whether the problems of the IMF arise because of lack of political accountability, or from too much political interference. Some, such as De Gregorio *et al.* (1999) argue for reforms that are in the opposite direction from those I have been arguing for, that the IMF should be made more independent, less politically accountable. They rightly see that many of the key failures are associated with interventions, especially by the Americans and French—the former pushing loans to Russia, for instance, the latter to Zaïre and Francophone West Africa, against

---

[11] Even when the agency does not act badly, the suspicion that it might adversely affects credibility. Thus, in the mid-1990s, in the United States, there was a major debate about biases in the consumer price index (CPI). Spearheaded by a bi-partisan Congressional commission chaired by the former chairman of the Council of Economic Advisers, Michael Boskin, a consensus developed that the CPI overstated the rate of inflation by between 1 and 2 percentage points a year—a significant amount. The discrepancy had implications for a variety of areas, including judgements about the seriousness of inflation and the indexing of social security payments and wages with cost of living increases. Determination of the CPI is entrusted to the Department of Labor, which has close ties to the labour movement. Unions were concerned that a downward revision of the CPI would adversely affect workers. When the Department of Labor resisted making changes in the CPI (at least at the speed that critics of the index thought desirable), some attributed it to general bureaucratic conservatism, but others saw a conflict of interest.

the better judgement of the staff. But pretending that the IMF is simply a technocratic body, helping the country adopt Pareto dominant policies, is simply wrong. There are key trade-offs, issues that should be resolved in the political process, and the IMF staff has repeatedly shown a failure to appreciate the distinction between providing advice concerning the set of 'Pareto optimal policies' and forcing a particular set of policies, a particular choice on the Pareto frontier, that reflects the interests of particular groups within society. (The trade-offs are particularly significant when there is uncertainty about the consequences of policies—which there always is, but which the Fund often fails to recognize publicly. Different policies entail different groups bearing risks.) Thus, letting the staff loose with even less political accountability could well make the problems identified earlier worse. I would argue that more direct public accountability holds open the promise of checking the kind of direct interference that has been the source of so much failure. It is at least conceivable that loans to Mobutu might not have proceeded if there had been a public debate exposing the corruption, noting that the funds were more likely to enrich Mobutu than the people of the country, who would be left with increased debt and little to show for it. Perhaps the loan would have gone forward anyway—a clear testimony to the importance of geo-political considerations in the cold war period—but at least there would be little pretence about what the money was for.

In the end, the most important reforms—and the hardest to achieve—will be in governance: to whom the IMF is *directly* accountable. Governance affects organizational behaviour. To be sure, in some sense, the IMF is accountable to its member countries. But any observer of political processes knows that different agencies within a government reflect more closely different interests within the polity: finance ministries reflect the interests of the financial community far more than they do the interests of labour, to say the least. That the IMF is accountable to finance ministers and central bank governors (many of whom themselves are not directly accountable)[12] undoubtedly has an effect on the IMF, and especially the policies that it advocates. It is more than likely that the IMF would have been far more concerned about the effects of its policies on unemployment and wages if it reported directly to labour ministers!

If the IMF were only a 'club' of central bankers, facilitating the clearing of checks, for instance, all of this would make little difference. But the policies of the IMF have profound effects on every aspect of the economy—and hence the lack of representativeness, both *across* countries and *within* countries, undermines the legitimacy of the institution, especially calling into question policies that go beyond, or are contrary to, its original mandate.

I am, however, not completely sanguine about the reforms discussed so far fully addressing the concerns raised earlier and ensuring that the institution really does pursue global economic stability in ways that reflect broad global interests. Further reforms will be needed in its modes of operation, with perhaps further restraints on the

---

[12] And indeed, one of the main items in the IMF agenda in recent years has been to increase the independence of the central banks—making themselves accountable to those who are even less democratically accountable.

kinds of actions it can take. An important step in the right direction will be to require *ex ante* assessments of the likely impact of a programme, not only on inflation and the exchange rate, but also on poverty, growth, and unemployment, and periodic reviews by independent outsider commissions not only of the accuracy of those assessments, but also of the overall effectiveness of crisis prevention and management policies.[13]

2.2. *The World Bank*

The fifth global public good described earlier, the provision of international humanitarian assistance, provides the rationale for the World Bank's mission of helping developing countries grow faster and eradicate their poverty. Originally, it saw its mission as addressing a market failure—the imperfections in capital markets that impede the flow of capital from developed to less developed countries. Standard theories at the time suggested that what caused lack of development was a shortage of capital. Lower capital–labour ratios in poor countries *should* have resulted in high returns, which *should* have, with well-functioning capital markets, led to a flow of capital from the developed to the less developed countries. But that was not happening. Now we recognize that what separates developed from less developed countries is not just a disparity in capital, but gaps in knowledge; and one of the functions of the World Bank is to reduce those gaps.[14]

The World Bank also sees as one of its functions the production and dissemination of knowledge about development and about the kinds of policies and institutions that are most conducive to development. Knowledge, policies, and institutions can all be thought of as complements to capital. Increases in knowledge or improvements in institutions and policies can raise the marginal productivity of capital, increasing not only the effectiveness of aid, but also inducing a flow of private capital.

Research in the economics of information over the past quarter of century has helped us understand why capital markets are often imperfect: why, for instance, there is likely to be rationing, or why equity markets typically provide only limited opportunities for firms to divest themselves of risk. Just because flows of capital from the developed to the less developed countries have increased so much over the past decade, we should not be lulled into thinking that there are no capital market imperfections, and that therefore there is no role of the World Bank in providing capital. We have already noted that most developing countries still do not have ready access to capital especially for funds that can be used broadly, say for health or education. Not only might they have to pay very high interest rates, but they may also actually face credit rationing. And when the economy goes into a recession, and they need funds to finance a fiscal deficit to help restore the economy's strength, private lenders are likely to retract rather than extend lending—flows are all too often pro-cyclical.

---

[13] For more extensive discussions of the kinds of reforms that might be desirable, see Independent Task Force (1999); Meltzer Commission (2000); and Overseas Development Council (2000).

[14] For a discussion of these issues, see World Bank (1998c).

There is thus a role for international financial institutions in general, and the World Bank in particular, in providing capital to the developing world. The benefits may be more related to *access* in bad times (though not necessarily just times of crisis), than to reduced borrowing *costs*. (The lower interest rates on IFI loans do not necessarily translate into lower costs overall. Since IFI loans have seniority over other debts, more IFI borrowing to some extent decreases the ability to repay other debts, and thus other creditors demand a higher interest rate to compensate for their higher risk.)

It is likely that capital markets for middle-income countries will continue to improve, and it is conceivable that, accordingly, the role of the World Bank in providing capital to those countries may diminish. But there is often a linkage between the transfer of knowledge and the provision of credit, especially when the capital is provided to finance particular projects. It appears that this is at least one of the reasons that China, which is sitting on huge amounts of reserves that earn lower interest rates than what it has to pay to the World Bank on its loans, continues to be among the Bank's largest borrowers. For the middle-income countries, the World Bank acts much like a credit cooperative. Indeed, the Bank actually earns a profit on its middle-income lending, part of which goes to cross-subsidize lending to lower-income countries. If, in the future, it turns out that improvements in capital markets effectively eliminate the value of the credit enhancement provided by the 'credit cooperative', and the Bank is unable to deliver non-lending (knowledge) services that are valued, then middle-income lending will, over time, diminish.[15]

3. INTERACTIONS AMONG GLOBAL PUBLIC GOODS

While the international financial institutions naturally focus on issues of *economic* global public goods and externalities, there are important interactions between these global public goods and other public goods and externalities. For instance, there is a clear relationship between economic stability and global security issues. Policies that increase unemployment or dramatically lower real incomes can lead, and often have led, to civil unrest, ethnic conflict, and strife not only within countries but among them. The policies pursued in Indonesia, including the elimination of the food and fuel subsidies just as incomes were plummeting and unemployment soaring, predictably led to riots that not only caused enormous bloodshed but further undermined the economy. The IMF has, at other times, strongly urged Jordan to remove food subsidies at a pace that the government felt might have led to riots there. Jordan's government managed to resist the IMF pressure; had it not, and had the government's worries materialized, Middle East security could have clearly been jeopardized.

High interest rate policies and scarcity of credit in Indonesia and elsewhere have contributed to faster exhaustion of natural resources. Cutting down forests is an easy

---

[15] Thus, I disagree with the Meltzer Commission report's recommendation that the World Bank withdraw completely from middle-income lending. There is a small implicit subsidy (associated with the credit enhancement provided by the Bank's original capital contributions and the potential further backing of the 'shareholders' should that prove insufficient), but, taking account of the cross-subsidy to low income countries, possibly the net effect is a tax on middle-income lending.

way of raising cash. Thus, there can be marked environmental consequences of economic policies. At the same time, putting in place good environmental policies may be costly, and when the benefits are a global public good (such as reduced atmospheric concentrations of greenhouse gases), it is appropriate that those most able to bear the costs of providing for these global public goods should do so. The Global Environmental Facility administered by the World Bank provides some funds, but clearly more funds are needed. The Bank has been using some of its 'leverage' to advance better environmental policies, for example by encouraging the elimination of energy subsidies, an action that would both improve the environment and economic performance.

Similarly, World Bank health programmes can not only be of enormous benefit to the people in the country, but can also reduce the global threat of contagious diseases. In that way, the World Bank contributes to another one of the global public goods.

4. CONCLUSIONS

The recognition that there are global public goods and global externalities, requiring collective action at the global level, represents a major change in thinking. Research has demonstrated the difficulties *within countries* of collective action. Markets by themselves are powerful, but important and extensive market failures provide scope for collective action. Unfortunately, that collective action does not always work as we would hope. Agency problems are pervasive. Public bodies are sometimes captured by special interest groups, and politicians sometimes pursue agendas of their own. Limited competition in the provision of public goods has adverse effects on efficiency and effectiveness.

To date, unfortunately, collective action at the international level has not been subjected to the same kind of analytic scrutiny that has occurred at the national and local level. This chapter is intended to be an initial contribution, identifying the *objectives* (the rationales for global collective action). It also begins to assess whether policies have been well directed at achieving those objectives, or, as so often happens at the national level, they more accurately reflect the interests of the bureaucrats that run international institutions or the special interests that they serve.

More broadly, at the international level, collective action is, if anything, even more difficult. The international community, having recognized the need for collective action, has been struggling with the problem of global governance without global government. In some arenas there has been more reliance on consensus; in other arenas, there has been more delegation to specialized bodies, supposedly run by 'experts', with little direct accountability.

The two arenas in which global collective action has been most advanced—reflecting their importance—relate to international economic and political stability. In this chapter, I have tried to argue that while there is a real rationale for collective action, the actions undertaken by the IMF have arguably not been well directed at *correcting* the market failure. In some cases, it may actually have exacerbated the problems. I have speculated about why that might be the case, and have proposed reforms that might go some way toward making it more likely that its policies will not only be more effective, but more directed at correcting global economic market failures.

REFERENCES

Collier, Paul (1999). Consensus-building, knowledge, and conditionality. Paper presented at the International Symposium on Global Finance and Development, Ministry of Finance of Japan and World Bank, 1–2 March. Tokyo.

De Gregorio, José, Barry Eichengreen, Takatoshi Ito, and Charles Wyplosz (1999). *An Independent and Accountable IMF*. Geneva Reports on the World Economy, 1. International Center for Monetary and Banking Studies, Geneva.

Feldstein, Martin (1998). Refocusing the IMF. *Foreign Affairs*, 77(2), 20–33.

Furman, Jason and Joseph E. Stiglitz (1998). Economic crises: Evidence and insights from East Asia. *Brookings Papers on Economic Activity*, 2, 1–114. Brookings Institution, Washington, DC.

Hellmann, Thomas, Kevin Murdock, and Joseph E. Stiglitz (2000). Liberalization, moral hazard in banking and prudential regulation: Are capital requirements enough? *American Economic Review*, 90(1), 147–65.

Independent Task Force (1999). Safeguarding prosperity in a global financial system: The future international financial architecture. Report of an Independent Task Force sponsored by the Council on Foreign Relations. New York.

Meltzer Commission (2000). Report of the International Financial Institution Advisory Commission. March. Washington, DC.

Overseas Development Council (2000). The future role of the IMF in development. ODC Task Force Report. April. ODC, Washington, DC.

Stiglitz, Joseph E. (1995). The theory of international public goods and the architecture of international organizations. Paper presented at the meeting of High Level Group on Development Strategy and Management of the Market Economy, 8–10 July. UNU/WIDER, Helsinki, Finland.

——(1996). Some lessons from the East Asian miracle. *World Bank Research Observer*, 11(2), 151–77.

——(1998). Must financial crises be this frequent and this painful? McKay Lecture, 23 September. Pittsburgh, PA.

World Bank (1998a). *Global Economic Prospects and the Developing Countries 1998/99: Beyond Financial Crisis*. World Bank, Washington, DC.

——(1998b). *Assessing Aid: What Works, What Doesn't, and Why*. Policy Research Report. Oxford University Press for the World Bank, New York.

——(1998c). *World Development Report 1998/99: Knowledge for Development*. Oxford University Press for the World Bank, New York.

10

From the GATT to the WTO and Beyond

S. P. SHUKLA

1. INTRODUCTION

The object of this chapter is to analyse the evolution of the international trading system from its inception as the General Agreement on Tariffs and Trade (GATT) in 1947 to its latest incarnation as the World Trade Organization (WTO), comprising the complex array of agreements forming its substance and mandate. It focuses on the adequacy or inadequacy of the system as it evolved and functioned in an environment of changing international economic and political reality. It also attempts to grapple with the more difficult question of looking at the future prospects of the system, the strains it will need to face and subsequent changes that are called for in its approach, content, and functioning, taking into account the future governance needs of the world economy and polity.

The chapter consists of six parts. The second section provides a synopsis of the functioning of the GATT through three decades from 1947 to 1979. The third section analyses the crisis that gripped the system in the 1980s and the denouement that followed at the conclusion of the Uruguay Round negotiations in 1994. The fourth section is devoted to a brief analysis of the outcome of those negotiations (viz. the World Trade Organization) and the subsequent paradigm shift. The fifth section attempts to look at the forces propelling the WTO from triumph (1994) to fiasco (1999), while the last section concentrates on what is to be done, outlining strategic considerations and defining certain institutional and programmatic initiatives.

2. THREE DECADES OF THE GATT (1947–79)

The General Agreement on Tariffs and Trade, which came into being on 30 October 1947, was designed to deal with international, that is, cross-border, trade in goods. The GATT was to be guided by the fundamental principle of non-discrimination, but it accorded recognition to the then existing preferential systems and, in practice, provided room for substantial deviation through lax application of its rules on free-trade areas and customs unions. It banned quantitative restrictions, but concurrently carved out significant exceptions. Much like the American reciprocal trade agreements that preceded it, the GATT supported reciprocity in tariff negotiations as well as an emergency clause to be evoked in the event of import surges. It made retaliation possible by permitting the withdrawal of concessions from trading partners who reneged on their part of the bargain. The GATT advocated the democratic principle of 'one member–one vote' and reinforced it further by stipulating that any amendment to the basic principle of non-discrimination was possible only with unanimity.

During the three decades ending with the conclusion of the Tokyo Round of Multilateral Trade Negotiations (1973–79), the GATT was characterized by notable achievements and serious shortcomings. True to its objective, the agency launched impressive tariff reduction measures but at the same time overlooked, connived at, and even presided over glaring breaches of its basic tenets. It tried to respond to the changing political and economic environment but could not quite adjust to new realities, or to the emerging aspirations of most of its members. The GATT tried to grapple with a new generation of trade problems but ended with a challenge to its integrity. In confronting issues of concern, the GATT was torn between adherence to its rules and recognition of the weight exerted by the trading powers. All in all, it is a mixed story.

2.1. *Tariff Reduction and Trade Expansion*

Let us first review the GATT's main *raison d'être*—tariff reduction. This was pursued systematically in seven 'rounds' of trade negotiations, and remarkable cuts with expanding coverage were achieved in conjunction with the Geneva Round at the inception of the GATT, and the subsequent Kennedy Round (1963–67), and Tokyo Round (1973–79). Reductions largely affected the fast growing sectors of industry, but not agriculture or textiles and clothing. With the implementation of the Tokyo Round, '...the average import weighted tariff on manufactured products maintained by industrialized nations declined to about 6 per cent' (Hoekman and Kostecki 1995: 19). The impact of tariff cuts was far less on export products from developing countries.[1]

Starting from 1950, the next 20 years were a remarkable era of economic growth. Without doubt, an important stimulus for growth in this period was trade, which continued to expand as large inflows of American capital were used to reconstruct production facilities in war-devastated Europe and effective demand was kept at a high level by the continent's expansionary policies. Removing exchange and trade restrictions facilitated larger volumes of trade and more efficient use of resources to serve bigger markets, exploiting economies of scale. Mass consumption of standardized goods expanded rapidly in the early post-war period and American steel, chemical, automotive, rubber, and electronics industries faced insatiable demand. Given the GATT philosophy and the ensuing process of non-discriminatory tariff reduction, these American industries enjoyed the prospect of maintaining their leading position, while letting the European economies share the growth. For them, 'free trade promised nothing but expanding exports' (Reich 1983: 780).

---

[1] See Hoekman and Kostecki (1995: 17–18); Tussie (1987: 17, 29); and Hudec (1987: 62, 75).

Later, significant structural transformations took place. These included rapidly increasing international mobility of capital among the developed countries; narrow segment-specialization leading to a fast increase in intra-industry trade; increasingly oligopolistic organization of industrial production; and, an intra-corporational but also international division of production processes.[2] The cumulative impact of these structural changes eventually led to a vast escalation in intra-corporation trade. They also led to the internalization of tariffs and to what Diana Tussie calls 'painless tariff-cutting' (1987), but these tariff-cutting measures appear to be more of a consequence—rather than a cause—of trade expansion. Or, put more accurately, both phenomena were caused by basic changes in investment patterns as well as in organizational aspects of production.

Another factor underlying tariff reductions was linked to the political and strategic objective of the cold war.[3]

Interestingly, impressive tariff reductions were achieved in the Kennedy (1963–67) and Tokyo (1973–79) Rounds, the former coinciding with the final years of remarkable growth and the latter at a time when the expansionary phase was already faltering. Moreover, these tariff reductions have to be viewed in conjunction with the major exceptions that continued to persist within the system. We will turn to these elements later, in the context of the GATT's other major area of activity.

All in all, the GATT responded to and participated in a complex process shaped and conditioned by various political and economic factors, which were unique to its historical environment. Thus, the widely held belief that the GATT tariff reduction caused the phenomenal trade expansion (and growth) does not seem warranted. Even less sound would appear the claim that such causal linkage is valid for all situations and times.

2.2. *Developing Countries: The GATT's Response*

Let us turn to the question of developing countries, the second major area of the GATT's activity in this period. As a result of decolonization and the subsequent emergence of new nations, the GATT witnessed a large upsurge in members during the second and third decade of its existence, and in the 1960s, its composition changed overwhelmingly in favour of the developing countries. The desire to bring new nations into its sphere, however, had already started to influence the thinking in the GATT in the 1950s and specific problems of the developing countries were included in its deliberations.

Two initiatives followed. First, inclusion of Article XVIII in 1954–55 recognized the right of developing countries to use import restrictions to protect infant industries and to safeguard balance-of-payment situations. This Article also upheld developing country autonomy in policy-making in respect of the latter. Second, an expert panel under the chairmanship of Mr Haberler furnished a report in 1958 on developing

---

[2] See Tussie (1987: chapter 3).

[3] 'With the advent of the cold war, . . . exclusion from MFN treatment could be used as a threat or punishment, inclusion as a bribe or reward. Trade policy was a vehicle for moving western countries into closer alliance.' President Kennedy 'expressly linked (his initiative for the 1963–67 Round) to the question of western unity in the face of the Soviet threat' (see Pincus 1986: 245–7).

country trade problems, such as low export growth, fluctuating commodity prices, and protectionist policies of the industrial countries in terms of agriculture.[4]

The Haberler Report triggered debate in the GATT and led to developing countries calling for the agency's reform. Developments in other forums, which eventually led to the establishment of UNCTAD (United Nations Conference on Trade and Development) in 1964, influenced the course that the GATT took. The GATT deliberations on reform culminated in the inclusion of Part IV titled 'Trade and Development' in the GATT's mandate in February 1965.

Part IV was impressive in its format and general declaration of principle. But as an instrument to correct the distortion in the GATT's structure and functioning with specific obligations targeted to industrialized countries, its value was limited. The only operationally significant provision was related to the interpretation of the reciprocity concept in the context of developed/developing country relationships. But even here, the entire negotiating mechanics was left to the discretion of the stronger parties.

Two other elements of the GATT's response to the demand for reform should be noted. The first relates to waivers granted to developing countries, who had been pushing for a legal basis that would permit preferential treatment in their favour. With the creation of UNCTAD, the demand gained momentum and in 1971 the GATT granted two waivers. These waivers, valid for ten years, permitted implementation of the generalized system of preferences (GSP) which enabled industrialized countries to extend preferences to developing countries, and allowed developing countries to exchange preferences amongst themselves.

The second element relates to the Framework Agreements articulated in the Tokyo Round (1973–79). These agreements granted a permanent legal basis to what had been secured for 10 years with the 1971 waivers. However, the preferential element, introduced to modify the GATT's principle of non-discrimination or 'most-favoured-nation' treatment was counterbalanced by 'graduation', a concept based on the assumption that developing countries—as their economies progressively developed—would participate more fully in the framework of rights and obligations. The Framework Agreements also included a declaration on balance-of-payment measures. This was the first move by the developed countries to circumscribe that part of Article XVIII which allowed developing countries a substantial degree of policy-making autonomy with regard to measures to safeguard their balance-of-payment positions.

Developing countries, who formed the GATT's overwhelming majority, were interested in establishing effective trade-development linkages. The GATT's response—regardless of whether evaluated in terms of the Haberler Report or according to the expectations of developing countries—was inadequate, both conceptually as well as politically. Inadequacy was compounded by the major divergence from rules that the GATT permitted or encouraged. And here we turn to the systemic and chronic exceptions referred to earlier. These relate to agriculture and textiles and clothing, the two areas of particular interest to developing countries.

---

[4] 'The substance of the report was that the predicament of the underdeveloped countries was due in no small measure to the trade policies of the developed countries' (see Dam 1970: 279).

While growth in agriculture and in textiles and clothing was crucial to development in many developing countries, these two sectors of the economy in the industrialized world had not been affected by the structural transformation taking place in the other major industries, where increased mobility of industrial capital across national borders, increasing intra-industry and intra-corporation trade, and the emergence of transnational corporations had significantly promoted production and trade. This partly explains the persistence of the continuing exceptions.[5]

2.3. *Agriculture*

At the time of the GATT's inception, an exemption was incorporated in Article XI, which prohibited quantitative restrictions, in order to adapt it to America's policy of domestic agricultural support. This was inadequate to meet domestic exigency, and the United States obtained a very liberal waiver in 1955, enabling it to continue with wide-ranging agricultural protection. Later, the EEC's CAP (Common Agricultural Policy) came into effect. The EEC's domestic production was effectively isolated from world market forces by its border mechanism of variable levies, and exporters were paid the difference between domestic support prices and competitive world prices through 'export restitution' measures. In due course, the CAP with its double mechanism transformed agriculture in Europe, converting it from a large importer to a massive exporter of farming products.

Considering the track record of the two major powers, it is no surprise that the GATT's agricultural regime was marked by lax discipline on quotas, lesser bindings of tariffs, and little discipline on domestic support or subsidization, and a mere appeal to avoid export subsidies, which could disturb the relative shares of world markets. All this grossly hurt the trade prospects of efficient producers, many developing countries included.

2.4. *Textiles and Clothing*

A discriminatory, quota-based and restrictive trade regime was clamped on efficient producers, beginning with Japan. Later, on the grounds that imports from 'low-wage' regions were causing 'market disruption', this was extended to cover all textile exporting countries in the developing world. In the process, there was a total reversal of the GATT philosophy and rules, and with every successive renewal, the regime became more extensive in scope and more restrictive in content. Conceived as a temporary measure to enable the textile industry in the developed world to adjust to market forces, the system remained in position throughout the GATT's lifetime and beyond. Paradoxically, it had originated with the trade liberalization measures launched in the GATT.[6] Concurrently as developments were taking place in textiles sector

---

[5] Later as the agri-business came to dominate agriculture, pressures for bringing the agricultural sector under the GATT discipline acquired new momentum in the 1980s.

[6] It was during the Dillon Round of tariff negotiations (1960–61) that the short-term arrangement came into being. The US textile industry had linked its support to the Trade Agreement Act of 1962 with the restrictions it wanted to be imposed on 'market disrupting' imports from 'low-cost' countries. A successful

under the GATT's benign supervision, a good deal of activity was being carried out by the same agency, with the ostensible purpose of providing special and more favourable treatment for the developing countries. The irony of the situation is obvious.

The trade regime for textiles and clothing encapsulated the basic contradiction of the system: the continuing need for expansion on the one hand, and, on the other, the built-in tendency to pass the relevant costs of adjustment onto weaker constituents. This generated recurring internal tension, eventually threatening the system's viability. This was obvious in the contradiction between ongoing processes of integration (acquiring new members and territories, and eventually, new issues and activities) and exclusion (building in exceptions; evasion in the application of basic norms and principles; bending of the rules and discrimination against weaker members; creation of exclusive sub-systems). The process can be characterized as 'exclusion built into integration'.[7]

The third decade of the GATT was marked by incipient strains in other industrial sectors that were to plague the system into the 1980s. Steel and automotive industries in the United States as well as in the EEC were in trouble. The American economy was already showing signs of ill health. But causing greater concern were the developments in the world monetary system, as the underpinnings of the post-world war system were unravelling, and this environment contributed to pressures that endangered the trading system in the 1980s.

2.5. *Conflicting Reactions*

Two major reactions ensued. One accentuated the system's inherent tendency of exclusion, while the other focused on the hope of reforming, if not replacing, the system, and resulted in the third world initiative of the United Nations—the 'new international economic order' (NIEO).[8] The grandeur of the concept, introducing a grand, mutually beneficial, international bargain of technology and finance in exchange

conclusion of the long-term arrangement was considered by the US Administration as necessary to obtain legislative authority for negotiations in the Kennedy Round (1963–67). Likewise, the negotiating authority for the Tokyo Round (1973–79) was obtained by promising stronger protection to the US textile industry through what came to be known as MFA (see Low 1993: 107–8; and Hoekman and Kostecki 1995: 219).

[7] The contradiction manifested itself, in a manner of speaking, during the US–UK negotiations on the shape of the postwar world trade order, and later in the course of negotiations leading to the ITO Charter, although it can be said that the element of integration was relatively stronger in those negotiations. Soon ITO vanished into the archives and the GATT came into being in an environment of substantial attenuation, if not abandonment, of multilateralism, and more important, largely as an instrument of consolidation of Western Europe against the perceived threat of the USSR, as part of the cold war strategy. The beginnings of the GATT thus were rooted in the exclusion of the Soviet bloc. In the postwar period, Japan's entry into the GATT provides a classic example of integration on the pain of exclusion in terms of the unprecedented boycott Japan faced from almost all Western European countries through resort to the non-application clause and later, the imposition of restraint on its textile exports. The process continued unabated *vis-à-vis* developing countries and culminated in the emergence of the WTO and its operations during the five-year period of its existence (see Shukla (2000) and also notes 3 and 5 above).

[8] UNCTAD, maintaining a high profile, opened wide-ranging negotiations on the Common Fund for Commodities, a Code on Transfer of Technology, a Set of Principles for the Control of Restrictive Business Practices, and supported initiatives for revision of the Paris Convention, Economic Cooperation among

for resources and markets, was matched only by its naïveté. The idea did not survive the 1970s and was obliterated by a counter-initiative launched by the GATT's industrialized members in the 1980s.

The tendency of exclusion manifested itself in various ways. The textile and clothing regime adopted a more restrictive and extensive form of the Multifibre Arrangement (1973–77); proposals for trade reform were introduced to elude the 'force-of-numbers' logic and to keep control of the decision-making process with the trading majors;[9] and, the so-called 'code' or 'side agreement' approach emerged prominently at the GATT.

In the Tokyo Round (1973–79), 'codes' were defined for such non-tariff procedures as government procurement, subsidies, dumping and countervail. Unlike tariffs, these codes impinged more closely on domestic policies and required a degree of commonality in approach and circumstances. There was a tendency among the trading majors to limit code negotiations to a small group of industrial countries, to present the outcome to other members as, more or less, a *fait accompli* and to extend benefits to signatories only. Developing countries viewed these negotiations with misgiving. Codes thus articulated and conditionally and selectively applied, violated the basic principle of non-discrimination and threatened the integrity of the GATT system, perpetrating yet another exclusion.[10]

2.6. *Halfway Solutions*

Emergence of the 'side agreement' approach, the US predilection for conditional MFN, and the underlying distrust in the 'force of numbers' were all symptoms of the basic tensions that were affecting the world at large and causing tremors in the GATT. On the one hand, because the era of expansion was coming to an end, the system needed, more urgently than before, enlargement space offered by worldwide markets. Competition and tension between the EEC, Japan, and the US were becoming sharper, and the underpinnings of the system, which had facilitated growth in the industrialized capitalist world while maintaining the relative dominance of the US, had disappeared.

Developing Countries, the question of linkages between trade and finance, and the reform of the international financial system (see UNGA Resolutions 3202 (S-IV), May 1974; 3281(XXIX) December 1974).

[9] A typical expression of this concern is found in the following: 'With certain exceptions, decisions in GATT are taken by simple majority vote and it has become increasingly obvious that countries which accept legally binding and serious obligations governing their mutual trade would not indefinitely submit to a situation in which the administration of the trade rules would be governed by a body in which a vast majority of the members (and an increasingly organized majority), while enjoying all the benefits of the Agreement, has no equivalent commitments and yet by force of numbers has effective control of the decision-making process'. Eric Wyndham-White, the first director-general, who 'was a predominant and omnipresent factor in GATT from the beginning to his retirement in 1968' (see Dam 1970: 339) wrote this in his foreword (1975) which was put forward in the context of the Tokyo Round. The proposal advocated, among other things, a 'code' approach to accomplish strengthened disciplines in the GATT.

[10] In regard to the code on subsidies, the US insistence that benefits of the 'material injury test' be made available only to the signatories of the code and their further insistence on having 'commitments' in regard to the subsidy regime from developing country signatories created conceptual and real problems for the GATT. Although the issue was settled by the concerned parties outside the 'court', so to say, the legality of the US position was in serious doubt.

On the other hand, the third world, which held the promise of expanding markets, was vociferously demanding for a new international economic order. Faced with these diverging interests, the trading majors in the GATT had to settle for halfway solutions. These included (i) the tightening of restrictions on textiles and clothing; (ii) the reduction of tariffs to a new, historically low level; (iii) the concession to preferential treatment with concurrent measures, such as the 'graduation' principle, to minimize its effects; (iv) promotion of the 'code' approach but without full endorsement for the GATT Plus arrangements; (v) tackling of the non-tariff barriers question and the attempt to introduce a modest level of harmonization of domestic policies and standards; and, (vi) deferment of the difficult problem of agriculture, and waiting for the euphoria of the third world to subside. Thus ended the third decade of the GATT.

3. CRISIS AND DENOUEMENT (1980–94)

The years 1980–94 in the GATT's history were turbulent and troublous, because of pressures induced by the changing global economic environment and the inability or unwillingness of the trading majors to abide by the rules they themselves had set up. The turbulence and troubles were exacerbated because of the characteristic manner in which the majors tried to force a denouement to their overwhelming advantage, finally succeeding. It is this aspect that we turn to now.

The 1980s witnessed increasing pressures on the GATT system. The United States was facing growing competition in the manufacturing industries not only from Germany and Japan, but also from such newcomers as South Korea, Brazil, Mexico, Taiwan, and Singapore. The EEC emerged as a mega-exporter of agricultural products, threatening America's share of the world markets. Demands for protection grew rapidly in the US. But neither was the EEC immune from competition by Japan and the newcomers. According to the GATT discipline, safeguard measures were to be undertaken in a non-discriminatory manner. In certain circumstances, safeguard efforts could result in compensatory claims. Consequently, there was a natural disposition for the two majors to introduce, with the consent of the affected party, bilateral, extra-GATT agreements or understandings on import restrictions that would not be contested in the GATT. Thus, these 'grey area' measures replaced the GATT principle of 'open markets—nondiscrimination—competition' with an approach characterized by 'market sharing—discriminatory bilateralism—managed trade'. Under protectionist pressures, the coverage of these measures—anti-GATT, but not strictly GATT-illegal—expanded to industries such as iron and steel, automotive, electronic products, footwear, and even semi-conductors.

In the US, these measures were further reinforced by what Bhagwati (1991) has dubbed 'aggressive unilateralism', and two far-reaching legislative acts, namely the Trade and Tariff Act of 1984 and the Omnibus Trade and Competitiveness Act of 1988, were passed.[11] 'The legislation was a culmination of severe pressure from

---

[11] The Trade and Tariff Act of 1984 established negotiating objectives in new areas including services, intellectual property rights, and trade related investment measures and expanded the scope of application of Section 301, under which a US executive, utilizing the option of withdrawal of tariff concessions, or

Congress on the Administration to "do something" about trade.' Apart from being a response to protectionist pressures, it appeared to be 'more about unilateral armament to make demands for reciprocity effective and decisively influence the shape of the future international trading system' (Low 1993: 62–3).

3.1. *Measures by the United States: A New Round with New Issues for the GATT*

3.1.1. *Services and the Punta del Este Compromise*
The search for new opportunities by the United States was extended to high technology industries, services, particularly banking, insurance and other financial services, audio-visual services, telecommunications, and other measures to increase operational space for transnational corporations. It also included a move for bringing agricultural trade under effective GATT discipline, an effort that was mainly aimed at the EEC. The US initiative in the GATT was guided by this two-pronged approach. It first found expression in the 1982 GATT ministerial meeting and was later consolidated in May 1983 in the demand for a new GATT round *with the new issues*. The 1982 meeting exposed two major controversial elements in the GATT: US confronting the developing countries on the issue of services, which at that time was the most contentious 'new' issue and the US versus the EEC on the old agricultural question. The US initiative on a new GATT round was mired in controversies, moves and countermoves, and induced laborious negotiations at the formal as well as the informal levels. It was only after the longest gestation period and the most trying discussions ever experienced in the GATT that in September 1986, the new round could be launched at the Punta del Este ministerial meeting.[12]

For the United States, the services issue was at the core of its agenda, not only because it occupied the dominant position in this field, but also because the services issue was the key to the transformation of the GATT. Services, transcending the narrow confines of the cross-border exchange of goods, were envisaged to make the agency into an effective instrument that would support and promote the transnational corporations. Opposition by the developing countries was, at one level, rooted in their collective memory of the colonial period. At another level, the rationale of opposition was a sophisticated analysis of the contemporary stage of development of global capitalism and its perceived dangers to the third world in its autocentric pursuit of development. Developing countries were concerned that gaining access to the industrialized markets for their goods would be made conditional on the third world opening its markets for services from the developed countries. And in the early stages, developing countries were able to put up a united front of opposition. Arguing that the

imposition of high punitive tariffs, can exercise his authority to enforce the 'rights' of the US in international trade relations. The Omnibus Trade and Competitiveness Act of 1988 dealt with a range of issues affecting mutual relations between the US and its economic partners, and the decline of US competitiveness. It further strengthened Section 301 and introduced 'Special' and 'Super' 301s, calling for the categorization of foreign practices whose elimination would be imperative for expanding US exports.

[12] For an account of the developments leading to the Punta del Este meeting in September 1986, see Shukla (1994, 2000).

issue lay outside the legal competence of the GATT, they succeeded in hedging the conclusion of the 1982 ministerial meeting considerably (although they were unable to prevent the United States from placing the issue on the GATT agenda). Later these countries were also successful in hindering the preparatory work for the new round. Under pressure, however, the number of countries opposing the move by the United States dwindled to ten nations that remained firmly opposed.[13]

Meanwhile, a behind-the-scenes compromise was worked out between India, Brazil, and the EEC (which was initially ambivalent on the issue of services, but fearing a build-up of pressure on agriculture and on the CAP which constituted a sensitive element in the regional integration process, it was also cool to the idea of a new round). The compromise included three important elements: (i) in an effort to respond to the issue of the GATT's legal competence, negotiations were to be bifurcated into two independent tracks: goods, within the GATT's jurisdiction and services outside the GATT; (ii) development orientation was to be provided to the services negotiations; and (iii) national regimes in services sectors were to be respected. This was a far cry from the position originally proposed by the United States that had simply intended to graft services onto the existing GATT and used the leverage in goods to access the protected services markets of developing countries. The compromise was accepted with certain modifications that did not affect its substance.[14] This was possible legally because the United States could not pursue its design through the amendment option and possible politically because the EEC, for its own reasons, was party to the compromise. The Punta del Este compromise of September 1986 on services cleared the way for the launch of the Uruguay Round.

The other two new issues, namely trade-related investment measures (TRIMs) and trade-related intellectual property rights (TRIPs), were tackled largely within the confines of relevant GATT articles, with the outcome that resulting mandates were modest, and did not transgress the GATT framework.[15]

---

[13] Argentina, Brazil, Cuba, Egypt, India, Nicaragua, Nigeria, Peru, Tanzania, and Yugoslavia.

[14] The commitment to respect national laws and regulations in the services sector was changed to the commitment to respect the policy objectives thereof. The question of the *inter se* relationship of the outcomes of the two streams of negotiations was not postponed indefinitely, but linked to the implementation of the results at the end of the Round, when a decision would have to be reached on whether the services discipline could be integrated with the rest, with a common enforcement mechanism. The GATT secretariat would service the negotiations.

[15] Article XX (d) recognized that member countries may follow their own regimes in terms of patents, copyright, etc., but also stipulated that measures to enforce such regimes should be applied in a manner so as not to constitute arbitrary or unjustifiable discrimination between countries or disguised restriction on international trade.

The mandate was to clarify GATT provisions and elaborate, as appropriate, new rules and disciplines with a view to reducing distortions and impediments to international trade and of ensuring that procedures to enforce intellectual property rights do not themselves become barriers to legitimate trade. In this effort, 'the need to promote effective and adequate protection of intellectual property rights' was to be taken into account. Thus, what the US wanted to be *the* negotiating objective appeared ultimately as just a factor to be taken into account while carrying out an exercise which was in accordance with the extant approach of the GATT. It was a very restrictive mandate.

The other new issue was the trade-related aspects of investment measures. The mandate was equally restrictive and was confined to the examination of the operation of GATT articles related to the trade

3.1.2. *Offensive on TRIPs*

Soon after the Punta del Este meeting, another major thrust of the US offensive surfaced in its determined pursuit to stretch the mandate on TRIPs beyond the GATT's jurisdiction. Once the coalition of American, European, and Japanese drug and pharmaceutical industries launched a powerful offensive,[16] the three GATT majors, disregarding the Punta del Este consensus, united to include the substantive issue of norms and standards of intellectual property rights (IPR) within the scope of negotiation. They proposed to enforce global protection standards for all forms of intellectual property through an international regime singularly oriented to the requirements of IPR holders and firmly lodged in the GATT.[17] Developing countries opposed the issue, perceiving it as yet another challenge to their economic sovereignty and a threat to their development and public welfare policies.[18] The issue remained deadlocked throughout the mid-term ministerial meeting held in December 1988 in Montreal.[19]

In April 1989, however, in the name of a compromise, developing countries capitulated, virtually accepting the stand of the industrial countries with the addition of some qualifying verbiage.[20] Inevitably, this reversal was to undermine the whole

---

restrictive and distorting effects of investment measures. It also visualized elaboration of further provisions, if necessary, to avoid adverse effects on trade.

[16] See The Intellectual Property Committee/Kaidanren/UNCIE (1988).

[17] The industry coalition, and subsequently the industrial countries, felt that the limitations on the rights that were placed on the grounds of public interest in national legislation amounted to licensing piracy. They wanted to compel various national regimes on patents, such as those in India, Brazil, South Korea, and Argentina, to fall in line with their conception of a global regime. Such a regime lodged in the GATT would equip them with the power of the enforcement mechanism that was not available in the other forums like the World Intellectual Property Organization.

[18] Developing countries were not opposed in principle to a reasonable and functionally necessary protection of intellectual property rights. But they argued that a balance between such rights and the requirements of public interest had to be worked out by the concerned countries in terms of their national legislation; there could be no globally applicable standard formula. Furthermore, the subject was entirely outside the scope and jurisdiction of the GATT. And finally, they argued, insistence on bringing the subject into the GATT amounted to a breach of the consensus on which the Round was launched.

[19] Three alternative formulations, two of which were variants of the approach of the developed countries and one putting forward the view of developing countries, had to be sent to the ministers for consideration at the Montreal meeting (see GATTMTN.TNC/7(MIN) PP21).

The deadlock at Montreal was reflected in the two diametrically opposite drafts on the table at the last stage of the meeting; one was the so-called chairman's proposal which embodied the developed countries' position, and the other, put forward by India, incorporated the stand of the developing countries (see unnumbered documents circulated in the green room at the Montreal Ministerial Meeting).

[20] The decision on TRIPs brought the substantive issue of norms and standards and their enforcement within the ambit of negotiations. The reference to 'public policy objectives' was weak and virtually redundant as all it said was that 'in the negotiations, consideration will be given to concerns raised by participants related to the underlying public policy objectives of the national systems . . .'. This was in sharp contrast to the formulation in the mandate for services negotiations agreed at Punta del Este, which prescribed that 'such framework (i.e. the multilateral framework of principles and rules for trade in services) shall respect the policy objectives of national laws and regulations'. More significant was the fact that the mandate of TRIPS was altered in this way, while it still remained an integral part of the GATT negotiations or the goods track (i.e. Part I of the Ministerial Declaration launching the Uruguay Round), there was no decision on legally separating these negotiations from the GATT track, as was done in the case of services.

process of keeping extraneous subjects off-limits, and marked the beginning of a new enlarged agency, resembling the American conception of the GATT. It also marked the end of developing country resistance that had been voiced since the 1982 ministerial meeting.[21]

3.1.3. *Agriculture*

On the other major front relating to the old issue of agriculture, the EEC had succeeded at the 1982 meeting in resisting pressures for substantive negotiations. However, at Punta del Este in 1986, the agreement on agriculture that emerged was a true compromise between the positions of the US and the EEC,[22] but these two positions continued to chafe each other and eventually led to the failure of two ministerial meetings. At the mid-term ministerial meeting of 1988, differences between the US and the EEC on agriculture were too large to be bridged.[23] The five Latin American nations, who had been prominent in the agricultural–exporter country coalition, insisted that all other issues be deferred until the agricultural question was resolved. This signalled the failure of the Montreal meeting.

By April 1989, a compromise had been reached,[24] enabling the negotiations to continue. Their chequered course, however, was to cause the failure of yet another ministerial session, Brussels in December 1990, as the EEC was not ready to take on substantial commitments. It was not until the EEC was faced with 'the realization that from a budgetary perspective its support policies were unsustainable' (Low 1993: 222) that it (i.e. the EEC) was prompted to reform the CAP, thus making the US–EEC accord on agriculture possible in November 1992.

Two more developments of systemic significance intervened, clearing the way for conclusion of the Uruguay Round: the Multilateral Trade Organization and the Final Act.

---

[21] How did this dramatic reversal in the position of developing countries come about? The event was widely covered in the local Indian press and other third world media (see *Economic and Political Weekly* 1989; SUNS April–May 1989; Raghavan 1990; Shukla 1994). The US had fashioned the powerful weapon of 'aggressive unilateralism' since 1984. It was used against Brazil prior to the April 1989 events. India was also targeted during this period and actual use followed in May 1989. The internal political situation in both countries was fluid and diminished the political willpower to stand firmly in their positions. The arm-twisting was to have its effect, and the Indian–Brazilian coalition weakened, inducing a lack of consultation and coordination that dented mutual trust. As the two countries faltered, the opposition they had laboriously built against the US initiative also collapsed. Industrial countries seized the opportunity to press their advantage.

[22] It recognized the 'urgent need to bring more discipline and predictability to world agricultural trade by correcting and preventing restrictions and distortions including those related to structural surpluses...' which was the EEC argument. It further said that negotiations shall aim 'to achieve greater liberalization of trade in agriculture', which was theme of the US.

[23] The US wanted the EEC to recognize the long-term goal of the total elimination of border protection and all trade-distorting subsidies. In the short run, the US wanted agreement on freezing export subsidies, domestic support and measures of border protection. The EEC was not prepared to go that far.

[24] The long-term goal was defined as 'substantive progressive reduction' in border protection as well as all trade-distorting support measures; and a freeze on the domestic and export support levels calculated with reference to an agreed base level of 1987–88 was to be made effective immediately.

3.2. *The Multilateral Trade Organization*

The first development was the proposal to set up a new organization, then known as the Multilateral Trade Organization (MTO), to provide institutional underpinning for the outcome of the Uruguay Round. More important, it was intended to provide a solution to what was considered by the trading majors to be the 'problem' of amending the GATT, particularly for the purpose of enjoining new obligations or con-ditionalities on members who were reluctant to accept them, but who retained their right to continued enjoyment of their MFN privileges. Recourse via the amendment route prescribed in the GATT was admittedly difficult.[25] Indeed, major traders agreed to the Punta del Este compromise of separate negotiations for services to be conducted outside the GATT's juridical framework because they realized that they would fail, should they adopt the amendment route to include services within the ambit of the GATT. The April 1989 capitulation in TRIPs undermined the possibility of another, legal–cum–political challenge similar to the services issue, and encouraged fresh attempts to expand the GATT's ambit. Within a year, the MTO concept was intro-duced. The Punta del Este mandate for the new Round had not provided for nego-tiations on such a radical issue. The proposal did not originate in the course of the negotiations proper, but was developed by an outside expert, and implanted with the support of the industrial countries, particularly Canada and the EEC, at the penul-timate stage of negotiations. By the end of 1991, heralding the paradigm shift, a full-fledged proposal for the establishment of MTO had emerged.

3.3. *The Draft Final Act*

The second initiative was the introduction of the Draft Final Act by the director-general on 20 December 1991 (the GATT Secretariat 1991). It was not a consensus document. Put forward by the director-general on his initiative, the document con-tained the MTO proposal (albeit without agreement on its basic features or provisions on the scope of the MTO) and the integrated dispute settlement mechanism that sanctioned 'cross-retaliation'. In plain language, this amounted to the legitimization of trade-leverage in goods to force open markets for services, for example, or to impose new disciplines in IPR, for example, on unwilling members. The document also included the TRIPs Agreement which had brushed aside a whole range of counter-proposals and reservations advocated by the major developing countries since the restart of the negotiations in April 1989. The Draft Final Act also incorporated the TRIMs Agreement containing an addendum to its review clause which, strangely, far exceeded the scope of the agreement itself and made mention of 'investment and competition policy'.

The consensus ruling, working back-to-front, made it impossible to deviate from the provisions of the Draft Final Act unless, of course, such a departure was approved by consensus! Consequently, no modifications could be introduced. An exception was the agricultural provisions on which substantive amendments were made later, where

[25] See Dam (1970: 345) and Jackson (1992: 52).

the two majors (the US and the EEC) had agreed on the changes. The rest of the draft, remaining largely as presented by the director-general, eventually became the text of the Final Act[26] that was approved for adoption by the ministers at Marrakesh in April 1994. Bypassing straightforward legal avenues available in the GATT treaty, this process of achieving a consensus was non-transparent and undemocratic, and forced a paradigm shift on reluctant members.

4. THE WTO: A PARADIGM SHIFT

The Marrakesh meeting outcome was more than just 'GATT-phase II' or 'GATT Plus'—it constituted a fundamental shift in philosophy.

The GATT was primarily associated with cross-border trade in goods, with the understanding that the institution avoided involvement in domestic policy-making. The GATT also conferred the privilege of most-favoured-nation treatment on its members. This MFN right could not be abridged or infringed with new conditionalities or additional obligations except by amendment to Article I that had unanimous agreement of all contracting parties. The current WTO system (that is to say, the complex range of agreements, declarations, decisions, and understandings that comprises the WTO agreement) has suspended both principles.

The WTO system is no longer confined to cross-border transactions in tangible goods and currently extends to transactions in intangibles, such as services. Overstepping the border paradigm, it is involved in the supply of services through the presence of commercial enterprises in foreign countries. The system is no longer restricted to exchange transactions, but rather stipulates the criteria that determine the permissibility of policies and practices that may restrict production or trade options of investors. It is establishing a bridgehead for the future introduction of norms with regard to investment and competition policy, and is laying down for its member countries a model law for the protection of IPR. And finally, it is promoting a common enforcement mechanism for all binding multilateral disciplines encompassed within the system. Thus, the system makes its own rules on intra-border transactions, and imposes norms and standards for domestic policies of member countries, making these enforceable through the denial of MFN treatment in regard to trade in goods to those who fail to accept the new system.

Equally far-reaching is the potential power of the WTO to bring any new subject within its ambit with a two-thirds majority decision at a ministerial conference and enforce it on recalcitrant member(s) with a threat of expulsion. The WTO provides room for making MFN treatment in goods contingent on the acceptance of *new* conditionalities and obligations that may be imposed in the future. Clearly, under the new system, the veto implicit in the unanimity requirement for derogating the most-favoured-nation principle or linking it to future acceptance of further obligations has been rendered ineffective. Earlier, irrespective of their trade weight, the veto was available to all GATT members.[27]

[26] See GATT Secretariat (1993).   [27] For a detailed analysis, see Annex in Shukla (2000).

4.1. *Elements of the WTO System: Old and New*

The WTO system not only introduced new disciplines, it also substantially modified some 'old' elements. In regard to these old issues, agriculture, textiles and clothing, and some systemic issues need mention.

4.1.1. *Agriculture*

In sharp contrast to the erstwhile doctrine of minimal interference, the Agreement on Agriculture takes a more integrated view of agricultural trade; tries to reduce the trade distorting effects of border protection, domestic support policies and export subsidies, and attempts to subject trade and domestic support regimes to a comprehensive discipline. The underlying approach, however, does not adequately recognize the vastly different roles of agriculture, on the one hand, in large countries like India and China and, on the other, in a number of smaller countries in the non-temperate zones, including the least developed countries of Sub-Sahara for whom the priority is food security, not trade expansion. The Agreement incorporates a measure of discipline, particularly for industrial countries which should benefit small and efficient exporter countries, to some extent. Commitments, however, by industrialized nations with regard to the reduction of domestic support and export subsidies are modest in comparison to prevailing levels of subsidization.[28] In contrast, a large number of developing countries may find the discipline too burdensome.[29]

4.1.2. *Textiles and Clothing*

The pace of integration of this sector, the absolute pariah of the system, into the GATT as mandated in the Agreement on Textiles and Clothing is very slow and 'back-loaded', that is, half of the quota regime is to be liberalized by the end of a ten-year integration period. However, tariffs will continue to be as high as 12 per cent even after integration has been concluded, and it is possible that instead of gaining the

---

[28] As far as border protection is concerned, tariffs of the industrial countries were pegged. Quantitative restrictions (QR) are to be converted into tariff equivalents. Over a six-year period, tariffs are to be reduced by 36 per cent. A minimum import access of 5 per cent is to be provided. As regards to domestic support, a mutually accepted measurement of such support has been devised, which takes into account direct as well as indirect support. As was to be expected, the definition does not reflect sound economic rationale but rather the requirements of the two major negotiating partners. Consequently, the measure excludes vital elements, is limited in scope, and includes loopholes. Its main objective is to reduce, in six years, support levels by 20 per cent compared to those prevalent in an agreed base-period. A support equivalent of 5 per cent of the value of the output is to be allowed; for developing countries, the support percentage is 10. Considering the high levels of support extant in both the US and the EEC, commitment is very modest. Implementation of the commitment is to be conducted on a global basis, and not on a product-by-product basis, which leaves scope for minimizing the trade expansion effect and selecting its direction. In terms of export subsidies, these are to be reduced by 36 per cent in value terms and 21 per cent in terms of volume over a six-year period. Developing countries are to be allowed to provide transport and marketing subsidies. Here again, considering the high levels prevailing in the industrialized countries, the commitment is modest.

[29] The higher level of permissible subsidies may not bring much advantage because of the inherent inadequacy of resources in the third world for the purpose. The obligation to peg all agricultural tariffs is inequitably onerous for developing countries, as it would rob them of any flexibility in utilizing border measures, which were enjoyed by the industrial countries throughout the GATT's history.

momentum it should have, the entire integration process will become frustrated as industrialized countries become more nervous over talk of 'social dumping'.

4.1.3. *Systemic Issues*
The Agreement on Safeguards succeeded in bringing about a considerable measure of discipline with regard to 'grey area measures'. But the Agreement provides some room for selectivity in application of quantitative restrictions (QRs) and this could be a wedge for discriminatory action against imports from low-wage countries. On the whole, however, it constitutes a forward step in preventing abuse of the escape clause.[30]

The weakening of GATT Article XVIII (a process which started with the Tokyo Round) is further compounded by the understanding on the balance-of-payments, which introduces stipulations that effectively circumscribe the only substantive right exclusively enjoyed by developing countries in the GATT system.

The Understanding on Rules and Procedures Governing the Settlement of Disputes (DSU) is notable for two features. The erstwhile system was prone to being blocked at almost every stage by the party complained against. This is no longer the case, as the process of adoption of findings/decisions of the dispute settlement panel/ the appellate body has been made virtually automatic. A vast improvement over the dilatory processes of the past, it also allows the appellate body considerable room to evolve judicial law. Considering the expanding scope and intrusive role of the WTO, this aspect of DSU is a cause for concern.

The other important aspect of DSU is the integrated system of enforcement that sanctions 'cross-sector' and 'cross-agreement' retaliation.[31] Embodying the punitive mechanism of the paradigm shift, it also provides a motivation for overloading the WTO agenda with extraneous issues.

---

[30] See Articles 11.2 and 11.3 in the Agreement on Safeguards. A safeguard measure can be evoked only when a member has determined that imports of the product in question are being made in increased quantities so as to cause or threaten 'serious injury' to the 'domestic industry'. The terms 'serious injury' and 'domestic industry' have been defined carefully to prevent abuse. A quantitative safeguard measure is to be applied in a manner so that imports are not ordinarily reduced to levels lower than the average of the past representative period, and the relative proportions of supplying members in imports are maintained. However, a degree of selectivity is permitted in cases where 'imports from certain members have increased in disproportionate percentage in relation to the total increase in imports' (Article 5). The period of validity of a safeguard measure is to be up to four years and can, under certain circumstances, be extended to a maximum of eight years. All measures will be progressively liberalized so that termination becomes feasible (Article 7).
[31] Before taking recourse to cross-retaliation, however, the possibility of withdrawal of concessions or suspension of obligations in the same sector/under the same agreement has to be exhausted. But, in practice, the prescribed sequence may achieve little to limit the tendency of industrialized countries to resort to cross-retaliation in goods to enforce compliance in new disciplines. This is possible because of the skewed distribution of issues of new disciplines, as between developed and developing countries. So long as this distortion remains, resort to cross-retaliation cannot be moderated, much less eschewed, through the prescription of a procedural sequence. The futility of such procedures should not come as a surprise: efforts to bring extraneous issues within the GATT's ambit were, in the first instance, motivated by the desire to use the leverage in goods trade to impose disciplines in the so-called new issues.

4.2. *New Disciplines*

4.2.1. *The TRIMs Agreement*

The point of departure for the TRIMs Agreement was based on the GATT's national treatment requirements with regard to imported products; in other words, no measures should be applied to restrict the use of imported products in production. The Agreement expands the principle further to include such practices as export obligations, import entitlements based on export performance, and export–import balancing requirements. Even with this addendum, the approach of the Agreement emulates the GATT in the sense that despite the ban on certain practices, there is no attempt to introduce a global policy or law on investment *per se*. A significant move in that direction is the TRIMs article which stipulates that the review process of the Agreement undertakes consideration of whether the Agreement should be complemented with provisions on investment policy and competition policy.[32]

4.2.2. *The TRIPs Agreement*

The TRIPs Agreement is not so much an effort to harmonize the policies of all member governments as it is an attempt to align or upgrade the policies and laws of developing countries to those of major industrial countries, or rather to the requirements of transnational corporations.[33] This implies that the balance struck by the concerned polity between considerations of public interest and the private interests of IPR owners has to be replaced by norms and standards incorporated in the international agreement, an agreement that did not result from willing participation or objective assessment of the issues involved, but was largely the outcome of pressure by powerful IPR lobbies and trade intimidation by the major industrial countries.

An important feature that deserves to be noted concerns the so-called transitional arrangements. The complex challenge of development has been reduced to the simple formula of granting the transition a few more years of grace and the provision of technical assistance.[34] Even though many industrial countries have suppressed IPR protection for more than half a century and have thus reaped substantial benefits with inexpensive replication and reverse engineering, the TRIPs Agreement prescribes that

---

[32] See Article 9 of Agreement on TRIMs.

[33] In the case of patent laws of developing countries, for example, coverage has to be expanded and the exclusions removed. The terms of patents are to be uniformly extended. Provisions regarding compulsory licensing have to be minimized so that they become redundant, and no ceiling on the issue of royalties is to be allowed. In short, the welfare and development objectives, if not given up altogether, are to be relegated to the background.

TRIPs covers an entire range of intellectual property issues, including industrial patents, copyrights, geographical indications, plant varieties, micro-organisms, bio-technological processes, layout designs of integrated circuits and trade secrets. The underlying approach is the same as the one guiding TRIPs, namely to create a right where none exists, to strengthen existing rights, to minimize the scope for possible limitation on the grounds of public policy, to establish not only norms and standards, but also legal procedures, and to enforce model law through the cross-retaliation mechanism.

[34] See Articles 65, 66, and 67 of the Agreement on TRIPs. For developing countries to attain the level of patent protection currently prevalent in the industrial countries, particularly in the US, an additional four-year transitional period has been provided; for introducing a product patent where it is not

even the least developed countries achieve, in a mere ten-year period, protection levels to match those currently prevalent in the industrial world. The promise of technical assistance is offered only for the 'preparation of laws and regulations on the protection of intellectual property rights as well as for the prevention of their abuse'. The bias of TRIPs is much too obvious.[35]

4.2.3. Services

The General Agreement on Trade in Services (GATS) extended its potential jurisdiction to the erstwhile national domain, and broadened the connotation of trade to include production, distribution, marketing, sale, and delivery.[36] The first round of negotiations, however, produced only moderate results as the Agreement had built-in checks and balances and the negotiating mechanism was tuned to the requirements of the development process.[37]

A major shortcoming of GATS was that it virtually overlooked the labour sector.[38] There is strong economic justification in favour of providing access to the employment markets of labour-deficit economies for workers from labour-surplus economies.[39] But

permissible, the period is 9 years. However, transition, even in the case of LDCs, must be completed in ten years.

[35] See the following two assessments: 'The final outcome of the negotiation suggests that US pharmaceutical, entertainment, and informatics industries, which were largely responsible for getting TRIPS on the agenda, obtained much, if not most, of what was desired when the negotiations were launched. It is fair to say that developing countries agreed to substantially more than even an optimist might have hoped for in 1986 when the Round began' (Hoekman and Kostecki 1995: 156). Any comment here would be superfluous. And the following sums up its impact: '...TRIPs is a redistributive issue; irrespective of assumptions made with respect to market structure or dynamic response, the impact effect of enhanced IPR protection...will be a transfer of wealth from (developing country) consumers and firms to foreign, mostly industrial-country firms' (Rodrik quoted in Hoekman and Kostecki 1995: 157).

[36] See Articles I.3(b) and (c) and XXVIII (b) of GATS.

[37] The modality of exchange of concessions was based on a positive list approach, that is to say, every country was to indicate which service sector or subsector or activity it would like to table, rather than presuming that everything was on the negotiating table, except to the extent indicated otherwise. Furthermore, such offers could be subjected to specific conditions and limitations. Most important, national treatment was not to be included in the agreement as an unqualified, basic principle governing national regulations or policies in regard to service sector transactions. The question of considering the application of national treatment can arise only after access is granted, and access is left to the decision of the member country concerned. At best, national treatment is a goal to strive for, and its application can be subjected to various limitations and conditions, as may be specified by the access-granting country.

This rather modest approach has been criticized by those who see the elements of GATS which made possible the adoption of such an approach as the main 'weaknesses' of the system (Key 1997). This is in tune with the original stand of the proponents of the services negotiations, but it must be remembered that without these 'weaknesses', wider participation in GATS would not have been possible: GATS would then have become as unequal and biased as TRIPs.

[38] Although the definition of 'service' included the supply of services 'through the presence of natural persons' in a foreign country, the Annex on Movement of Natural Persons Supplying Services under the Agreement made it clear that, 'The agreement shall not apply to measures affecting natural persons seeking access to the employment market...nor shall it apply to measures regarding citizenship, residence or employment on a permanent basis'.

[39] See Nayyar (1988, 1989) and, in this volume for a comprehensive treatment; Bhagwati (1986) and Hindley (1991).

the whole issue of labour services was dismissed arbitrarily, which benefited capital-
and technology-intensive services, and, consequently, also industrial countries.[40] Thus
the possibility of vast potential gain from the exchange of services has been pre-
empted. Developing countries with a surplus of unskilled, semi-skilled, or particular-
skilled workers lost in the deal.

While the WTO Agreement supplied the legal and institutional infrastructure of the
paradigm shift, TRIPs and GATS provided its architecture, and the TRIMs Agreement the blueprints of its future expansion. The old peripheral regimes on textiles and
agriculture were rectified with certain immediate amendments, but these consisted
more of promise and less of performance with reference to the future. The emergency
safeguard route was cleansed of extra-legal activities, but a danger continued to exist,
particularly for those concerned with the textile regime. The WTO infrastructure is so
vast that it can easily support not only further expansion of the existing regimes, but also
their variations on newer issues. No wonder that prospective beneficiaries of this
'magnificent' structure expressed their triumphal mood through the famous remark
that its completion marked 'a defining moment in history'. But this definition affected
different participants differently in ways that embodied built-in contradictions.

5. FROM TRIUMPH TO FIASCO (1995–99)

As was evident from the early 1980s through to the emergence of the WTO, the trend
of the GATT/WTO mandate has been to transcend national frontiers and enter
domestic policy areas on a whole range of new issues. Initiatives since the Marrakesh
meeting through to Seattle—whether they concern the EEC's push for a global
investment regime,[41] the insistence of the United States on linking labour standards to
trade issues,[42] the proposal to bind tariffs at zero level on 'e-commerce',[43] or, for that

[40] The agreement will in no way moderate or liberalize the ubiquitous and strong barriers that are in
existence in all industrial countries to prevent the inflow of labour. The scope of movement of natural
persons is narrowly limited to selected high-skilled categories, largely associated with specific projects or
activities. This stands in sharp contrast to the broad definition of 'supply of services' in GATS.

[41] The first WTO ministerial meeting in Singapore (1996) introduced the issue of 'investment' onto its
agenda. While ostensibly only a study was initiated at that time, the EEC tabled a full-fledged proposal on a
global investment regime at the Seattle ministerial meeting (1999). The EEC was pushing for an ambitious
and far-reaching regime, but their enthusiasm has since abated and a 'thin' multilateral discipline with the
obligations of MFN treatment and transparency is being proposed now. A difference of approach between
the US and the EEC is being reported, with the US favouring the stronger discipline first developed in the
OECD, which would be multilateralized in the WTO at a later stage. Many developing countries oppose
the idea of a global regime in the WTO.

[42] It seemed for a while that the Singapore ministerial meeting had succeeded in shelving the issue of
'social clause' or 'labour standards', but it was to surface in Seattle with renewed vigour. The US would
like to see a WTO working party take control of the issue. This is a new *avatar* of the erstwhile phobia of
low-wage country competition causing 'market disruptions', but is presented in a more sophisticated form.

[43] Americans have proposed binding tariff rates at zero level for the e-commerce sector. Accordingly,
there will be zero duty on transactions conducted through the electronic medium of the internet; similarly,
products of the 'medium-is-the-message' variety, such as audio-visual transmissions, will also be duty free,
while the same product in more tangible form, such as compact disc, continues to carry duty. Various
services supplied through the electronic medium will also be entitled to a duty free entry into the market.

matter, judicial law tailored by the dispute settlement and appellate panels of the WTO[44]—all unmistakably reinforce that trend. The process is described as harmonization or deeper integration. The GATT's integration, achieved through the international exchange of goods and relevant international disciplines, was 'shallow'. Deeper integration seeks to achieve the standardization of domestic policies in a wide range of issues including investment, competition, technology, government procurement, taxation, labour standards, and what are perceived by foreigners as 'structural impediments', a term which can be given an all-encompassing connotation.[45] And the process may not stop there.[46]

Decades ago, Kenneth Dam wrote in a different context about the GATT's efforts to cultivate 'new business'.[47] The GATT/WTO's appetite for new business acquired

Prima facie, industrial countries are better equipped to benefit from this proposal and will resort to 'e-commerce' to escape the tariff walls or other restrictions that would otherwise impede market access to the developing countries.

[44] Some decisions by the dispute settlement panels and the appellate body in the last few years of the WTO's existence have given rise to serious concern as they have far-reaching implications. In a dispute raised by the US against India in regard to the latter's alleged failure to fulfil the transitional requirements under TRIPs to provide exclusive marketing rights and make arrangements to receive product patent applications in the interim period, India cited adequate executive action undertaken to qualify as meeting the obligations. But the appellate body, maintaining that mere executive action was not enough, stipulated that the Indian government amend its patent law to provide 'adequate legal security' to other members and economic operators. This amounted to an interpretation of the fundamental law of a member country and, in attempting to prescribe what agenda it should adopt in a particular matter, an infringement of its sovereign legislature.

Interestingly, the dispute settlement panel of the WTO came to a contradictory conclusion in its recent finding on the question whether US trade-sanction laws (Sections 301–310) were in violation of the WTO trade rules. While accepting that provisions of the US law were *prima facie* in violation, the settlement panel ruled that the statement by the US Administration (which accompanied the legislation but did not constitute a part of it) was an adequate guarantee that no provisions of law would be used in violation of the WTO rules to the detriment of other members. Apparently, in the eyes of the WTO's dispute settlement mechanism, executive action by one member-state is not as good as that of another member-state! (see Raghavan 2000: 2–5).

Similarly, the panel has passed rulings which have eroded the discipline on general exceptions as mandated in the GATT, directly implying that, under certain circumstances, a country can take trade-restrictive measures for actions that are beyond its jurisdiction, or for actions that induce effects outside its jurisdiction. Panel rulings have also allowed the filing of briefs and opinions by persons and organizations not accredited with governments (see Das 1999: 36).

These rulings are indicative of the direction in which the judicial process of the WTO is moving. It is enhancing the intrusive role of the WTO with regard to the sovereign authority of member countries beyond the limits of what the WTO Agreement itself specifies. There seems to be an implicit bias in the sense that the rulings have affected, or have the potential of affecting, weaker members or developing countries adversely.

[45] The discussions on the Structural Impediment Initiative between the USA and Japan are a case in point: '...The gist of complaints against the Japanese is that they study too long and too well, that they work too hard, they consume too little, and they save too much. These odd complaints are made with a straight face' (see Palmeter in Bhagwati and Patrick 1990: 61).

[46] 'As broad and complex as the WTO mandate is, it is clear that there is potentially much more that could be encompassed...(T)here are a number of puzzling link issues that will require the attention of the new organization, such as...links to human rights practices and democratic institutions, links to monetary policy, questions of trade in armaments and globalization effects on the cultural values of particular societies' (Jackson 1998: 103).   [47] See Dam (1970: 376–7).

in the formative years, has recently grown enormously. And, unlike in its early phases of 'underemployment', new business is not solicited by the secretariat or accredited GATT representatives. It is being imposed on the organization by strong and deep-rooted forces which govern the working of the economic system. Trading is only one element of the system. The logic of capitalism with its compelling 'requirements of profit maximization, capital accumulation, the constant self-expansion of capital' (Wood 1999) are at work at the national as well as the global level. This need for 'constant self-expansion' is at the root of the GATT/WTO's search for new activities.

The propelling force behind this stupendous exercise arises from the economic power exercised by developed countries on behalf—or at the behest—of transnational corporations with home-bases in the industrial world. The compelling functional requirement of transnational corporations is the need for deeper integration, and the economic–theoretic construct of 'internationally contestable markets'[48] seeks to rationalize this requirement. It is argued that such markets, because they would ensure more efficient production, would be welfare-enhancing. But this rationale overlooks the reality of the existence of vast multitudes of people with little or no ability to participate in market processes. The distributive implications of these processes have also been ignored, as have the adverse effects for employment, increasing dependence and vulnerability of national economies, or long-term social, political, or cultural considerations which may necessitate state intervention.

The other infirmity of the deeper integration approach at the operational level, is that it minimizes the sheer complexity of the exercise involved. The problem of the different regulatory levels in various countries is not easy to handle in an international norm-setting exercise, and the experience of the EEC is noteworthy. The EEC was a relatively homogenous group of nations bound by common history and culture. The postwar reconstruction in the context of the cold war fostered still greater solidarity in the EEC, but progress towards harmonization was slow.[49]

The deeper the process of integration, the more glaring the basic contradiction in the system (reviewed in the first section of this chapter). The shallow integration of the GATT variety practised exclusion by establishing discriminatory/protectionist rules for trade in textiles and agriculture, thus limiting weaker members' access to markets. The new discipline of TRIPs (the first major essay in deeper integration) practises exclusion by denying weaker members options such as inexpensive replication and reverse engineering, thereby restricting their access to technology. The newer regimes

---

[48] An internationally contestable market 'would mean that the conditions of competition prevailing in that market allow for unimpaired market access for foreign goods, services, ideas, investments and business people, so that they are able to benefit from opportunities to compete in that market on terms equal or comparable to those enjoyed by local competitors. Hence market access conditions and, more generally, the competitive process should not be unduly impaired or distorted by the totality of potential barriers, including traditional border barriers, investment conditions, structural impediments, regulatory regimes as well as private anti-competitive practices' (Zampetti and Sauve 1996: 333–43).

[49] For example, the Treaty of Rome (Articles 59–66) stipulates that, 'there shall be free trade in services within the European Community. Nevertheless, until the 1992 initiatives there had effectively been no movement towards actually freeing trade in most of the service sector of the EC. The basic reason for this failure was the prior existence of different national levels of regulation' (Hindley 1991: 135).

being designed for labour and environment standards are also likely to limit weaker members' access to markets. Deeper integration carries the process of exclusion much further, with the ultimate outcome that people are barred from the law-making processes of their countries.[50] In effect, the legislative power of a country is transferred to the invisible control of the transnational corporations who have vested interests in creating 'internationally contestable markets'. In this sense, the process of deeper integration is anti-democratic.

The WTO has not improved on the GATT legacy of functioning in a non-transparent, 'green room' fashion,[51] nor has it replaced the 'trade weight' criterion in its decision-making process. The WTO is also committed to deeper integration. As a result, legitimate governments are being excluded from the decision-making process. National norms and standards established through democratic procedures by sovereign parliaments are being trumped by global standards set at the behest of powerful transnational corporations. This is being justified on the ground that providing 'internationally contestable markets' is a fundamental goal to which every member country must subscribe. It is no wonder that the WTO's 'democratic deficit' is burgeoning.

The WTO system seemed to be moving in an inexorable trajectory, without any plans to confront or moderate its propelling logic—or so it seemed until it received an unprecedented jolt at the Seattle ministerial meeting (November–December 1999). A failed ministerial meeting is not a unique experience in the history of the GATT–WTO. What was new at Seattle, however, was the manner in which the meeting was derailed. Tensions and contradictions caused by the ambitious expansion plans of the WTO majors finally collided in a total deadlock. There was nothing to show for the week of intensive deliberations, persuasion, subterfuge, and arm-twisting. Concluding remarks, which dealt largely with procedural inadequacies and ducked the substantive divide that had derailed the meeting, were preceded by criticism from many developing countries in Africa, Latin America, and the Caribbean region, decrying the

[50] The concept of 'contestable markets', as it has been put forward and is used to buttress a harmonization process that is to be carried out in the one-sided manner under duress in the WTO forum, recalls to mind the establishment of factories and acquisition of rights to customs-free trade in India by the English East India Company in the seventeenth century or the race amongst the European powers for the establishment of extra-territorial enclaves in China during the last decade of the eighteenth century. The factories and the enclaves were the ancient ancestors of 'contestable markets', regardless of their unsophisticated appearance or violent and corrupt ways. They were the vanguard of the first and, perhaps, the deepest integration that engulfed the world (see Roychaudhuri and Habib Irfan 1984: 390–4, and Hobsbawm 1987: 281).

[51] The 'green room' procedure refers to the selective, informal consultations that the director-general of the GATT conducted confidentially, apparently to make his own assessment of a possible consensus or a way out, on a given, difficult issue under discussion. Consultations were usually carried on in a small meeting room with grey–green walls, hence the name. The director-general's sensitivity to trade weights led to restricting these meetings to the trade majors and a few others, who, for one reason or another, were deemed important enough to be included, but to the exclusion of a large majority of members. No records were kept. Later, when the outcomes of the 'green room' discussions were introduced as a consensus at the more formal GATT meetings, some non-participants disassociated themselves from—or even strongly opposed—these conclusions. The procedure, at its best, helped the director-general to understand the requirements of the trade majors; at its worst, it was a backroom manoeuvre, mostly at the behest of the trade majors, to foist decisions on the unwilling or unsuspecting majority in a manner not quite regular or democratic.

absence of transparency, openness, and participation. Many bluntly refused to be part of a 'consensus' that was being forced on them by the trade majors.[52]

There were deep disagreements between the industrial and developing countries on issues relating to labour standards, investment, and competition policy. There were also large differences between the EEC and the US on agriculture, and between the US and Japan on the anti-dumping discipline.

Domestic politics on the eve of the presidential election year, no doubt, contributed to the exaggerated demonstration of the US position in favour of labour standards, an issue judged by some to be the major factor responsible for the failure of the Seattle meeting. Similar circumstances, perhaps, encouraged the EEC to stand firm on the agricultural question and not to yield too much to the lame duck, the Administration of the United States. There were clearly a number of factors that operated simultaneously to contribute to the failure. But the significance, in terms of the system, of open defiance by a large number of 'exclusion' casualties (literally both in terms of Seattle, and operational effects of the WTO system to date) can hardly be exaggerated. Final collapse was triggered by the deep dissatisfaction of developing countries over the palpable exclusion approach that had extended to substantive negotiations. The fact that the trading majors attempted to introduce some face-saving outcome, albeit without success, also acknowledges the strong impact made by the outburst of frustration by the developing countries.

The Seattle meeting proved that exclusion can be defeated through collective opposition by those being excluded. The frustration of the developing countries, without a doubt, manifested itself as the united front on procedural issues, but not necessarily substantive ones. But, in a way, the procedural issue is the most relevant because at its core is the inherently biased integration practice of the WTO. As the Seattle meeting demonstrated, integration that is not aligned with economic or political realities and is unresponsive to the principles of equity and democratic functioning, can throw the whole process of the WTO into an impasse.

6. WHAT IS TO BE DONE?

6.1. *Strategic Considerations*

The chance for some degree of moderation, if not redress, to the ongoing process of inequitable integration is possible only if formal democratic representation, as mandated in the constitution of WTO, is effectively exercised by those majority members who bear the costs of integration, which far exceed the gains. In the GATT's earlier framework, adroit use of the consensus principle in conjunction with a mutual awareness of the legal strength of the implicit veto provided even a small group of countries with an effective means to influence decisions to an extent. This possibility has eroded as a result of the paradigm shift and the South's voting strength will have to

---

[52] Texts of the statements were reported in *Third World Economics* (1999: box on page 4); Aslam (1999: 10–11) and Raghavan (1999: 12).

be strategically mobilized. For this to happen, two conditions need to develop. First, all members must recognize that as the WTO extends its mandate beyond the cross-border exchange transactions to become engaged in the harmonization of norms and standards for domestic policies and regulations, trade weights lose their relevance. The principle of 'one member–one vote' is more appropriate than ever before. Second, the solidarity of the South should be based on a shared understanding of the specific issue at hand as well as a more general approach to the overall functioning of the global economic system. The strength of Group 77, based on the recognition of the North–South divide, arose out of the latter. The Informal Group of Developing Countries in GATT was most effective when its operational methods resembled those of Group 77. The scope for similar coordination increased in the 1980s, precisely because the GATT was moving away from its traditional agenda. However, a certain lack of perspective on the part of developing countries—combined with the tactical moves made by the United States, presumably with the dual purpose of pressurising the EEC on the agricultural issue and neutralizing the developing country coalition on new issues-led to 'issue-based' coalitions being formed at the expense of a more general approach to reflect the mutual interests of the South. This could not, however, obliterate the basic divide. In Ricupero's words, '. . . (T)he North–South dimension pervaded all the negotiations, somewhat like sex in Victorian England—ostensibly ignored but nevertheless present everywhere' (1998: 15).

It should be possible to enter an issue-specific, tactical agreement with an industrial country group or even with one of the trading majors, without adverse effects to the solidarity of the South. Differences in the industrial world are being minimized through transnational corporations, enlargement of the EEC, and the emergence of new regional groupings. These developments should reinforce the validity of the South-based approach. Since the brunt of the inequitable integration process is being borne by the countries of the South, possible correction of the WTO trajectory can result only from their collective effort.

Integration with its built-in element of exclusion is evident not only at the global level in *inter se* relationships between industrialized core countries and developing countries, but also at the national economy level. Exclusion deepens the social and political divide *within*, highlights the 'democratic deficit' of the process and the unaccountability of the forces behind it. This environment should provide the South with renewed motivation for revitalizing the region's solidarity so as to enable it to capture the allocated democratic space as prescribed by the constitution of the WTO. This calls for certain institutional and programmatic initiatives.

6.2. *Institutional and Programmatic Complement*

6.2.1. *Revival and Strengthening of the Informal Group of Developing Countries*
The first step is to revive and strengthen the Informal Group of Developing Countries in the WTO. Indeed, it need no longer be 'informal'. With the replacement of the purely contractual, tariff negotiation-oriented GATT with the all-embracing and harmonization-oriented WTO, the group of developing countries should also acquire

a more formal and institutional character. The Group, within itself, should clearly acknowledge the sub-group of the LDCs as a necessary element of the solidarity of the South. The revival and re-enforcement of the Group should serve to restore a measure of balance in the WTO's functioning and, in times of crisis, also provide a safety valve. Needless to say, this step by itself would not require an amendment of the WTO's constitution: all that is required, is the explicit recognition of the political reality by all member states.

6.2.2. *'Standstill' and 'Rollback'*[53]

The second important—and formal—step is for the WTO to declare a 'standstill' on the ongoing process of deeper integration. In order to restore confidence in the functioning of the WTO, all new issues (such as labour standards and global investment regime) should be deferred for the time being; further strengthening of the TRIPs and TRIMs disciplines should be postponed. The Group of Developing Countries should take the initiative in this regard. A declaration of a standstill would make it possible to conduct a collective assessment of how integration efforts to date have affected member countries, particularly those of the South and, among them, the poor and the least developed countries. Such an evaluation simply cannot be allowed to become just another in-house exercise of the WTO secretariat. To be meaningful and acceptable, the assessment needs to be performed by external experts who have credibility with member states, particularly those of the South. However, before this review is possible, a waiver on the legal compliance of new disciplines such as TRIPs and TRIMs needs to be issued by the concerned WTO organs. The future of these disciplines should be decided in accordance with the findings of the assessment.

Considering the complex nature of the new TRIPs discipline and the difficulties it generates for developing countries, it may be necessary to introduce a 'rollback'. The demand for a TRIPs review that surfaced in connection with the built-in implementation agenda also supports the need for a rollback. It is possible that the assessment exercise proposed above may produce sufficient material evidence and rationale to initiate the rollback of the integration process, as necessary.

Although the options of standstill or rollback could serve as instruments for immediately restoring the confidence of majority members in the WTO, it is necessary to initiate institutional reforms to make the system more equitable and truly universal. The formally democratic constitution of the WTO makes it amenable to such a

---

[53] The terms 'standstill' and 'rollback' came into use in the GATT in the context of tariffs and non-tariff measures. The former implied a collective commitment to refrain from new non-tariff measures or from increases in the prevalent non-bound tariff rates, pending further multilateral negotiations, or on the eve of a new round of GATT negotiations. The aim was not to aggravate competitive worsening of the bad situation. Also, it was used for maintaining the *status quo* prior to the commencement of negotiations.

Rollback referred to collective agreement to rescind past measures which were in violation of the GATT, as a commitment to the principles of the GATT and with a view to creating a more congenial atmosphere for the multilateral negotiations. The GATT ministerial meeting of 1982 placed considerable emphasis on the standstill and rollback commitments for restoring GATT morale. No binding commitments, however, emerged from the meeting; all that could be offered was only a 'best endeavour' statement. The terms standstill and rollback are used here in a wider context, without distortion to their basic intent.

possibility. Nothing should be done in the name of so-called 'efficiency' or the 'reality of the trade weights' to erode or dent this unique aspect. On the contrary, lessons need be learned from recent events. More accommodating and equitable forms of international negotiation and decision-making should be evolved. This will require action at four different levels.

1. *Plurilateral agreements*

First and foremost, the modality of plurilateral agreements should be taken out of its present limited context and used more liberally, whenever there is a lack of unanimity among the member countries or the presence of strong reservations on the part of some, on the proposed disciplines on new issues calling for deeper integration. According to Article II.3 of the WTO agreement, 'The Plurilateral Trade Agreements do not create either obligations or rights for members that have not accepted them'. They are essentially 'optional' agreements. This modality is ideal in instances where, because of different stages of economic development of the members and the diversity of their social goals and priorities, it is neither feasible nor desirable to attempt to subject all of them to a uniform discipline modelled on the systems of a few advanced countries and yoked to the interests of transnational corporations. This modality permits those members of the universal system who are desirous of new transnational disciplines on new issues to proceed with deeper integration without having to adjust their style to suit the position of less enthusiastic members merely in the name of a consensus. Indeed, should the new disciplines promote universal welfare, they would attract larger membership in due course.

It would be legitimate for members of such a plurilateral agreement to refrain from extending the benefits of the arrangement to non-members. They should not, however, be allowed to impose it on non-members in the form of a new conditionality for continued enjoyment by the latter of their trade rights flowing from the MFN principle under the GATT. In other words, the sting in the paradigm shift brought about by the WTO agreement should be removed. No new agreement involving deeper integration should be allowed to be added as an integral part that is 'binding on all members'. This will not call for any amendment of the WTO agreement as it stands today. It will require an explicit understanding or a decision at the level of the highest legislative organ of the WTO, namely ministerial conference, to the effect that no more additions of new disciplines are to be made to the WTO Agreement under Clause 2 of Article II. Whether any of the agreements already annexed to the Agreement under this clause need to be converted into a plurilateral agreement or otherwise modified will have to be decided by means of a formal amendment to be considered in the light of the assessment referred to in the context of the standstill and rollback proposed above.

2. *Reform of Understanding on Rules and Procedures Governing the Settlement of Disputes (DSU)*

This approach to reforming the WTO will necessitate two other concurrent moves. Both relate to the DSU. The mechanism provided in Article II.2 of the WTO Agreement is backed by the coercive sanction provided in cross-retaliation in DSU.

It will be only logical that a decision to give up the resort to Article II.2 in future is complemented by a decision to give up cross-retaliation prospectively. As far as its application to the agreements already included in Annex 1 is concerned, the standstill and rollback decisions should appropriately provide for keeping cross-retaliation in abeyance.

Secondly, the provisions of DSU would need to be formally amended to ensure that the dispute settlement and appellate panels do not continue to enjoy unfettered authority to make new laws by means of judicial pronouncements furthering deeper integration. One way of achieving this result would be to group the decisions of these bodies in two categories: (i) decisions that relate to the compensation and suspension of trade concessions and (ii) rulings and pronouncements which are in the nature of laying down judicial law. While the former should follow the present provisions regarding appeal and finality, the latter should not follow the virtually 'automatic' and 'no-further appeal' route. Having the potential of trumping the national laws or handing out new domestic law for the member countries, such judicial law-making, should be subjected to political approval at the highest WTO legislative body. And there too, decisions should be made by the highest majority, that is, three-quarters majority. Alternatively, the decision should be made by a two-thirds majority, but should be applicable to a member only upon acceptance by it.

3. *Group system for negotiations*
The recent experience has highlighted the need to introduce transparency and make negotiations and decision-making truly participative. The opaque 'green room' procedures are no longer sustainable. The large membership of the WTO also makes the negotiations an increasingly cumbersome process. The considerations of efficiency cannot, however, be allowed to subvert democratic functioning. In the circumstances, resort to some version of a 'group system' of negotiations seems inevitable. The need to revive and strengthen the Group of Developing Countries becomes reinforced in this context. The group system, as it functioned in UNCTAD, had been criticized in the past, and there is an element of truth in that negotiations thus conducted tended to settle at the lowest common denominator. But in a diverse world, that kind of a denouement is perhaps inevitable. The recent pursuit of efficiency and highest possible levels of international discipline in the GATT/WTO forum has produced disastrous results.

4. *Constitution of a three-tier structure*
The most important institutional reform that the WTO needs, is to make it truly equitable in its approach, operations, and form. Formal equality in terms of 'one member–one vote' is crucial but is not sufficient to bring improvement. Through the history of the GATT, the concern over this has been visible, but not very productive. Indeed, in the late 1970s and, more so in 1980s, an offensive to minimize the concern was launched and, as we have seen, succeeded only too well. Events seem to be making a full circle. What the WTO needs is not a ritualistic reiteration of the principle of 'non-reciprocal, more favourable and differential treatment' in favour of developing

countries, but a formal constitution of a three-tier system, on the one hand, and institutional arrangements to offset the structural deficiency in their negotiating capability, on the other.

Taking the latter first, negotiations in the GATT/WTO have been marked by the non-participation or ineffective participation of a large number of small developing countries, particularly, least developed countries. Maintaining a permanent mission in Geneva is in itself an onerous multilateral obligation. To have a mission with sufficient strength and quality is a problem which even relatively larger and better equipped developing countries do not find easy to solve. What is essential, particularly for the LDCs, is to have a WTO/UNCTAD-supported institutional arrangement that would enable these countries to keep abreast of developments. Some form of financial support would allow these members to engage experts to help them to formulate their position on complex issues.

With regards to the former issue, differences in the capacity of developing countries to take on the obligations of a multilateral system must be recognized. The least developed countries should be entitled to the full and unreserved benefits of the system from all members without being enjoined to take on obligations. In this regard, other developing countries should also be prepared to extend the LDCs benefits without making claims for counter-concessions. The next tier in the structure should include other developing countries, who should be entitled to similar treatment from developed countries as prescribed in the Framework Agreements of the Tokyo Round. The developing countries of this tier should also be prepared to take on additional obligations in line with their development. However, as enunciated earlier, they should have an assurance that the process of deeper integration is entirely optional and their trade rights and benefits would not be subjected to additional obligations and conditionalities. The third tier, consisting of industrial countries, should be free to initiate disciplines to strengthen deeper integration amongst themselves, without converting these into additional conditionalities for other members.

In other words, the structure and functioning of the WTO should be guided by the values of democracy and equity. If integration is promoted within a democratic framework, it is less likely to be inequitable. Integration, as pursued at present, breeds built-in exclusion and is occasionally confronted by elective exclusion.[54] But the contradiction cannot be resolved this easily. What is needed is a conscious effort—through institutional and political initiatives—that strives for equitable integration. And in that process, the solidarity of the presently 'excluded' members will play a decisive role.

The strategy and the plan of action outlined above are undoubtedly rooted in the Southern perspective. This is inevitable because the WTO's current impasse has a lot to do with the impact its operations have on the South. More important, if the process of inequitable integration pursued in the GATT/WTO system has to be redressed, the Southern perspective has a crucial, functional significance. Structural reforms and

---

[54] The case of the People's Republic of China from 1950 through to the late 1980s is illustrative of 'elective exclusion'.

other initiatives here suggested are intended to contribute to the evolution of more equitable and viable international trading system, which should be a universal concern.

REFERENCES

Aslam, Abid (1999). Developing countries assail WTO dictatorship. *Third World Economics: Trends and Analysis*, 223, 10–11 (16–31 December).

Bhagwati, Jagdish (1986). Economic perspectives of trade in professional services. *Chicago Legal Forum*, 1(1), March.

——(1991). *The World Trading System at Risk*. Harvester Wheatsheaf, New York.

—— and Hugh T. Patrick (eds) (1990). *Aggressive Unilateralism: America's 301 Trade Policy and The World Trading System*. Harvester Wheatsheaf, New York.

Dam, Kenneth W. (1970). *The GATT: Law and International Economic Organization*. University of Chicago Press, Chicago and London.

Das, Bhagirath L. (1999). How the WTO rules and system are inequitable against the south. *Third World Resurgence*, August–September. Third World Network, Penang, Malaysia.

Economic and Political Weekly. (1989). Intellectual property rights: The Geneva surrender. 3 June. Bombay.

GATT Secretariat (1991). Draft final act embodying the results of the Uruguay Round of multilateral trade negotiations. MTN.TNC/W/FA, 20 December (UR-91-0185).

——(1993). Final act embodying the results of the Uruguay Round of multilateral trade negotiations. MTN/FA, 15 December (UR-93-0246).

Hindley, Brian (1991). International trade in services. In A. Koekkoek and L. B. E. Mennes (eds), *International Trade and Global Development: Essays in Honour of Jagdish Bhagwati*. Routlege, London and New York.

Hobsbawm, Eric (1987). *The Age of Empire, 1875–1914*. Weidenfeld and Nicolson, London.

Hoekman, Bernard M. and Michael M. Kostecki (1995). *The Political Economy of the World Trading System: From GATT to WTO*. Oxford University Press, Oxford.

Hudec, Robert (1987). *The Developing Countries in the GATT Legal System*. Trade Policy Research Centre, London.

Jackson, John H. (1992). *The World Trading System: Law and Policy of International Economic Relations*. MIT Press, Cambridge, MA and London.

——(1998). *The World Trade Organization: Constitution and Jurisprudence*. Royal Institute of International Affairs, London.

The Intellectual Property Committee (USA), Keidanren (Japan), UNCIE (Europe) (1988). *Basic Framework of GATT Provisions on Intellectual Property: Statement of Views of the European, Japanese and United States Business Communities*.

Key, Sydney J. (1997). Financial services in the Uruguay Round and the WTO. Occasional Paper 54. Group of Thirty, Washington, DC.

Low, Patrick (1993). *Trading Free: The GATT and U.S. Policy*. The Twentieth Century Fund Press, Washington, DC.

Nayyar, Deepak (1988). The political economy of international trade in services. *Cambridge Journal of Economics*, 12(2), 279–98.

——(1989). Towards a possible multilateral framework for trade in services: Some issues and concepts. In *Technology, Trade Policy and the Uruguay Round*. United Nations, New York.

Palmeter, David (1990). Commentary. In J. Bhagwati and H. T. Patrick (eds), *Aggressive Unilateralism: America's 301 Trade Policy and The World Trading System*. Harvester Wheatsheaf, New York.

Pincus, J. J. (1986). Why have US tariffs fallen since 1930s? In R. H. Snape (ed.), *Issues in the World Trade Policy: GATT at Crossroads*. Macmillan Press, Houndsmill.

Raghavan, Chakravarthi (1990). *Recolonization: GATT, the Uruguay Round and the Third World*. Third World Network, Penang, Malaysia.

—— (1999). Africa, Caribbean and Latin American regions protest non-participation, threaten walkout. *Third World Economics: Trends and Analysis*, 223, 12 (16–31 December).

—— (2000). WTO panel upholds US sanctions law. *Third World Economics: Trends and Analysis*, 225, 2–5 (16–31 January)

Reich, Robert B. (1983). Beyond free trade. *Foreign Affairs*, 61(4), 780.

Ricupero, Rubens (1998). Integration of developing countries into a multilateral trading system. In J. Bhagwati and M. Hirsch (eds), *The Uruguay Round and Beyond: Essays in Honour of Arthur Dunkel*. Michigan University Press, East Lansing.

Roychaudhuri, Tapan and Habib Irfan (1984). *The Cambridge Economic History of India*, vol. I. Orient Longman in association with Cambridge University Press, Delhi.

Shukla, S. P. (1994). The emerging international trading order: A story of the Uruguay Round. In G. S. Bhalla and Agarwal Manmohan (eds), *World Economy in Transition: An Indian Perspective*. Har-Anand Publications, New Delhi.

—— (2000). From GATT to WTO and beyond. *WIDER Working Papers* No. 195. UNU/WIDER, Helsinki.

Snape, R. H. (1986). Introduction. In R. H. Snape (ed.), *Issues in the World Trade Policy: GATT at the Crossroads*. The Macmillan Press, Houndsmill.

Third World Economics: Trends and Analysis (1999). Closing remarks by conference chair, Charlene Barshefsy, 16–31 December.

Tussie, Diana (1987). *The Less Developed Countries and The World Trading System*. Francis Pinter, London.

Wood, Ellen Meiksins (1999). Unhappy families: Global capitalism in a world of nation-states. *Monthly Review*, July–August. Monthly Review Press, New York.

WTO (1995). *The Results of the Uruguay Round of Multilateral Trade Negotiations: The Legal Texts*. GATT Secretariat/WTO, Geneva.

Wyndham-White, Eric (1975). Foreword. In *GATT Plus—A Proposal for Trade Reform*. Praeger Publishers, New York.

Zampetti, Americo B. and Pierre Sauve (1996). Onwards to Singapore: The international contestability of markets and the new trade agenda. *The World Economy*, 19(3), May.

PART IV

GOVERNANCE

11

Reforming the International Financial Architecture: Consensus and Divergence

JOSÉ ANTONIO OCAMPO

The Asian crisis and its rapid spread to Russia and Latin America in 1997 and 1998 gave rise to a broad consensus on the need to reform the international financial architecture in order to reduce the inherent instability of the current system. The recovery of the economies affected and the tendency for financial markets to normalize have reduced the sense of urgency in these reforms; but this could also be seen as an opportunity to set in motion a balanced, representative process for strengthening international financial governance. This chapter critically reviews the ongoing debate from the developing country perspective and argues the case for a thoroughgoing reform of the current architecture. Section 1 takes a brief look at four basic propositions that must underlie any relevant reform in this area. This serves as the basis for a closer look, in sections 2 and 3, at the current controversy which is organized in terms of distinguishing the areas in which there is some agreement from those in which there is still a considerable divergence of opinion. This is an expository device, based on the author's personal perception of existing consensus and divergence. As we will see, however, even in areas where some agreement is said to exist, there are considerable differences in the interpretation or in the relative emphasis given to each specific component of the reform. The chapter focuses on reforms needed to prevent and manage financial crises—what may be called the 'narrow' financial architecture—leaving aside issues relating to development finance, in particular.[1] Section 4 draws some conclusions from the analysis.

Parts of this chapter draw from the Report of the Task Force of the Executive Committee on Economic and Social Affairs of the United Nations (UN Task Force 1999), which the author coordinated. Thanks are due to grateful to Manuel Agosin, Yilmaz Akyüz, Guillermo Calvo, Michel Camdessus, Nitin Desai, Nicolás Eyzaguirre, Ricardo Ffrench-Davis, Stephany Griffith-Jones, Gerald Helleiner, Barry Herman, Daniel Heyman, Jan Kregel, Deepak Nayyar, Rubens Ricupero, Joseph Stiglitz, Lance Taylor, Camilo Tovar, Andrés Velasco, René Villarreal, and Rocío de Villarreal for discussions and comments.

[1] A broader set of issues is analysed in Ocampo (1999).

1. FOUR ESSENTIAL PROPOSITIONS FOR A RELEVANT REFORM

Any meaningful reform of the international financial architecture must be based on four basic propositions. The first one is that the instability of the system reflects 'information problems' that are largely unsolvable, as financial market behaviour is determined as much by *opinions* and *expectations* as by information, in the precise meaning of that term (i.e. factual information).

The central role that imperfect information plays in generating market failures in the financial sector is well known.[2] Improved information is thus central to a better market performance. However, we have seen in recent years how sophisticated and increasingly informed financial markets have continued to be extremely volatile. There are many reasons for that. The most important is probably the fact that much of the relevant information to which the market reacts comes only with a significant lag, and depends on macroeconomic conditions that are not entirely known in advance. Thus, for example, some investment decisions made before the Latin American debt crisis of the 1980s or before the 1997 Asian crisis may have been unsound to start with, but the magnitudes of the losses associated with them were determined even more by the major macroeconomic shocks that these regions experienced, which were probably unpredictable—certainly with respect to their magnitude—and were indeed unpredicted by even the best observers. The increasing information that is relevant for improving microeconomic efficiency may, thus, do very little to reduce *macroeconomic* volatility.

The economic factors that determine such macroeconomic volatility are, thus, central to financial market performance. We should mention first in this regard, using Joan Robinson's terms, that 'historical time' involves *uncertainty*. Thus, the investment and savings decisions that determine macroeconomic behaviour and performance are based on opinions and expectations of the uncertain evolution of economic variables rather than of risk probability distributions that can be known *ex ante*. In a word, markets are necessarily imperfect when time is involved, as the information necessary to correct such 'market imperfection' will never be available.

The way information is processed to form such opinions and expectations poses additional problems. A fundamental microeconomic factor in this regard is the fact that the processing of information for individual decisions is subject to sharply increasing marginal costs, particularly when it involves financial actors that constitute complex decisions. Thus, a board of directors of a financial institution faced with a decision to invest in a particular country (or sector), or even whether to invest at all, will not be able to take into account the rich information that the direct market operators of that institution may have on the strengths and weaknesses of all specific firms in that country (or sector). Much simpler information and even rules of thumb would be necessarily used, and the tendency to conform to the 'average opinion' that may exist in the market at that time would be very strong.[3] Regardless of the rationality

---

[2] See, for instance, the classic paper by Stiglitz and Weiss (1981).

[3] This idea was captured by Keynes' concept of the 'beauty contest'. See Eatwell (1996).

involved in forming such an 'average opinion' (or the lack of it), it is clear that the changes that it may experience will have major effects on markets. Indeed, the interrelation of the 'information' that financial actors manage at any particular time—that is, the 'information cascades'—or, rather, the interrelation of the opinions and expectations that is formed from such information, is central to the rich contemporary literature on self-fulfilling booms and busts.

Changes in opinions through time indicate that the *same* information may be interpreted in a totally different way at different times. Moreover, the mix between the simple way opinions and expectations are formed with today's sophisticated markets implies that markets may actually become *more* volatile in the face of changed expectations. This is the opinion of the chairman of the Federal Reserve Board, who has argued that the 'size of the breakdowns and required official finance to counter them is of a different order of magnitude than in the past' (Greenspan 1998). Indeed, certain characteristics of sophisticated markets may enhance instability. This is, first of all, an effect of improved communications and 24-hour trading around the world. Specialized information in today's markets may have the same result. In the case of emerging markets, for example, there is strong evidence that grading agencies may have increased rather than reduced volatility (Larraín *et al.* 1997). Also, changes in the opinions of those investors who are considered to be 'informed' may lead to overreactions by non-informed ones, who rely on the former to make their decisions (Calvo 1998). It is also generally accepted that the unbundling of risks through derivative operations and the corresponding concentration of certain risks in specific agents imply that even if improved regulation and supervision of these operations were designed, a breakdown in that corner of the market would have amplified implications.

The second proposition is that, as in any other case, self-insurance is a costly option in the area of international finance. This sounds self-evident and should probably be left aside from the discussion altogether, were it not for the fact that many proposals, particularly those involving developing countries, imply that in the current order, a degree of self-insurance is inevitable. Indeed, the line that divides national policies aimed at preventing crises from self-insurance is a fuzzy one. Thus, high levels of international reserves, building stronger credibility through the introduction of deflationary biases in macroeconomic policy, the adoption of prudential regulations stronger than those recommended by the Basle Committee, and discouraging excessive short-term external borrowing through price-based or quantitative capital controls, that is, the whole array of national policies recommended to developing countries in a world of volatile capital flows (with the particular preference depending on the author), all have elements of self-insurance attached to them.

All these exclusively national options are costly. Thus, although the prevention of excessive risks is an essential element in the design of any insurance system, the basic architecture of the international financial system cannot rely solely or even fundamentally on strengthening these forms of 'self-insurance'. Rather, it should aim at devising at the international level appropriate institutional mechanisms that reduce the costs involved in relying exclusively on national policies, and in choosing the less costly among them. In the case of developing countries, the greater volatility associated

290 J. A. Ocampo

with capital flows and/or terms of trade fluctuations implies that exclusive reliance on a high level of international reserves or deflationary policies to manage downside macroeconomic risks may be very costly. Stringent domestic regulations to manage financial risks may be necessary, but they are also costly. Thus, a well-designed international system must complement those policies with institutional mechanisms that allow these costs to be minimized. We will argue below that, from the perspective of national policies, the advantages of discouraging short-term external borrowing lie precisely in the fact that it reduces (though it certainly does not eliminate) the need to rely on other, more costly alternatives.

The third proposition that is essential to the analysis of international financial reform is the recognition that nations, particularly the industrialized countries but also many developing countries, are willing to give up their economic sovereignty only very partially, if at all—or, in the case of countries in the European Union, only to a regional organization. The positive and negative sides of this fact can be extensively argued over, but any viable reform must take it into account. This indicates that the 'financial safety nets' that have been developed at the national level to manage market instability cannot be replicated in the international system, or can be copied only in a partial and imperfect way. This is true of central banks, prudential regulation and supervision, deposit and credit insurance and guarantees, and bankruptcy procedures. This implies, in turn, that an essential task in the design of the international financial architecture is to guarantee that a system which will continue to rely essentially on a network of *national* institutions (regional in the case of some EU ones) takes adequate account of their international linkages. It also implies that options that are closed at the national level (such as strong restrictions on certain market activities, or even unilateral standstills on debts) should probably be left as open options at the international level.

The fourth proposition is that no international financial design is neutral in terms of the equilibrium in international relations. Thus, the particular balance that each alternative involves, as well as the *procedures* by which reforms are discussed and decided upon, should be a central concern for developing and small countries (UN Task Force 1999; Group of 24, 1988; Helleiner and Oyejide 1998). It will be strongly argued in this chapter that an international system that relies on one or a few international institutions is less neutral than one that relies on a network of regional institutions and on peer review among national institutions. More democratic forums are superior to closed ones, in terms of generating stable consensus by all players, powerful or not. A broad agenda, in which all relevant issues are placed on the table, is also preferable to a limited one. Given its unique character as a global forum, certainly the most democratic of its kind, the United Nations should play a role in this area, through an improved Economic and Social Council or the Economic Security Council recommended by the 1995 Commission on Global Governance, the mandates of which would obviously cover a broader set of economic, social, and environmental issues. Finally, but no less important, a country with very limited power in the international arena will be better off if it has access to a broader menu of alternatives to manage a potential crisis than if it is restricted to a few options.

The combination of these four propositions is what makes the desired system, and the routes to it, so complex. It will be argued here that only an integral system, which includes all the areas considered in this chapter, is desirable. In a sense, the desired system is complex largely because it includes many 'second best' or even 'nth-best' components, as no single, optimal solution is available. Moreover, even if an agreement were reached to replicate national financial institutions at the international level, it is unclear whether that system would be desirable to smaller international players, given the nature of world relations. The route is also made more complex by the fact that some major players do not perceive themselves to be facing fundamental problems, and by the additional fact that the simpler decision-making system that characterized the design of the Bretton Woods system in which the two dominant powers negotiated between themselves, would be unacceptable today. We should probably add that this is also the reason why some perceive that only a limited reform is viable, and why viable alternatives should build on existing institutions rather than relying on the creation of new ones.

2. AREAS OF GROWING CONSENSUS

2.1. *The Need for Expansionary Policies in Industrialized Countries During Crises and for Emergency Financing for Countries in Difficulties*

A clear consensus has been building up in some areas, though in most cases it is accompanied by significant differences in interpretation or in the emphasis given to each specific component of the reform. There is, first of all, a consensus that an inter-national financial crisis requires expansionary policies in the industrialized world. This is an essential difference between the recent crisis (as well as the 'tequila' episode of 1994) and the Latin American debt crisis of the early 1980s, when high interest rates induced by contractionary monetary policies in the United States clearly increased the severity of the contraction (Díaz-Alejandro 1988: chapter 15). Curiously, the shift towards this recent consensus has been building up only since mid-1998 and, despite the incomplete normalization of capital flows to emerging markets, it was replaced by a new shift in the stance of monetary policies in the United States and the European Union in mid-1999. This incomplete normalization reflects the limited 'trickling down' of the expansionary policies of industrialized countries, that is, its limited (or lagged) effects in terms of restoring confidence in emerging markets during crises.

The limited 'trickling down', as well as the strong evidence of contagion, is the basic reason for the growing consensus on the need to increase the supply of emergency financing in times of crisis that is made available *before*—rather than after—interna-tional reserves are depleted. Moreover, such financing should include countries facing contagion, as was recognized with the creation of the Contingency Credit Line created in April 1999, though under very restrictive eligibility criteria. These principles of intervention are a major advance, not only with respect to those adopted in Bretton Woods, based on the concept of a 'fundamental disequilibrium' in the balance of payments, but also with respect to experience accumulated since the 1994 Mexican and the 1997 Asian crises, when emergency funds were approved only after the crisis had been unleashed. Still, the effectiveness of the new type of contingency financing may be limited, for several reasons: (i) because it may serve to postpone the adjustment considered inevitable; (ii) because the negotiation process is too cumbersome; and, probably more importantly, (iii) because the market judges that the intervening authorities (the IMF, supported by some development banks and a few industrialized countries) are unable or unwilling to supply funds in the quantities required to stabilize speculative pressures. These difficulties are compounded by controversies over the nature of conditionality involved in the use of funds and moral hazard issues on the side of private lenders. We will return to these controversies below.

2.2. The Need to Improve the Institutional Framework in which Financial Markets Operate

A third area of consensus relates to the need to improve the information provided to financial markets, to adopt common minimum standards in prudential regulation, supervision and financial accounting, codes of conduct in fiscal, monetary, and financial policies, and principles of sound corporate governance, that is, to improve the institutional framework in which financial markets operate. There is, in particular, a broad agreement on the important role that information plays for adequate microeconomic performance in financial markets, and on the need for strong regulation and supervision to guarantee financial stability.[4] Disagreement remains, however, on what authorities would be given broader responsibilities in the area of prudential regulation and supervision, on what types of additional regulation would be required to reduce volatility and on how much additional information, regulation, and supervision would contribute to stability.

On the first of these topics, bolder reform recommendations include the proposal to create a World Financial Authority responsible for regulatory practices and effective risk management procedures, overseeing the development of credible guarantor and lender-of-last-resort functions and the accountability of the IMF and the World Bank (Eatwell and Taylor 2000). Less ambitious suggestions are based on strengthening the BIS (Basle Committee) and International Organisation of Securities Commissions (IOSCO) activities in the areas of domestic regulation and supervision, which would require extended membership by developing countries in these organizations. Peer review can also be used more extensively in this area.

There is now a broad agreement, which includes the authorities in developed countries, to extend prudential regulation and supervision to high leveraged institutions and offshore centres. But, clearly, reforms should go beyond that. In the case of industrialized countries, prudential regulation of financial institutions, including mutual and hedge funds, should clearly give greater weight to the high risk associated with operations in countries incurring large net borrowing, particularly of a short-term character—indeed, reforming the bias towards short-term lending implicit in current

---

[4] See Camdessus (1998); IMF (1998); IMF Interim Committee (1998); Group of Seven (1998); UN Task Force (1999); Miyazawa (1998); Rubin (1999); Eatwell and Taylor (2000); Eichengreen (1999); Griffith-Jones (1998), and Wyplosz (1999), among others.

Basle standards. This would discourage this type of lending at the source. On the borrowing side, international standards and the corresponding domestic regulation should include or give greater weight to risks related to the accumulation of short-term liabilities in foreign currencies (Furman and Stiglitz 1998; Rodrik and Velasco 1999), to the growth of credit, to currency mismatches of assets and liabilities, and to the valuation of fixed assets as collateral during episodes of asset inflation. Depending on the operation, higher capital standards, matching liquidity requirements or caps on valuation of assets should be established (UN Task Force 1999; ECLAC 1998*b*).

Also, due account should be taken of the links between domestic financial risk and changes in key macroeconomic policy instruments, notably exchange and interest rates. This indicates that prudential regulations should be stricter in developing countries, where such links are more important, and that they should be strengthened in periods of financial euphoria to take into account the increasing risks which financial agents are incurring. Indeed, otherwise, the application of strict prudential regulations may become a pro-cyclical element of economic policy since their effect is more stringent during a downswing, when provisioning standards and their effects on capital requirements affect the capacity to extend credit. Moreover, due to the important externalities which large non-financial firms could generate on the domestic financial sector, particularly in the context of an exchange rate depreciation, the unhedged external liability exposures of these firms should also be subject to regulation (UN Task Force 1999; ECLAC 1998*b*).

The information problems which regulation and supervision face should not be underestimated, however (UNCTAD 1998: Part I/ch. 4). Regulation will almost necessarily lag behind financial innovations, and indeed regulations will induce innovations. Moreover, since regulation always focuses on the activities of specific intermediaries rather than on financial services as such, an important form of innovation is the creation of new, unregulated agents that provide the same services. Supervisors can only review a limited number of individual operations by financial intermediaries, and that information will necessarily be partial and be available with a lag. Indeed, the experience of supervision worldwide indicates that many high risks are really known by the authorities only when it is too late to avoid some (even large) insolvencies from occurring. Moreover, this information comes as a significant surprise even to the (profit-motivated) financial and non-financial private firms involved, a fact which places significant doubts on whether the decisions that underlie such high risks could have been avoided in the first place. This is largely associated with the fact that unprofitable and loss-making investment decisions (and, thus, their real riskiness) are known only years after they have been made and, as we have pointed out, depend on macroeconomic as well as microeconomic factors, many of which are only known (and can only be known) *ex post*.

On the other hand, although an essential role of prudential regulation and supervision is to make financial intermediaries more risk-conscious, there are clear limits to the appropriateness of discouraging private risk undertakings. After all, this is the basic role of private entrepreneurship, and an essential role of financial systems is to facilitate the undertaking of risky ventures. Some classic roles of regulation may also become useless under major macroeconomic shocks: diversification of risks at the national level may turn out to be an inadequate safeguard under these conditions; attempts to avoid this problem by diversifying into assets and liabilities in foreign currencies generate new risks associated to currency mismatches, and capital requirements necessary to avoid some (hopefully) unusual circumstances may be so high as to entirely discourage important financial services.

Moreover, though prudential regulation is an essential activity, it involves some price signals (e.g. higher capital requirements as a counterpart to riskier assets, and higher liquidity requirements for short-term liabilities), but also a whole array of quantitative restrictions (e.g. outright prohibitions, or explicit limits on certain types of operations, such as matching requirements between certain assets and liabilities and limits on credits to related parties). On the other hand, prudential supervision is necessarily a discretionary public sector intervention. Thus, it involves two forms of intervention that are generally viewed today as subject to important 'government failures'. Indeed, a peculiar paradox in the recent literature is that authors, who are unwilling to accept that quantitative restrictions and discretionary government intervention and even public sector intervention at all are good in other areas of economic policy (e.g. trade policy or capital account regulations), are fervent in the defence of quantitative controls and discretionary policies in this particular case.

Although the argument in favour of stricter prudential regulation and supervision is a compelling one, there are thus limits to what these instruments can achieve in terms of avoiding financial crises, and there are also costs to stricter regulation that cannot be ignored. The lags in regulatory practices and the limits to what supervisors can do, on the other hand, are strong arguments to emphasize the *internal* regulation system that banks and other financial intermediaries develop, and to focus an important part of supervisory activities on analysing the functioning of such internal regulations.

Similar comments can be made about information. As we have argued, improved information may enhance microeconomic efficiency but may not improve macroeconomic stability, which is dominated by the evolution of opinions and expectations rather than information, in the correct sense of that term. During periods of financial euphoria, enhanced information has been unable to avoid excessive risk-taking in developed and developing countries alike. On the other hand, in today's informed but volatile markets, market discipline may generate a strong deflationary bias in macroeconomic policy during crises, and thus a more procyclical performance of economic activity, as authorities try to build credibility (Eatwell 1996). Under these conditions, stronger mechanisms for the authorities to 'lean against the wind' in times of financial euphoria may be necessary, as well as alternatives to manage the crisis—in particular, regulation of capital flows and standstill provisions, respectively.

2.3. *Consistency, Surveillance, and Consultation of National Macroeconomic Policies*

Given that economic sovereignty would be given away only in a very partial way, stronger mechanisms to guarantee that the externalities generated by macroeconomic policies events are adequately dealt with are necessary. In the case of industrialized countries, this is essential to guarantee the global consistency of their macroeconomic policies, that is, their collective ability to avoid both world inflationary and deflationary pressures. In the case of developing countries, evidence of contagion calls for similar mechanisms to develop collective lines of defence in the face of financial boom–bust cycles and to internalize at least partially the regional effects of macroeconomic policies.

The three essential problems are the weaknesses of the current arrangements, lack of adequate representation of the developing countries, and the considerable asymmetry between the two phases of the business cycle. With respect to the first of these problems, the Group of Seven is a weak mechanism of consultation; IMF Article IV reviews can be ignored rather easily by countries which do not require Fund financing, and there are no mechanisms of consultation (less so of surveillance or coordination) at the regional level in the developing world. In relation to the second problem, developing countries and the smaller industrialized countries obviously have no voice in the Group of Seven, and their representation on the IMF Interim Committee is less than desirable. The asymmetry between the two faces of the business cycle is reflected in the fact that, whereas the combination of market discipline and IMF conditionality is a very strong mechanism in the downswing, there are no similar mechanisms in the upswing when most of the risks that are later reflected in the crisis, incur. In a word, crisis prevention is essentially the role of policies adopted to manage booms, when 'market discipline' is perverse, as it rather encourages 'irrational exuberance' (to use Alan Greenspan's term), and there are no constraints on the adoption of national procyclical policies.

Thus, although stronger organs are required to guarantee the global consistency of macroeconomic policies, their creation should be accompanied by an improved representation of the developing countries in the corresponding institutions. This should go together with a strong emphasis of the critical role that Article IV consultations and parallel regional mechanisms should play in this area. It is also crucial that all these surveillance and consultative mechanisms give greater weight to the management of booms, when financial crises are incubated.

2.4. *Internationally Sanctioned Standstill Provisions to Guarantee an Adequate Sharing of the Burdens of Adjustment*

Through its chaotic effects on exchange and interest rates and on domestic economic activity, disorderly capital flight generates significant damage for debtor countries, and considerably increases the probability that illiquidity may turn into insolvency. It is also bad for creditors, as it reduces the probability that many of them will be repaid. Under these conditions, the unilateral suspension of debt servicing also generates significant damage. It destroys the credibility of national authorities and thus may worsen, rather than improve, conditions in the short term. The experience of many developing countries indicates that it leads to a repeated exercise of debt rescheduling, which interrupts investment and growth for protracted periods. On the other hand, under these conditions, the provision of emergency financing by international institutions and official sources may serve to bail out many private creditors, raising moral hazard issues and serious concerns over the distribution of the burden of adjustment.

These considerations are the basis for the growing consensus on the need to create internationally sanctioned standstill provisions (also referred to as orderly debt work-outs) in the area of international finance. These provisions would play the same role as national bankruptcy procedures play in domestic affairs. The preventive suspensions of debt service and agreed rescheduling under an internationally agreed procedure would serve to solve the coordination problems implicit in chaotic capital flight, and thus avoid some of its worst effects. If, aside from illiquidity, there are problems with the debt burden of the country concerned, this mechanism would also serve to distribute more equitably the costs of adjustment and, particularly, to force private creditors to pay (also in an equitable way among themselves) a part of the burden.

Due to the effects that the use of this mechanism may have on the credit reputation of the borrowing countries and its collateral effects on trade financing, the countries concerned are unlikely to use these provisions, except under severe difficulties. However, to avoid moral hazard on the side of borrowers, they must be subject to some control. According to UNCTAD, which has provided probably the most forceful defence of this mechanism, there could be two alternatives (UNCTAD 1998: Part I/chapter 4; UN Task Force 1999; and Akyüz and Cornford, Chapter 5, this volume). The first would be to explicitly give the IMF the power to sanction such standstills, to lead the renegotiations and to facilitate 'lending into arrears' only in these cases. The second alternative would be to allow countries to unilaterally call the standstill, but then to submit it for approval to an independent international panel, whose sanction would then give it legitimacy. A third, complementary possibility would be to draft *ex ante* rules under which debt service would be automatically suspended or reduced if certain macroeconomic shocks are experienced. These rules, at times, have been incorporated into debt renegotiation agreements.

We should emphasize that this mechanism has four implications. First, to avoid free riding, the mechanism requires the *generalized* adoption of 'collective action clauses' in international lending. Secondly, 'bailing in' should be encouraged, by giving preference to lending that is given to the country involved throughout the period during which the standstill is in effect and a later phase of 'normalization' of capital flows. Thirdly, debt renegotiations under this framework must have a strictly agreed, short time-horizon, beyond which the IMF or the international panel would have the authority to determine the terms of rescheduling. To avoid repeated renegotiations, which have been one of the most troublesome features of debt rescheduling over the past two decades, the renegotiation should aim for a definite settlement, that is, in which the debt burden is sustainable. The external debt, public and private, should thus be classified in three portions: (i) the first component to be subject to normal servicing, which would include the 'bailing in' operations; (ii) the contingent portion to be paid totally or partially, depending on certain external and domestic conditions (e.g. terms of trade and normalization of borrowing, in the first case; economic activity or unemployment, in the second); and (iii) the third portion to be written off. Finally, utilizing this mechanism would necessitate the use of explicit controls on capital flows, which must extend for some time beyond the successful conclusion of renegotiations.

2.5. *Social Safety Nets*

In recent debates, emphasis has also been correctly placed on the role that multilateral financial institutions, particularly development banks, should play in financing social safety nets in developing countries. Strong social safety nets are, indeed, essential in managing the social repercussions of financial vulnerability in the developing world. The concept itself is subject to some confusion, as it is used to refer both to the design of long-term social policies and to specific mechanisms to protect vulnerable groups during crises. The term should probably be used to refer specifically to the latter, although these arrangements should be part of a stable mechanism of social protection. Multilateral banks have been involved in the former for a long time and have also accumulated some experience with the latter.

Recent analyses have come to some basic conclusions about these programmes. Firstly, safety nets must be a part of *permanent* social protection schemes, as only a permanent scheme guarantees that the programme coverage will respond without lags to the demand of vulnerable sectors for protection during crises (Cornia 1999). This implies, in turn, that financing must be fundamentally of a domestic character, with external financing contributing marginally, if at all, during crises. Secondly, given the heterogeneity of labour markets in developing countries, a combination of several programmes with different target groups is necessary (Márquez 1999). Thirdly, these programmes must be adequately financed and should not crowd out resources from long-term investment in human capital. This, it must be said, leads to a fourth con-clusion: that the effective functioning of social safety nets requires that public-sector expenditure should include anti-cyclical components. This would be impossible—without generating inefficiencies in the rest of public-sector expenditure—unless fiscal policy as a whole is countercyclical. In the absence of this anti-cyclical fiscal pattern, external financing from development banks during crises will be unnecessary or, at best, illusory, as overall net fiscal financing requirements will actually decrease despite the increased spending associated with social safety nets.

3. AREAS OF DISAGREEMENT

3.1. *The Provision of Adequate Emergency Financing*

As we have pointed out, the agreed principle that emergency financing should be available has not been matched by a clear agreement on how to make funds available in adequate quantities to be really effective. The current principles of IMF intervention were summarized in the April 1998 Interim Committee Communiqué: 'The Fund cannot be expected to be able to finance whatever large balance-of-payments deficit. Its role is essential to catalyse other sources of financing, and, when needed, to coordinate support from other sources.' However, as we have pointed out, under crisis condi-tions, its 'catalytic' and 'coordination' roles would be largely ineffective if the market judges the intervening authorities to be unable or unwilling to supply funds in the quantities required. Thus, insufficient resources may turn two correct principles—emergency financing and the catalytic role of the Fund—largely into a dead letter.

Thus, even if no true lender of last resort were devised (as we assume it will not), a well-funded 'emergency financier' would certainly be required. This, for developing countries, must be a *sine qua non* of any reform effort. As bilateral financing and contributions to the IMF will continue to be very scarce, the best solution is certainly to allow additional issues of SDRs under critical financial conditions, to create the additional liquidity required. These funds could be reallocated once financial conditions normalize (UN Task Force 1999). This procedure would, by the way, create an anti-cyclical element in world liquidity management and would give SDRs an increasing role in world finance, a principle that developing countries advocated in the past and should continue to do. Second best alternatives are to make more active use of central bank swap arrangements under IMF or BIS leadership, or to allow the IMF to raise the resources needed in the market.

3.2. IMF Conditionality

IMF conditionality has long been an area of contention. However, in recent years—and even decades—the issue has become increasingly troublesome for three different reasons. First, the scope of conditionality has been gradually expanded to include not only the realms of other international organizations, but also of domestic, economic, and social development strategies and institutions which, as the United Nations Task Force has indicated, 'by their very nature, should be decided by legitimate national authorities, based on broad social consensus'.[5] Indeed, although not referred explicitly to IMF conditionality, this point has been made in strong terms by the president of the World Bank: 'We must never stop reminding ourselves that it is up to the government and its people to decide what their priorities should be. We must never stop reminding ourselves that we cannot and should not impose development by fiat from above, or from abroad' (Wolfensohn 1998). Secondly, whereas the legitimacy of conditionality is indisputable when domestic policies are the source of macroeconomic disequilibria that lead to financial difficulties, it is unclear how this principle applies when such difficulties are generated by contagion. Moreover, it is even less clear why conditionality should be mixed in this case with adverse credit conditions (higher interest rates and shorter maturities), as has been advocated by the Group of Seven and agreed to in the case of the new credit windows created in recent years. Finally, evidence of overkill in some IMF programmes has accumulated and has led to mounting criticisms on the specific macroeconomic analysis implicit in the programmes. Due to this fact, with a significant lag, the IMF itself facilitated countercyclical fiscal management in the depressed Asian economies (Fischer 1998).

Even if the legitimacy of the principle of conditionality is accepted—or, as it is sometimes alternatively stated, 'support in exchange for reforms'—these are reasons that should lead to a major revision of the characteristics of such conditionality. Indeed, the perception that conditionality has gone too far in practice may undermine

---

[5] See UN Task Force (1999: section 5). Actually, the strongest statement in this regard has come from Feldstein (1998), a conservative critic of the Fund.

its legitimacy, and weaken the international consensus on which the IMF itself is built. Thus, a strong argument can be made that the way to restore full confidence in the principle of conditionality is by reaching a renewed international agreement on how it should be used.

Several principles can be advanced in this regard. Firstly, conditionality should be restricted to the macroeconomic policies that were its purview in the past. It should be used when expansionary policies are clearly associated with the generation of macroeconomic imbalances, or when a country needs to draw Fund resources beyond some automatic low-conditionality facilities if the source of the imbalance is an international shock. Reforms of domestic prudential regulation and supervision may also be required, but parallel agreements should be made with the corresponding international authorities (a still controversial issue, as we have seen). Secondly, low-conditionality facilities should be available in adequate quantities when the source of the imbalance is an international shock. This principle should be clearly applied to the case of contagion, where *ex ante* criteria could be used to determine eligibility for the available windows. Thirdly, more stringent credit conditions should not be used as a complement to conditionality, as it undermines the 'credit union' character of the IMF without really approaching 'market conditions' that, under such circumstances, would be very stringent. Fourthly, automatic rules should be agreed when signing an agreement with the Fund, by which the restrictiveness of policies would be eased should evidence of 'overkill' become clear. Finally, regular official evaluation of IMF programmes, either by an autonomous division in the Fund (as it is done in the World Bank) or by outside analysts, should be introduced and the major conclusions of these evaluations, when reviewed by the Board, should be explicitly introduced into regular Fund practice.

3.3. *Preservation of the Autonomy of Developing Countries to Manage the Capital Account*

Massive evidence of capital account liberalizations that induced major external and domestic financial crises in many countries has led to several agreements in this area.[6] It is now generally agreed that such liberalizations should be gradual, should emphasize longer-term flows and be extremely cautious with shorter-term and volatile funds (such as short-term credits and portfolio flows), and should be preceded by the development of strong prudential regulation and supervision, and consistent macroeconomic policies. Moreover, it is also accepted that any international agreement in this area should include safeguard mechanisms that would allow a temporary use of controls under certain, critical conditions. The consensus stops at this point. A strong argument has been made by some analysts to place well-managed capital account liberalization as the final objective of policy, on the basis that freer capital markets are inherently good for growth. If these assertions were correct, the use of capital controls should be essentially a temporary device. These are the arguments that underlie the current discussion on the introduction of capital account convertibility into the

---

[6] For a recent survey, see Williamson and Mahar (1998).

Articles of Agreement of the IMF. A strong argument can be made, however, on the advantages of maintaining the autonomy of developing countries to manage capital accounts, on at least four grounds.[7]

First of all, some of the fundamental assumptions that underlie full capital account liberalization are wrong. There is no evidence that capital mobility allows an efficient smoothing out of expenditure in developing countries through the economic cycle. On the contrary, in these countries the volatility of capital flows is clearly an additional source of instability. There is also no evidence of an association between capital account liberalization and economic growth, and some evidence in the opposite direction.[8] A simple way to explain this result is to argue that, even if it is true that freer capital markets, through their effect on a more efficient savings–investment allocation, have positive effects on growth, the additional volatility associated with freer capital markets has the opposite effect.

Secondly, capital account regulations are obviously costly, but they also generate benefits. In particular, if they are not used as substitutes for appropriate macro-economic management, the additional degrees of freedom they provide to economic policy are important. During financial booms, a form of tax or control on inflows provides an additional mechanism to 'lean against the wind' and thus avoid excessive borrowing, particularly of a short-term character, thereby acting as an effective mechanism to prevent financial crisis. In countries that use some form of managed exchange rate flexibility, they also help to avoid an excessive appreciation of the domestic currency in the face of favourable terms of trade or capital account shocks, avoiding the generation of current account positions that become unsustainable once these favourable shocks cease. In terms of our discussion in Section 1, they may be one of the least costly forms of 'self-insurance' that a country may choose. It is certainly preferable to allowing the economy to boom without restrictions, accumulating excessive risks, and may be better than sterilized reserve accumulation, a policy that has been found to be self-defeating in many developing countries. During crises, controls on outflows provide additional 'room for manoeuvre', if they are not used as a substitute for fundamental macroeconomic adjustment. As we have argued, they are also a necessary complement to debt standstills, generally viewed as an important ingredient of a necessary financial architecture (Krugman 1998).

Thirdly, it can be argued that some capital account regulation on inflows used by some developing countries during boom years may be not only more effective but actually preferable to alternative prudential regulation and supervision. Indeed, the boundary between some forms of capital controls and prudential regulation is a thin one. This is associated with the fact that capital account regulations have both macro and microeconomic effects, and may thus serve in the latter case as a substitute for prudential regulations aimed at avoiding unsustainable credit booms or guaranteeing a

---

[7] For a more extensive analysis of these issues, see UN Task Force (1999); UNCTAD (1998: Part I/ chapter 4); ECLAC (1998a: Part III); Akyüz and Cornford (Chapter 5, this volume); Eichengreen (1998, 1999); Griffith-Jones (1998); Grilli and Milesi-Ferretti (1995); Krugman (1998), and Rodrik (1998).

[8] See, in particular, Eatwell (1996) and Rodrik (1998).

certain structure of assets or liabilities of financial intermediaries. As we have pointed out, prudential regulations in some cases establish not only price signals, but also quantitative restrictions, and although financial supervision is an essential activity, it is not free from significant information problems, or those associated with discretionary public sector interventions. Certain types of regulations of the capital account may thus be equivalent to or a near substitute for traditional quantitative prudential regulations (e.g. explicit prohibition of a certain type of external borrowing, or a minimum stay period for portfolio capital) or may introduce a price signal to substitute for quantitative restrictions (such as a Tobin tax, or the system of reserve requirements on capital flows to discourage the short-term indebtedness extensively used by Chile and Colombia in the 1990s) (Agosin and Ffrench-Davis 2000; Ocampo and Tovar 1999), reducing the need for more discretionary interventions. Equivalent practices, such as the selling fees imposed by mutual funds on investments held for a short period, are actually used by private agents in order to discourage short-term holdings (Morgan 1998: 23). Moreover, whereas prudential regulation and supervision cover only financial intermediaries, capital account regulations have a more extensive coverage. Given the significant externalities that non-financial agents have on domestic financial stability, this is a significant advantage.

Finally, but no less important, it is unclear why developing countries, in the absence of an adequate international financial safety net, should give away their autonomy in this area. This is a crucial point. Why should developing countries give up this degree of freedom if they do not have access to adequate emergency financing with well-defined conditionality rules? In terms of our discussion in Section 1, this is a particularly crucial issue for countries without significant power in the international arena, for whom renouncing any possible means to manage a crisis is a costly alternative.

Thus, at least in the case of developing countries, a flexible approach is superior to capital account convertibility. Thus, the mandate of the IMF should not be for convertibility, but rather for analysing and spreading good practices in this area. Based on the Latin American experience, three issues may be pointed out.

1. Capital account regulations during booms, which have a preventive character, would be preferable to the establishment of strong quantitative controls on outflows during the ensuing crises, which generate severe credibility issues.
2. Price-based regulations (such as reserve requirements on capital inflows) are an alternative to quantitative controls, but simple quantitative controls (e.g. flat prohibitions on certain activities or regulations) may be preferable in underdeveloped regulatory regimes.
3. A permanent regulation or control regime that is tightened or loosened throughout the economic cycle is clearly superior to the alternation of a free capital account regime during the boom and quantitative controls on outflows during the crisis. This type of sporadic, crisis-driven controls generate serious credibility issues and are generally ineffective, as a tradition of regulation and supervision is necessary to make them operative.

3.4. *Freedom to Choose which Exchange Rate Regime should Continue*

In the face of recent events, some authors have strongly argued that the only stable regimes in the current globalized world are either a convertibility scheme or a totally free exchange rate. According to this point of view, the IMF should stop countries from adopting exchange rate regimes that are assumed to be unstable. This argument is obviously only one step from arguing that the exchange rate regime should be subject to conditionality, a step that would certainly be unfortunate.

The free-versus-floating exchange rate controversy is an old one and indicates that no optimal regime exists. Currency boards certainly introduce built-in institutional arrangements that provide for fiscal and monetary discipline, but they reduce the room for stabilizing macroeconomic policies and may thus generate strong swings in economic activity and asset prices. Probably as a result of this, these arrangements are not speculation-proof, as the experience of Argentina in 1994–95 or Hong Kong in 1997 indicates. On the other hand, the classic arguments in favour of floating rates are that these provide a market mechanism to face both trade and capital account shocks, and allow authorities an additional degree of freedom to manage monetary policy to respond to domestic anti-cyclical goals. However, exchange rate volatility increases the costs of trade transactions and thus reduces the benefits of international specialization. During periods of financial euphoria or exceptional terms of trade, appreciation may generate Dutch disease effects. The existence of financial liabilities in foreign currencies generates additional difficulties, as exchange rate fluctuations generate significant capital gains and losses, which tend to be strongly pro-cyclical. Probably as a result of these links between the exchange rate and financial structures, the essential advantage of a floating exchange rate—that of allowing authorities to determine monetary policy on the basis of domestic factors—does not always materialize. Contrary to that rule, the experience of both domestic policies and IMF programmes is that under floating rates, authorities tend to use monetary policy to counteract market pressures on exchange rates.

In practice most countries choose intermediate regimes, such as adjustable and crawling pegs, exchange rate bands and dirty floatation. The basic argument for an intermediate exchange rate regime is that it may counteract some of the adverse characteristics of free floating, while maintaining the advantages of utilizing the exchange rate as a policy tool. However, at several stages in the business cycle, such intermediate regimes may lead authorities to use interest rate management as a support for exchange rate management. This may be socially very costly if an inappropriate exchange rate is defended.

As long as no compelling argument exists in favour of one or a few specific alternatives, countries should be free to choose the exchange rate regime that they find preferable. National authorities and IMF surveillance and conditionality should recognize in this case, however, that other policies might have to be adjusted accordingly. In particular, domestic regulation will have to take into account the specific macroeconomic risks that financial intermediaries face under a particular regime. Equally important, complementary capital account regulations may be useful to moderate shocks in either direction. Thus, regulation or controls on inflows may be useful during the boom to avoid reducing interest rates in a pro-cyclical way and thus feeding the expansion of aggregate domestic demand. In turn, controls on outflows during crises may be a useful alternative to high domestic interest rates, which have strong effects on aggregate demand and on the stability of the domestic financial system.

3.5. *The Role of Regional Institutions in the New Architecture*

There are at least three arguments in support of a strong role for regional institutions in the new financial order. The first one is that globalization also entails open regionalism. The growth of intraregional trade and investment flows is, indeed, a striking feature of the ongoing globalization process. This increases macroeconomic linkages and thus the demands for certain services provided by the international financial system which we have analysed in previous sections: surveillance and consultation of macroeconomic policies, and mutual surveillance of each other's mechanisms for the prudential regulation and supervision of the financial system, in particular.

Secondly, it is unclear whether there are strong scale economies to justify international institutions in specific areas. Traditional issues of subsidiarity are thus raised. For example, macroeconomic consultation and surveillance at the world level would certainly be inefficient to manage the externalities of macroeconomic policies among neighbours in the developing world (or even within Europe). Due to differences in legal traditions and the sheer scale of the diseconomies involved, surveillance of national systems for the prudential regulation and supervision of financial sectors, and even the definition of specific minimum standards in this area, may be dealt with more appropriately with the support of regional institutions. Also, although regional and international contagion implies that the management of the largest balance-of-payments crises should be assigned to a single world institution, it is unclear how far we should push this assertion. Strong regional institutions can serve as regional buffers; the postwar Western European experience provides the best example in this regard. Moreover, even in major crises, regional reserve funds can play a role (as the experience of the Andean [now Latin American] Reserve Fund indicates) and, if expanded, could even provide full support to the small and medium-size countries within some regions.

The third argument was already put forward in Section 1: for smaller countries, the access to a broader menu of alternatives to manage a crisis is relatively more important than the 'global public goods' that the largest international organizations provide (e.g. global macroeconomic stability) and upon which they will assume they have little or no influence. Due to their small size, their negotiation power *vis-à-vis* large organizations would be very limited, and their most important defence is, therefore, competition in the provision of financial services from such institutions to them.

There may be a fourth, political economy, argument: countries are likely to take quite different attitudes to the analyses made by international and regional organizations (and to the attached conditionality). They are thus more likely to 'own' the latter, as they feel they have a stronger voice in the analyses made by regional organizations, a fact that will improve rather than reduce effectiveness.

Thus, although the current discussion has underscored the fact that some services provided by international financial institutions, including some clear 'global public goods', are being undersupplied, it would be wrong to conclude from this statement that an increasing supply should come from a few world organizations. Rather, the organizational structure required should, in some cases, have the institutional nature of the networks that provide services required on a complementary basis, while in other instances, it should function as a system of competitive organizations. The provision of services required for the prevention and management of financial crises should probably resemble the first model, but it would also be desirable if various parts of the network compete with each other (e.g. regional reserve funds versus the IMF in the provision of emergency financing to smaller countries).

This implies that the International Monetary Fund of the future should not be viewed as a single, global institution, but rather as the apex of a network of regional and subregional reserve funds. To encourage the development of the latter, incentives could be created by which common reserve funds could have automatic access to IMF financing and/or a share in the allocation of SDRs proportional to their paid-in resources—in other words, contributions to common reserve funds would be treated as equivalent to IMF quotas. As noted, regional reserve funds could provide most of the exceptional financing for smaller countries within a region, but also part of the financing for larger countries, and they could also serve to deter, at least partly, would-be speculators from attacking the currencies of individual countries.

This model should be extended to the provision of macroeconomic consultation and surveillance. This would complement, rather than substitute, regular IMF surveillance. In the area of prudential regulation and supervision, more elaborate systems of regional information and consultation, including the design of specific regional 'minimum standards', can also play a positive role. Again, peer reviews should be part of this system. In the case of debt standstills and workouts, regional mechanisms should at least play a role in assessing the specific regional impacts that they may have.

An institutional framework such as that suggested would have two positive features. First of all, it would bring more stability to the world economy by providing essential services that can hardly be provided by a few international institutions, particularly in the face of a dynamic process of open regionalism. Secondly, from the point of view of the equilibrium of world relations, it would be more balanced than a system based on a few world organizations. This would increase the commitment of less powerful players to abide by rules that contribute to world and regional stability.

4. CONCLUSIONS

This chapter argues that the instability experienced by the international financial system in recent years (and decades) not only reflects characteristics that are inherent in financial markets, but also flaws of the 'narrow' international financial architecture relating to the prevention and management of financial crises. These shortcomings are extremely costly for developing countries. A comprehensive reform is therefore needed, including not only areas in which, according to the author's personal evaluation, there is some degree of agreement, but also those in which significant divergence of opinion remains.

At the outset, the chapter sets forth four essential propositions that must be taken into account in any substantive reform. Firstly, the 'information' problems that generate market instability are largely unsolvable, since financial market behaviour is determined as much by opinions and expectations as by factual information. Accordingly, a greater flow of information is unlikely, by itself, to make financial markets more stable and, indeed, the asymmetry between the sophistication of financial markets and the simple way opinions and expectations are formed could cause greater flows of information to increase instability rather than reduce it. Second, as in any other area, 'self-insurance' is a costly option in international finance. So although preventive policies need to be adopted by developing countries, they are costly and insufficient by themselves. Thirdly, any system would have to rely largely on networks of national institutions, since countries are unlikely to give up financial sovereignty entirely. Finally, no international financial design would be neutral in terms of equilibrium in international relations. This is particularly important for small players, who would prefer more democratic forums with more—rather than fewer—institutions.

The chapter identifies five areas in which some degree of agreement exists. The first of these is the need for industrialized countries to implement expansionary policies during crises. Second, the system requires emergency financing to be made available before international reserves are depleted rather than afterwards; a basic conceptual change *vis-à-vis* the principle of 'fundamental disequilibrium' in the balance of payments adopted at Bretton Woods. Thirdly, the institutional framework in which financial markets operate should be strengthened, so as to provide markets with more information, and adopt common standards in prudential regulation and supervision, together with codes of conduct in several areas. On the other hand, the chapter argues against the excessive optimism that some institutions and authors place on this as the crucial (and even sole) area of reform. In the fourth place, the system needs stronger mechanisms of macroeconomic consultation and surveillance, with adequate developing country representation, which operate during booms as well as during crises. These mechanisms should guarantee the global consistency of the macroeconomic policies of industrialized countries. Fifth, the system also requires the design of internationally sanctioned standstill provisions (orderly debt workouts) so as to ensure an adequate sharing of the burdens of adjustment between countries and private financial agents during crises.

The chapter identifies five areas that must also be dealt with in a comprehensive reform of the current system, on which significant difference of opinion remains. The first of these is the need to have adequate funds available for emergency financing during crises, for which the chapter strongly argues in favour of countercyclical issues (and retirements) of SDRs. Secondly, the chapter argues against extending the scope of IMF conditionality, which has expanded excessively over the past two decades; this should be confined to the macroeconomic areas that were its purview in the past.

Third, the chapter argues strongly in favour of preserving the autonomy of developing countries to manage their capital accounts. Indeed, it claims that, given the inherent instability of financial markets and current flaws in the system, the regulation of capital inflows by developing countries during booms is essential for averting financial crises, and it may even be necessary to adopt other preventive policies as well. Along the same line of reasoning, the chapter also argues for maintaining total autonomy for developing countries to choose their exchange rate regime. Finally, the chapter argues in favour of a leading role for strong regional institutions in the new architecture. In this particular area, competition in the provision of international financial services is particularly important for smaller countries which suggests that more, rather than fewer, institutions are required for a more balanced international financial architecture.

REFERENCES

Agosin, Manuel and Ricardo Ffrench-Davis (2000). Managing capital inflows in Chile. In S. Griffith-Jones, M. F. Montes, and A. Nasution (eds), *Short-Term Capital Flows and Economic Crises*. Oxford University Press, Oxford.

Calvo, Guillermo (1998). Contagion and Sudden Stops. University of Maryland (November), Baltimore. Unpublished.

Camdessus, Michel (1998). Opening address at the Annual Meeting of the Board of Governors of the IMF. *IMF Survey*, 27 (19 October).

Cornia, Giovanni Andrea (1999). Social funds in stabilization and adjustment programmes. UNU/WIDER Research for Action, 48. UNU/WIDER, Helsinki, Finland.

Díaz-Alejandro, Carlos F. (1988). *Trade, Development and the World Economy, Selected Essays of Carlos F. Díaz-Alejandro*. Andrés Velasco (ed.). Basil Blackwell, Oxford.

Eatwell, John (1996). International financial liberalization: The impact on world development. Discussion Paper No. 12. Office of Development Studies, UNDP, New York.

——and Lance Taylor (2000). *Global Finance at Risk: The Case for International Regulation*. The New Press, New York.

ECLAC (1998a). *América Latina y el Caribe: Políticas para mejorar la inserción en la economía mundial*, second version, revised and updated. Fondo de Cultura Económica, Santiago, Chile.

——(1998b). Preventing and handling financial crises. *The International Financial Crisis: An ECLAC Perspective* (LC/G.2040) (October). ECLAC, Santiago, Chile.

Eichengreen, Barry (1999). *Toward a New International Financial Architecture: A Practical Post-Asia Agenda*. Institute for International Economics, Washington, DC.

——(1998). Capital Controls: Capital Idea or Capital Folly? University of California-Berkeley (November), Berkeley. Unpublished.

Feldstein, Martin (1998). Refocusing the IMF. *Foreign Affairs*, 77(2), 20–33.

Fischer, Stanley (1998). Reforming world finance: Lessons from a crisis. *IMF Survey*, Special Supplement (19 October).

Furman, Jason and Joseph E. Stiglitz (1998). Economic crises: Evidence and insights from East Asia. *Brookings Papers on Economic Activity*, 2, 1–114. Brookings Institution, Washington, DC.

Greenspan, Alan (1998). The structure of the international financial system. Remarks at the Annual Meeting of the Securities Industry Association, 5 November, Boca Raton, FL.

Griffith-Jones, Stephany (1998). *Global Capital Flows—Should They Be Regulated?* Macmillan, London.

Grilli, Vittorio and Gian Maria Milesi-Ferretti (1995). Economic effects and structural determinants of capital controls. *IMF Staff Papers*, 42(3) (September).

Group of 7 (1998). *Declaration of G-7 Finance Ministers and Central Bank Governors.* 30 October.

Group of 24 (1998). *Communiqué.* 3 October.

Helleiner, G. K. and Ademola Oyejide (1998). Global economic governance, global negotiations and the developing countries. Background Paper for the *Human Development Report 1999* (December).

IMF (1998). *Toward a Framework for Financial Stability.* IMF, Washington, DC.

IMF Interim Committee (1998). *Statement.* IMF, Washington, DC. 16 April.

Krugman, Paul (1998). Curfews on Capital Flight: What Are the Options? The MIT Press, Cambridge, MA, Mimeo.

Larraín, Guillermo, Helmut Reisen, and Julia von Maltzan (1997). Emerging market risk and sovereign credit ratings. OECD Development Centre Technical Paper, 124 (April). OECD, Paris.

Márquez, Gustavo (1999). Labor Markets and Income Support: What Did We Learn from the Crises? Inter-American Development Bank (IDB), Washington, DC. Unpublished.

Miyazawa, Kiichi (1998). Towards a new international financial architecture. Speech at the Foreign Correspondents Club of Japan. 15 December.

Morgan, J. P. (1998). *World Financial Markets.* New York. 7 October.

Ocampo, José Antonio (1999). International financial reform: The broad agenda. *CEPAL Review*, 69, December. ECLAC, Santiago, Chile.

——and Camilo Tovar (1999). Price-based capital account regulations: The Colombian experience. Financiamiento del Desarrollo Series. ECLAC, Santiago, Chile.

Rodrik, Dani (1998). Who needs capital-account convertibility? In S. Fischer (ed.), *Should the IMF Pursue Capital Account Convertibility?* Princeton Essays in International Finance. Princeton University, 207, Princeton, NJ.

——and Andrés Velasco (1999). Short-term capital flows. Paper prepared for the ABCDE Conference at the World Bank. Mimeo.

Rubin, Robert E. (1999). Remarks of the treasury secretary on reform of the international financial architecture to the school of advanced international studies. *Treasury News*, Office of Public Affairs (21 April).

Stiglitz, Joseph E. and J. Weiss (1981). Credit rationing in markets with imperfect information. *American Economic Review*, 71(3), 393–410.

UNCTAD (1998). *Trade and Development Report 1998.* United Nations, New York and Geneva.

United Nations Task Force (of the Executive Committee on Economic and Social Affairs of the United Nations) (1999). Towards a new international financial architecture. ECLAC, Santiago.

Williamson, John and Molly Mahar (1998). A survey of financial liberalization. *Essays in International Finance*, 211 (November).

Wolfensohn, James D. (1998). The other crisis. Address to the Board of Governors, 6 October. Washington, DC.

Wyplosz, Charles (1999). International financial instability. In Inge Kaul, Isabelle Grunberg, and Marc A. Stern (eds), *Global Public Goods: International Cooperation in the 21st Century.* Oxford University Press, New York.

12

Developing Countries in Global Economic Governance and Negotiation Processes

G. K. HELLEINER

1. INTRODUCTION

The economic dimension of the globalization that is now receiving so much popular and analytical attention is by no means the only one. But it is an extremely important one which has profound implications for public policy. As a global economy emerges, there arises the same need for the performance of certain 'public' functions at the global level as has long been recognized within individual national market economies. Global 'public goods' (defined, strictly, as those that are non-rival and non-excludable in consumption) are at present only weakly supplied, if they are supplied at all, in the global economy. Nor are there yet public sector mechanisms for the support of private activities that create positive externalities (or the control of those that create negative ones) that flow beyond national borders. In the consideration of international or global public policies, some emphasize the degree to which public goods (and bads) derive from or are linked with the existence or potential existence of such international spillovers of positive and negative externalities (e.g. Kaul *et al.* 1999).

Global public goods in the economic and social realms include global macro-economic management so as to reduce the prospect of crisis and instability; the provision of 'firefighting' responses to crises within the global economy; the formulation and policing of rules for international exchange and investment; the provision of some elements of global infrastructure (that typically result from the adoption of a longer time horizon for planning purposes than is typical within markets); research in such socially important spheres as public health and improved technology for poor farmers; and the management of the global commons (oceans, electromagnetic spectrum, etc.).

Beyond the supply of such public goods, governments are also usually expected to undertake efforts to set a floor under levels of human living, and seek to achieve a

This chapter draws significantly, and with permission, upon my earlier paper co-authored with Ademola Oyejide, 'Global Economic Governance, Global Negotiations and the Developing Countries', published in *Globalization with a Human Face, Human Development Report 1999, Background Papers, Vol. 1* (UNDP 1999: 109–22). I am grateful to Ademola Oyejide for his input to that paper and thus to my thinking, and to Deepak Nayyar for his comments on it. Neither is to be held responsible for the contents of this work.

reasonable degree of equity in the distribution of income and wealth; some would characterize such public activities as the provision of public goods, because of their importance to social order. In any case, much 'aid' rhetoric notwithstanding, there is only limited attention to such public activity at the global level.

There is virtually zero prospect of global 'government' within any foreseeable future. Yet, as the full implications of a globalized economy become more apparent, many of the *functions* of government, in particular the supply of public goods and the pursuit of social objectives, will somehow have to be undertaken at the global level. Institutions for the purpose will therefore be constructed; and international rules, laws, and dispute settlement mechanisms will evolve. So, probably, will international private sector codes and standards, introduced on a voluntary basis, and, in some instances, 'hybrid' private–public arrangements to achieve the same ends (Clapp 1998). Government is not the only instrument of economic governance.

Generally, the industrialized (OECD) countries entrust far more responsibility for economic 'governance' activities to private market actors, working voluntarily in their perceived collective interest, than is typically the case in developing countries. The same is true of their approaches to the establishment of international regimes. For instance, in the International Organization for Standardization (ISO), founded in 1946 to promote global standardization and compatibility of products and technical specifications, most of the developing country members (only about half the developing countries are represented at all) are governmental standard-setting organizations whereas OECD countries are mainly represented by organizations that are either private or have heavy private sector involvement (Clapp 1998: 301). Similarly, in the intergovernmental discussion of possible regimes for foreign investment, OECD governments have worked assiduously, under the pressure of heavy financial sector and transnational corporate (TNC) lobbying, to leave as much rule-setting as possible for market participants themselves. That they *can* seek to control and regulate in this sphere, if they really want to, is illustrated by the extraordinary lengths, including heavy pressure on developing countries to cooperate, to which OECD governments have gone to control money laundering and the trade in drugs at the international level.

OECD governments are also typically more responsive to the representations of non-governmental organizations (NGOs) and civil society than are the governments of developing countries. In the emerging discussions of global governance arrangements Northern NGOs are likely to make their voices heard whereas the interests of the people of the developing countries will be represented only by their governments (or, in some instances, by Northern NGOs purporting to speak for the disempowered in the developing countries). How (or whether) to involve non-governmental actors—whether profit-oriented or charitable—in future global governance (or negotiations with such an objective) is a large question, too large for this chapter, the focus of which is upon intergovernmental relations and governance arrangements.

There should be no illusions as to where the bulk of the power in decision-making relating to the global economy is likely to continue to rest—that is, with those countries, firms, and organizations that are economically the strongest. Economic interdependence among nations or firms of unequal strength is inherently asymmetrical in that the weaker party to any relationship with a stronger one is more vulnerable to the effects of its discontinuation (or even the threat thereof). And the world's economic decision-making processes and institutions reflect that asymmetry.

Still, universally recognized (at least at the rhetorical level) democratic principles provide for equal participation of weak and strong individuals in political processes. These principles cannot, of course, be casually translated into a case for UN-style 'one country, one vote' global governance systems. But one can certainly make a strong case for attempting, at the global as at national levels, to construct global governance arrangements that, at least to some degree, reflect democratic principles. Until now, such global economic governance as has existed has been profoundly undemocratic. The peoples of the developing countries, accounting for over 85 per cent of the world's population (and that percentage is rising), are severely under-represented. Decision-making on key global economic issues remains highly concentrated in the major industrial powers; and there still seems to be deep resistance to much relinquishing of their power.

On the basis of experience to date, there is reason to fear that the future evolution of governance arrangements for the global economy will continue to be seriously biased in favour of the interests of industrial countries, particularly the G-7 countries, whose governments and private firms (and even, in some cases, NGOs) now exercise disproportionate influence over global economic affairs. To the extent that future global governance arrangements are undertaken through or in conjunction with the private (or non-governmental) sector, they are likely to be even more biased toward Northern interests and perceptions than they already are in intergovernmental institutions and processes. Above all, there must be concern as to whether emerging global economic governance arrangements will grant sufficient weight to the imperative of global development and the struggle against human poverty (Culpeper and Pestieau 1995; Commission on Global Governance 1995: chapter 4).

There are essentially two kinds of representational problems in the development of appropriate global economic governance processes and arrangements.

1. The central intergovernmental institutions in today's global economy are still those of the major industrial powers (the G-7) and the international financial institutions (the International Monetary Fund, the World Bank group and the Bank for International Settlements) which they control. Although they account for most of the world's people and nearly 50 per cent of its gross output, the developing countries still have only limited influence in the key international economic institutions or in the development of reforms and improvements therein. If new processes and systems are to carry credibility and legitimacy (and therefore be sustainable) they must provide for greater collective influence and power for the developing countries.

2. The poorest people and smallest countries are at particular risk within the emerging global economy; their problems and their potential marginalization therefore require focused consideration at the global level. In this case, the problem is not the system's failure democratically to respond to the needs of the majority so much as its potential failure to protect the rights and welfare of particular 'minorities'. These

'minorities' should be thought of as including the poorest and most vulnerable within the larger and wealthier countries of the international system, as well as those in the poorest and smallest countries.

As developing countries increasingly realize their previously underutilized economic potential and thereby acquire increasing economic strength, they will grow in import-ance to the functioning of the industrial economies and to overall global welfare. Since their economic performance is typically subject to much greater volatility than that of the industrialized countries, the closer integration of developing (and transi-tion) economies into the global system and their greater importance to it will also pose increasing risks—not only to themselves but also (systemically) to the entire global economy. There are bound to be more Mexican, East Asian, and Russian-style crises in the years to come. Thus, the economic and political security of the G-7 countries now rests significantly and increasingly upon events in the rest of the world. From this will undoubtedly flow some efforts, on the part of the industrial countries, to accom-modate the interests of the more economically significant non-G-7 countries, at least those whose problems may create systemic risks. Within the financial sphere, such efforts have already begun. It may prove much more difficult, however, to motivate, within the industrial countries, the full inclusion of the poorest and weakest or effective protection of their interests within efforts to reform the current system of global economic governance.

In Sachs's words, ' . . . developing countries are not trying to overturn Washington's vision of global capitalism, but rather to become productive players in it. Only if they are shut out might they change their minds. But the developed world should not fear dialogue with the developing world. It should join it urgently, for our mutual well-being' (1998a). Again, speaking of the G-7 finance ministers' end-October 1998 statement, he observes that 'for all its advances [it] still reflects a haughty disregard for the rest of the world. There is no talk about negotiation with the poorer countries, no talk about finding a fairer voice for those countries in the new international system. The rest of the world is called on to support the G-7 declarations, not to meet for joint problem-solving. . . . Until the poor are brought into the international financial system with real power, the global economy cannot be stable for long' (Sachs 1998b).

It will be a major challenge not only substantively to envisage and design appro-priate institutional and legal requirements for global economic governance but also to develop effective and legitimate processes—processes that are participatory and fair—to move the world toward its required new governance system. If the global rules system is to be 'harmonized' through deeper integration among national economies within an agreed overall framework, as most now forecast and many advocate, there must be full and reasonably democratic representation as the rules and framework are created and implemented. There can be 'no harmonization without representation'.

This chapter on developing country roles and objectives in global economic gov-ernance is organized around themes in negotiation processes rather than the specific objectives of improved global governance themselves. These objectives are considered, of course, but they are discussed within the context of a discussion of better process.

Section 2 addresses the prospect for fairly short-term and modest reforms, mainly relating to governance and negotiation processes for reform, within the key current multilateral economic institutions—the International Monetary Fund (IMF), the World Bank and the World Trade Organization (WTO). Section 3 focuses upon the importance of the selection of the agenda and the choice of appropriate forums and processes for moving toward longer-term and more fundamental reforms in the global economic governance system. In Section 4 the particular problems of the smallest and poorest countries in the global economic system are considered. Section 5 addresses the potential for improved developing country cooperation within existing systems. There follows a brief conclusion.

2. REFORMING TODAY'S KEY INSTITUTIONS

In official perceptions, the weakest dimension of current global economic governance arrangements—and that which is therefore now receiving the most official attention—is in the realm of international finance. Difficulties created by volatile short-term private capital flows and financial crises in developing countries, the evident need for further supervision of private international financial institutions and markets, and the growing impact of turmoil in international financial markets upon national and global economic performance, have combined to elicit intense discussion of the governance requirements (or architecture) for a stable global financial system. This in turn has engendered widespread reconsideration of the roles of the existing multilateral institutions, the creation or strengthening of new ones, and intensified turf struggles between the IMF, World Bank, WTO, Bank for International Settlements (BIS) and the International Organization of Securities Commissions (IOSCO), among others, for jurisdiction and influence. There is also more active discussion of the possible future role of stronger regional financial institutions—not only development banks but also monetary associations (Mistry 1998; Ocampo, Chapter 11, this volume; UN Task Force 1999).

The central multilateral institutions concerned with the overall functioning of the global economy and the global monetary and financial system are the IMF and the World Bank Group. The representation of the majority of the world's population within these institutions is particularly weak. Formal voting power therein is determined by a formula assigning primary weight to economic strength with the result that their governance is, by far, the least democratic of the major multilateral bodies. Whereas developed countries, as defined by the World Bank, account for only 17 per cent of voting strength in the United Nations (and in the Global Environmental Facility), 24 per cent in the WTO, and 34 per cent in the International Fund for Agricultural Development (IFAD), they account for 61–62 per cent in the World Bank and IMF (Woods 1998).

Decision-making in international organizations is often done by 'consensus' rather than via formal voting, but even then the underlying voting power influences outcomes profoundly. Moreover, key appointments and staffing decisions/practices, which are fundamental to effective governance, are also somewhat problematic. By custom, for instance, the president of the World Bank is appointed by the United States; and the managing director of the IMF has always been a European. Although there may have been a rationale for such disproportionate voting arrangements and undemocratic management selection procedures within these institutions at the time of their foundation, it is difficult to defend them today—particularly when both institutions press borrowing countries to improve their own governance via conditions on their lending.

Far as the IMF and World Bank are from reasonably democratic governance, they at least incorporate *some* degree of developing country representation and participation. But, in the various meetings of industrial countries on economic and financial matters in the G-7/G-8 Economic Summits; the meetings of G-7 and G-10 finance ministers; the meetings of central bank governors in the BIS; and the various committees of the OECD, there has been virtually no developing country representation. Within the past few years, the BIS has invited the participation of several of the larger and more significant developing countries, and the OECD has incorporated Mexico and Korea into its membership; but these are marginal changes, in the nature of symbolic gestures, rather than substantive changes in the nature of these organizations.

It is probably more significant that several emerging market economies have been invited to participate in the Financial Stability Forum (from 1998 onwards) and the new Group of Twenty (from 1999 onwards), both of which were initiatives of the G-7 to carry forward the international discussions of financial architecture, outside the Bretton Woods institutions. (Some fifteen emerging market countries were also included in the unilateral, *ad hoc*, and short-lived initiative of the US Treasury in 1998 to create a Group of Twenty-Two for similar purposes.) Increased developing country representation in the key current discussions of international monetary and financial reform is to be welcomed. Both of these initiatives, however, are primarily directed at the prevention and resolution of *systemic* financial crises, rather than the much wider range of reform issues in the financial system that require attention, and are flawed in other ways as well.

In particular, the new G-20, initially chaired by the Canadian finance minister, is severely flawed in that it contains no representation either from the poorest and smallest developing countries or from the European 'like-minded' countries (the Nordics and Dutch) who, on the basis of prior experience, might be expected periodically to speak on their behalf. (Developing country members are: Argentina, Brazil, China, India, Mexico, South Africa, and South Korea. Russia, Saudi Arabia, Turkey, and Australia are also members. The others are the G-7, the EU, and the IMF/Bank, which is counted as one.) Presumably, this is because the poorest and smallest are unlikely ever to constitute any systemic threat. Nor are there any mechanisms for reporting or accountability to the broader international community, such as the constituency system provides within the IMF and World Bank, or provisions for non-governmental inputs or transparency. As discussed below, both the agenda and the forum in which it is discussed and negotiated are important to the eventual outcome of such international initiatives. It is unfortunate that this potentially important initiative is so narrow in its scope, less than fully representative, and lacking in accountability to the full global community.

The concerns of the smallest and poorest countries are more likely to be heard and discussed in the forthcoming UN conference on financing and development, in which participation and the agenda are much broader. They are also discussed in the periodic international (UNCTAD) conferences on the least developed countries. Unfortunately these UN-sponsored meetings carry limited influence in developed countries' finance (or trade) ministries.

Reforms in IMF/World Bank governance are badly needed. It is unlikely, however, that those countries that now exercise disproportionate power and influence within these institutions will give them up lightly. In the medium term, there will have to be efforts at internal reforms *within* the current institutions and systems, and *within* the constraints of current power relationships. There is much that can and should be done in this respect.

Improvement of institutional accountability is an obvious priority in the reform of current international governance arrangements. Powerful international organizations are fallible. To ensure accountability (and effectiveness) they require a modicum of transparency, independent evaluation, and (ombudsman-like) mechanisms for protection of the weak against abuse of their power.

Within the World Bank, there is an independent Operations Evaluation Department (OED) which assesses performance of projects and programmes on a regular basis and publishes its reports. In 1993, the Bank also established an inspection panel, which is mandated to investigate local citizens' complaints concerning harm done because of violations of Bank policies or procedures (and when agreed by the Board); thirteen cases have so far been filed from eight developing countries. The panel's operations have frequently been impeded by politicization and delay in the Bank's Board, not least by the governments of developing countries; clearly it is not as independent as it needs to be to play its role effectively, and its future role remains uncertain. The World Bank is also at present embarking, on a pilot basis, on a new form of 'partnership' relationship with some of the poorest countries to which it lends (and to which bilateral aid donors contribute), with the borrowing countries more clearly 'taking the lead'. (Similar aspirations have long been agreed by bilateral donors in the Development Assistance Committee of the OECD, although their translation into altered practices has lagged [Helleiner 2000]). This initiative receives firm support from developing countries. Its progress itself deserves careful and independent monitoring and evaluation.

In the IMF, however, purportedly for prudential and security reasons, there are traditions of greater secrecy, internal discipline, and centralization of power. Transparency has increased somewhat in recent years but there is still no permanent institution for independent evaluation of IMF performance. In 1996 its Executive Board initiated an *ad hoc* 'pilot' project on external evaluation which generated an independent (external) evaluation of its Enhanced Structural Adjustment Facility (ESAF) programmes in 1997–98. Tellingly, this proved far more critical than a previous internal review had been. Independent assessments of IMF surveillance and research activities in 1999 also generated criticisms which internal reviews had missed (or suppressed). But these have only been modest first steps. A recent independent consideration of transparency and evaluation issues in the IMF by a committee of experienced Washington hands concluded that the IMF 'should establish a permanent evaluation office and endow it with a maximum of independence' (Polak *et al.* 1998: 15); and it is difficult to understand why this was not done long ago.

As far as 'partnership' initiatives are concerned, the IMF also lags behind the Bank. Defending its more heavy-handed approaches, it argues the need for speed in responding to crises and the continuing need for a 'short leash' (i.e. stringent conditionality for its lending) on critical matters of monetary and fiscal discipline. At the same time the IMF has increasingly been imposing conditions on its lending that relate to structural and longer-term developmental issues, and most recently even to poverty reduction, none of which has ever previously been within its mandate, expertise, or experience. Paradoxically, it emphasizes at the same time that the country stabilization and adjustment programmes it supports are their 'own'. When slippages and interruptions occur, IMF staff tend to attribute them to national-level deficiencies rather than to inappropriate programme design or limited local ownership. There are obviously profound differences of perception on these issues. There is also intense debate as to the proper role of the IMF in developing countries *vis-à-vis* the World Bank and bilateral aid donors. Many, both in developing countries and in the industrial world, would prefer to see the IMF return to a narrower role, focused on short-term balance-of-payments problems and their resolution, and reduced IMF effort to play a development role for which it is not suited. Absent an ombudsman, independent evaluations, an agreed role, or a power structure more responsive to developing country concerns, the IMF seems doomed to continuing controversy and hence probably declining influence and respect.

As a young and still small entity, the WTO is not, of itself, so powerful a player as the international financial institutions (Krueger 1998). It has been argued, for instance, that, even in respect of pressure to amend trade policies, African countries at present probably have less to fear from the WTO than from the IMF and World Bank (Elbadawi and Helleiner 1998). Moreover, its formal voting structure and its dispute settlement system both allow, in principle, for greater input from its smaller and poorer members, and create the potential for more equitable outcomes for them—if *only* they can get their collective act sufficiently 'together' to realize the opportunities.

In reality, however, the capacity of many, perhaps most, developing countries to participate effectively in the WTO system—to take advantage of their rights and to defend their interests, indeed even to meet their obligations in the WTO—is very much in doubt. The WTO is a member-driven organization in the sense that, since it has no permanent executive board, delegates from member countries are actively involved in its day-to-day activities. If they are not, their interests are ignored. A 'continuous dialogue' takes place in the WTO. It is estimated, for instance, that the continuous WTO process involves at least 45 meetings per week in Geneva (Blackhurst 1998). The requirements for effective participation place an enormous strain on resource-constrained smaller and poorer countries.

Most of the smaller and poorer developing countries are either not represented at all or not adequately represented at WTO headquarters in Geneva and hence cannot be part of the consensus-building consultations that go on inside and outside the formal meetings. When they are represented, their staffing is weak and clearly inadequate for handling the ever-increasing complexity of issues and the rising number of meetings and obligations characterizing the WTO process. A recent study of this issue suggests that almost 60 per cent of the total number of developing country members of the WTO suffer from one handicap or another that renders their effective participation suboptimal (Michalopoulos 1998).

Because of the increasing 'legalization' of trade and investment issues and disputes (Ostry 1998), WTO procedures are often extremely difficult for poorer countries to utilize effectively. As the WTO grows and its mandate quite possibly expands to include investment, competition, and even environmental and labour issues, its role in the governance of the global economy is likely to increase in relative importance. Because of its basic structure, developing countries have a chance to influence its evolution—its governing structures, its rules, its financing, etc.—but such an outcome is obviously far from assured. Developing countries need to plan together how better to exercise their potential influence in the future of the WTO.

The WTO's predecessor, the GATT, was a fairly secretive institution with its major decisions, despite its formal structures, disproportionately influenced by the major industrial powers. The less than fully transparent nature of the negotiating process also contributed to the disenfranchisement of the developing countries. Often, the most critical issues were discussed and 'resolved' in meetings between the director-general and a limited group of the more powerful countries. As was the case in most of the earlier rounds, decision-making in the Uruguay Round negotiations was 'pyramidal' in structure in that the major trading countries (those at the 'top') had implicit, but nonetheless effective, veto power over the negotiations' overall outcome (Winham 1998). Thus, through various informal consultations, the larger developed countries agreed among themselves with respect to the major issues and presented the results to other members, essentially for ratification. In particular over the last two years of the Uruguay Round negotiations, the decisive voices were those of the US and EU.

These GATT traditions seem to have been carried forward, by the developed countries, into their plans for the functioning of the WTO in its own first round of global negotiations. But the 'deeper integration' which is now on the WTO negotiating agenda has generated greater public concern in the North (and, to some degree, also in the South) and greater challenge from many governments of the developing countries. At the same time, more developing countries appear to have realized the costs of their failure to be sufficiently prepared, involved, and united in the Uruguay Round negotiations under the GATT, and the creation of the WTO. Many of them not only view the outcome of those negotiations as fundamentally harmful to their interests but also now recognize their greater potential for influence in future global negotiations under the WTO.

Developing countries prepared more carefully, individually and collectively, for the so-called 'Millennium Round' of negotiations, which was to have been launched in Seattle in November 1999, than they had ever done before. Roughly half of the substantive proposals for inclusion in the proposed text of the Seattle framework document came this time—and for the first time—from developing country governments. They included significant and detailed proposals for alteration of existing regimes, notably that on intellectual property. In this case, the developing countries called for changes in the previously negotiated provisions so as to recognize the rights of those who cultivate traditional crop varieties; prohibit the patenting of life forms or biological processes; bring WTO provisions on intellectual property rights into line with the International Convention on Bio-diversity and the International Undertaking on Plant Genetic Resources; ensure access to essential medicines at reasonable cost; and provide more time for developing countries to bring their domestic laws into compliance with WTO obligations. It is noteworthy that some of the most important of these proposals for reform originated with relatively minor trading countries who had never previously been active in such negotiations; in this case, for instance, Kenya played a particularly important role. At the same time, the developing countries were vigorous and united in their opposition to proposals from the industrial countries for the addition of such new areas for negotiation in the WTO as labour and environmental standards, and investment.

The result was that very little had been agreed prior to the Seattle ministerial meeting. In such circumstances, the probability of failure was already high, before anyone even arrived there. NGO protests and demonstrations in Seattle were certainly noteworthy; and there can be little doubt that NGOs' demands for greater transparency and public accountability on the part of governmental negotiators (in whatever forum) and the WTO secretariat will influence future negotiation processes. But it would be stretching the facts to suggest, as some have done, that these public protests themselves 'derailed' the WTO negotiation processes. The negotiations were already in serious trouble. Nor were North–South disagreements the only, or even, in the end, the most important, source of this trouble. Disagreement among the US, EU, and Japan, particularly over approaches to the agricultural sector, was probably the single most important contributor to the collapse of the Seattle meeting. But the increased activism of the developing countries within the WTO, already signalled earlier in the year by the bitter struggle over its leadership, will certainly have to be reckoned with in the evolution of global governance arrangements for trade and trade-related economic policies in the future. Cosmetic devices, such as the launch of bargaining rounds in the developing world (as in Uruguay) or the effort to label the next one as a 'development round' (as some now suggest), are unlikely to satisfy.

One of the early casualties of the current difficulties in reaching agreement among WTO-member governments is likely to be its present overall system of governance. Some more efficient system of representative decision-making will probably have to be devised for a membership organization of such unwieldy size and such vast and complex a mandate. Failing its development, whatever its formal structures, WTO decision-making may revert to previous 'Green Room' practices in which the main players exercise inappropriate and disproportionate influence behind closed doors, or be seen as reverting to them, or both. To maintain equity in representation and improve overall transparency of processes will be major challenges as the required new system is developed.

Another casualty should be the newly minted (Uruguay Round) concept of the 'single undertaking' in which member countries are required to agree on (and abide by) the *entire* set of rules that is multilaterally negotiated within the WTO and to continue to do so in all its future negotiations and activities. More flexible arrangements for joining and/or opting out of particular subagreements within the overall organization, while maintaining a 'fundamental core' of tenets and practices to which all subscribe—arrangements analogous to those in the later stages of the GATT—would be more conducive to future agreements among so large and so varied a membership.

It would also be helpful, at an early stage, to declare poverty reduction and the development of the lowest-income countries as among the fundamental objectives of the WTO. At present, even though its charter formally commits it to poverty alleviation and the promotion of sustainable development, these are not generally seen as primary WTO objectives; but they should be, and WTO decisions and practices should, in future, reflect them. Such changes, as long as they go far beyond cosmetics, could go some distance in restoring flagging developing country confidence in the WTO.

3. THE CHOICE OF AGENDA AND FORUMS FOR DISCUSSION AND NEGOTIATION

It is obvious that the choice of the agenda for international discussion and negotiation, whether inside or outside the existing major multilateral economic institutions, is fundamental to eventual decisions as to the arrangements—rules, institutions, practices—for global economic governance. It is equally clear that the countries and private interests with the greatest economic power have always had disproportionate influence over international agenda-setting. The drive towards the universal liberalization of capital accounts and the amendment of the IMF's Articles of Agreement to facilitate this objective, in the second half of the 1990s, suited the interests of the Northern banks and other financial institutions, and the governments that represent them. There was certainly no groundswell of worldwide or democratic upset or even concern over the fact that many governments, particularly in developing countries, found it socially useful to maintain some direct or indirect controls over international private capital flows. Similarly, the successful US push to include services, investment measures, and intellectual property in the Uruguay Round of the GATT, and hence in the WTO (and, later, electronic commerce in the WTO), did not stem from a global consensus that there were issues in these spheres that urgently required multilateral action. It was the product of US perceptions of its own national economic interests and, more particularly, the pressures of lobbies representing the American telecommunications, financial, and pharmaceutical industries.

The management and staff of the major multilateral institutions, notably those of the IMF and World Bank, have also carried influence in agenda-setting. Different presidents of the World Bank and managing directors of the IMF have led their institutions in quite different directions. The composition, background and training of the staff of these institutions (now including the WTO) certainly also influences institutional perceptions as to which issues should be on the international agenda and how they should be approached. In all of the major international economic institutions, the primary qualification for professional employment is postgraduate training in economics on the North American model. This imparts a particular (liberal, economistic) slant to their analysis of international issues which are not always themselves totally 'economic' in their nature. Imagine, as a mental experiment, what agendas and solutions would arise from these institutions were the majority of their staff trained in other disciplines and/or in Japan, China, India, or even France.

Agendas have also, from time to time (and increasingly frequently) been influenced by organized not-for-profit pressure groups, non-governmental organizations (NGOs), that have developed specialized interest and expertise in particular areas, for example the preservation of the global environment or, more recently, poor countries' international debt. Some argue that such groups are likely to become more influential at the international level as their capacity for global organization increases through e-mail and the travel/telecommunications revolution. Since their only weapons are information and persuasion, however, it seems unlikely that they will acquire any more influence over the global agenda than they have at present in democratically governed countries (where it is usually fairly marginal). As emphasized throughout this chapter, the world is far from democratically governed. It is therefore even less likely that they will have more than marginal influence over the main global agenda. Such influence as there is will continue to derive from Northern NGOs' influence over Northern governments, rather than from genuinely democratic pressures from the globe's peoples upon global institutions that are accountable to them.

The choice of the forum for discussion and negotiation of international economic issues is also fundamentally important to the determination of outcomes. This has repeatedly been the experience in the past, for example, in respect of investment and trade regimes (which we discuss below); and it is likely to be the case in forthcoming discussions and negotiation of a new international financial architecture. In no sphere has this been more dramatically evident than in approaches to a global regime for investment, and, in particular, for transnational corporations and foreign direct investment. There has been fairly universal agreement that this is an important agenda item; but there is little consensus as to what to do.

In the 1970s, when negotiations were based in the United Nations system, they focused on a 'code of conduct' for TNCs, which was to set restraints on some of their activities. Parallel discussions took place in the UNCTAD on 'rules and principles' governing restrictive business practices in the international arena, and on another code of conduct on the transfer of technology. In each case, developing countries' concerns were assiduously advanced. Industrial countries, on the defensive, worked to keep the proposed codes and rules legally non-binding and to limit their impact; and, of course, they succeeded.

The recent discussions of the proposed Multilateral Agreement on Investment (MAI), within the OECD, were utterly different—not so much, as some suggest, because of a global change of approach to TNCs as because of the common interests of OECD members as home bases for TNCs. The draft MAI set out to protect foreign owners of capital, in a wide variety of forms and activities (not just foreign direct investors), from the 'distorting' policies of governments. It sought national treatment for *all* foreign 'investment', even prior to establishment within a country. Yet, it did *not* seek to impose any rules or limits to the degree to which national governments might favour or subsidize foreign investors. Its draft provisions proved too restrictive upon national sovereignty even for some OECD governments (notably that of France). They would never have been acceptable to most developing countries (Ganesan 1998; Agosin 1998). Investment issues (at least some of them) now may land within the jurisdiction of the WTO, where no doubt developing countries' concerns will have some influence. (In the meantime, UNCTAD was asked to undertake research on developing countries' potential interests in a multilateral framework for foreign investment, and on the developmental implications of foreign direct investment.)

More fundamentally, the globalization of business activity will eventually require a globalized system of accounting, audit, and disclosure standards; corporate taxation; competition laws and the like. Current disputes over transfer pricing, tax revenue-sharing, and the role of tax havens are a harbinger of the multilateral negotiations that will be required to usher in an agreed global corporate tax system. The problems created for tax authorities by mobile capital and globalized firms are already widely recognized and will soon have to be systematically addressed. No doubt they would be best addressed within the context of an overall assessment of the need for 'global taxes' to finance global public goods and other global objectives (Mendez 1992) but they need not await such an overall approach and they probably will not. Similarly, current debates, within the WTO and elsewhere, over the appropriate use of anti-dumping duties and the link between trade and competition policies are a foretaste of the inevitable future negotiation of a global competition regime for transnational corporations. Where these matters are addressed will again influence the outcomes.

The choice of forum will similarly be extremely important to current negotiations over future architecture for the international financial system. Some indication of how important this choice may be can be gleaned from the major and substantive differences in approach to future capital account regimes, as between the IMF and the UNCTAD. Dominated by G-7 governments and financial interests, the IMF has pressed for capital account liberalization not only via its technical advice but also through a proposed amendment to its Articles of Agreement that would add this objective to its basic purposes and expand its jurisdiction to this end. It has done so despite continued expressions of reservation and caution on the part of the G-24 and other developing country spokespersons (Helleiner 1998). In the UNCTAD, on the other hand, where developing country interests are better represented, the risks of capital account liberalization and the potentially important role for capital account taxes and controls have always been highlighted (UNCTAD 1998 and 1995). Only in the aftermath of the Asian crisis have IMF positions begun to converge toward UNCTAD and developing country ones; and, of course, significantly different orientations remain. There are also longer-term jurisdictional issues to be resolved—as between, for instance, the IMF, World Bank, WTO (in financial services), BIS, IOSCO, a possible new World Financial Authority (as suggested by Eatwell and Taylor 1998, and Kaufman 1998, among others), and even the UN itself. Most *immediate* is the question as to the appropriate *process* for moving the current global financial system towards some new agreed architecture.

Since the IMF and World Bank's voting and power structures are so unbalanced, they would certainly *not* be the developing countries' venue of first choice; nor would their Interim or Development Committees which, in any case, have been discredited as serious negotiating or decision-making bodies. On the other hand, they would not like to see the G-7 or the OECD or the BIS, in which their voices are scarcely heard at all, become the prime *loci* for key decisions on the future of the international monetary and financial system.

In 1998, as noted above, the US government unilaterally initiated a discussion of international financial issues (notably increasing accountability and transparency, strengthening national financial systems, and managing international financial crises) among G-7 countries and a selection (by the US) of fifteen middle-income countries, together constituting the so-called Group of Twenty-Two. Apart from its limited aspirations and timetable, the G-22 was not fully representative—it totally excluded the poorest and smallest, not to speak of such 'like-minded' or 'middle powers' as the Scandinavians, Dutch, and Australians. Moreover, disproportionate influence within it was wielded by the US Treasury. A more representative and legitimate forum for such negotiation and discussion was urgently required.

One possibility that has been actively discussed, indeed formally recommended by the G-24, is the re-creation of some version of the *ad hoc* Committee of Twenty on 'Reform of the International Monetary System and Related Issues' of the 1970s. This committee was made up of ten developing countries and ten industrial countries, reflecting the (then) constituencies of the IMF's Executive Board. It functioned through a Committee of Deputies (senior national officials), a supervisory Bureau, and seven Technical Groups on particular topics (for a brief summary, see Mohammed 1996). In the current context, because of the breadth of its required mandate, it would not be appropriate for such a committee to function solely as a committee of the IMF's Board, as it did then. What is required is an intergovernmental Task Force answerable and reporting not only to the IMF but also to the World Bank, the BIS, IOSCO and the Economic and Social Council (ECOSOC) of the UN. Now, as then, it could be helpful to have parallel unofficial research on and discussion of the key issues by academics and other knowledgeable persons, as was done in the so-called 'Bellagio group' in the 1970s. Now, however, one would require much more input into such an unofficial group from the developing countries.

The terms of reference for such an intergovernmental Task Force and the objects of focus for its Technical Subcommittees are suggested by the current problems and issues in the international monetary, financial and trading systems. In broad terms, the mandate would be to find improved means for the governance of the newly globalized economy. More specifically, it would seek to provide an appropriate system for global macroeconomic management, including provision for adequate liquidity and emergency responses; a stable system of development finance for all developing countries and for development-related research; an agreed framework of rules and obligations for the conduct of international trade and investment (including provision for prudential regulation of international financial markets and institutions), with a capacity for their effective and equitable application; and, most important of all, provision of the key elements of human development for all of the world's population. The topics it would most urgently need to address in the financial system include, as suggested by the G-24, the following:

(1) the capacities and modalities of the international monetary and development finance institutions to prevent, and to respond in a timely and effective manner to, crises induced by large-scale capital movements;
(2) the appropriateness of the conditions prescribed by these institutions to deal with such crises;
(3) the equitable sharing of the costs of post-crisis financial stabilization among private creditors, borrowers, and governments;
(4) the more effective surveillance of the policies of major industrialized countries affecting key international monetary and financial variables, including capital flows;
(5) the strengthening of social safety nets as integral elements of stabilization and adjustment programmes to protect the most vulnerable segments of the population;
(6) the increased representation and participation of developing countries at the decision-making level of international financial institutions to properly reflect developing countries' growing role in the world economy, including through the revision of the bases determining the voting power in these institutions; and,
(7) the need to enhance the role of SDRs in the international monetary system to achieve greater stability, particularly in view of the prospect of an emerging polarization around three major currencies.

(G-24 communiqués, 3 October 1998 and 14 April 1998; Caracas Declaration, 9 February 1998)

These seemingly reasonable and good-faith public proposals from the principal developing country group within the international financial institutions have been met by the G-7, as has been seen, with a much more narrowly focused 'Group of Twenty' (to replace the US-sponsored G-22). The G-20 is again less than fully representative and accountable to no one; it is therefore unlikely to move very far in the direction of effective and appropriate global economic governance arrangements. What is required is a broader overall agenda for the reform and/or creation of global economic institutions and systems of economic governance; and a credible, accountable and fully representative process for negotiating the details.

As long as developing countries acquiesce in the decisions made by today's most influential global economic actors as to the agenda for change in the way in which international economic affairs are conducted and/or the forums in which such change is negotiated, they will continue to face inequitable and otherwise unsatisfactory outcomes. There have recently been some signs of greater activism on the part of developing countries, both in the Bretton Woods institutions and in the WTO. That this increased activism has not as yet been to much effect reflects the current dispensation of international economic influence and power. If such activism continues, however, there is a real prospect that, within the context of an ever more integrated and interdependent global economy, today's major powers will eventually be forced to pay more attention and to respond more appropriately to it.

4. THE PARTICULAR PROBLEMS OF THE SMALLEST AND POOREST COUNTRIES

It is sometimes argued that small countries derive exceptional benefits from their interaction with the international economy and, to some degree, this is true. On the other hand, the smaller and poorer members of the international community are typically much more open to global influences and vulnerable to external bullying than larger countries. At the same time, they obviously have much less influence in overall global events. Their vulnerability to external shock and their inability to influence the rules of the global economic system or the manner in which they are implemented can involve them in severe costs. To portray them as disproportionate 'winners' from international exchange within the global economy is therefore a gross oversimplification (Helleiner 1996; see also Commonwealth Secretariat 1997). Small and poor countries, like others, must and can find ways to interact with the global economy so as to maximize their gains and minimize their risks.

As they do so, they typically experience severe difficulties in making their voices heard within the international community. Their small size and limited incomes make it difficult for them to finance diplomatic and/or legal representation in international negotiations, conferences or other events. Their interests are therefore frequently defended only within larger constituencies. Even then, however, their interests inevitably tend to be relatively neglected. In the IMF and World Bank, for instance, one executive director seeks to represent twenty-three African countries. Within such large 'constituencies', representatives of individual countries must patiently await their turn for actual representation in decision-making circles. In the WTO, as has been seen, most of the smallest and poorest are not represented at all.

In any case, the small professional cadre of a small, poor country is typically fully occupied in the management of national affairs and has little opportunity for detailed involvement in multilateral economic diplomacy. Those who represent the small and poor countries are typically working 'on their own', without support or instruction from national capitals. These countries' role in the negotiation of future rules, institutions, and arrangements is therefore likely to be quite limited. Moreover, the attention and expertise directed by international institutions towards the problems of the smallest and poorest of their members, while perhaps showing some positive per capita 'small country effects', tend to be left to their most junior and least experienced staff. Such staff, apart from their other deficiencies, are typically unwilling and/or unable to make on-the-spot discretionary deviations from 'normal' headquarters instructions and practices in response to country-specific circumstances when they are needed: this can impart undue rigidity to national-level negotiations with inevitable consequent frustration and annoyance on the part of the countries concerned.

Negotiations in the Uruguay Round of the GATT illustrate well the enormous difficulties encountered by smaller and poorer countries, particularly the African ones. Only a limited number of these countries, those few able to maintain a permanent presence in Geneva, managed to play any role at all. (Of the twenty-nine 'least developed countries' that belong to the WTO—of a total of 48—only twelve had missions in Geneva, and these were required to service a number of other international organizations as well (Michalopoulos 1998: 9)). Most African countries were unable to participate effectively in the negotiations. Constrained by inadequate understanding of the complex issues being negotiated and lacking access to in-depth analysis of how the various agreements might affect them, they could not effectively defend their national interests (Ohiorhenuan 1998).

Factors limiting the effective participation of African countries were not limited to those associated with their Geneva-based negotiators but extended back to their capitals as well. In particular, there were typically few, if any, effective interministerial consultative mechanisms in their national capitals for debating the issues, reaching agreement, and sending instructions to Geneva. Erratic and sporadic communication characterized the weak connections between national negotiators in Geneva and their principals in the capitals. The few instructions that came through often lacked specificity since they were usually not based on detailed analysis. The contrast between the weak back-up for these countries' trade negotiators and the batteries of trade lawyers, economists, industry specialists, and lobbyists surrounding OECD members' negotiators could hardly be more stark.

As indicated earlier, the WTO's mandate already covers a wide variety of complex issues. The results of the GATT's Uruguay Round and its creation of the WTO clearly imposed on the smaller and poorer developing countries more obligations than had any previous GATT rounds. In particular, these countries acquired substantive legal obligations to fulfil with respect to a large number of agreements ranging from agriculture to intellectual property, and only a limited 'transition period' in which to do so before facing potential penalties for shortfalls in their required reforms. In addition to these, they were to comply with approximately 160 notification requirements under the WTO agreements, failure in the implementation of which in turn would affect their substantive rights.

It is difficult to imagine that African governments, let alone civil society, could have had any sense of 'ownership' of the results of the Uruguay Round. Yet now the WTO offers technical assistance, when it does so at all, to assist these countries to implement the rules systems that they had no role in drafting and that, in some cases, for example, the intellectual property regime, are costly to implement and inappropriate to their circumstances!

To participate effectively in the WTO process, any country needs to have, in Geneva, officials with the requisite technical skills, knowledge, and experience of how the WTO process works. These officials would also have to be supported by the provision of timely and adequate technical analysis, advice, and directives from their country's capital. Furthermore, the country needs to have the institutional framework and administrative support structure for meeting its WTO obligations and, in particular, for carrying out its notification requirements. For virtually all the smaller and poorer

WTO members, paucity of human and material resources and a limited national knowledge-base constitute real constraints on their ability to be effective members. These are key areas in which technical and other forms of assistance are required (Oyejide 1997; Ohiorhenuan 1998). In particular, many of the smaller and poorer countries badly need assistance for human resources training and for developing institutional support within their countries. They also need assistance in building negotiating capacity, including the provision of policy analysis and identification of national interests and policy options.

Failure adequately to involve all the parties in the Uruguay Round resulted in gross underestimation of the problems now being encountered in many developing countries that are short on relevant legal expertise, as they seek to implement the agreement. Dispatching teams of Northern lawyers to redraft the trade and intellectual property laws of African countries is hardly a realistic solution. What is required is a careful, deliberate, and participatory reconsideration of many elements of the Marrakesh agreement, not least those relating to transition periods and the obligations of the least-developed countries. In particular, it seems clear that, with minor exceptions, the 'more favourable treatment' of developing country members promised at the launch of the Uruguay Round negotiations and finding expression in the WTO agreements on transition periods, differences in threshold levels for certain obligations, and offers of technical assistance, rather than substantive exemptions, was too haphazardly and arbitrarily put together and is ineffective. The length of these transition periods and the threshold levels for various obligations are not linked to specific and objective indicators of levels of development, or any considered assessment of what institution-building, strengthening of administrative capacity or other resources, or duration of time would be required to bring the relevant developing countries up to the point at which their 'favourable' treatment might appropriately end.

The smallest and poorest countries (and firms) are also at an enormous disadvantage when they attempt to *play* by the agreed 'rules of the game' for trade and investment, whatever these rules may be. In principle, rules systems and pre-agreed dispute settlement mechanisms should help to protect the weak against bullying by the strong. In practice, however, such protection is not always realized. Today's rules systems are complex and their implementation requires legal inputs that are expensive. The mere threat of US or European anti-dumping action, for instance, is enough to discourage small exporters without the wherewithal to launch a legal defence. Similarly, when large countries breach the agreed rules at the expense of the small and poor, the cost of a legal challenge may exceed the financial capacities of the latter (or, in some cases, even the relevant trade losses).

Within many national jurisdictions, the legal rights of those who are unable to afford legal costs are protected by publicly-funded provision of legal aid. Analogous international provisions are required to permit international rules systems to function effectively and, in particular, to protect small and poor countries against bullying by the strong in the areas of international trade and investment.

In the context of the WTO and its dispute settlement mechanism, various options have been suggested to protect more effectively the interests of the smaller and poorer countries (Whalley 1989; Blackhurst 1998). One is for the WTO to have a larger and more activist Secretariat, in which the smaller and poorer countries are adequately represented, and in which the strengthened Secretariat is endowed with the power to monitor and investigate violations of WTO rules, and to initiate dispute settlement cases against offending members. Not surprisingly, such major reforms of the WTO win little support from its more powerful members and are therefore not in prospect. A second suggested option which has, to a degree, already been acted upon is the establishment of an international legal advisory service to help the smaller and poorer members protect their interests in the WTO system. In 1999, a small 'centre' of this type was launched, with the financial support of a consortium of developing countries and the more progressive aid donors, in Geneva. Its efficacy is obviously still untested but it seems unlikely that it can make more than a minor dent in the (quite major) problem. A third suggestion, recognizing the inability of this group of countries to support an adequate level and number of representatives in Geneva, is that the WTO should itself provide funding to enable each country to keep a minimum number of professionals working full-time on WTO activities. This has not found much support either.

As already noted, analogous problems for the smallest and poorest countries are found in the international financial institutions (IFIs). Since these countries' problems are unlikely to pose 'systemic threats', it is implicitly argued, there is no need to provide them with special crisis finance, such as has been developed for potential crises in 'more important' countries or to involve them seriously in discussion of international financial reforms. It is not sufficiently appreciated that small and poor countries are also vulnerable to volatile flows of private capital and they too can experience major financial crises requiring external support. Even if the absolute size of such flows is small, their repercussions for small and poor countries can be enormous. Facilities for 'exceptional finance' to assist such countries in times of crisis have not been created, presumably because they are not systemically needed (Helleiner, 1999). At the same time, these countries are uniquely dependent upon IFIs for finance, and therefore more vulnerable than others to the imposition of their (often inappropriate) conditions and advice.

Conceivably, increased transparency and the use of the internet could be disproportionately helpful to the smallest and poorest countries in the global economy. Some of their problems might also be tackled by the poorer and smaller countries themselves seeking to compensate for their individual inadequacies by pooling resources through joint representation in the context of regional and sub-regional groupings or similar arrangements (Oyejide 1997; Yeo 1998). Such cooperation among groups of developing countries raises larger issues to which we now turn.

5. DEVELOPING COUNTRY COOPERATION IN THE EXISTING SYSTEM

Whatever the formal structure of governance and decision-making in international organizations, there is underutilized potential for increased influence on the part of the small and poor through increased cooperation with one another. Such cooperation can take many forms—ranging from merely *ad hoc* issue-specific collaboration to more institutionalized arrangements for information exchange and the development of common positions.

Developing countries have not as yet been very successful in efforts at collective action within the principal multilateral economic institutions—the IMF, the World Bank group, and the WTO. They have had neither an effective equivalent of the G-7 Economic Summit nor anything remotely resembling the industrialized countries' Organization for Economic Cooperation and Development (OECD). Such cooperative research and technical support operations as they have had, have been quite weak. Developing country interests have therefore tended to be analysed at greatest length in the multilateral organizations themselves; such analyses are subject to obvious constraints and biases (not least the influence of the industrialized countries within these bodies) from which more independent work would be free.

For this weakness the developing countries have largely had themselves to blame. It is true that the economic and political interests of individual developing countries often diverge, that mutual fears and suspicions (not to speak of armed conflicts) can be found within the developing country group, and that international cooperation can, in such circumstances, be difficult. But they also have extremely important elements of common economic interest in the global arena. In this same arena industrial countries with divergent interests pursue those that they hold in common to far greater effect.

Developing countries themselves are responsible for the fact that their collective multilateral organizations (including the G-77, G-15, and G-24) are not only each weakly funded but also poorly coordinated with one another. Their research and analytical capacities have been and remain minimal. The South Centre in Geneva, the product of the South Commission (1990), has only a tiny professional research staff. Nor do their purely regional organizations (e.g. SELA in Latin America or the Organization of African Unity) function much more effectively. Developing countries have so far simply not devoted the financial or technical resources to the joint pursuit of their common interests that would be required to achieve real impact in global economic affairs. (Perhaps the very poorest and smallest countries cannot be expected to devote significant resources to these 'larger' international and global issues since, even if they banded together, their influence would probably still be too small to justify their opportunity costs.) Negotiation has often been left to ill-prepared, technically deficient and/or overworked diplomats, while lobbying and public positioning have frequently been done by unaccountable (often Northern) NGOs and academics.

In the critically important realm of international finance, the developing countries' interests are represented in the IMF and World Bank by the Intergovernmental Group of Twenty-Four on International Monetary Affairs (G-24). Only in 1998, after more than twenty-five years of its existence, did G-24 finance ministers agree to fund a (very small) permanent 'liaison office' in Washington to maintain a collective 'memory' and assist developing country governors and executive directors in the IMF and Bank, and even now its funding remains precarious. The G-24 research programme offers some support to developing country representatives and decision makers but it is still primarily donor-funded and it has no full-time or on-site staff. Its annual budget is about one-twentieth of the annual cost of the World Bank's *World Development Report*!

Developing country collective representation in the WTO is, if anything, even worse. Whereas, as noted above, the WTO's formal voting structure allows for greater developing country power than in the international financial institutions, its governance does not incorporate a permanent executive board or equivalent body. If national interests are to be protected, member countries must each have permanent representatives in Geneva; but, of course, that is expensive and difficult for small and poor countries. (The Commonwealth Secretariat has therefore supplied a staff adviser to assist its smaller member countries in WTO matters.) There is as yet no equivalent of the G-24 (or its research programme) working in support of developing country interests in the WTO. The situation has been sufficiently alarming to G-24 finance ministers that they have authorized research on WTO issues, particularly those relating to financial services and investment, out of their own (very small) research budget. The staff of the UNCTAD have also been deployed to help with the provision of background papers on the developing countries' interests in particular issues in previous rounds of GATT bargaining and now in the WTO, despite the potential for tension with industrial countries and with the WTO itself that such activities create. Until the run-up to the Seattle Ministerial meeting of the WTO, developing countries had been unable effectively to develop and promote their own agendas in the WTO, leaving them forever searching merely for ways to respond to US and other initiatives.

Prior to the Uruguay Round negotiations, it was not unusual for the developing countries to operate through a bloc-wide approach using the G-77 framework. This approach appeared not to have been seriously considered during the Uruguay Round, partly because the bargaining format made the bloc-wide approach less workable and more fundamentally because the commonality of interests of the G-77 group seemed to have weakened over time as different countries developed in different ways (Whalley 1989; Oyejide 1990). The depth of most developing countries' disillusion with that Round's results and collective disagreement with Northern positions in the WTO, together with new perceptions of their collective power therein, have resurrected some of their cooperative spirit and effort. As noted above, in 1999, developing countries attempted, for the first time, to put many initiatives of their own on the agenda for the new round of multilateral bargaining. So far the only outcome has been stalemate; and the developing countries' inherent power and research capacity, particularly when not organized collectively, remains weak.

6. CONCLUSIONS

Governance is not simply a matter of designing an optimal system and then putting it in place through whatever mechanisms are available (including coercion if necessary). Rather, it should be thought of as a communicative and consultative *process* through which disputes are resolved, consensus is built and performance is continually reviewed. No less critical to its success than its policy instruments is the forum that a governance arrangement must provide for the expression of claims, review, and discussion of continuing reform. Above all, good governance is good process. To develop the required new arrangements for the effective governance of the global economy, one must therefore *begin* with an effective and credible process—ideally a process involving civil society and business as well as governments and existing international organizations.

Current efforts to improve governance in the newly globalized economy are heavily biased towards the interests of the governments, firms, and peoples of the wealthiest countries of the world and this bias will not easily be overcome. Whereas there are signs that larger and potentially more influential developing country players in the global economy may eventually be admitted to global governance and decision-making councils, in the interest of their very effectiveness and efficiency, the smallest and poorest risk continuing exclusion.

It would be presumptuous to try to prescribe the ultimate changes in global economic governance arrangements that 'should' result from 'better' global economic decision-making processes. It may nonetheless be helpful to offer some ideas (most of which have already been presented above) as to the first steps toward appropriate change that already seem feasible and at least potentially realistic. The most obvious starting point in any attempt to move toward more effective global governance arrangements is reform in the key multilateral economic institutions—the IMF, the World Bank, and the WTO. Each requires greater transparency, increased accountability, more independent evaluations, and effective ombudsman-like and/or legal-aid mechanisms to protect the weak against the strong. Particular effort will have to be made to protect the interests of the smallest and poorest countries, and the poorest peoples everywhere, in such reform efforts.

Transparency and evaluation procedures are ripest for reform in the IMF. Whatever the eventual mandate for the IMF (and it may be either reduced or expanded), there is no reason why a systematic and independent evaluation mechanism cannot fairly quickly be introduced to its current structure; the principal resistance to such reform emanates not so much from powerful member countries as from the IMF's own staff. It should also be quite feasible to continue the process of increasing the transparency of its procedures, budgets, reports, and agreements (subject to reasonable limits on matters of high sensitivity). If the IMF continues to offer balance-of-payments finance for the poorest and smallest countries (and, as noted above, many believe it should not), it must provide for the offsetting of exogenously originating shocks in a manner no less favourable than that provided for emerging market countries. The relative importance of its role as a 'gatekeeper' for other (larger) external sources of finance in the poorest countries should, in any case, be reduced in favour of the World Bank and the regional development banks, which adopt longer-term perspectives and, accordingly, can better promote local ownership of government programmes. The recent debacle over the selection of a new managing director for the IMF also suggests that the time is ripe for the reform of the anachronistic current customs governing the appointment of the chief executive officers of both the IMF and the World Bank.

In the World Bank (as well as in the IMF) the most immediate and hopeful reform issue is the achievement of a transition to effective local 'ownership' of country programmes, an issue in which bilateral aid donors are also, of course, heavily involved. The World Bank's rhetoric with respect to 'comprehensive development frameworks' under local national leadership has yet to be effectively translated into practice; doing so, and achieving genuine donor coordination in the process, should be a matter of the highest priority, and, while undoubtedly difficult, it is inherently feasible. Independent monitoring of Bank and donor performance, as well as that of developing countries, at the individual recipient country level, can be a powerful stimulus to appropriate reforms. (Local ownership of IMF programmes should also be a major reform objective but crisis response typically implies shorter-term perspectives which render participatory processes more difficult; the IMF's modes of operation are more difficult to change.)

The WTO may still be young enough to permit more 'fundamental' debate as to its rules system, its decision-making systems, the role and composition of its secretariat, and the capacity of all its current or prospective members to benefit from it; such debate should be fully participatory and transparent. The most immediate and feasible reform priorities are: the development of a more effective (while fully representative) WTO decision-making system; the significant strengthening of 'trade-legal aid' arrangements for the poorest; the abandonment of the concept of the 'single undertaking' as the overarching rule for future negotiations; and reconsideration of the most egregious of the mistakes of the Marrakesh agreement (notably the capacities of the poorest to understand and implement all of its provisions during the time periods provided, and the consistency of the full range of intellectual property provisions with broader developmental objectives).

To provide a common framework, a common point of reference, and systemic monitoring for all of these discussions of reform and thereby to improve the prospect of a coherent overall system of global economic governance, it would make sense to constitute a special committee of the United Nations or a subcommittee of its Economic and Social Council or even some high-level independent body to formulate agreed principles (e.g. full participation or representation, transparency, independent evaluation, ombudsman facilities, assistance to the weakest, mutual consistency, etc.) for the emerging governance arrangements and systematically to monitor their translation into practice on a regular basis.

The most immediate need is for appropriate process and participation in the current and forthcoming discussion of a new international financial architecture. This discussion is the one to which economic policy makers in the North are now most committed. The G-7-initiated Group of Twenty may be seen as a step in the right direction; but, as noted above, its agenda is too narrow, its representativeness and accountability are flawed, and its future, in any case, is uncertain. It is inadequate, as at present constituted, for carrying these issues forward towards appropriate outcomes. It therefore should be replaced, as quickly as possible, with a representative and accountable body that addresses the full range of financial architectural reform issues and carries full legitimacy. Such a change is eminently feasible.

The WTO debacle in Seattle has generated fresh pressures for rethinking and reform in the architecture for global trade as well. It would therefore make sense either to expand such a new body's mandate or to constitute a parallel body, along similar lines, to address the future of 'deep integration' and its implications for the trade regime and related issues.

At present, proposals for change in the global financial and trading systems originate almost exclusively in G-7 governments, Northern businesses and Northern universities—and they are typically brought to the world in the pages of the *Financial Times*, the *Wall Street Journal*, or the *International Herald Tribune*. There has not as yet been much comparable detailed developing country discussion of their own interests in international economic architectural issues. (Honourable exceptions are to be found in the UN-sponsored Task Force on international financial architecture (1999), the annual UNCTAD *Trade and Development Reports* and UNDP *Human Development Reports*. None of these, strictly, present the views of developing country governments or peoples. They do, however, present challenges to the views of the major powers and the multilateral economic institutions that they dominate.) Where are the true voices from the South in these critically important architectural discussions?

Greater effort will have to be made by developing countries themselves, who, despite increased activism in some areas, have still been fairly quiescent in recent years, to develop positions that are in their agreed collective interest and then to press them energetically in the relevant multilateral forums. An essential early step is for an organized effort to be made, within the South, to exchange ideas and formulate their own agreed positions on international financial architecture and the future role and functioning of the WTO, wherever such agreement is possible, *prior* to entering into detailed discussion and negotiation with the more powerful actors who still are accustomed to setting the terms for international policy debate. Negotiations toward improved arrangements for the governance of the global economy, if they are to be truly effective, require that the developing countries be better prepared for them; and that they take place in a mutually agreed and representative forum. Better preparation will require increased resources, and the strengthening of relevant research activities and capacities within the developing countries and their regional and other cooperative institutions. Such reforms are perfectly feasible and long overdue. Developed countries' long-term interest in effective global economic governance should lead them both to assist in such strengthening of developing country capacities and to the development of improved negotiation processes and forums—ones that carry broader legitimacy and therefore have better prospects of genuine success.

REFERENCES

Agosin, Manuel (1998). Capital account convertibility and multilateral investment agreements. *International Monetary and Financial Issues for the 1990s*, vol. X. United Nations, New York and Geneva.

Blackhurst, Richard (1998). The capacity of the WTO to fulfil its mandate. In Anne Krueger (ed.), *The WTO as an International Organization*. University of Chicago Press, Chicago.

Clapp, Jennifer (1998). The privatization of global environmental governance: ISO 14000 and the developing world. *Global Governance*, 4, 295–316.

Commission on Global Governance (1995). *Our Global Neighborhood*. The Report of the Commission on Global Governance. Oxford University Press, New York and Oxford.

Commonwealth Secretariat (1997). *A Future for Small States: Overcoming Vulnerability*.

Culpeper, Roy and Caroline Pestieau (eds) (1995). *Development and Global Governance*. North–South Institute/International Development Research Centre, Ottawa.

Eatwell, John and Lance Taylor (1998). International capital markets and the future of economic policy. CEPA Working Paper Series III, Working Paper No. 9. Center for Economic Policy Analysis, New School for Social Research, New York.

Elbadawi, Ibrahim and G. K. Helleiner (1998). African development in the context of new world trade and financial regimes: The role of the WTO and its relationship to the World Bank and the IMF. African Economic Research Consortium, Nairobi. Mimeo.

Ganesan, A. V. (1998). Strategic options available to developing countries with regard to a multilateral agreement on investment. *International Monetary and Financial Issues for the 1990s*, vol. X. United Nations, New York and Geneva.

Helleiner, G. K. (1996). Why small countries worry: Neglected issues in current analyses of the benefits and costs for small countries integrating with large ones. *The World Economy*, 19(6), November.

——(ed.) (1998). *Capital Account Regimes and the Developing Countries*. Macmillan, New York and London.

——(1999). Small countries and the new financial architecture. *Capitulos* (SELA) May/August.

——(2000). External conditionality, local ownership and development. In Jim Freedman (ed.), *Transforming Development*. University of Toronto Press, Toronto.

Kaufman, Henry (1998). Address to G-24 Ministerial Meeting, Caracas.

Kaul, Inge, Isabelle Grunberg, and Marc A. Stern (eds) (1999). *Global Public Goods: International Cooperation in the 21st Century*. Oxford University Press, New York and Oxford.

Krueger, Anne (ed.) (1998). *The WTO as an International Organization*. University of Chicago Press, Chicago.

Mendez, Ruben P. (1992). *International Public Finance. A New Perspective on Global Relations*. Oxford University Press, New York and London.

Michalopoulos, Constantine (1998). Developing countries' participation in the World Trade Organization. Policy Research Working Paper 1906. World Bank and World Trade Organization, Washington, DC and Geneva.

Mistry, Percy (1998). Coping with financial crises: Are regional arrangements the missing link? *International Monetary and Financial Issues for the 1990s*, vol. X. United Nations, New York and Geneva.

Mohammed, Aziz Ali (1996). Global financial system reform and the C-20 process. *International Monetary and Financial Issues for the 1990s*, vol. VII. United Nations, New York and Geneva.

——(1998). The Future of the G-24. G-24 paper. Mimeo.

Ohiorhenuan, John (1998). Capacity building implications of enhanced African participation in global rules-making and arrangements. Paper prepared for the African Economic Research Consortium's collaborative research project on 'Africa and the World Trading System'. AERC, Nairobi. Mimeo.

Ostry, Sylvia (1998). Reinforcing the WTO. Occasional Paper 56. Group of Thirty, Washington, DC.

Oyejide, T. A. (1990). The participation of developing countries in the Uruguay round: An African perspective. *The World Economy*, 13(3).

——(1997). Africa's participation in the post-Uruguay Round world trading system. PSIO Occasional Paper, WTO Series No. 6. WTO, Geneva.

Polak, J. *et al.* (1998). *IMF Study Group Report: Transparency and Evaluation*. Center of Concern, Washington, DC.

Sachs, Jeffrey (1998a). Global capitalism: Making it work. *The Economist*, 12 September.

——(1998b). Stop preaching. *Financial Times*. 5 November.

South Commission (1990). *The Challenge to the South*. Oxford University Press, Oxford.

UNCTAD (1995). *Trade and Development Report 1995*. United Nations, New York and Geneva.

——(1998). *Trade and Development Report 1998*. United Nations, New York and Geneva.

United Nations Task Force (of the Executive Committee of Economic and Social Affairs) (1999). Towards a new international financial architecture. CEPAL, Santiago.

Whalley, John (1989). *The Uruguay Round and Beyond*. Macmillan, London.

Winham, Gilbert R. (1998). Explanation of developing country behaviour in the GATT Uruguay Round negotiation. *World Competition*, 21(3).

Woods, Ngaire (1998). Governance in international organizations: The case for reform in the Bretton Woods institutions. *International Monetary and Financial Issues for the 1990s*, vol. IX. United Nations, New York and Geneva.

Yeo, S. (1998). Trade policy in sub-Saharan Africa: Lessons from the Uruguay Round experience. AERC, Nairobi. Mimeo.

13

Processes of Change in International Organizations

DEVESH KAPUR

1. INTRODUCTION

Although international institutions are a ubiquitous feature of international life, little is known about their trajectories of change. This chapter attempts to address this lacuna by examining processes of change in international institutions, in particular the subset of international institutions known as intergovernmental organizations (IOs). The purpose of this chapter is not to develop a general theory of change in international institutions but rather to develop limited generalizations about causal mechanisms and their consequences. It first examines the rationale and purposes of international organizations—before we can ask how and why particular types of organizations change, we need to understand why they exist in the first place. It then examines the trajectories of change in international organizations by posing three, interrelated, questions. One, what factors drive (or hinder) change in international institutions and organizations and what are the principal instruments and mechanisms that leverage change? Two, what factors explain variations in the pace and direction of change? And three, what are the consequences of change both for the institutions themselves and for their members?[1] Finally the chapter concludes by examining some normative aspects of change in the context of global governance distinguishing between the feasible and the desirable.

2. RATIONALE AND PURPOSES OF INTERNATIONAL ORGANIZATIONS

International institutions are mechanisms for transnational cooperation and collective action. Institutionalization serves to anchor international cooperation, be it through

The author would like to thank Deepak Nayyar and Richard Falk for their suggestions and comments and participants at the project meeting at Helsinki in May 1999.

[1] The paper uses 'change' rather than 'reform' in order to avoid the latter's normative implication of an improvement over the status quo. While change is often motivated by a desire to improve matters at least in some aggregate sense, change has complex consequences and, at least in the case of international institutions, it is difficult to demonstrate that change is Pareto-superior.

formal intergovernmental organizations such as the UN and Bretton Woods institutions or less formal arrangements, for example, the GATT (before its formal constitution as the WTO) or the various groupings of countries as in the G-7, G-10, G-22, G-24, and G-77. Whether their memberships are intergovernmental or non-governmental, they serve similar purposes: they lower transaction costs for members and produce information; they encourage members to think about their future ('lower their discount rate'); create linkages across issues; and they serve as agents that both create and diffuse ideas, norms, and expectations. The rules embedded in the IOs' charters provide for more stable expectations. Their organizational structures and administrative apparatus provide a durable negotiating forum for direct interaction among members, enhancing iteration and reputation effects. The secretariats of IOs provide consultative and supportive services for their members, which influence the terms of member interactions, help shape understandings, elaborate norms (from human rights to narrow technical standards), and mediate members' disputes.

While a creature of their members (states in the case of multilateral institutions), IOs have the authority to act with a degree of autonomy (which varies across IOs and over time) in defined spheres. States delegate a variety of functions to IOs in part because they provide domestic cover for activities that may be unacceptable in direct state-to-state form, but more palatable otherwise. As agents, IOs act as subcontractors for the global system of states, managing a vast array of operational activities. They serve as trustee or escrow agents as well as allocate scarce resources (with attendant distributional consequences and conflicts). They are arbiters, both in a facilitative and binding form as well as managers of enforcement of rules, either in the form of sanctions, conditionalities, or direct force. IOs also embody, however faintly (and for many, naively), an aspiration for a certain cosmopolitanism binding a global community of states. The shortcomings of individual institutions notwithstanding, IOs have been a successful institutional mechanism of global cooperation in part because they enjoy economies of scale by pooling activities, assets, and risks. While IOs' processes and the norms they propagate reflect the disproportionate influence of their more powerful members, they also bind the latter's actions to some degree.

In general, international cooperation is more likely to occur the greater the commonality of interests (or the narrower the issue area) across actors (and correspondingly the less their conflicting interests), the fewer the number of actors, and the more the 'shadow of the future' looms large in actors' decision-making (Ruggie 1992; Martin and Simmons 1998). Prominent theories of international cooperation share a presumption that interstate bargaining, entailing as it does the investment of time, money, energy and personnel, is inherently costly. The assumption of high transaction costs in the formation of international institutions (whether in the broad 'international regime' manifestation or in the narrower sense of international organizations) has led observers to conclude that international institutions are inherently sticky. Were this not the case, the suboptimality of most international bargaining outcomes (of which international institutions are the product) would encourage governments to perennially negotiate and renegotiate agreements underpinning international institutions (Abbot and Snidal 1998).

The 'stickiness' of international institutions means that change is gradual and does not occur easily. Indeed, institutional change as a broader phenomenon is invariably incremental, evolutionary, and, in some cases (and to some observers), even glacial. Public organizations are embedded in a complex web of rules. These limit both institutional autonomy to a greater extent relative to private organizations, as well as their access to the different pathways through which private organizations change (for instance mergers and acquisitions). International organizations would seem to lie somewhere in between the two extremes of autonomy enjoyed by private firms and national public organizations, since unlike the latter, they are not embedded in a 'thick' institutional matrix that limits autonomy. Within a national context the legislative, executive, and judicial branches of government as well as an autonomous central bank, all place constraints on the degrees of freedom enjoyed by each other. These horizontal constraints arise because these institutions are embedded within a broader set of rules—namely the national constitution. Since the latter does not have an international equivalent, such horizontal constraints are more limited for international institutions, which enjoy greater autonomy *vis-à-vis* other international institutions, relative to national institutions. Although their autonomy may be more circumscribed in other dimensions because of multiple principals, by playing off their principals against each other IOs can sometimes enjoy a greater *marge de maneuver* than national public institutions.

Consequently, it should not be surprising that IOs—the public institutions run by much maligned international bureaucrats—do change and even disappear altogether. One analysis of IOs in the 1980s found that hundreds were created and died during this period. Only two-thirds of the IOs that existed in 1981 were still active in 1992—a surprisingly high mortality rate. During this period slightly more IOs were created than were cast off, but most new IOs were created *not* by governments but by other IOs. Emanations—second generation IOs created through actions of other IOs—are likely to be of less importance than traditionally created IOs but both connect states through a web of shared goals, and institutional rules, and commitments.[2] Emanations constituted 70 per cent of the population of IOs in 1992, up from 64 per cent a decade earlier (Shanks *et al.* 1996).

The relatively high rate of mortality of IOs seems at first glance puzzling given the proposition that international institutions are inherently sticky. Three factors explain this. First, the demise of the Eastern bloc and the political and economic travails of Africa led to a decline in IOs from these regions. Second, mortality rates were higher for emanation IOs ('second or third generation') than treaty IOs ('first generation') where expectedly issues of stickiness are most apparent. Finally, there is strong survivor bias, that is, the longer institutions have been around the longer they are likely to exist, as is evident from an increase in the average age of IOs from 18.4 years in 1981 to 25.4 years in 1992.

---

[2] Examples of second generation IOs include IDA, IFC, and MIGA in the case of the World Bank, UNDP and UNCTAD in the case of the UN, etc.

3. SOURCES OF CHANGE IN INTERNATIONAL ORGANIZATIONS

A simple typology of sources of change would seek to distinguish between exogenous and endogenous sources of change. Analytical simplicity aside, the distinction is rarely as sharp, except at the edges. The forces driving change may be exogenous to the system—broad structural changes and shocks in the form of disasters and crises are two important factors. In some cases the locus of change may be endogenous to the system but exogenous to individual actors constituting the system. That is, change is not a choice variable for an individual actor but rather the result of the aggregation of changing preferences and interests of actors—change resulting from competition and changing norms are examples. In other cases, change is endogenous to the system but exogenous to the IO. Leadership and domestic politics in the systemically powerful countries are examples of this source of change although, as we shall note later, the former can also be endogenous to the IO. Finally, the source of change can be endogenous to an IO—institutional 'learning' leading to adaptive change is a good example. In general, the greater an IO's institutional autonomy, the greater the likelihood that the source of change is at the endogenous end of the spectrum.

3.1. *Structural Changes*

IOs are embedded in the broader global system, and structural changes lead to 'critical junctures' that create distinctively new conditions and pressures for institutional change. Over the last decade, the end of the cold war, the weakening of the state relative to both civil society actors (such as NGOs) and markets, an acceleration in the pace of global economic integration ('globalization'), and the informatics revolution have been the most significant changes in the external environment of international institutions. These changes have affected international institutions in somewhat contradictory ways.

Globalization would seem to increase the demand for global public goods. Since international institutions supply global public goods (much as the state supplies national public goods), the increased demand for their services should result in an expansion of IOs. However, this is tempered by other structural changes. Since IOs are creatures of nation states, the relative weakening of states means that the increase in demand for global public goods has been met more by non-governmental organizations than intergovernmental institutions. Thus, non-governmental development NGOs now provide more funds for economic development activities and disaster relief than the UN. Global rules and norms are being shaped to a much greater extent by a variety of non-governmental and 'hybrid' actors that includes state and non-state bodies whose activities range from regulation of myriad financial instruments to environmental issues to land mines.[3] Second, the end of the cold war and the emergence of the

---

[3] These range from the International Standards Organization (ISO), whose standards, ranging from products to internal corporate procedures to environmental standards, are increasingly becoming the 'norm' for market actors; the International Securities Markets Association, a private regulator that oversees

US as the lone superpower, have reduced its incentives to support multilateralism as a broad norm. Instead, the US has become much more selective in its support for IOs, which, as we shall note later, has implications on the type and direction of change. The incentives for the US in supporting the family of IOs, are further reduced by the pre-eminence of US based institutions, both among non-profit transnational NGOs as well as market actors (MNCs). This has meant that the web of international rules being woven by these actors has a greater degree of conformity (although they are by no means identical, especially in the case of NGOs) with domestic US norms.

Finally, the informatics revolution has weakened the role of IOs as informational intermediaries that reduce the transaction costs of cross-national interactions. The range and sources of information and the ease with which information can be accessed has profoundly changed. Information can now be obtained directly and rapidly from original sources, consequently reducing the importance of intermediaries. However, IOs still retain their comparative advantage as a relatively neutral 'seal of approval' on the quality and relative comparability of information.

3.2. *Crises and Disasters*

Change often follows shocks. And shocks, in the form of crises and disasters, tend to lay bare the limitations of existing arrangements and policies. Indeed, the origins of existing international institutional arrangements, ranging from the United Nations to the Bretton Woods Institutions, are (for the most part) attributable to the crises and disasters faced by the international system in the 1930s and 1940s.

In recent years, disasters have been a strong impetus for change. The agreement on the new International Criminal Court (ICC) in 1998 came from a broad consensus that existing international institutional arrangements were poorly suited to addressing the juridical issues arising from events in the former Yugoslavia and Rwanda. The International Court of Justice (ICJ—the so-called World Court) resolves disputes between governments and does not get involved in intra-state issues. The UN can impose economic sanctions or press for military intervention. The impact of sanctions falls most heavily on the general population, while military intervention imposes the heaviest costs on the rank-and-file soldiers on the front line. In contrast, the ICC is designed to direct the threat of justice more precisely on the political and military leaders who are responsible for mass slaughter.

Analytically, however, disasters and crises are not necessarily exogenous to IOs as a factor driving change. There is considerable endogeneity in some cases, where IOs have been intimately involved in precipitating crises, although the degree of respons-ibility is quite contentious. The massacres that followed the fall of the Bosnian enclave of Srebrenica in 1995, changed the basic tenets of UN peacekeeping operations and

international trade in private securities markets—the world's second-largest capital market after domestic government bond markets; the International Organization of Securities Commissions (IOSCO) which has become a leading force in coordinating international enforcement of securities laws; the International Association of Insurance Supervisors (IAIS) on insurance; the International Union for the Conservation of Nature (IUCN) on environmental issues, etc.

forced the UN to rethink its peacekeeping philosophy of neutrality and non-violence in civil conflict. Henceforth, the UN would become more willing to take sides and to insist on deploying a well-armed fighting force instead of lightly armed peacekeepers into environments where there was no ceasefire or peace agreement.

Well-publicized environmental fiascos (Transmigration in Indonesia; Narmada in India; Polonoreste in Brazil) were critical in making the World Bank rethink the way its infrastructure projects were conceived and implemented. The criticisms related to these failures forced the World Bank to incorporate greater transparency and participation in its projects and to employ stricter environmental impact assessment procedures.[4] The IMF has been slower to change despite perceived failures, but nonetheless, after recent financial crises, it retreated from its insistence on pressuring countries on capital account convertibility and has also moved toward greater transparency (albeit from a low threshold) in response to fierce criticism.

Financial crises have also forced an acknowledgement of the growing economic and financial importance of the larger developing countries and have resulted in some efforts to engage them in hitherto closed groups. The OECD has expanded at the margin, admitting Mexico and South Korea, and it has recently begun to invite non-members to its annual ministerial meeting.[5] Over the past few years, the BIS (which has been a key forum for discussion of international monetary questions) whose membership was long confined to the G-10, has over the past few years begun to invite officials from the central banks of larger developing countries, irrespective of whether or not those institutions are BIS shareholding central banks. US frustration with the European dominance in the G-7 and G-10 led it to sponsor the G-22, although the latter's expansion (to thirty-three members) at the behest of the smaller European countries undermined its objectives. Subsequently, in early 1999, the G-7 initiated the Financial Stability Forum (FSF) which, in addition to significant international financial centres (Australia, Hong Kong, Netherlands, Singapore) included international financial institutions (IMF, World Bank, BIS, and OECD); sector-specific international groupings of regulators and supervisors (Basle Committee on Banking Supervision, International Organization of Securities Commissions and International Association of Insurance Supervisors); and committees of central bank experts (Committee on Payment and Settlement Systems, Committee on the Global Financial System).

Disasters can, however, impede change as much as they promote it, particularly when filtered through the prism of domestic politics. The UN's intervention in Somalia had far-reaching consequences. It was pivotal in reversing US policy on UN operations from a stance of promoting 'assertive multilateralism' to refusing to accept virtually any new UN peacekeeping operations. Reaction to the Somali debacle led directly to the UN's colossal failure in Rwanda. By the early summer of 1994, the United States had dug in its heels about avoiding any risk in UN operations, and the Security

---

[4] See Fox and Brown (1998).

[5] The countries are Argentina, Brazil, China, India, Indonesia, Slovakia, South Africa, and Russia. *Financial Times*, 25 May 1999: 6.

Council not only refused to strengthen the UN force in Rwanda but cravenly reduced it. The possibility of multilateral peacemaking, particularly through the UN, suffered a severe setback.

3.3. *Competition*

Competitive pressures for resources and mandates—among IOs and between IOs and national bodies, market institutions, and NGOs—have been an important factor driving change. IOs faced little competition in the 1950s and 1960s. It was an expansionary era for IOs and alternative transnational institutional mechanisms, both market and non-market, were limited. But even then competition forced change in the few instances that it did occur. During the 1950s, the IBRD discouraged the idea of soft-loan lending to developing countries in contrast to the UN, which had been more proactive (through its Special UN Fund for Economic Development proposal). When it appeared that the United States would launch a soft-loan facility in any case and that it might be lodged in the UN, the IBRD reversed its stance. The result was IDA, which fundamentally changed the character of the World Bank. Similarly, the IBRD softened its opposition to lend for social sectors after the creation of the Inter-American Development Bank (IDB), which had no such inhibitions.

Competition (or lack thereof) from alternative sources of funds—whether bilateral aid, government export agencies, private-sector lending or other multilateral development banks and agencies—was for long a critical factor in explaining the tightness of the lending standards ('conditionalities') of the Bretton Woods institutions. Conditions were tighter when alternative sources of funds were limited (during the 1950s, 1960s, and 1980s) and looser when alternatives abounded, as in the 1970s. The IMF's burst of low conditionality lending in the late 1970s and early 1980s was similarly driven by a fear of institutional irrelevance when the surge of commercial bank lending threatened to undermine its liquidity function. In general it would appear that the conditionality regime has become tighter in the 1990s. Although this reaffirms the competition hypothesis in the case of Africa and countries struck by economic and financial crisis, where few alternatives exist (especially since cold-war rents have vanished), nonetheless the conditionalities of the Bretton Woods institutions have become tighter even where there has been greater competition (particularly from private sources). This change, as we shall discuss later, is due to structural changes and changing norms on the use of conditionalities.

During the 1990s the environment for IOs has become much more competitive. This is especially true of development-oriented IOs which have seen their market share shrink, either at the hands of the private sector in infrastructure-related projects (hitherto the bread-and-butter of multilateral development banks) or NGOs in poverty and social sectors. Competition among IOs has also increased. While in part this represents old-fashioned turf battles among bureaucracies, it has also been propelled by the decline in the overall resources available to the family of IOs. The share of contributions to multilateral institutions in total net flows of financial resources from OECD countries to developing countries and multilateral institutions declined by half between 1986–87 and 1996–97 (averaged over two years)—from 17 to 8.5 per cent.[6] While the decline in real terms was less (from about $17 billion to $16 billion, at 1996 prices and exchange rates), the resources made available to IOs were spread out over more countries (with the inclusion of countries from East Europe, Central Asia, and Indochina after 1990) and faced substantially greater demands from burgeoning humanitarian and civil conflict crises.

Competition also drives changes in international institutional arrangements, leading to the formation of new IOs. Following the Cuban revolution, once the US agreed to the demands of Latin American countries for a regional development bank (the Inter-American Development Bank), other regions responded by setting up similar institutions—and the African Development Bank, Asian Development Bank, and a host of sub-regional development banks followed suit despite the existence of the World Bank. More recently, the formation and/or resuscitation of regional groups has been driven by competition from other regional groups. Following the example of the EU and NAFTA, trade has become the pivotal issue in driving regional institutional arrangements, whether ASEAN, Mercusor, the Andean Group, SAARC, or SAADC.

3.4. *Norms*

Human rights, neoliberal economic agendas, governance, gender, and the environment are just a few norms that have come to occupy centre stage in the agenda of IOs in recent years. Norms are complex sets of meanings including permissions and prohibition, through which people understand and act in the world. Historically constructed norms, ideas, and discourses have played an important role in institutional change, albeit one where precise causality is difficult to prove. Norms serve a regulatory purpose—they constrain. They may also have constitutive effects, by shaping forms of behaviour, roles, and identities through practice. Although the argument that norms are simply a function of power and interest and thus are redundant as an analytical category has considerable merit, it is more likely that the constraining and constitutive effects of norms mutually shape and reshape each other. In particular by shaping preferences, norms can enter into, and change, interests.

The origins of the norms, the mechanisms by which those norms exercise influence and the conditions under which they are more likely to be influential are hard to identify with much precision.[7] This complexity is further enhanced by the long time it takes for norms to diffuse and change the behaviour of IOs. Some norms gradually garner legitimacy on the basis of mounting evidence that is underpinned by a solid body of research. The WHO's anti-smoking campaign and the emphasis placed by development agencies on girls' education are examples of this phenomenon. Systemic changes and crises can accelerate the acceptance and diffusion of hitherto latent norms in international institutions. Environmental norms diffused more rapidly within the multilateral development banks after the brouhaha surrounding several of their

---

[6] Data from OECD. Available at http://www.oecd.org/dac/htm/TAB02e.HTM
[7] A good survey of the issue can be found in Finnemore and Sikkink (1998: 887–917).

projects cited earlier. The increasing importance of governance in the agendas of the IFIs and the UN system during the 1990s was the result of the continued development crisis in Africa and the problems faced by the transition process in East Europe on the one hand, and the weakening of the norm of sovereignty on the other.

As the last example indicates, the acceptance of norms cannot be understood without reference to context, and the changing constellation of key actors, their beliefs and preferences, and their interests, and relative bargaining power. The last is a reminder that norms can also serve as a fig leaf for more prosaic material interests. There is understandable scepticism that richer countries are long on norms when they are short on resources, and the increasing attention to norms of governance even as development budgets decline is perhaps not entirely coincidental. As long as the cold war was on, 'crony capitalism' in Indonesia was not considered a problem. Nor was it a problem while the East Asian 'miracle' was being trumpeted. But when the Asia crisis of 1997–98 erupted, 'norms' of corporate governance were strenuously advanced to deflect attention from broader issues of the nature and quality of international financial regulation.[8] Similarly, while the virtues of the norm of democracy are trumpeted within states and intranational governance, the same norm is seen as faintly ridiculous in international governance. On the other hand, poor countries often waive the norm of sovereignty when their domestic governance leaves much to be desired.

3.5. *Domestic Politics*

Domestic politics has been an important, albeit less predictable, factor in shaping change in international institutions. Expectedly, the importance of domestic politics as a factor affecting change in IOs matters only in the case of the more powerful states. In recent years, IOs have often been whiplashed by domestic US politics. The ill-fated raid by US Rangers to capture General Mohammed Aidid in Mogadishu, and the accompanying televised images of a dead American helicopter pilot being dragged through the streets of Mogadishu, led to a major backlash in Washington and proved devastating for the UN. There were furious recriminations against the UN in the United States, although the operation had been conceived and commanded exclusively by the United States without the prior knowledge of the UN (or even of senior US officers in the UN). The results for the UN peacekeeping operations are well documented and were an important factor in the US decision to block Boutros Boutros-Ghali's re-election as secretary-general (Urquhart 1999).

International institutions have often served as a convenient whipping boy in domestic US politics, particularly in the 1990s. The end of the cold war relaxed the pressures for a broad bipartisan consensus on US foreign policy. Funding for IOs was invariably ensnared in partisan politics, which in the 1990s pitted a Republican Congress against a Democratic president. The domestic politics of abortion in the United States has led to unilateral (and therefore unacceptable) riders on UN support for family planning initiatives and to forced budget cuts. Indeed in some instances, as

---

[8] See Wade (1999: 134–49).

in the case of UN reform, the US failure to pay its dues stymied the very changes it had been pressing so hard to promote in the first place, as other countries balked.

International trade is perhaps the most salient issue area where politically powerful domestic lobbies have either forced change or blocked change. Japanese and EU agriculture lobbies stymied agreements in the Uruguay Round as well as at Seattle, while textile and pharmaceutical interests in the United States were instrumental in the MFA and TRIPs agreements. The US push for environmental and labour standards in the Seattle Round was driven by President Clinton's desire to regain 'fast-track' authority to negotiate free-trade agreements for which he needed the support of environmental and labour groups as well as the desire for support from influential labour groups for Vice-President Gore's presidential aspirations. Similarly incumbent left-of-centre governments in the EU, plagued by high levels of unemployment, pressed for labour standards to be included in the Seattle Round to placate key labour constituencies.

3.6. *Leadership*

International institutions are not a passive set of rules or impassive structures but are active sites of bureaucratic politics that empower international officials who wield transnational influence and act as agents of change. It is hardly surprising that leadership change and institutional change (institutions as rules or as organizations) go hand in hand. Indeed, if there is no desire for change, then there would be little need for changing leadership. This is as true for political leaders and voters as for CEOs and shareholders (through board members) and for IOs and their member countries as well. In recent years, more rapid leadership turnover and clamour for change in IOs have gone hand in hand.[9]

But just how important is leadership for change in international institutions in general and IOs in particular? And under what conditions is leadership likely to be more important than other factors? Does leadership really lead or does it lead only to the extent it is allowed to by an IO's principals? A considerable body of research has documented the importance of 'supranational entrepreneurship'—informal political leadership by high officials of international organizations—in influencing the outcomes of multilateral negotiations, although the mechanisms and degree of importance are contested.[10] Robert McNamara played a singular role in transforming the World Bank in his thirteen-year stint as president of that institution (1968–81) as did Raul Prebisch in the case of ECLA (Economic Commission for Latin America) in the 1950s. Could they, however, have been as successful in changing their institutions in the 1980s, when the atmosphere for multilateral institutions was much more hostile? Not as much to be sure, but during the 1970s while the Word Bank flourished, UNESCO under Amadou Mahtar M'Bow, languished in the same environment. Similarly,

---

[9] Frustrated with the lack of change in the WHO, its members voted for a new leader in July 1998, and when Gro Brundtland succeeded Hiroshi Nakajima she immediately launched significant organizational changes.

[10] For an analysis of the phenomenon in the European Community (EC) see Moravcsik (1999: 267–306).

ECLA's counterparts in other regions were much less successful in institutional change and adaptation, even in the period when ECLA flourished. Was leadership the deciding factor that explained not just the degree of change, but also the direction of change that allowed one institution to emerge much stronger at the end of the 1970s?

The importance of the variable 'leadership' (relative to other factors) in shaping the contours of change is an increasing function of an IO's relative autonomy and the institution's relative importance. While we defer the discussion on the variables that affect IOs' autonomy to the next section, two points need emphasizing here. One, an IO's leadership has considerable agenda-setting power, which affects not just *which* issues are brought to the table but, critically, *when*. Second, an IO's leadership also has considerable discretion in internal organizational matters, ranging from budgetary procedures and priorities and financial controls, to personnel and procurement policies. Although these factors seem rather prosaic in the larger scheme of things, these micro dimensions are critical to organizational effectiveness, and in turn to an IO's legitimacy and autonomy. Poor leadership in particular can undermine the internal workings of an IO with surprising ease. Agency problems are severe in IOs and accountability mechanisms involving an IO's leadership are weak except for renewal or denial of another term (it is virtually impossible to sanction leaders of IOs until their term is completed).

If the intensity of lobbying and conflict over the selection of the leadership of IOs is any indication, the principals of IOs (member states) clearly believe that leadership matters. In recent years, bitter disputes, strong-arm tactics and side payments to some members have accompanied the selection of leaderships of IOs, ranging from the African Development Bank, ITU, UNESCO, WHO, and more recently, WTO and IMF. But if leadership matters, what are the selection mechanisms? One explanation stems from the severe agency problem characteristic of IOs mentioned earlier. Since principals (member countries) have few instruments to reward or sanction their agent (an IO's leadership), they look upon leadership contests as an opportunity to choose a 'good type' of leader, one who shares their preferences and would act on behalf of their interests (Stichcombe 1968).[11] Re-elections would be opportunities for sanctioning behaviour inimical to the country's interests. But how does a country determine that a prospective leader would act on behalf of its interests? In the absence of complete information about a candidate, countries choose nationality and region as surrogates of the likelihood of the candidate reflecting their policy preferences. In addition, countries vote strategically in leadership contests, backing candidates simply to block third candidates (who they believe reflect interests inimical to theirs) or garner payoffs in other issue areas. In some cases the desire of a country to secure a leadership position for its own nationals may have symbolic implications, with the intention of projecting or signalling some intent by the state in question.[12] The large resources deployed by Japan in this regard are a case in point, as Japan seeks to project an image of global leadership and become a permanent member of the Security Council. In other cases,

---

[11] This mechanism draws upon models of electoral accountability. See Fearon (1999).

[12] The original argument of how and why states project desired images is Jervis's (1970).

countries push their nationals for candidates of IOs for domestic political reasons, either as reward or to remove them from the domestic political arena.

The above discussion suggests that leadership, as an analytical category shaping change, straddles both exogenous and endogenous categories. But are the selection mechanisms of leaderships of IOs random, or are there reasons to believe that there is a systematic bias in the choice of leadership, which in turn shapes the trajectory of change?

Our hypothesis is that the more autonomous an IO and the more it is involved in the distribution of economic resources or the greater its sanctioning authority, the greater the desire to maintain exclusionary mechanisms for leadership selection or, in their absence, the greater the intensity of conflict over leadership choice. Exclusionary mechanisms are evident in the leadership of the Bretton Woods institutions, which enjoy a primacy among economic organizations. Thus the president of the World Bank is a US national, the managing director of the IMF is from West Europe even though choosing a candidate from a global pool would improve the probability of a better candidate. Among the regional development banks, the Asian Development Bank (ADB) is exceptional in that its President is a Japanese national while the others draw from a regional pool. The WTO is a good example of an IO whose actions are seen to be critical to the interests of member countries. Hence the intensity of the conflict in the selection of its director general in 1999, with the unprecedented outcome of the six-year term being split into two three-year terms, to accommodate the two rival camps.

In the case of the UN, the secretary-general's post is off limits to the major powers but only because they enjoy veto power on critical matters. Even otherwise, the fear that the secretary-general would be capable and autonomous has been an important reason for the selection of pliable leaders and in the rare exception where this was not the case (Boutros Boutros-Ghali), the re-election was torpedoed.

3.7. *Learning*

Change may also occur simply due to organizational learning. But what determines learning? In what ways are organizations capable of learning? Among the kinds of learning that organizations are capable of, which ones are desirable? Several of the factors discussed earlier, affect change in IOs, both directly as well as indirectly by their impact on learning. Competition, failures, and changing norms, and epistemologies are all likely to spur learning. The consequences of an international institution's own actions may lead to wider systemic learning which, in turn can shape future change in that institution. The Uruguay Round was quite successful for global trade, but relatively less so for developing countries. The lessons were clearly carried over into the bargaining at Seattle, and the failure of the trade negotiations at Seattle stemmed at least to some degree from the type of success achieved in the earlier trade round.

Institutional learning is likely to be Bayesian, that is, institutions update their beliefs in response to new information. However, the ability to process information is not equal across IOs. A large literature on organizational learning stresses the importance of an organization's capabilities in affecting learning. Capabilities, in turn, depend on a variety of factors ranging from recruitment criteria (the stock of human capital), organizational structure and systems of authority, and staff and managerial turnover (long-serving staff are more likely to defend the status quo than new staff but may simply reinvent the wheel) (Argyris *et al.* 1996). Even if it were possible to correctly gauge an IO's capabilities, it is unclear how one could analytically distinguish change in IOs due to learning from the factors discussed earlier.

4. VARIATIONS IN DEGREE AND CHARACTERISTICS OF CHANGE

The above analysis of the factors driving change in international institutions does not, however, explain why change is faster in some institutions than others or why the content of change varies across institutions. This variation, I argue, can be explained primarily by the interaction between institutional history and the type of exogenous changes discussed earlier. The former affects key characteristics of an IO—its goals and instruments, governance, and financial structure—which shape the specific trajectory of change of different IOs consequent to exogenous changes.

The importance of path dependent change is strongly supported from the evidence that founding conditions become imprinted on organizations and mould their subsequent development (Stichcombe 1968). This is true not only at the meta-institutional level but also at the meso-organizational level, where initial institutional design exerts an indelible and enduring influence on the trajectory of change in organizations (Barnett and Carroll 1995; Becker 1989). Institutional characteristics are key to determining the varying contours of change across institutions and organizations that result when exogenous factors initiate change. These characteristics of organizational ecology include the charter (or 'articles of agreement') that delineates membership criteria and mandated functions, institutional governance, and internal organizational processes such as recruitment practices and budgetary sources, factors that are generally ignored in most analysis of IOs.[13]

The institutional grid of the current international system was essentially laid out in the mid-1940s. The period was a historic 'critical juncture' when the rules of the game of the current international order were mapped out. While at the outset rule-making processes were relatively open, they became much more closed as time went on. But at Dumbarton Oaks and at Bretton Woods, barely a quarter of the current members of IOs were present when the rules were being crafted. These countries would join as rule-takers and not as rule-makers. At a given point of time, power is unequally distributed and certain actors are in a position to impose rules on others. This imparts a strong element of path dependency as those power relations get reproduced over time despite a marked change in circumstances. The resulting institutional rigidities mould the characteristics of change.

---

[13] Peabody makes this point in the case of the WHO (Peabody 1995: 731–42).

Perhaps the most rigid consequence of institutional history is structures of governance of IOs (distribution of voting power, veto points, participatory structures). Expectedly, they shape the trajectory of change in directions that reflect the structure of power in these organizations. A relative concentration of power and limited recourse to veto rules can certainly affect the speed and direction of change. The Uruguay Round of the GATT is a good illustration. However, the lack of a more democratic and participatory structure reduces legitimacy and therefore longer-term sustainability. The very governance structure that led to the 'success' of the Uruguay Round laid the seeds of failure of the succeeding Seattle Round in 1999.

But the correspondence between the formal structures of governance, including forms and degree of participation and democracy, and change in international organizations, should not be overdrawn. The different multilateral development banks (AFDB, ADB, EBRD, IBRD) vary considerably (though not radically) in their structures of governance, but their trajectories of change have been more or less similar. There can be little doubt that governance structures—including types and forms of representation, voting and majority rules and veto points—matter. But that does not mean that international institutions can (let alone will) be democratic. An unpleasant reality of international institutions is that whatever form of governance and decision-making prevails in international organizations, they will not be democratic in the sense that democracy is a system of popular control over decision-making.[14] Structurally IOs will always face a democratic deficit. As Robert Dahl has argued, even in countries with deep-rooted democratic structures it is 'notoriously difficult' for citizens to exercise effective control over key decisions on foreign affairs; their influence on international institutions is likely to be much less. One country, one vote (as in the UN) might seem more democratic than one dollar, one vote (as in the Bretton Woods institutions) but both violate the notion of democratic equality inherent in one person, one vote.

Expectedly, charters pose one of the more difficult barriers to change, since changes to charters, like changes to constitutions, require super majorities that are not easily achieved. The articles of the World Bank have been amended just twice since it was established and in the IMF's case three times, despite the enormous change in the scope and substance of the institutions' work. This apparent incongruity has been possible for a number of reasons. The original articles themselves were not very confining (and when they appeared so the institutions' lawyers were skilful in their creative interpretation). And in recent years, when even creative interpretation has not been possible, the institutions have managed to skirt the spirit if not the letter of the articles, because the issues involved only affect developing countries while the voting rules are heavily weighted in favour of industrialized countries.

Nonetheless, institutional rules pertaining to veto points and super majorities pose barriers that are exceedingly difficult to breach. In the Bretton Woods institutions, the super majority required for a formal amendment to the Articles of these institutions or for a capital increase (in the case of the World Bank) or quota increase (in the case of

---

[14] See Dahl (1997). Dahl's scepticism at the possibility of designing democratic international organizations is shared by Tobin (1997).

the IMF) effectively gives veto power to one country, the United States.[15] In the UN's case, Articles 108 and 109 of its charter require that any formal amendment be ratified by two-thirds of the member states, including all the permanent members of the Security Council. The circumstances under which such a majority can be mustered are truly exceptional and certainly is not the case at present. Any change regarding the veto—the fundamental rule of UN decision-making as well as the most direct expression of the inequality of states—is even more unlikely. While the veto is fundamentally undemocratic, it keeps the big players in the game—and there is no game without them. The states currently entitled to it will not agree to any meaningful limitations. Aspirants such as Germany and Japan are unlikely to accept a veto power inferior to that of the incumbents while developing countries, who have jointly fought the veto for decades, are split into those who now aspire to permanent membership and the veto and those who maintain a negative stance.

Membership in some organizations is open to all states, while others limit membership according to criteria such as geography, historical association, or shared purpose. Some organizations have broad general mandates; others limit themselves to specific functions.

Collective action in international institutions which limit membership according to pre-specified criteria is relatively easier and therefore these organizations are more likely to reach a consensus on change. The relative ease with which NATO shifted tack after the end of the cold war despite the demise of its *raison d'etre*, illustrates this point. On the other hand, the common criteria for membership may also result in stronger risk correlation across members inducing institutional stresses that may paralyse decision-making. The failure of most international commodity organizations (ranging from the International Rubber Organization to the International Tin Organization to OPEC), the OAS during the Latin American debt crisis, ASEAN's poor performance during the 1997–99 Asian crisis, and the stresses in regional trading arrangements like Mercusor during the economic downturn in Latin America in 1998–99, are cases in point.

Path dependency also affects changes in organizational processes, which over time have significant consequences for organizational effectiveness and (critical for public institutions), legitimacy. This is particularly important in the case of staffing and recruitment practices which are key to the creation of Weberian bureaucracies, which, in turn, have been critical agents of change in a variety of national and international settings. However, meritocratic recruitment does not mean an absence of bias in the embedded norms of bureaucracies. Consequently, although the Bretton Woods institutions and the WTO have some of the most meritocratic recruitment processes within international institutions, their selection criterion is biased toward economists from elite US universities. Not only has this meant that the norms common in elite US economics departments dominate these institutions, but also that experience is

---

[15] Indeed one of the two amendments to the World Bank's Articles (in 1989) was to increase (from 80 to 85 per cent) the voting majority for approving a capital increase to ensure that the United States retained its veto power even as its share in the capital declined.

undervalued relative to academic credentials because of limited attention paid to horizontal recruitment. However, the more senior the managerial position, the more the relative balance between nationality considerations and merit shifts in favour of the former.

It is often alleged that the bureaucracies in IOs are 'hidebound' and deeply resistant to change. But evidence would suggest otherwise. In the World Bank, for instance, staff are frequently supine—terrified of losing their substantial benefits (and for many, their visa status) and consequently prone to jump at the smallest presidential twitch. If anything the 'obstructionist' charge has been a convenient cover for the current chief executive allowing him to remove senior managers who have dared voice dissent (Kapur 1999a).

The UN family, particularly the Secretariat, faces a different problem. Nationality quotas are relatively more important and they have contributed to mediocrity and nepotism.[16] It is unfortunately true that for many LDC nationals the difference between wages in their home countries and earnings as international bureaucrats is substantial, which means that LDC élites are often nominated by their governments for these jobs.[17] To the extent their opportunities for wages are substantially fewer, this group is more likely to resist change, especially any change that may threaten their jobs. It is likely that the creation of an international civil service with specified rules and selection criteria would mitigate these problems, but there is little support for such a service.

The importance of path dependency notwithstanding, it alone does not explain the variance in the content of change across IOs. Rather, the *content* of change is shaped by the interaction of institutional history with the precipitating factors driving change. In recent years, three factors have been particularly important (in turn resulting from changes in structural power, interests, and preferences). First, financial pressures on IOs have substantially increased. As a result, IOs with greater financial autonomy, that is, those less dependent on direct appropriations of public funds, are becoming relatively more important. Second, as a result of a growing congruence between norms and interests of the more powerful member states of the international system, there is an increasing reliance on punitive measures relative to incentives. As a consequence, the mandate of those IOs equipped with punitive instruments has been expanding relative to those that use principally incentive or 'development'-oriented instruments. Third, an increase in disasters and crises has forced a shift in the time-horizons of the activities of IOs. The 'discount-rates' of IOs have increased and consequently their attention to long-term 'development'-related activities has been declining. Furthermore, crises have also enhanced the 'liquidity premium' of IOs since a rapid response to crises requires quick access to additional financial resources. Consequently, IOs

---

[16] For instance, in the case of the UN, the retiring head of the Office of Internal Oversight Services remarked that the organization, 'until very recently, has never chosen senior staff on their management abilities'. *New York Times*, 15 November 1999: A10.

[17] It is interesting to note that despite all the noises about 'diversity' in recruitment to international bureaucracies, to the extent diversity is valued in recruitment it is on the basis of nationality and gender, but never class. There are undoubtedly practical reasons for this, but self-interest is also evident.

which can commit new resources rapidly—inevitably IOs with greater financial autonomy (the international financial institutions) relative to their counterparts that are more dependent on government funds—are in greater demand.

A critical institutional characteristic that shapes the content of change is an IO's financial structure. Financial autonomy is the key to bureaucratic autonomy and can also be the crucial instrument to leverage change. The salience of this issue is quite different for the IFIs relative to the UN family since the former enjoy greater financial autonomy. Since the mid-1980s the UN family has faced much tighter budget constraints. In some cases, key donors have exited and in others they have simply refused to pay pending specific 'reforms'. In the 1990s, virtually every multilateral organization was in the throes of 'reform' designed to make it more 'efficient, effective, and responsive', but the dimensions of these changes have differed.

In the UN system these changes have entailed zero budget growth, programme cutbacks and staff cutbacks principally through attrition. The UN Secretariat established an Office of Internal Oversight Services (OIOS) in late 1994 and appointed a former CEO of a major international accounting firm as UN under-secretary-general for administration and management. The aim was to establish standards for management accountability and to overhaul personnel, procurement, and planning systems— the basics of a modern management structure. An efficiency review was launched in November 1995 and the General Assembly had three groups studying reforms, including reform of the Security Council and the institution's finances.[18]

The story has been similar for other organs of the UN. Following UNCTAD VIII in February 1992, the United Nations Conference on Trade and Development (UNCTAD) initiated major institutional changes which emphasized consensus building as opposed to the earlier approach which attempted to negotiate binding international agreements or resolutions among its traditional four-group system. UNCTAD's acceptance that economic policies based on market forces were the best basis for achieving development, in contrast to its earlier emphasis on the role of the state, ensured its continued survival. UNIDO launched a major restructuring in 1993 and refocused its services when several major industrialized countries threatened to leave. The WHO, whose budget has been declining in real terms for the past fifteen years, proceeded with a list of forty-seven reforms in 1993. In 1998, under a new director-general, further restructuring ensued when more than fifty programmes were merged into ten divisions. Faced with a stagnant budget and pressed by its donors, the UN Development Programme (UNDP) cut its administrative budget by 10 per cent, reduced headquarters staff by a quarter and senior executive positions by 15 per cent while tightening its focus on poverty eradication. The WIPO (the World Intellectual Property Organization) cut its thirty-one programmes down to nineteen. The list goes on.

The story has been different, however, for the IFIs which enjoy greater financial autonomy. For the multilateral development banks and the IMF, the central focal

---

[18] There has been no shortage of reform proposals for the UN since its inception. A recent compilation reprinting every major reform proposal laid out for the UN runs into three thousand-page volumes (Muller 1997).

points for major shareholder pressure have been capital increases and quota increases (in the case of the IMF). Since these increases are few and far between (averaging once a decade), donors have focused on alternative mechanisms to influence change. The principal mechanism has been replenishment of soft-loan windows, which occurs every 3 to 4 years. In the case of the World Bank, the IDA tail began to wag the Bank dog since the early 1980s. The annual budget approval process and the use of net income have become powerful levers for change (Kapur 1999*b*). In the case of both the UN and the IFIs, donors willing to commit resources but lacking in political clout (particularly the Nordics and Japan) began using off-budget financing to influence the agendas of these institutions. By supplementing the institution's budgetary resources through 'trust funds,' which have grown rapidly both in number and volume, these countries have sought to shape institutional priorities by bypassing the regular budgetary process. To the extent that budgets reflect the priorities of an institution, the growing share of off-budgetary funds in financing administrative expenses changes micro incentives within organizations. It provides a mechanism for change from below, even when change from above is stymied by the lack of change in formal institutional governance structures.

A second factor shaping change among IOs—in particular their relative importance *vis-à-vis* each other—has been the increasing preference for punitive instruments over incentive-based instruments in international relations. Bilaterally this has been most evident in the increasing use of sanctions as an instrument of US foreign policy in areas as disparate as trade to nuclear proliferation to drug control to human rights, despite their quite limited effectiveness.[19] Given the influence of the United States in IOs, this shift in US preferences in favour of punitive instruments has diffused into multilateral institutions and is reflected in the choice of IOs as new agendas are placed on the international system. The privileging of the WTO, a recent addition to the family of IOs, relative to other IOs, in common issue areas illustrates the point. Although for long intellectual property rights were the purview of WIPO, the enforcement of the IPR regime was placed within the WTO and not WIPO. A similar rationale has been evident in the drive by the United States and the EU to keep global labour standards in the WTO and not the 'toothless' ILO. Indeed President Clinton, in pressing for a working group on labour standards within the WTO, was clear that [the working group] 'should develop these core labour standards, and then they ought to be part of every trade agreement, and ultimately I would favour a *system in which sanctions would come for violating any provision of a trade agreement.*'[20] For similar reasons, despite the existence of the UNEP (an IO explicitly created for the purposes of addressing global environmental concerns), the WTO has become the preferred institutional vehicle for environmental standards for the United States and the EU. For similar reasons, issues of governance, which have explicitly political ramifications, are being principally addressed through the Bretton Woods institutions, which are financial institutions and are enjoined by their charters to eschew political considerations in their lending, and

[19] See, for instance, Haas (1998); Elliott and Hufbauer (1999: 403–8); and Pape (1997: 90–136).

[20] Interview with President Clinton, *Seattle-Post Intelligencer*, 30 November 1999, emphasis added.

not through the UN which has a more explicit political mandate. In all cases institutional choice is guided by whether an IO is equipped with punitive instruments or not, rather than institutional mandate and comparative advantage *per se*.

A third factor influencing the content of change in IOs has been the growing importance of disasters and crises in driving change. Crises influence the content of change in IOs by increasing the discount rate of the principals of the IOs. As a result those IOs whose goals are geared to emergency response (such as UNHCR) are becoming more privileged while others are changing their programmatic focus to short-term emergency responses. In the case of the UN, the size of its peacekeeping budget relative to its regular budget has tripled over the last decade—from around a quarter in the late 1980s to more than three-fourths in the late 1990s (Mendez 1999: 402). Over two decades, the World Food Programme's (WFP) resources devoted to emergencies increased from less than a fifth in 1977 to 85 per cent in 1997. While earlier, three-fourths of the resources devoted to emergencies were a response to physical disasters (such as droughts), two decades later three-fourths of the resources were devoted to 'man-made' disasters. In the process WFP was transformed from a development organization focused on creating long-term assets (and the largest UN agency in resource transfers) to a humanitarian response agency (Hopkins 1998: 71–91). The resulting shift in the time-horizons of IOs is short-changing long-term programmes.

5. CONSEQUENCES OF CHANGE

There is little doubt that both the UN and the Bretton Woods institutions are under much greater pressure to change than in the past. Many IOs are caught between a rock and hard place. They can either agree to the changes demanded by the major powers but in the process undermine their independence or, alternatively, maintain their agency but risk being marginalized. For the UN that marginalization was evident in Kosovo where the United States and West Europe relied on NATO rather than face a possible veto in the Security Council. Global economic issues have also been largely negotiated outside the UN, especially in the framework of the 'Group of Seven' and, to a lesser degree, in the BIS, IMF, the WTO, and the OECD.

In part, this is an inevitable consequence of a unipolar world where problems akin to those of monopolies in other economic and political settings are bound to arise. The earlier bipolar world had many problems, but it did have some of the benefits of competition. If the cold war made change difficult, with each camp often seeing change only too frequently as a zero sum game, now change is only possible if it proceeds in particular directions. But differences in institutional governance structures—ranging from patterns of representation, funding, and veto points—mean that change in particular directions is more likely to occur in some institutional settings than others. Consequently, some institutions get privileged over others in the expansion of mandates and resources. In all these instances, the *ex post* institutional choice is clearly one where membership is restricted or influence is skewed in a particular direction, despite the existence of institutional alternatives *ex ante*.

The trajectory of change in IOs is resulting in a 'corner solution'. Those international institutions that are relatively autonomous financially or are equipped with rule-enforcement powers (such as conditionalities, force, or sanctions) are changing by expanding the scope of their activities. In opting for a 'full menu' approach to their mission—which means catering to the needs of nearly 200 member states—these IOs are adopting an approach akin to the US Department of Defence's practice of spreading defence contracts across states to maximize congressional support. The practice is designed to ensure that all members are kept reasonably happy. Since member states are increasingly susceptible to pressures from civil society (or in any case use it as an excuse), the expansive agendas also increasingly cater to 'stakeholder' concerns, although much of this is 'feel good' rhetoric and programmes. On the other hand, international institutions that are financially more directly dependent on their members are moving to reduce the scope of their activities—hoping that a narrower focus will help them retain support from a core clientele. As a result of these changes, the variance in the size distribution of international organizations is likely to increase with a few large, broadly focused and financially autonomous organizations with rule-enforcement capabilities and a large cluster of IOs dependent on public funding with a narrower reach and scope.

6. CONCLUSION

To the extent that IOs are found wanting in their capacity to change in a manner that has positive consequences for global welfare, the failure is less theirs than that of their principals. Much has been written about the failure of western political imagination and the botched effort in re-creating the post cold war system (Maynes 1999). The poverty of political imagination is as true of the attempts to change IOs, which have been stymied by the limited vision and commitment of the leaderships of major countries to change the IOs in a manner that reflects broader global long-term interests rather than parochial short-term interests. Consequently, in the absence of a major systemic crisis, IOs are unlikely to change in a manner and degree that is anything other than incremental.

Moving from the feasible to the desirable, a critical change that would be desirable in IOs is for more democratic structures of governance. However, a fundamental structural reality of international organizations should be recognized. While all organizations depend on delegation of power and responsibility, the greater the degree of delegation in decision-making the further removed is the *demos* from final decision-making and the less democratic is the political system. In international organizations, delegation in practice is so extreme that the system slips below a democratic threshold.

Three systemic changes can mitigate (although by no means resolve) this dilemma. First, in concordance with the global movement recognizing the benefits inherent in decentralization, the structure of international organizations should also promote the principle of subsidiarity with greater resources and responsibilities devolving to regional (and sub-regional) organizations.

Second, and especially given the limited 'voice' option available to poor countries, membership should be voluntary and 'exit' should not impose onerous costs—then on the lines of Hirschman's suggestion, governance by voice is not necessary for legitimacy. For a majority of poor countries exit is not a low-cost option—alternative mechanisms for acquiring legitimacy in the absence of voice do not exist. The 'market' for international organizations is, for the most part, not contestable except in the few areas where both regional and global institutions exist. Thus, in development projects, borrowers had some choice between a regional development bank and the World Bank. In some cases, countries can engage in forum-shopping—for instance Canada, Mexico, and the United States can choose between NAFTA and the WTO dispute settlement mechanisms in cases of trade dispute resolution (Busch 1999). But in many important areas this is not true. Following the onset of the Asian crisis, the United States shot down the idea of an 'Asian monetary authority' as well as severely criticized the Asian Development Bank when it attempted to adopt a position different from the prescriptions of the IMF. The monopoly power of the IMF was confirmed, and the possibility of exit denied. This means that a multiplicity of IOs, even with some overlapping (especially vertical) jurisdictions, is preferable to a few centralized global IOs.

Finally, while it would be unrealistic to expect a radical redistribution of power in IOs, it would be desirable to raise the price of power, both through higher financial contributions and greater accountability. A permanent seat on the Security Council would come with a significant premium, reflected in higher contributions to the UN budget. Higher quotas in the IMF and a capital share in the World Bank would automatically lead to a higher share in the contributions to IDA (or other soft-loan lending windows). By raising the marginal cost of power held in IOs, those with a greater share of power would be somewhat less inclined to force these institutions into excessive risk-taking.

REFERENCES

Abbot, Kenneth and Duncan Snidal (1998). Why states act through formal international organizations. *Journal of Conflict Resolution*, 42(1), 3–32.

Argyris, Chris, Donald Schon, and Michael Payne (1996). *Organizational Learning II: Theory, Method and Practice*. Addison Wesley, Reading.

Barnett, William P. and Glenn R. Carroll (1995). Modelling internal organizational change. *Annual Review of Sociology*, 2, 217–36.

Becker, Warren (1989). Strategic change: The effects of founding and history. *Academy of Management Journal*, 32, 489–515.

Busch, Marc (1999). Overlapping institutions and global commerce: The calculus of forum shopping for dispute settlement in Canada–US trade. Paper presented at the Annual Meeting of the International Studies Association. Washington, DC.

Dahl, Robert (1997). Can international organizations be democratic. In Ian Shapiro and Casiano Hacker-Cordon (eds), *Democracy's Edges*. Cambridge University Press, Cambridge.

Fearon, James (1999). Electoral accountability and the control of politicians: Selecting good types versus sanctioning poor performance. Mimeo.

Financial Times (1996). 25 May, 6.

Finnemore, Martha and Kathryn Sikkink (1998). International norm dynamics and political change. *International Organization*, 52(4), 887–917.

Fox, Jonathan and David Brown (1998). *The Struggle for Accountability: The World Bank, NGOs and Grassroots Movements*. The MIT Press, Cambridge, MA.

Haas, Richard (ed.) (1998). *Economic Sanctions and American Diplomacy*. Council on Foreign Relations, Washington, DC and New York.

Elliott, Kimberly Ann and Gary Hufbauer (1999). Ineffectiveness of economic sanctions: Same song, same refrain? Economic sanctions in the 1990s. *American Economic Review, Papers and Proceedings*, 89(2), 403–8.

Hopkins, Raymond (1998). Complex emergencies, peacekeeping and the World Food Programme. *International Peacekeeping*, Winter, 71–91.

Jervis, Robert (1970). *The Logic of Images in International Relations*. Princeton University Press, Princeton.

Kapur, Devesh (1999*a*). The changing anatomy of governance of the World Bank. Paper presented at conference on Reinventing the World Bank at Northwestern University, May.

——(1999*b*). Global governance and the common pool problem: Insights from the World Bank's net income. Dept. of Government, Harvard University, Cambridge, MA. Mimeo.

Martin, Lisa and Beth Simmons (1998). Theories and empirical studies of international institutions. *International Organization*, 52(4), 729–57.

Maynes, Charles (1999). Squandering triumph: The west botched the post-cold war world. *Foreign Affairs*, Jan/Feb.

Mendez, Ruben (1999). Peace as a global public good. In Inge Kaul, Isabelle Grunberg, and Marc Stern (eds), *Global Public Goods, International Cooperation in the 21st Century*. Oxford University Press, New York and Oxford, p. 402.

Moravcsik, Andrew (1999). A new statecraft? Supranational entrepreneurs and international cooperation. *International Organization*, 3(2), 267–306.

Muller, Joachim (ed.) (1997). *Reforming the United Nations: New Initiatives and Past Efforts*. Kluwer Law International, Boston.

New York Times (1999). 15 November, A10.

OECD. Data available at http://www.oecd.org/dac/htm/TAB02e.HTM

Pape, Robert (1997). Why economic sanctions do not work. *International Security*, 22, 90–136.

Peabody, J. W. (1995). An organizational analysis of the World Health Organization— Narrowing the gap between promise and performance. *Social Science and Medicine*, 40(6), 731–42.

Ruggie, John G. (1992). Multilateralism: The anatomy of an institution. *International Organization*, 46, 561–98.

Seattle-Post Intelligencer (1999). 30 November.

Shanks, Cheryl, Harold Jacobson, and Jeffrey Kaplan (1996). Inertia and change in the constellation of international governmental organizations, 1981–1992. *International Organization*, Autumn, 593–627.

Stichcombe, Arthur (1968). Social structure and organization. In J. G. March (ed.), *Handbook of Organization*. Rand-McNally, Chicago, IL. pp. 142–93.

Tobin, James (1997). Comment on Dahl's scepticism. In Ian Shapiro and Casiano Hacker-Cordon (eds), *Democracy's Edges*. Cambridge University Press, Cambridge.

Urquhart, Brian (1999). The making of a scapegoat. *The New York Review of Books*. 12 August.

Wade, Robert (1999). Gestalt shift: From 'Miracle' to 'Cronyism' in the Asian crisis. *IDS Bulletin*, 30(1), 134–49.

14

The Existing System and the Missing Institutions

DEEPAK NAYYAR

1. INTRODUCTION

The process of globalization in the world economy has brought about profound changes in the international context. It could have far reaching implications for development. The reality that has unfolded so far, however, belies the expectations of the ideologues. The development experience of the world economy from the early 1970s to the late 1990s, which could be termed the *age of globalization*, provides cause for concern, particularly when it is compared with the period from the late 1940s to the early 1970s, which has been described as the *golden age of capitalism*. Any such periodization is obviously arbitrary but it serves an analytical purpose.[1]

Available evidence suggests that the past twenty-five years have witnessed a divergence, rather than convergence, in levels of income between countries and between people. Economic inequalities have increased during the last quarter of a century as the income gap between rich and poor countries, between rich and poor people within countries, as also between the rich and the poor in the world's population, has widened.[2] And income distribution has worsened. The incidence of poverty increased in most countries of Latin America and Sub-Saharan Africa during the 1980s and in much of Eastern Europe during the 1990s. Many countries in East Asia, Southeast Asia and South Asia, which experienced a steady decline in the incidence of poverty, constitute the exception. However, the financial meltdown and economic crisis in Southeast Asia has led to a marked deterioration in the situation. In the developing countries, employment creation in the organized sector continues to lag behind the growth in the

I would like to thank Amit Bhaduri, Andrea Cornia, Nitin Desai, Gerry Helleiner, Devesh Kapur, John Langmore, and Lance Taylor for helpful discussion on the theme of this chapter even before it was written. For comments and suggestions on a preliminary draft, I am grateful to Amit Bhaduri and Shrirang Shukla.

[1] The quarter century that followed the Second World War was a period of unprecedented prosperity for the world economy. It has, therefore, been described as the *golden age of capitalism*. See, for example, Marglin and Schor (1990) and Maddison (1982). The *age of globalization*, however, is not a phrase that was used in the literature to describe the world economy during the last quarter of the twentieth century. It is suggested here by the author, as this periodization facilitates comparison.

[2] For supporting evidence, see UNCTAD (1997) and UNDP (1999). See also IMF (1997).

labour force, so that an increasing proportion of workers are dependent upon low productivity and casual employment in the informal sector. Unemployment in the industrialized countries has increased substantially since the early 1970s and remained at high levels since then, except in the United States, while there has been almost no increase in the real wages of a significant proportion of the workforce in many industrialized countries. Inequality in terms of wages and incomes has registered an increase almost everywhere in the world. In most countries, the share of profits in income is higher while the share of wages is lower than it was in the early 1980s. Over the same period, the rate of growth in the world economy has also registered a discernible slowdown. And the slower growth has been combined with greater instability. It would seem that, in some important respects, the world economy fared better in *the golden age* than it has in the *age of globalization*.

It is obviously not possible to attribute cause-and-effect simply to the coincidence in time. But it is possible to think of mechanisms through which globalization may have accentuated inequalities. Trade liberalization has led to a growing wage inequality between skilled and unskilled workers not only in industrialized countries but also in developing countries.[3] As a consequence of privatization and deregulation, capital has gained at the expense of labour, almost everywhere, for profit shares have risen while wage shares have fallen.[4] Structural reforms, which have cut tax rates and brought flexibility to labour markets, have reinforced this trend. The mobility of capital combined with the immobility of labour has changed the nature of the employment relationship and has reduced the bargaining power of trade unions. The object of managing inflation has been transformed into a near-obsession by the sensitivity of international financial markets, so that governments have been forced to adopt deflationary macroeconomic policies, which have squeezed both growth and employment. The excess supply of labour has repressed real wages. Financial liberalization, which has meant a rapid expansion of public as well as private debt, has been associated with the emergence of a new rentier class. And the inevitable concentration in the ownership of financial assets has probably contributed to a worsening of income distribution.[5] Global competition has driven large international firms to consolidate market power through mergers and acquisitions, which has made market structures more oligopolistic than competitive. The competition for export markets and foreign investment, between countries, has intensified, in what is termed 'a race to the bottom', leading to an unequal distribution of gains from trade and investment.

Globalization has, indeed, created opportunities for some people and some countries that were not even dreamed of three decades ago. But it has also introduced new

---

[3] Some evidence on the increase in profit shares in industrialized countries and the decrease in wage shares in developing countries is reported in UNCTAD (1997). Stewart (2000) develops a similar argument that globalization may have led to an increase in inequality through an increase in returns to capital as compared with labour.

[4] For evidence in support of this proposition, see UNCTAD (1997). In addition, see Wood 1994, 1997. Stewart (2000) also suggests that trade liberalization, associated with globalization, provides an explanation for rising inequality and cites supporting evidence.

[5] This argument is developed in UNCTAD (1997).

risks, if not threats, for many others. It has been associated with a deepening of poverty and an accentuation of inequalities. The distribution of benefits and costs is unequal. There are some winners. But there are many losers. However, the exclusion of countries and of people from development has become much less acceptable with the passage of time.[6] The proposition that economic growth, or economic efficiency, will ultimately improve the lot of the people is far less credible today than it was fifty years earlier. The democratization of polities, even if it is much slower than the market-ization of economies, has enhanced the importance of time in the quest for develop-ment. Now, almost three-fourths of the world's people live in pluralistic societies with democratic regimes. And even authoritarian regimes need more legitimacy from their people. Poverty, or austerity now for prosperity later, is no longer an acceptable trade-off for people who want development here and now. Clearly, the time has come to evolve a new consensus on development where the focus is on people. For the welfare of humankind is the essence of development. As we enter the twenty-first century, therefore, ensuring decent living conditions for people, ordinary people, should be the fundamental objective of the conception and the design for global governance. Such an underlying worldview is an imperative.

This chapter endeavours to draw together the conclusions that emerge from the chapters in this volume. In doing so, it does not attempt a summary or a synthesis. Instead, it seeks to develop an overview, for the whole is different from the sum total of the parts. Section 2 considers the *institutions*, with a focus on the United Nations, the Bretton Woods institutions and the World Trade Organization, to sketch some con-tours of reform and change necessary in the existing system. Section 3 sets out the *issues*, of emerging significance in the contemporary world, to suggest that there are some missing institutions, which are needed. The issues selected, global macro-economic management, international financial architecture, transnational corporations, cross-border movements of people, or international *public goods* and *public bads*, are illustrative rather than exhaustive. Section 4 explores some important elements of *governance*, such as structures of representation or decision-making in institutions, international rules or norms, evolution or change in institutions, and the role of the nation state, which are critical for any vision about the future.

2. THE EXISTING SYSTEM

2.1. *The United Nations*

During the second half of the twentieth century, the evolution and the experience of the United Nations system have been strongly influenced by two divides in the world.

---

[6] Exclusion is no longer simply about the inability to satisfy the basic human needs of food, clothing, shelter, health care, and education for large numbers of people. It is much more complicated, as the consumption patterns and lifestyles of the rich, associated with globalization, have powerful demonstration effects. People everywhere, even the poor and the excluded, are exposed to these consumption possibilities because the phenomenal reach of the media in our age has spread the consumerist message far and wide. This creates both expectations and aspirations.

The East–West divide, which was responsible for the cold war, shaped what the UN could or could not do in terms of maintaining peace or ensuring security, which was largely in the realm of politics. The North–South divide, which was associated with decolonization and development, shaped what the UN could or could not do in terms of reducing disparities and promoting development, which was largely in the sphere of economics. In both cases, it was conflict, rivalry and limited, even forced, cooperation, which functioned as checks and balances in the system. And, in an almost dialectical sense, these factors provided the driving force, but also slowed things down. The world has experienced a dramatic change during the 1990s. The distinction between East and West has disappeared with the collapse of communism. The distinction between North and South is much more diffused, while the dominance of the Washington consensus has brought divergent perceptions about development closer together. This represents a sea-change. The conflict is much reduced, even if it has not been replaced by harmony. However, the long term implications of a unipolar world in the realm of politics and a new orthodoxy in the sphere of economics are yet to unfold in entirety.

Yet, it is clear that changes in the world, particularly during the past decade, have eroded the legitimacy, the effectiveness, and the credibility of the UN.[7] The unipolar world has eliminated the erstwhile *competition between systems*. As competition has vanished, the urge for cooperation has diminished. This has reduced both the relevance and the role of the UN. The dominance of the Washington consensus is just one aspect of the outcome. There are others. Some new nation states remain economically fragile and politically unstable. A few nation states have fractured as they have slipped into ethnic strife or civil war. The legacy of death, displacement, and destruction is awesome. There is still no system in place to take care of, let alone prevent, complex humanitarian emergencies. The process of globalization has also given rise to new problems and governance needs. The United Nations system has not quite adjusted to these changed realities. The responsiveness of the UN to issues of our times has been limited to global meetings such as the Earth Summit or the Social Summit. This is perhaps a form of representation for peoples' concerns. Even if these initiatives have not yielded concrete results, the UN has provided a sounding board for new ideas and, at the same time, given them an international visibility. It is, perhaps, a silver lining to the cloud. The moral authority of the UN, however, is seriously undermined because its laws or principles are enforced selectively when it suits the interests of the rich and the powerful.

The problem is compounded by the fact that there is a democratic deficit in the United Nations system. It was an integral part of the original design. And it has not diminished with the passage of time. In terms of decision-making, the principle of one country, one vote has not translated into a democratic mode in a world of unequal

---

[7] This erosion is vividly illustrated by the response of the international community to the crises in Iraq and Kosovo during the 1990s. The response to crises before then, whether inside or outside the United Nations system, provides a sharp contrast. At the time of the Korean War, the UN provided a critical input. The Cuban crisis was resolved outside the United Nations system essentially through the balance of power in the cold war era. The problem of apartheid in South Africa was addressed through the UN.

partners, just as much as the principle of one person, one vote does not make citizens equal in a political democracy. Matters are made worse in the UN for two specific reasons. First, the veto clause and the restricted membership of the Security Council are clearly undemocratic. Second, in the General Assembly, any vote on a decision is seen as a failure while any consensus is seen as a success. The latter, experience shows, can be far from democratic. In terms of representation, the UN is essentially an intergovernmental organization. In a more democratic set-up, there should be representation not only for the state but also for civil society. There is some attempt to involve non-governmental organizations and corporate entities but there is no attempt so far to reach out to people at large.

All the same, the UN is the core of any international system of governance. Therefore, it is essential to contemplate reform that would make it more credible, more legitimate and more effective.[8] It must act in accordance with its charter. It must be democratic in achieving representation and making decisions, through participation, transparency, and accountability. It must move towards political independence in relation to the powerful geopolitical actors. Some institutional changes are obviously desirable. First, it is imperative to enlarge the membership of the Security Council and to circumscribe its veto powers. This structure was created more than half a century earlier. The world has changed since then. These changes have to be recognized rather than ignored or wished away. Second, it is necessary to explore possibilities of alternative modes, at least partial, of independent financing. This would loosen the reins of political control now exercised by the powerful member states. For the issue of financing is less about money and more about political control. It would also ease the pressures on the UN that have been attributable to resource constraints. Some version of the Tobin tax, say on international foreign exchange transactions or stock market transactions, and some charges on the use of the global commons, are possible means of such independent financing. Third, the establishment of a high quality Volunteer Peace Force would be of great benefit. It would depoliticize intervention by the UN and enable it to provide a prompt collective security response wherever humanitarian emergencies arise. Fourth, it is worth thinking about a Global Peoples Assembly, modelled on the European Parliament, which would provide people with opportunities for participation. It would run parallel to the General Assembly. But it would be the voice of global civil society. Fifth, the creation of an Economic Security Council has become essential as a means of governing globalization. It would ensure that the UN provides an institutional mechanism for consultations on global economic policies and also, wherever necessary, the international regulatory authority.

2.2. The Bretton Woods Institutions

The Bretton Woods institutions were created more than fifty years ago. At the time, their object was to manage the international payments system and to assist in the

---

[8] For a detailed discussion, see Richard Falk, Chapter 7. See also Commission on Global Governance (1995) and Ruggie (1993).

reconstruction of Europe. There was an underlying worldview about the pursuit of full employment, which was shaped by memories of the great depression. This conception also recognized the logic of international collective action in situations where markets did not work and there was a role for government intervention. The world has changed since then. So have the Bretton Woods institutions. But their concerns have become much narrower with the passage of time.

The IMF adapted to the change from a regime of fixed exchange rates to a regime of floating exchange rates, just as it has attempted to cope with the move from capital controls to capital mobility. It had more success with the former than it has had with the latter. The World Bank adapted to the change in its role from reconstruction to development, just as it moved from project lending mostly in infrastructural sectors to sectoral lending, programme lending, and structural adjustment lending. Both the institutions became much more influential and powerful in the process. The influence and the power were directly attributable to the evolution of conditionality. Such conditionality was, ostensibly, a means of ensuring repayment but, in effect, it also performed a surveillance role for international banks. At the same time, it helped shape domestic economic policies in developing countries and transitional economies.

The orthodoxy of the Bretton Woods institutions, however, has not resolved the economic problems of borrowing countries.[9] Indeed, the solution has often turned out to be worse than the problem. But that is not all. There are two fundamental flaws in the performance of the Bretton Woods institutions. The failure to manage the international financial system, reflected in the instability of exchange rates and the volatility of capital flows, which together compound the adjustment problem, is one flaw. The essence of the problem is international capital flows without any international controls. The failure in promoting development, which is reflected in persistent poverty and growing inequalities, is another. The crisis of development has, in fact, been accentuated in the era of globalization. These flaws are, in part, attributable to the *virtual ideology* of the Bretton Woods institutions, which does not recognize the importance of public action in coping with market failure. It would seem that the logic of international collective action, which was an integral part of their original design, is forgotten.

As we enter the twenty-first century, therefore, reform and change in the Bretton Woods institutions is an essential element in any design for governing the world economy. Of course, the Bretton Woods twins have much in common in their need for reform and change. Nevertheless, their roles and functions are different enough, so that it is logical to consider the suggested changes separately for each of the institutions.

2.2.1. *The International Monetary Fund*
The time has come to redefine the role of the IMF. In terms of governance, this means a constructive role in managing and stabilizing the international financial system,

---

[9] There is an extensive literature on this subject. See, for example, Taylor (1988), Williamson (1990), Cooper (1992), Taylor (1993), and Killick (1995).

not only through crisis management but also through crisis prevention.[10] The sustainability of the exchange rate, of the current account deficit, of short-term debt and of outstanding portfolio investment, is relevant in thinking about the objectives of a reformed international financial system. However, the preoccupation with the instability and volatility of capital flows associated with financial crises is so great that there is a tendency to understate the importance of managing exchange rates and current account deficits. The world, it seems, has come a full circle from a time when we thought only about current account macroeconomics to a time when we think only about capital account macroeconomics. But the adjustment problem, and for some countries even the liquidity problem, is not yet *passé*. Therefore, even as it adapts to its new role, the IMF must continue to perform its old role. In doing so, it is necessary to change the structure of governance and the mode of thinking.

Governance in the IMF needs much more representation, transparency, and accountability.[11] The representation embodied in voting rights that are based on quotas is far too unequal between member countries. The lenders are the principal share-holders in the IMF but the borrowers are the principal contributors to the income of the IMF. There is a clear need to restructure voting rights so as to make them more representative and less unequal. There is almost no transparency in the IMF. Indeed, its operations and programmes are shrouded in secrecy. The absence of public scrutiny means that there are almost no checks and balances. It is high time that the IMF practices what it preaches about transparency. This calls for a disclosure of information and an independent evaluation of operations. The accountability of the IMF is limited, at best, to finance ministries and central banks, which, in turn, have close connections with the financial community. The IMF has almost no accountability to governments in totality, let alone people at large, when things go wrong. Account-ability is an imperative without which the IMF could continue to pursue the interests of a subset of the international community, often to the detriment of the general interest of peoples and governments or the collective interest of the world economy.

Thinking in the IMF also needs to change. This is particularly necessary in the sphere of conditionality.[12] Its content leads to overkill. Its coverage extends beyond stabilization and adjustment programmes. And, quite often, it does not work. What is more, where policy reform is driven by the IMF and the World Bank, domestic political constituencies are often forgotten by governments. Such conditionality often subverts the domestic political process so that the question of ownership simply does not arise. Clearly, there is need for a fundamental reform in the practice of condi-tionality. The IMF also needs to reconsider its thinking in macroeconomics. There is now ample evidence to suggest that its stabilization programmes lead to adjustment through changes in output rather than through changes in prices.[13] The outcome is beggar-thyself policies where current account deficits are reduced or inflation is

---

[10] See Yilmaz Akyüz and Andrew Cornford, Chapter 5, as also José Antonio Ocampo, Chapter 11.

[11] See Jong-Il You, Chapter 8 and Joseph Stiglitz, Chapter 9.

[12] For an analysis and evaluation of IMF conditionality, see Dell (1981) and Williamson (1983). See also Kapur (1997).   [13] Cf. Taylor (1988) and Cooper (1992).

restrained through a contraction in output and employment. Last but not least, the IMF should rethink its perspective on capital account liberalization and capital account convertibility. In this sphere, it would be wise for countries to hasten slowly for, experience has shown, a premature integration into international financial markets is fraught with danger and can put development at risk.[14]

2.2.2. *The World Bank*

More than fifty years after it began life, the World Bank also needs to redefine its role.[15] Its primary task should be to respond to the crisis of development. Its subsidiary task should be to provide scarce capital to countries and to sectors which do not have access to international capital markets. The benefits may be more related to access in bad times than to reduced borrowing costs. The pursuit of these objectives, however, requires a change of mindset. The World Bank should cease to be a moneylender. It should transform itself into an institution more concerned with development. This is easier said than done but it is feasible. The World Bank should focus its activities on development in poor countries and for poor people. This would need reform in its structure of governance and its mode of thinking.

In terms of governance, more representation and more accountability are an imperative. The representation, as in the IMF, is asymmetrical and unequal. A very large proportion of the voting rights are vested in a very small number of industrialized countries as they are the principal shareholders in terms of paid-up capital. In contrast, a large number of developing countries and the transitional economies are vested with a small proportion of the voting rights even though they are the principal stakeholders, interest payments from whom provide most of the income of the World Bank. The need to restructure such a voting system is obvious. It is a necessary condition for change. The accountability also is limited, once again, to finance ministries and central banks. The comprehensive development framework is a step in the right direction but it represents a modest beginning. Moreover, in the World Bank, there is a difference between what is said and what is done, just as there is a difference between the thinking arm and the operational arm. The Operations Evaluation Department exists but learning from experience is not yet incorporated into management and executive board decisions. The independent evaluation must also begin in borrowing countries to assess projects and programmes supported by the World Bank. This would be the beginning of accountability to governments and to people.

In terms of thinking, there is a need for radical reform in the sphere of conditionality. The story is not very different from what it is in the IMF. Conditionality is characterized by overkill and overreach. And, quite often, it does not work. There is an obvious need to promote local ownership of country programmes. For this purpose, the World Bank must give up its attempts to micromanage economies through

---

[14] This argument is outlined in Nayyar (2000) and developed in Nayyar (2001). See also Helleiner (1998) and Eatwell and Taylor (2000).

[15] See Jong-Il You, Chapter 8, and Stiglitz, Chapter 9. There is, of course, an extensive literature on this subject. See, for example, Kapur *et al.* (1997) and Stiglitz (1999).

conditionality. It should, instead, seek to become a partner in development through local participation. For the World Bank, it is perhaps just as important to reorient its thinking about development, which attaches far too much importance to markets and to openness. Simplified prescriptions, which emphasize more openness and less intervention and which advocate a rapid integration into the world economy, combined with a minimalist state that simply vacates space for the market, are not validated by either theory or history. Economic theory recognizes and economic history reveals the complexity of the development process. The degree of openness and the nature of intervention are strategic choices in the pursuit of development, which cannot be defined and should not be prescribed irrespective of the time and space, for they depend upon the stage of development and must change over time.[16] And there can be no magic recipe in a world where economies are characterized by specificities in time and space.

The production and dissemination of knowledge about development and about policies or institutions that are most conducive to development is an important function of the World Bank. This function has been distorted, if not subverted, by the Washington consensus. Its policy prescriptions became increasingly influential as these were adopted by the World Bank, to begin with its research agenda and subsequently in its policy menu. The dominance in ideas soon turned into a propagation of ideology as the World Bank acquired a near-hegemonic status in thinking about development. The time has come to question this knowledge-hegemony. This process can begin the moment developing countries and transitional economies seek to influence and to shape the research agenda of the World Bank. This is neither implausible nor unreasonable because research budgets are supported by the income stream rather than the share capital of the World Bank. It is also important to recognize that over-centralized knowledge systems are like dominant ideologies, which do not have the checks and balances to introduce correctives when the need arises. Even in the sphere of knowledge, competition is desirable. Therefore, research about policies and institutions conducive to development must be progressively decentralized to regional institutions and national institutions. And it will not take long to build supportive research capacities.

The Bretton Woods institutions have been the most ardent advocates of economic reforms in recent times. It is time to reform the reformers. There are some critical elements of change, which deserve emphasis.[17] The structures of internal governance need to be democratized, in particular through a reform of voting systems. In addition, the Bretton Woods twins should practise what they preach in terms of transparency and accountability. There is also a strong need to rethink conditionality, which is often counterproductive. The standardized package of policies, which is inflexible, must be dispensed with simply because one size does not fit all. Above all, the Bretton Woods institutions must begin to question their belief system about the magic of the market to

---

[16] For an analysis of contending views about openness and intervention, see Nayyar (1997).

[17] For a detailed discussion on reform in the Bretton Woods institutions, see Haq (1995) and Woods (1998). See also Kenen (1994).